KU-167-465

GROWING UP

A young person's
guide to adolescence

26·7·96

To
Stephanie on your
11th Birthday
Love
your granma xxx
1996.

Merlion Publishing

CONTRIBUTORS

Dr Frances Ackland

Liz Burnell

Dr Kenneth R Fox PhD
Associate Director
Physical Education Association
Research Centre
University of Exeter, UK

Dr Diana Gibb MD MRCP
Honorary Consultant Paediatrician
Senior lecturer in Epidemiology
Institute of Child Health
University of London, UK

Mary Ingoldby

Dilwyn Jenkins MA

Dr Nicola McClure MBBS

Dr Lalitha Moodaley MB BS DO
MCOphth
Moorfields Eye Hospital and
University College
Hospital, London, UK

Geoffrey A Meek BEd MSc
School of Education
University of Exeter, UK

Heather Pinchen
Journalist and Sex Therapist

D Roberts-Harry BDS MSc
FDS MOrth
Senior Registrar in Orthodontics
University of Bristol
Dental Hospital, UK

Dr Michèle J Sadler
Consultant Nutritionist

Mal Sainsbury

Cyril Simmons BD MEd AFBPsC
CPsychol
Education Department
Loughborough University of
Technology
Loughborough, UK

Neil Stoodley BM BCh FRCS
Directorate of Children's Services
Bristol Royal Hospital of Sick
Children
Bristol, UK

Miss Gillian Turner FRCOG
Department of Obstetrics and
Gynaecology
Southmead General Hospital
Bristol, UK

Dr Joanne R Williams
Physical Education Association
Research Centre
University of Exeter, UK

B D Woods MSc NCSP DLC
Lecturer, University of Exeter, UK

Copyright © 1993 Merlion Publishing Ltd
First published 1993 by
Merlion Publishing Ltd
2 Bellinger Close
Greenways Business Park
Chippenham
Wiltshire SN15 1BN
UK

This book may not be reproduced in whole or in part in any form without written permission from the publishers.

All rights reserved.

Printed in Great Britain by BPCC Paulton Books
Typeset on Scantext by The Face Group

ISBN 1 85737 077 5

Designers	Tracy Carrington
	Jane Brett
	David Allen
	Paul Fielder
Editors	Felicia Law
	Josephine Paker
Production Manager	Julie Hitchens
Typesetting Co-ordinator	Gina Brierley
Picture Researcher	Claire Allen

Merlion photography by Mike Stannard and Bob Whitfield. Illustrations by Robert Geary, Jeremy Gower, Tony Herbert, Tony Kenyon (all B.L. Kearley Ltd.) and David Mitchell.

CONSULTANTS

Dr Frances Black BSc Med
MBBS FRACGP BA
St Ives
New South Wales, Australia

Dr Pushpa Bose
Senior Psychiatrist
Child Psychiatric Clinic
Singapore

Sue Bray BEd MEd FPEA
Lecturer in Education
University of Exeter, UK

Dr Eleanor T Elequin
Professor, Dept of
Educational Foundations
University of the Philippines
Quezon City, Philippines

Alan Emond MA MD MRCP
Consultant Paediatrician
(Community Child Health)
Bristol Royal Hospital for Sick
Children, UK

Dr Editha Marquez-Marcelo
Faculty Member, College of
Education
University of the Philippines
Quezon City, Philippines

Dr Jamshed S Moos MD
FRCP FCCP
Consulting Physician
Hon Professor of Medicine
(Retd)
Sir JJ Hospital and Grant
Medical College, Bombay,
India

Irene Pates
Singapore

Carla L La Rochelle
Teacher, Washington
Elementary School
Evanston, Illinois, USA

James C La Rochelle
Guidance Counselor
Haven Middle School
Evanston, Illinois, USA

Dr Michèle J Sadler
Consultant Nutritionist

Dr Richard Williams
Bristol Royal Hospital for Sick
Children, UK

CONTENTS

STAYING ACTIVE

LOOKING GOOD

EATING WELL

THOUGHTS & FEELINGS

CHANGING BODY

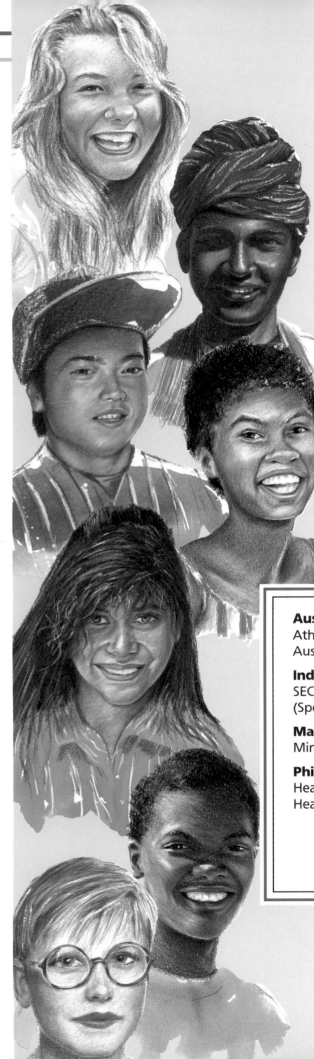

HELPLINES

Here's a list of organizations you could contact in case you'd like to find out more about some of the things discussed in this chapter. Whichever part of the world you live in, there are organizations that can answer your questions. These organizations will be happy to give you useful information and advice.

Australia
Athletics Australia
Australian Sports Commission

India
SEC Day School, Agripada
(Sports for disabled)

Malaysia
Ministry of Sports

Philippines
Heart Foundation and
Heart Center

South Africa
National Council for the
Physically Disabled

UK
British Sports Association for the
Disabled
Sports Council

You should be able to find the telephone numbers in your local telephone directory or by phoning directory enquiries.

1
STAYING ACTIVE

A young person's guide to fitness

Bodies are made to move! They are not designed to sit around in front of television or reading magazines. Keeping fit doesn't mean you have to be a super-athlete, and even a little exercise can give you a lot of fun. When you're fit and healthy, you'll find you look better and feel better. You'll have more energy and more self-confidence. In this chapter, you can read about how to keep your body fit and active.

Being active

Every time you move you are exercising. You are keeping your body tuned and in good running order. The human body is designed to bend, stretch, run, jump and climb, and to do a lot more besides. The more it does, the stronger and fitter it will become. Best of all, exercise is fun. It's what your body likes doing most of all – keeping on the move!

Feeling fit and feeling good

Feeling fit gives you confidence, which is a good feeling in itself. Training your body to be good at a particular activity is not only good for your health, but it also builds up your energy and stamina level.

Let's suppose you start swimming on a regular basis. The energy you use when you swim decreases as your skill and muscular strength improve with constant exercise. You will find that each session you can swim for a longer distance without getting tired. You increase the length of time you can exercise using the same amount of energy. You increase your stamina.

As your stamina grows, and your skill and strength develop, you will start to grow in confidence – not just in the particular activity but overall. Exercise is all about confidence and feeling great.

A question of routine

You may think staying active will take up a lot of your time. That need not be true. If you reserve part of your day for exercising regularly, it will become part of your routine. You may find you want to spend more and more time being active.

I'M STAYING HEALTHY

I'M FEELING HAPPY

I'M FEELING CONFIDENT

I'M CONCENTRATING BETTER

The benefits of exercise

People who exercise regularly will tell you that they find they have more energy to enjoy life. So have a go – you'll soon see the benefits!

6

A little each day

How fit you are depends on how much exercise you get every day. When you are young, you exercise a lot without realizing it. Little children can never keep still. They run around and leap up and down. When you're a bit older, you run to catch a bus, you reach for a book or you wash the car. These are all forms of exercise, and all involve keeping joints flexible and muscles firm. But when you're older, most of your exercise is what we call planned exercise. Dancing, walking, jogging and riding your bike are all forms of planned exercise and, providing you do it regularly, so is taking the dog for a walk.

Readers' views

"A new girl joined my class in school, and we became friends. She knew how to play tennis, but she didn't know anyone she could play with. I asked her to teach me. We started out by just hitting tennis balls over the net. She was very patient with me and we practised a lot. Now I've got so good, I'm playing as her doubles partner in the next tournament."
Rita

"Cycling is my favourite sport. I ride my bike everywhere, to and from school and visiting friends. My sports teacher at school gave me some extra coaching and encouraged me to enter for a local race. I won first prize! I'd like to try a national race next year."
Tom

"One day, a friend asked me to play in the volleyball team. I'd never played before but it looked like fun, so I went along. I don't think I was very good but I really enjoyed the game. Now I go every week and have a great time. It's not just playing the game that I like but meeting up with all my friends – I'm part of the team now."
Connie

"Roller skating was a real craze last year. Everyone could roller skate except me. I was sure I couldn't do it. I knew I'd lose my balance and fall over, and everyone would laugh. Then I was given a pair of skates for my birthday. My friend forced me to put them on and try them out. Of course, I fell over! And of course she laughed, but I bet everyone falls at first. I tried again, and again – and learned to keep my balance. I felt great! It was good to join the others and see their surprise. Now I can skate really fast."
Ben

How active are you?

How active are you? How much exercise do you tell people you take? And how much do you actually take? Nowadays, there are many ways of saving your legs and avoiding exercise. You can usually get a ride instead of walking, or you can hop into an elevator instead of climbing the stairs. Cars and elevators are wonderful inventions, but they can be a short cut to a flabby body if you use them all the time.

Chart your actions

You can find out how active you are by keeping a diary of all the different kinds of exercise you do in a week. It might be interesting to fill in the times when you watch television as well. Does this make up a large part of your time? Well, you're not alone. On average young people in the United States of America watch seven hours of television in a week. In the United Kingdom, it's 17 hours.

Compare your chart with a friend and see who leads the healthier lifestyle. This is a good way of finding out if either of you needs to change your habits!

How active should you be?

Does your diary have at least one period of exercise written down for every day of the week? If the answer is yes, then you're active enough. And there's no need to worry if there's only one day without exercise. But if you have more blanks than entries on your chart, you're definitely not getting enough exercise. You probably didn't need the chart to tell you that. Are you out of breath at the top of the stairs? Does your skin look blotchy? Do your joints creak when you move? Does everyone tell you you're just plain lazy? These are all signs that you need more exercise.

It's easy to plan an exercise regime which starts tomorrow – or the day after – or even next week. So start today with the easiest kind of exercise – walking.

MONDAY

TUESDAY

WEDNESDAY

THURSDAY

FRIDAY

SATURDAY

SUNDAY

MORNING
Helped with paper round – 1 hour on my bike.

Missed bus. Walked to school – 2 kilometres with all my kit!

Shopping. 2 kilometres round the mall with loads of bags.

This is how your exercise chart might look

AFTERNOON
Swimming 1 hour

EVENING

Badminton Club
1½ hours

2 hours of dancing at the
Youth Club – great!

Watched 2 hours of TV –
very strenuous!

Helped around the house
2 hours – hard work!

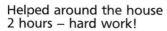

> You should do some kind of energetic exercise for at least 20 minutes, at least two or three times every week. The important thing is not so much what activity you do, but how often you do it.

Walk anytime, anywhere, and with anyone you please.

There's no excuse!

One of the simplest ways of keeping fit is to walk as much as you can. Perhaps it's easier to catch a bus or get a lift with a friend, especially if you are the kind of person who is always late! But walking to school or to a friend's house is much better. All you have to do is plan your time so you set off earlier. Walking is relaxing. Walk tall – a good posture, with back straight and stomach tucked in, gives your lungs room to work.

Work out a rhythmical stride, letting your arms swing naturally – it will be much easier than if you slouch along. If you have to carry a load, like books or shopping bags, try to divide the weight so that it is evenly split and balanced on either side of you.

Exercise for your mind

Physical exercise is not only good for your body. People who get regular exercise are usually happier, more relaxed and more alert than people who sit around all day. Try an experiment! Next time you're in a bad mood, go for a walk or play a ball game in the park. See how much better you feel after an hour.

When you take up any form of exercise, you have to learn to concentrate on what you are doing. You have to learn to control and co-ordinate your muscle movements. Developing your powers of concentration like this means you have to block out other things, which allows you to relax and stop worrying. When you finish, you feel mentally refreshed.

Which exercise is best for improving mental well-being? There is no simple answer to this question. Different benefits come from different types and amounts of exercise. It seems that using large muscle groups such as the muscles in your legs in some form of activity for 20 or 30 minutes is most likely to help.

Body and mind

Your mind and body cannot be separated. Exercise seems to prove this point. Most people who exercise regularly say that the exercise makes them feel better. This sense of mental well-being can be experienced as a warm glow, reduced tension, increased alertness, a sense of achievement, or simply a happier mood.

People whose jobs involve a lot of sitting around are often the ones who suffer most from stress. Exercise can also help people reduce their stress levels or handle their stress better. Exercise has even been helpful in treating people with illnesses such as depression.

Scientists have been hard at work trying to find out how exercise produces these benefits. Several answers seem possible. After you have finished an exercise like brisk walking, jogging, cycling or swimming, the electrical activity in your muscles is very much reduced. This produces tension-free muscles and feelings of relaxation.

SALUTE TO THE SUN
Yoga is an activity that is particularly good at helping to turn bad moods into good ones. Try this routine, called Salute to the Sun:

4. Bend your left knee between your hands and stretch your right leg out behind you. Look directly ahead and feel the stretch in your spine.

3. Gently bend your body forward. Tuck your head in and try to touch the floor with your hands.

1. Stand with your feet slightly apart and your palms pressed together in front of your chest.

2. Slowly bring your arms above your head as if touching the sides of a large, rounded Sun.

The pain killer

A recent exciting discovery was that chemicals called endorphins are released into the bloodstream during exercise. These chemicals are similar in effect to mild doses of pain killers used in hospitals. Endorphins may explain the pleasant state of mind called 'runner's high' which some people say they reach after several kilometres of running.

The mood changer

Most people find that exercise simply puts them in a better mood! They become more mentally alert. Their feelings of frustration or anger are replaced by feelings of calm or contentment. The cause of these changes is not yet understood, but it may be due to increased oxygen supply reaching the brain.

The confidence booster

A sense of achievement is another benefit of exercise. People feel good about themselves when they know they have improved their appearance and fitness. This can help self-confidence and boost self-esteem.

Yoga

This is a form of mental and physical exercise that grew out of the ancient Hindu religion in India. It involves a combination of exercising the body, concentrating, and breathing slowly and evenly. There are at least 200 poses, called postures, in yoga. These are divided into standing and sitting poses. There are also poses which refresh you after all this work, called recuperative poses. In the western world, most beginners learn Hatha yoga, which concentrates on the easier postures. People who wish to study yoga in more detail will find that there are eight different types of yoga, called disciplines.

Yoga is not competitive. The exercises keep your muscles flexible and toned. The regular breathing exercises make you feel calm and relaxed. Yoga is often recommended for people who are very tense or worried.

5. With your hands firmly on the ground, bring your left leg back to join your right, putting your knees on the floor as you do so.

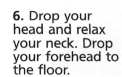

6. Drop your head and relax your neck. Drop your forehead to the floor.

7. Gently push your head and upper body backwards.

8. Push your bottom up to the ceiling, keeping your head down. Now repeat the first 3 positions in reverse order to finish upright.

Which activity do I choose?

Getting fit and staying fit is fun and there are hundreds of ways to do it – from archery to abseiling, from trampolining to Tai Chi. The list is almost endless. How will you know which to choose?

What's available?

First you'll need to find out what's available. Look in the telephone directory, or ask in the library and find out where your nearest sport or leisure centre is. See what activities they have on offer. Also look for any specialist sports clubs in your area – there might be a tennis club, or a riding school, for example. A sporting goods store might be a useful resource for community information, too. As you narrow your choices, you need to make some decisions.

How much time do you have?

When does your free time occur in the day? You may be free for an hour at 7 o'clock in the morning which is great for jogging or keep-fit exercises, but you may not find anyone around then to play tennis with you.

What can you afford to spend?

Will your new activity cost anything? Depending on what pursuit you choose, there may be very little to spend, or several costs involved. Work out how much money you have, and what you would have to pay for the fares to the sports centre, the cost of admission and the cost of lessons.

Don't worry about expensive clothes and equipment. Many sports clubs and leisure centres can supply beginners with everything they need. When you decide to get your own equipment, look on the notice board for second-hand bargains. If you are really broke, there are still things you can do. You don't need to join classes or clubs to take up walking or jogging. If you have a bike, cycling is free, too.

When do I start?

When you've decided what you want to do, get started straight away. You may try several different activities before you find the one that's just right for you. You might even end up with several new things to do, all fun and all good exercise.

Beating a bully

"I was getting picked on at school by a bully. I couldn't do anything about it because he was much bigger and stronger than I was. One day, I saw a film about a karate expert and wished I could be like him. So I signed up for a karate course at the sports centre.

It wasn't at all what I expected. The instructor taught us that martial art is about being fit and defending yourself, not about getting your own back on your enemies. First of all, we learned all the different movements. As the weeks went by, I got much fitter and stronger. And I did loads of practice at home as well. Now I really look forward to each lesson.

Maybe the bully heard that I was going to karate, or maybe I just wasn't afraid of him any more. He left me alone. Now I am a purple belt and working on my next grading. I can't imagine being bullied now I know how to take care of myself. I'm also keeping an eye open in case that bully is annoying other kids. I might be able to help them."

Go it alone?

Another decision you should make is whether you like doing things on your own. Also, do you have the self-discipline to set exercise targets and stick to them without someone else goading you on?

Go with the group?

Many people enjoy company, and taking exercise is a good opportunity to meet new people and work together. If you're a social person, head for activities that involve a group.

It sometimes takes a little courage to join a sports club and meet new people in different surroundings. The best idea is to go with a friend. Friends who set realistic targets can encourage and work together. But if you can't find anyone to go with, be brave and go on your own. Also try to join the first class in a course. Then there will be other beginners who all feel the same as you. By the second session, you will probably be much more confident, by the third you will be an old hand! The most important thing is to have a go.

Playing in a team

There are two kinds of team sports. Some games, such as basketball, volleyball and soccer, can only be played by a group of people working as a team against another. Others, such as singles tennis and wrestling, are played by two people and one tries to beat the other. In these one-to-one sports the results of different games are added to make a total score.

Team sports are usually very competitive since each individual member of the team has an opposite number to play against, and the whole team must pit its skills against the other team and work as a group. Wanting your team to come out on top can inspire you to play your best. There are other advantages to being a member of a team, – some of which have nothing to do with the sport!

Winners and losers

Unfortunately, one team must always lose in competitive team sports. Sometimes the point of the game disappears when winning or losing matters too much. This can cause stress for players who feel pressurised to win all the time. A game that becomes an ordeal is no fun at all.

But losing doesn't mean failure. A successful game is one where your team plays as well as it can, whatever the outcome of the match. You can learn how to lose a game but still feel that you have done your best.

Co-operative sports and games

The most important part of playing any game or sport is to enjoy it. For those who don't like to compete, there are team activities which don't have winners or losers – just the pleasure of playing the game! There are hundreds of games where the object is to create co-operation and trust between players, rather than winning.

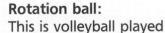

A friendly handshake after the match.

VOLLEYBALL
Here are three different fun versions of this popular game.

Rotation ball:
This is volleyball played with the standard rules. But after both sides have served, players take turns to swap over to the other team. Since there is no 'your side' and 'my side' nobody worries about the score and the game is simply enjoyed for itself!

Everyone in the team enjoys sharing in the success.

Takraw:
This fun game from Thailand and Malaysia is enjoyed by people of all ages. Players form a circle and one member of the group throws a small hollow ball up in the air. The aim of the game is to keep the ball in the air for as long as possible using only heads, knees, elbows or feet. No hands allowed!

Volley-volley ball:
The scoring system is changed in this game to allow everyone to share in the action. Each player can score from 1 to 3 points. If only one team member hits the ball before sending it back across the net, only 1 point is scored. If 3 different players hit the ball, the team get the full 3 points. The game is played to 35 points.

TEAM SPIRIT

Training and playing as a team is a skill in itself. Learning how to co-operate with others, to find your own special place in the group and to make decisions with others are skills you need in other areas of your life. Being a good team member is a useful skill for getting along with your family. And it is important when you finish school and get a job.

Members of a team help each other, supporting and encouraging the weaker members and backing up the stronger ones. Working as a team to solve problems and face difficulties together builds up courage and confidence. Being dependent on the other members of the team, with others depending on you, gives a sense of security and belonging.

A team will quickly develop its own identity, with members taking pride in the team's achievements and feeling great loyalty towards one another. It is a rewarding experience to know that you are a part of a successful team, and a challenge to be struggling to win!

One great advantage of team sports is that they are relatively cheap – you'll probably find that footwear is the most expensive item you have to buy. And being in a team can improve your social life. Meeting new people with similar sporting interests often leads to new friendships. Teams often like to socialise together away from the game, especially when they are celebrating a win!

Go it alone

Not all people who enjoy sports and physical exercise are members of a team or a club. There are many kinds of activity where you don't even need a partner. You can go it alone.

Cycling, swimming and riding are all hobbies that can be great fun in themselves. There are advantages to doing activities on your own — you don't have to rely on other people's schedules and you can set your own pace.

Some activities 'come naturally'. You don't need special abilities or equipment to enjoy them.

running

skipping

throwing

jumping

keep-fit exercises

TAKE A WALK!
Mobile bodies are healthy bodies. Most of us are able to walk, and this is a very simple, natural and healthy way to exercise.
Here are some activities that involve walking:

Orienteering
This is a way of finding your way around by reading a map and using a compass. In orienteering competitions you are given a map, and you are timed to see how quickly you can travel over a marked route.

cycling

ice skating

skiing

Some activities need to be learned, and usually involve using special equipment.

swimming

riding

Solo skills

If you want to enjoy any of these activities you'll have to learn a skill. That means training your body to move in a special way. Once you've learned the skill, you can really get going with your chosen sport.

All these kinds of sports can be enjoyed on your own as well as with friends. Feeling the wind in your hair, gaining the confidence that comes with controlling a horse or your own sense of balance or thrilling to an exciting sensation of speed are all very personal pleasures!

How do I learn?

Often, these skills can be learned from family and friends. If you don't know anyone who can teach you, find out what courses and classes are available locally by looking at notices in your library, community centre or leisure centre or in newspapers or the phone book. Tell your parents or teachers what you want to learn. They may be able to help you to find a good instructor.

If you don't have the right equipment, don't let this hold you back. Sports and leisure centres will usually hire out everything you need. Borrowing or sharing with friends are other possibilities.

You don't have to be an expert at something to like doing it. But sometimes you enjoy doing it so much, you become an expert! If you're interested in training seriously for a sport, turn to the Expert's view on page 21.

Never forgotten!

When you were young, it may have seemed very difficult to learn to ride a bike or balance on a skateboard. Some people have trouble learning to stay afloat in water, and ice skating on those two thin blades – that seems impossible! Yet if you persevere, you will train your body to learn these skills, and the great thing is that your body will not forget how to do them.

Stairs
Try climbing up and down a flight of stairs 10 times a day, then 15 times, then 20 ... You can do this easily at home, and it's a great way to get fit.

Warming up and cooling down

You've decided which exercise to do, and you're ready for action. But before asking your body to do anything energetic you must 'switch it on'. This is known as warming up. All athletes go through a warming up routine before they start exercising. Whether you are a beginner or a super-fit athlete, your body needs to be prepared for activity. There are three important reasons for this.

As you warm up, your circulation starts to work harder, taking blood and oxygen to your heart and muscles, getting your heart ready for the moment when you exert yourself. At the same time, the warming up exercises loosen your muscles and make them more elastic. This allows your body to stretch and bend easily. You can hurt yourself if you suddenly start to use muscles that are cold and stiff. Meanwhile, the cartilage in your major joints gets thicker and warmer as you move. The thickness improves the strength of the joints, and as a result you are less likely to injure yourself.

GET MOVING

The time you spend warming up depends on the kind of workout activity you are about to do. The basic rule is that the more energetic the workout activity, the longer you should take to warm up for it. There are different kinds of warming up exercises for various activities. It's a good idea to start any warm-up session with some gentle jogging.

Gently work on the exercises. Take your time to stretch thoroughly and warm up your body and remember to listen for messages from your body. If a particular movement hurts, stop! Give yourself a rest and then move on to another kind of exercise.

Here are some general warm-up exercises which will help your posture, your heart, and the muscles and joints throughout your body.

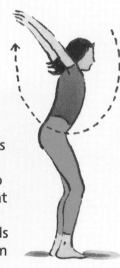

Twist from the waist to strengthen thighs and back.

Relax and slowly unwind to an upright position.

Exercise against a wall to strengthen leg muscles.

1. Stand upright with your knees slightly bent. Stretch one hand out to the side, and sweep it up over your head and back. Repeat five times then try it with the other arm. Now raise both hands above your head and wave them from side to side.

2. Standing with your knees slightly bent, put your hands at the top of your legs. Slowly bend the top half of your body from one side to the other 20 times.

3. Stand with hands stretched above your head. Bend your knees and in one sweeping movement, swing your arms down and up behind you in a circle. Without stopping, swing them forward again and up high over your head. Repeat this exercise.

4. Stand facing a wall and rest one hand against it. Grip your right ankle with your right hand, and gently pull your leg up until your heel touches your bottom. Let your leg go. Do this 10 times with each leg.

5. Stand an arm's length away from a wall. Face the wall and place both your hands flat against it. Bend your arms, leaning forward until your body touches the wall. Keep your body straight. Now push away from the wall until you are standing up again. Do 10 more push-ups against the wall.

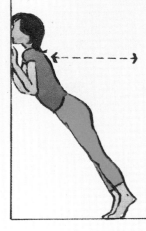

6. Finish your warm-up routine by jogging on the spot or skipping for a few minutes. Better still, put on your favourite music and dance. This will loosen up your whole body.

Cooling down

After exercise, it's just as important for your body to slow down gradually as it was for you to warm up. Cooling down gently allows your heartbeat to alter its rhythm easily from a fast, pumping action to its regular pace. If you stop exercising suddenly, when your heart is still racing, you may feel dizzy.

When your body is working hard, the muscles make a substance called lactic acid which builds up around your muscles. You need to allow the lactic acid to disperse by doing some slow stretches. If you stop your exercising suddenly, without cooling down, you'll feel very stiff the next day. Relax with a few bending and stretching movements. Take some deep breaths to help control your heartbeat.

Be sure you are completely cooled off before taking a shower. If you are still warm, the hot shower water may make you feel faint. After cooling down, enjoy a refreshing drink to replace the fluids you have sweated out while exercising. Fruit juice is a good choice, as it provides sugar, potassium and water.

Shoulder exercises loosen the muscles in the upper part of the body.

Feel the stretch throughout the whole of one side of your body.

Feel the stretch in the leg, buttock and lower back.

Serious training

Once you have started to get fit, your body will respond to any demand you may make on it. In fact, the more activities you enjoy, the fitter and healthier you will become. As you race around in an exciting ball game like hockey or basketball, there isn't time to think about how your body is working. You just concentrate on playing the game and your body gets on with the job of moving.

Getting off to a good start is an important technique in track athletics.

Young kayakers listen to their instructor.

Switch on and tune in

Taking regular exercise puts you in tune with your body. This means that you develop a good idea of how much you can do or can't do. Sometimes, you'll be surprised to find you can carry on exercising longer than you expected without getting tired. This happens when you have built up stamina through practice. You can read more about this on pages 28 and 29.

Get into the habit of exercise now and make it part of your daily routine. Switching on and tuning in to your body is like finding your favourite radio station – it gives you a lot of pleasure! The very least your body needs to keep in shape is twenty minutes' exercise three times a week. But if you can build up to four or five times a week that's even better. Bodies thrive on MORE exercise rather than JUST ENOUGH!

Enough is enough

At the same time, your body will soon tell you if you are overdoing things or going too fast. The basic rule is: listen for messages! If you run out of breath you will be forced to stop. But take notice of any sort of pain, whether it is a sharp one like a 'stitch' or a nagging ache somewhere. Your body is telling you to take a break. Take a few deep breaths and let your lungs catch up with the rest of you! If you feel dizzy, have a temporary black-out or get cramp, STOP AT ONCE.

If you find a sport you really enjoy, or show real talent in, you will probably want to train hard. You will want to beat your own records, or you may want to do well in competitions. Serious training will certainly improve your performance, but you'll need to remember to leave enough time for school work and other activities.

Coaching

Once you have built up some knowledge of a sport, you may want to take it up more seriously. This means concentrating on your skill to improve your performance. You will need to put aside more time for your sport, too. This may be hard – serious swimmers and track athletes often have to get up very early in the morning to train before school or college.

To help you achieve all this, you will need someone else's experience and advice. The best person to help you is a trained coach. Your coach will be the most important person in your sporting life and will help you to develop the skills you already have so that you can achieve more. Many coaches have been successful competitors in the past and know their sport backwards.

Once you are signed up, you will have to attend coaching sessions once or twice a week. Most will follow the same pattern. You will start the session with warming up, to build and tone your muscles for the more strenuous exercise to come. In some sports, especially contact ones, your coach will be building your body shape for maximum power.

Next, your coach will probably concentrate on specially designed exercises to develop co-ordination and skill in the most important aspects of your sport. Timing is an all-important element of most sports, which means that your hand-eye co-ordination must be extremely fast.

You may have to repeat these exercises over and over again for repetition is a very important part of training. Your coach will notice and correct your mistakes so that eventually you perform well without thinking.

Training for some sports will involve team skills. The coach will watch all of you, calling out advice and encouragement throughout the game. You may find yourself back in front of the blackboard, analyzing tactics and moves. If you play a game like American football, you will have to learn plays off by heart. The coach will also remind you about rules and discipline so that you will know how to behave when you take part in competitions.

Coaching sessions end with cooling down exercises. The coach may also take time to assess your progress. Expect some criticism. Every move you make will be analyzed. You will be expected to learn from your errors. Try to be self-disciplined enough to act on the advice you get.

TRAINING EXERCISES

Here are some of the exercises you might be asked to practise in a soccer coaching session:

1. Tapping
Move around touching the ball forwards and sideways using the inside and outside of one foot alternately. Swap feet.

2. Stopping
Tap the ball forward using the outside of the foot. Let the ball travel 3 or 4 paces then stop it using the underside of your foot. Aim to stop quickly and balance. Swap feet.

3. Turning
Stop the ball as before then pull it behind your body using one toe. Turn and face the opposite direction to retrieve the ball. Swap feet.

4. Dribbling
Use the inside and outside of your foot to control the ball in a 'snake-like' movement as you move forward. Swap feet.

Activity chart

Here is a chart that summarizes many of the sports and activities you might want to consider for exercise. Three stars means most beneficial, and one star means least beneficial for stamina, strength and flexibility.

In the last column there is a list of equipment you may need but don't forget that in most cases you don't have to get it all at once.

	Stamina	Strength	Suppleness	Minimum number of participants	Special equipment
Archery	*	*	*	1	Bow, arrows, arm guard.
Badminton	**	**	**	2	Racquet, shuttlecocks, rubber-soled shoes.
Baseball	**	**	**	2 teams of 9	Bat, ball, leather gloves.
Basketball	***	**	**	2	Basketball boots or sneakers, basketball.
Billiards	*	*	*	2	Billiard table, cues, balls.
Bowling (ten-pin)	*	*	*	2	Bowls, bowling shoes, lightweight loose-fitting clothing.
Boxing	***	***	*	2	Gloves, shorts, vest, boots, gum shield, head guard.
Canoeing	**	***	*	1	Canoe, paddle, life jacket, helmet.
Climbing stairs	*	*	*	1	
Cricket	*	*	**	2 teams of 11	Bat, ball, leg pads, gloves.
Croquet	*	*	*	2	Mallets, balls, hoops and pin, wear rubber-soled, flat-heeled shoes.
Curling	*	*	**	2 teams of 4	Stones, brooms, tee, rubber-soled shoes or boots with a sliding sole on one foot.
Cycling	***	**	*	1	A bicycle, goggles, gloves and a hard hat or crash helmet.
Dancing	***	**	***	1	Shoes suitable for the particular kind of dancing, for example, ballet slippers.
Darts	*	*	*	1	Darts, a dart board.
Digging in garden	**	**	**	1	A spade, strong shoes or wellington boots.
Driving	*	*	*	1	A motor vehicle and a driving licence.
Fencing	*	**	**	2	Face mask, padded jacket and glove. Foil, sabre or epée as appropriate.
Fishing	*	*	*	1	Rod, line, hooks, flies or sinkers as appropriate, net.
Football (American)	**	**	**	2 teams of 11	Football, helmet, face guard, padding for chest, shoulders, ribs, kidneys, crotch, thighs and shins, boots, team jersey, pants.
Football (soccer)	**	**	**	2 teams of 11	Football, team jersey and shorts, studded boots.

	Stamina	Strength	Suppleness	Minimum number of participants	Special equipment
Golf	*	*	**	1	Clubs, bag for clubs, balls, tees, studded shoes.
Gymnastics	*	***	***	1	Leotard, long gymnastic trousers for boys.
Hiking	***	**	*	1	Strong shoes or boots, lightweight waterproof.
Hockey	**	**	**	2 teams of 11	Hockey stick, shin pads, ball.
Horse riding	**	*	*	1	Horse, hard hat, jodhpurs (reinforced trousers), gloves, riding boots.
Housework	*	*	**	1	Duster, broom, vacuum cleaner.
Ice-hockey	**	**	**	2 teams of 6	Stick, skates, skate heel guards, protective face mask, gloves, pads for shoulders, elbows and shins.
Jogging	***	**	*	1	Loose comfortable clothing, flat, rubber-soled shoes.
Judo	*	**	**	2	Jacket and trousers, belt in appropriate colour for your grade.
Jumping (ski)	**	***	**	1	Skis, goggles, helmet, gloves, ski suit, boots.
Karate	**	**	**	2	Jacket and trousers, belt in appropriate colour for your grade.
Keep-fit	**	**	**	1	Leotard or track suit.
Lacrosse	**	**	**	2 teams of 10	Crosse, ball.
Mountain climbing	***	**	**	2	Hard hat, boots.
Mowing lawn	*	*	*	1	Lawn mower.
Orienteering	**	**	*	1	Orienteering compass, track suit or orienteering suit, studded athletic shoes.
Rowing	***	***	**	1	Boat, oars, life jacket.
Rugby (Union)	**	**	**	2 teams of 15	Studded rugby boots, headband or scrum cap, team jersey.
Running	***	**	*	1	Loose-fitting clothing, running shoes or trainers.
Sailing	*	**	**	1	Boat, life jacket.
Sawing wood	**	**	*	1	Saw.
Scuba diving	***	*	**	1	Wet suit, swim fins, buoyancy compensator, weighted belt, face mask, air tanks.
Sculling	***	***	**	1	Boat, oars.
Shooting	*	*	*	1	Shotgun, rifle or pistol for appropriate type of shooting, ear protectors, licence to use weapon.
Skating (ice)	**	**	*	1	Skates, boots.
Skating (roller)	**	**	*	1	Roller skates, knee pads, elbow pads.
Skin-diving	***	*	**	1	Wet suit, face mask, snorkel, swim fins.
Skiing (cross-country)	***	***	**	1	Skis, ski suit, boots, goggles, gloves, ski poles.
Skiing (downhill)	**	**	**	1	Skis, ski suit, boots, goggles, gloves, ski poles.
Snooker	*	*	*	2	Snooker table, cues, balls.
Squash	***	**	**	2	Racquet, non-marking shoes.
Surfing	**	**	**	1	Wet suit or baggies, surf board.
Swimming	***	***	***	1	Swimming costume, goggles, cap.
Table tennis	**	**	**	2	Bat, balls.
Tennis	**	**	**	2	Racquet, tennis balls, rubber-soled shoes.
Volleyball	**	**	**	2 teams of 6	Flexible heelless shoes, net, ball.
Walking briskly (over 1 hour)	***	*	*	1	Strong, comfortable flat-heeled shoes.
Washing/polishing car	*	*	*	1	Sponge, dusters, bucket, soap.
Water polo	***	**	**	2 teams of up to 13 – only 7 in water	Swimming costume, cap, ball.
Water skiing	**	**	**	2	Life jacket, skis, boat.
Weight lifting	*	***	*	1	Leotard, boots.
Wrestling	**	***	***	2	One-piece suit, heelless soft shoes.

Equipped for exercise

Sporty people can sometimes seem to be a totally different species! You might see them striding purposefully around, wearing special outfits, brandishing weird implements, and flexing parts of their anatomies that most of the rest of us don't seem to have!

But don't be put off. The most important piece of equipment you'll need when taking up a new sport or activity is your body.

For freedom of movement you'll need some loose-fitting, comfortable clothes. Cotton is the best fibre to wear while exercising, because it is cool and it absorbs sweat better than a man-made, or synthetic, fibre. It's very important to wear really comfortable shoes. You won't be able to concentrate on what you're doing if your feet hurt!

Buy sensibly

Before you rush out to buy the latest trendy sports gear, remember that sports clothing is a huge fashion industry. The makers want to tempt you into spending lots of money on attractive designs. Have a look in your wardrobe first – you'll probably find suitable clothes for most activities!

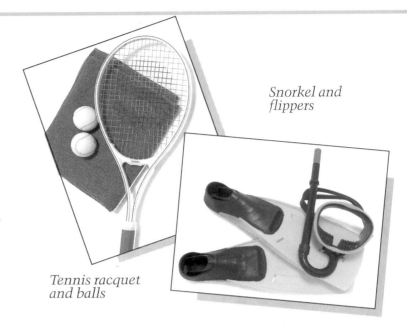

Snorkel and flippers

Tennis racquet and balls

Some sports do require special clothing or equipment, and you'll find out exactly what you might need after you've had your first lesson or two. Until you're sure that it's the activity for you, it's a better idea to hire or borrow the things you need. Once you have decided that you do want to continue with a particular sport, you should consider buying a special sports bra for girls, and an athletic supporter if you are a boy.

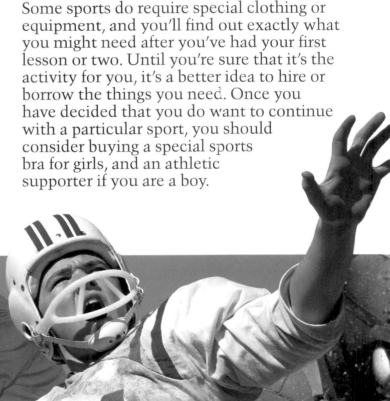

24

Protective gloves

Karate belts

Cycling and horse-riding helmets

Reflective clothing to wear at night

Serious spending!

Buying sporting equipment can be a very expensive business. From squash racquets to surfboards, mountain bikes to water skis, there's a big difference in the quality and price of different makes. Always get expert advice before spending too much money. And remember that it's worth looking out for second-hand bargains. With any luck, you may find that your sports club supplies the equipment, and you won't need to buy any at all!

Note the special clothing and protective gear worn in these photos.

SAFETY FIRST

Safety equipment is essential for some sports and activities, and should always be worn. Here are some of the sports that require protective clothing or equipment:

Life jackets are essential for sailing, boating and water-skiing.

Thermal suits are needed for skiing and deep sea diving.

Riders, go-cart racers and climbers always wear hard hats.

Ice hockey players must wear helmets with full face masks and special pads.

Fencers must wear full face masks, and should also wear padded jackets and a thick glove on their sword hand.

Cricketers should wear leg pads and gloves when they are batting.

Goalkeepers in sports like soccer, hockey and lacrosse wear padding all over their bodies, and face masks too. The same applies to catchers in baseball, and wicket-keepers in cricket.

More safety points

When you go off to any activity always tell someone where you are going and when you expect to be back.

Never swim alone at a pool or beach.

If you are exercising at night, particularly on roads, always wear reflective clothing so that you are visible.

Don't go jogging in lonely areas or in heavy traffic.

Getting energy

Food provides the energy your body needs to keep going. It is the fuel of life. Different foods contain body-building substances known as nutrients. These are proteins, carbohydrates, fats, vitamins and minerals. Your body needs all these nutrients to work properly.

When you eat a good variety of foods, you get the right amount of nutrients. This is known as getting a balanced diet. A balanced daily diet should contain about 50-60 percent carbohydrate, 20-30 percent fat and 12-15 percent protein, with vitamins and minerals in addition. Foods rich in carbohydrates include bananas, potatoes, rice, bread and pasta. Fat-rich foods are butter and oils, cheese and whole milk. Foods containing plenty of protein include meat, fish, eggs, cheese, beans, peas and nuts. Fruit and vegetables are rich in vitamins and minerals.

The secret of giving your body the high energy, top quality fuel it needs is a balanced diet. Eat as many different kinds of food as you can. Be sure to include fresh fruit and vegetables, meat, fish, low-fat dairy produce and cereals. These are all fuel for fitness. It's the combination of good diet and exercise that keeps you in top form.

Your body uses the energy in food in four main ways:

To live
As you know, food energy keeps your heart beating and lungs breathing. Everything you do — talking, sleeping, working, even laughing takes energy supplied by food. The carbohydrates found in foods such as bread and potatoes make them good sources of energy for people with an active lifestyle.

To grow
Growing takes a lot of energy. When you enter your teens, you are growing at one of the fastest rates in your life. This is why it is so important to eat well at this time. Foods rich in protein such as meat and nuts help you grow.

To be healthy
Your body needs vitamins and minerals to be healthy. If your body doesn't get enough of them, you may develop deficiency diseases.

Lack of iron, for example, leads to anaemia, which is a blood disorder. Calcium is essential for healthy bones and teeth. But to convert calcium into a form in which it can be absorbed, your body needs vitamin D. Fresh fruit, vegetables and dairy produce provide vitamins and minerals.

To make and store fat
The fat in your body protects the organs and bones in your body. It also insulates you, helping you keep warm. Your body can use its fat as a fuel store, converting it into energy. The fats you eat, including butter and margarine, also contain important vitamins.

BURN IT UP

Different kinds of exercise use up different amounts of calories.
Check to see how your favourite activity scores!
You'll burn up each hour:

175 calories	270 calories	355 calories	435 calories	740 calories
strolling	walking slowly	walking at a	walking briskly	sprint walking
rifle-shooting	badminton	normal pace	running slowly	normal running
table tennis	bowling (ten-pin)	gentle jogging	climbing	boxing
billiards	canoeing	basketball	football	handball
boules	dancing	cycling	skiing	rugby
bowls (green)	diving	fencing	swimming	squash
archery	rowing	gymnastics		water polo
cricket	softball	hockey		wrestling
croquet	baseball	orienteering		
golf	surfing	karate		
sailing		lacrosse		
		judo		
		rambling		
		skating		
		sub aqua		
		tennis		
		trampolining		

Calorie count

The energy in food is measured in kilojoules or calories. Some foods provide more energy than others. Most packaged food has its kilojoule or calorie value printed on the package. These labels also tell you how much protein, carbohydrate and fat is in the food, together with all the other ingredients.

How many calories you need depends on many factors, including how active you are. On average, adolescents between the ages of 12 and 16 need between 2,100 and 2,800 calories a day. Not just any calories, though. Many sugary treats and snacks supply calories without enough nutrients.

Eating and exercise

After eating a meal, you need some time to digest it. This is because your body tackles food by diverting blood to the stomach to break the food down. Taking on vigorous exercise at the same time puts a strain on your system and makes you feel sick. Wait at least two hours after a meal before doing anything very energetic.

If you eat foods high in calories but low in nutrients and if you don't take enough exercise to burn up the calories, you soon put on weight. If extra calories are not burned up in physical activity, they are stored in the body as fat.

Increase your stamina

To get fit and stay fit you need to build up your stamina. Having stamina means that you can be active for a long time without getting too tired or out of breath. You have plenty of energy. Building up stamina makes your body more efficient. This makes the aerobic system – your heart, lungs and blood circulation – work at its best. If you have an efficient aerobic system, it will give you the energy to get the best out of any kind of physical activity.

Building up stamina

There is only one safe and effective way to increase your stamina and that is to build it up gradually. Regular exercise over a period of time is the best way to develop staying power. Always start off slowly if you are not used to exercise, and stop when your body tells you it's time for a rest.

How much exercise?

As you start exercising, you should aim to exercise for twenty minutes three times a week. Then try to build up to exercising three or four times a week for at least half an hour. Quite soon, you will notice that you are able to go on for longer with less effort. Your body is becoming fitter and faster! Once you have built up your stamina, you can enjoy your favourite sport or activity without worrying about running out of steam. You'll have staying power!

What kind of exercise?

You could begin with some running on the spot, lifting your knees as high as you can. Start with only a minute or so, and gradually increase the length of time you run. Then you could try stepping up onto a bench or low stool. This sounds easy enough, but see what you feel like when you've done it 30 times with the right foot first, and then 30 with the left foot first!

Certain kinds of exercise, called aerobic exercise, are especially good for building up stamina. They involve taking more air into your lungs. Read more about this on pages 30 and 31. Choose an activity from the **Aerobic exercise** section.

Runners set out on a 'fun run' marathon.

RUNNING RULES

It is better to run on grass than on roads.

Keep your back straight and breathe evenly through your mouth.

Make your heel touch the ground first, so the weight on your foot rolls forwards, from heel to the toe.

Keep your arms and shoulders relaxed, elbows slightly bent.

Give your arms a shake every so often to stop them tensing up.

Always warm up before jogging and cool down afterwards.

Slowing down and growing up

Being fit isn't about pushing yourself all the time. Relaxing and resting are important parts of a healthy lifestyle, too. Sleep is a vital time for your body, allowing it time to repair and rebuild itself. You're growing fast during your teenage years and although it may seem surprising, most of this growing takes place when you are asleep! Make sure you have at least eight hours of sleep a night and more if you're very active. If you rest when you're tired, you'll have more energy when you need it. A balanced routine of exercise, rest, relaxation and sleep will build up your stamina, get you fit and keep you there.

LET'S JOG

Let's imagine that you have decided to take up jogging. In order to build up stamina, you will need a jogging routine. But don't overdo it! For most people a maximum comfortable jogging distance is 8-16 kilometres. It's important for your body to have times of rest and recovery. It is not a good idea to train vigorously more than five days a week.

1. First of all make sure you are wearing loose, comfortable clothing and suitable running shoes with flat, cushioned soles.

2. Take a brisk walk every other day. 10 or 15 minutes will be enough at first. Every so often, break into a jog for a minute or so. Keep the jogging pace slow and steady. If you feel a pain or run out of breath, slow down or stop until you are ready to continue.

3. As the weeks go by, increase the jogging periods bit by bit until you are jogging more than you are walking.

4. Aim to jog consistently for an entire 15 minutes and then very gradually increase the distance you run. Remember to stay at a comfortable pace.

Aerobic exercise

The word aerobics was first used by an American fitness expert called Dr Kenneth Cooper. Aerobic means 'with air'. Aerobic exercise is any exercise which makes you breathe deeper and take more air into your lungs. Your heart and lungs work with the blood circulating around your body to provide your muscles with a supply of oxygen. This process is called the aerobic system. Aerobic exercise strengthens your heart, making it beat faster. Aerobic exercise makes the aerobic system better at its job.

What is aerobic exercise?

Any form of rhythmic exercise which is kept up at a steady pace for 15 minutes to an hour can be called aerobic exercise. Aerobic exercise is wonderful for building up stamina, and will help you to go on exercising for longer without getting tired. Aerobic exercise can range from a gentle activity like walking, to a very energetic sport like cross-country skiing. Whatever level you choose, you need to exercise aerobically at least three times a week to stay healthy.

GET AEROBIC!
Here are some types of aerobic exercise:

Cycling
Either ride out and about or on an exercise bicycle.

Jogging
You can jog on the spot but like cycling, it's much more interesting to get out and look at the passing scenery!

Swimming
This is thought to be the best activity there is for strength, stamina and flexibility — the most important benefits of exercise. Your body is supported by the water as it moves.

Skipping
Keeping a steady rhythm is the best way to skip. After a while you will be able to skip for longer without tripping up or getting tired.

Rowing
Keeping a steady rhythm is the only way to row! This is another aerobic exercise which is good for developing stamina and improving co-ordination.

Squash and tennis
These sports are only aerobic if you spend more time playing than fetching the ball!

Don't forget to do some warm-up exercises before you start your aerobic exercises. They'll get blood and oxygen flowing to your muscles.

Team sports
Many team sports provide opportunity for both aerobic and anaerobic exercise. Players move up and down the field following the ball, but a sudden burst of energy is needed to sprint towards goal, tackle, or intercept a pass.

Ice skating and roller skating
Like all the other activities listed here, these sports need to be practised continually for at least 15 minutes to be aerobic. You will use a steady rhythm with lots of twists and turns.

Dancing
All kinds of dancing are aerobic, from tap dancing to disco. Exercise dance classes are a good form of aerobic exercise. You can also do dance routines at home with a cassette tape, record or video.

Cross-country skiing
The pace may be steady, but trudging relentlessly across snow-covered ground for ten to twenty kilometres requires strong lungs and muscles.

Ball games
Many ball games are aerobic if played at a steady, energetic pace.

How does it work?

Aerobic exercise makes you breathe more deeply and take more air into your body. More oxygen, carried in your blood, reaches all the organs, bones and muscles. Your body uses this oxygen to produce energy, which in turn allows you to do more. This is a very efficient, self-service system, which is a bit like an endless equation in maths: X (Exercise) $= O$ (Oxygen) $= X$ (Exercise) and so on.

Once you have built up some stamina with regular aerobic exercise, you can use this formula, just as long distance runners and swimmers do, to increase your staying power.

Anaerobic exercise

Not all exercise is taken at a steady pace. For example, when you're going for a goal, or running in a 100 metres sprint race, you may need a short burst of hard exercise. The aerobic formula can't provide enough energy for all this sudden exercise, so your body uses an emergency supply of energy which is already stored in the muscles. Exercising in this way is called anaerobic exercise. Anaerobic means 'without air'.

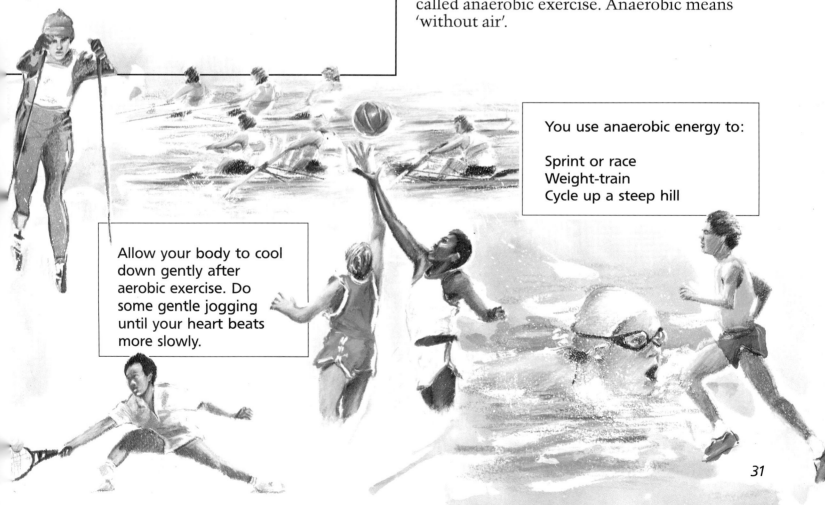

You use anaerobic energy to:

Sprint or race
Weight-train
Cycle up a steep hill

Allow your body to cool down gently after aerobic exercise. Do some gentle jogging until your heart beats more slowly.

Your heart

Your heart is a muscle that has a very special job to do. It pumps blood around the body, keeping you alive. Every day it pumps blood through about 96,500 kilometres of tubes called blood vessels. Your heart beats through every minute of your life, even when you are asleep. You don't even have to think about it. An adult heart weighs about 340 grams. You can feel yours beating by pressing the flat of your hand against the middle of your chest.

When you're young, you are likely to be as energetic as you will ever be, so your heart should be at its healthiest. But if you are lazy about exercising, or eating too much, your heart will already be under strain doing extra work. For example, every pound of excess fat on your body means your heart has to push blood through about 320 extra kilometres of tubes.

So it's definitely worth taking care of your heart while you're young! Think about what you eat and, most importantly, make sure you take some exercise.

The heart and exercise

The blood delivers oxygen from the lungs to all the muscles, bones and organs in your body. Muscles need oxygen to work. When you exercise, your muscles work harder and need more oxygen. This is why the heart beats faster when you take exercise of any kind. Since the heart itself is a muscle, it also needs more oxygen to beat faster.

Hearts thrive on exercise. Beating faster makes them stronger and bigger, which in turn makes them better able to do their job. More blood carrying more oxygen reaches the rest of the body. Exercise makes the blood move faster around your body and this is healthy for two important reasons.

The first reason is that waste deposits are less likely to build up as the blood washes through the system. And in addition, arteries and veins stay strong and flexible because the extra blood flowing through them keeps them working hard. Keeping your heart healthy will make sure that your body benefits from both these advantages.

HOW DOES THE HEART WORK?

The muscle fibre of the heart contracts and relaxes to pump blood. Blood is pumped away from the heart to the lungs, where it receives oxygen. It then returns to the heart to be delivered to the rest of the body. It is carried away through blood vessels called arteries. It travels around your body and then returns to the heart through much thinner blood vessels called veins. The blood's journey through the body is called circulation.

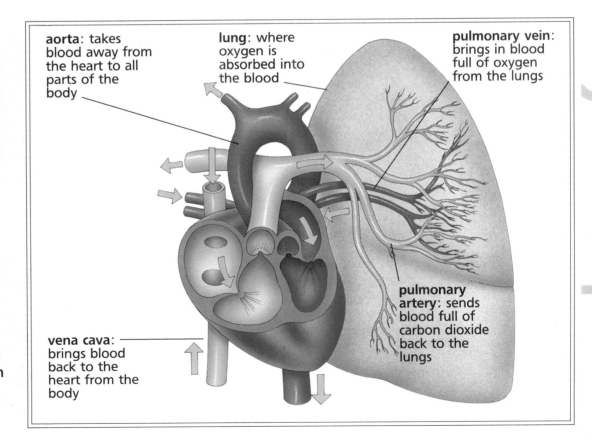

aorta: takes blood away from the heart to all parts of the body

lung: where oxygen is absorbed into the blood

pulmonary vein: brings in blood full of oxygen from the lungs

pulmonary artery: sends blood full of carbon dioxide back to the lungs

vena cava: brings blood back to the heart from the body

The rhythm of life

Every time the heart muscle pumps, there is a heartbeat. An adult who is relaxing will register about 70 heartbeats in one minute. This number of beats is known as one's resting pulse rate. Younger people have faster pulse rates.

The pulse is a throb, or wave, of pressure which passes through the arteries. Feeling and counting the pulse lets you know how fast and strongly your heart is beating. Try taking your pulse before and after physical activity and see how much faster your heart beats after exercise! An easy pulse to find is in your wrist.

Measure your pulse here.

You'll need a watch with a second hand.

HOW TO TAKE YOUR PULSE

1. Press two fingers lightly on the inside of your wrist. You are looking for a place near the base of the thumb.

2. If you can't feel a throb, move your fingers slightly. Don't press too hard.

3. Once you have found the pulse, you need to time it. Count how many times it throbs in fifteen seconds and multiply the amount by four.

This figure is your pulse rate, which tells you how many times a minute your heart is beating.

Measure your pulse rate as you exercise.

TRAINING AND PULSE RATES

People who are training hard for any sport think seriously about their pulse rate. They take their pulse rates before, during and after an exercise session. Keeping track of their pulse helps them to train in the right way. An extremely fit athlete will achieve a pulse rate of up to 180 beats per minute.

Pulse rate chart
Heartbeats per minutes after exercising

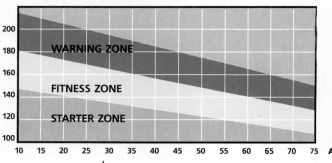

Next time you are exercising, stop and take your pulse. If your pulse rate is in the Starter Zone, which is purple on the chart, you need to work your body a little bit harder. Your pulse rate should be in the Fitness Zone, shown as blue on the chart.

Regular exercise makes your heart stronger. After a time, it is able to send more blood around the body with fewer beats. The added strength makes your pulse rate drop. Exercising a bit more and keeping your pulse rate in the Fitness Zone will improve your performance. The pulse beat can be irregular even in healthy young people, so just check again if you notice this.

If your pulse rate is pushed up to the Warning Zone, you probably need to stop for a while and give yourself a rest. It's better to strengthen your heart gradually.

Breathe in, breathe out

Lungs are your body's breathing equipment. When you are resting, you take air into the lungs at the rate of about 15 breaths a minute. Inside the lungs, oxygen is taken out of the air and absorbed into the bloodstream. Then your heart pumps it to the rest of the body. All the organs and muscles inside you need to draw on this oxygen supply to produce energy.

Lungs and exercise

Your body needs more oxygen when it is exercising, so you need to take faster and deeper breaths to handle the extra demand. The lungs must work especially hard to take in as much oxygen as they can to feed the muscles. Like various other parts of your body your lungs get stronger whenever you exercise. The connection between breathing and exercising is like a circle. Breathing helps exercising which in turn helps breathing, and so on. The lungs also help to keep your body temperature down. This is because you breathe in cool air and blow out warm air. You also lose moisture when you breathe out, especially during exercise.

Deep breathing

We all take breathing for granted. Air is all around us. We have got used to this free supply of oxygen and other gases. But few of us breathe properly. Most people in the western world use only a tiny part of their lung capacity, surviving on lots of short, shallow breaths.

In many eastern countries breathing is treated more seriously. When we are relaxed our breathing becomes deeper and slower. Many experts believe that it's good for us to breathe deeply from time to time, and learn to fill our lungs with air in one steady breath. Deep breathing stimulates the blood circulation, pumps more oxygen to the brain, calms the nerves and makes sure we get rid of stale air trapped in the system. Some eastern relaxation techniques, like yoga, combine breathing exercises with stretching.

HOW YOUR LUNGS WORK

You take in air through your nose or mouth. The air travels down a main passageway called the trachea, or windpipe.

The trachea branches into hundreds of air passages called bronchi, which end in thousands of air sacs called alveoli.

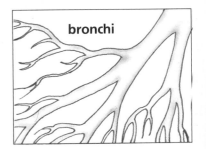

Although each alveolus is very tiny, if they were all spread out side by side they would cover an area larger than a singles tennis court!

A fine mesh of tiny veins called capillaries surround the alveoli. Capillaries are full of blood.

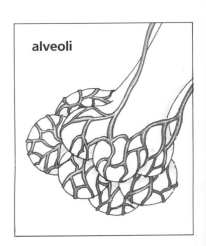

Here, the oxygen you breathe in is absorbed into the bloodstream and then it is carried around the body to the muscles and organs.

HOW YOU BREATHE

You have muscles in your chest that make you breathe. Some are fixed to your ribs and make your rib cage move in and out. Below your lungs is a strong muscle called the diaphragm.

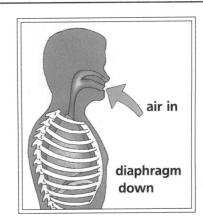

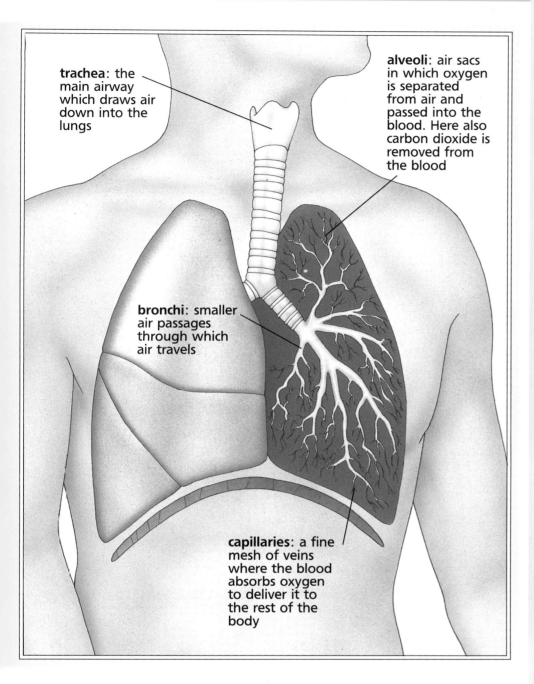

trachea: the main airway which draws air down into the lungs

alveoli: air sacs in which oxygen is separated from air and passed into the blood. Here also carbon dioxide is removed from the blood

bronchi: smaller air passages through which air travels

capillaries: a fine mesh of veins where the blood absorbs oxygen to deliver it to the rest of the body

As you breathe in, your diaphragm moves downwards and your rib cage moves out. This makes a bigger space for your lungs to move into. As you breathe out, your rib cage and diaphragm squeeze your lungs into a smaller space again.

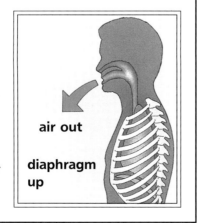

air out

diaphragm up

Lung problems

Any illness that interferes with the normal function of the lungs is going to affect how you perform physically. Bronchitis and asthma are two very common conditions where it becomes very hard to keep a good supply of air passing through the lungs. In fact it becomes difficult for the sufferer to breathe. No exercise should be undertaken if you have bronchitis, pneumonia or pleurisy.

Bronchitis is an inflammation of the bronchi which are the air passages in the lung. This infection often starts as a cold, or as an infection of the throat. Sufferers have a slight fever and a painful cough. It is treated by rest, antibiotics, inhalations and cough syrup.

Pneumonia is an infection of the lung tissues caused by bacteria, a virus or a fungus. Sufferers have a high fever, rapid pulse and breathing rate, cough and chest pain. Some sufferers become very ill. Mild pneumonia is treated by bed rest, breathing exercises and antibiotics.

Pleurisy. The pleura is a membrane which lines the inside of the chest and covers the lungs. It is usually moist, allowing the lungs to move smoothly when you breathe. If the pleura becomes inflamed, it dries, and the surfaces become rough and rub together. This is very painful, and the pain gets worse if you cough or take a deep breath. Sufferers are treated with pain killers and drugs that fight the inflammation.

Asthma see page 54-55.

Build your strength

How many times have you heard an adult say to a child, "Eat up all your food and you'll grow big and strong!" But eating well is only part of the story. People develop muscle and bone strength by exercising regularly, getting the right amount of relaxation, rest and sleep, and by eating a proper balanced diet.

These ingredients make up a simple recipe for fitness. Following it when you are young will help you to build a strong, healthy body to take you through the rest of your life. Exercise is not a magic spell. You won't miraculously turn into someone else. But a strong and fit body will make you feel physically and mentally better.

The right amount of sleep, rest and relaxation

Regular exercise

Eating a balanced diet

Getting in shape

Strength is one of the three important results of exercise, together with stamina and suppleness. But you don't have to be a body builder to become strong, nor do you have to be an Olympic sportsperson! There are other more relaxed and less demanding ways of exercising which will develop muscles and bones. You will notice the difference almost immediately. Your body shape will trim up, and you'll feel better about the way you look and move. And the more you do, the more you'll be able to do — and all with a new alertness and zest for life.

A body with a firm and attractive shape

Stamina and endurance so that you don't get tired so quickly

The confidence that comes from having a strong body

Muscles and strength

Voluntary muscles are made of two kinds of fibres called slow twitch and fast twitch fibres. You use slow twitch fibres for endurance work. Fast twitch fibres are used for bursts of power.

Fast twitch for power

Fast twitch fibres have a smaller blood supply but they are able to store energy. These muscle fibres spring into action with their emergency supply when you need more energy than the aerobic system can supply. They are used when you exercise hard in short bursts, as you might if you sprint, or throw a javelin. This kind of exercise is called anaerobic, meaning 'without air'. Anaerobic exercise is good for building up strength.

Slow twitch for endurance

Slow twitch fibres are used when you exercise aerobically. These muscle fibres have a rich blood supply. They use the oxygen in the blood as energy. This oxygen reaches your blood via your heart and lungs.

Who wants to be a "beefcake"?

Developing strength doesn't mean turning into a body builder! To turn into Mr or Ms Universe you would have to build up individual muscles with isometric exercise. This kind of exercise involves weight lifting and resistance training that includes pushing and pulling weights and springs on special equipment. Only consistent, hard isometric training, together with a particular diet, produces muscles like this!

Members of the aerobic class spend at least 20 minutes developing 'slow twitch' muscle strength.

Mr Universe flexes his muscles in the course of the famous competition.

Muscle power

Exercises which strengthen the fast twitch fibres will develop your muscles. Using your own body weight in press-ups and pull-ups is a good way to do this.

All kinds of exercise are good for general fitness and building up muscle power, but some activities, like canoeing and weight-training, are especially good for making you stronger. Isometric exercise and resistance training make single muscles and groups of muscles strain their hardest against heavy or immovable objects. If you are an adult, this eventually makes the muscles big and bulging. You can read more about developing muscles on pages 40 and 41.

But while you are still growing, you should avoid this kind of exercise for several reasons. First, growing bones and muscles can be injured. Also, young people don't have the same hormones as adults and can't develop bulging muscles even if they try!

37

Fit feet

How often do you think about your feet? Probably not often, but they are well worth considering. With every step you take, that is, each time your foot hits the ground, your foot takes the full impact of your weight – that's 50 times a minute for each foot if you're walking at a normal pace. In your lifetime you may walk 105,000 kilometres. That means your feet will have hit the ground tens of millions of times! It definitely makes good sense to take care of your feet, especially when you're exercising. Wearing the right shoes that fit well is the best way to do this.

Short riding boots

Walking boots give support to your feet

These trainers have holes in them to keep feet cool

The right shoes for exercise

Trainers and running shoes are suitable for many kinds of sports, but not for sports like skiing, skating or riding. For these sports, you will need special shoes. If you are buying trainers or running shoes, look for shoes which have thick soles, so your feet are cushioned. Plastic shoes are cheaper to buy, but plastic does not allow your feet to breathe in the same way that leather does, so they will make your feet too hot. This may lead to smelly feet. Remember that trailing laces are **dangerous**. Keep laces short and properly tied.

YOUR FEET

Your feet are very complicated structures. Did you know that each foot contains at least 26 bones as well as a complex system of joints which connect them together? Then there are the ligaments, lengths of stringy tissue, which strengthen the joints and hold them in place.

Each foot also contains many muscles which are attached to the bones. Twelve of these are found in the lower part of the leg, not the foot. They control the foot by means of long tendons that pass through the ankle and join up with various bones.

The right fit

Your shoes must fit properly to support and protect your feet. When you buy new shoes, make sure there is about one centimetre of space between the end of your toes and the shoe. Your shoes should also fit across the widest part of your foot without pinching. Also check that they don't rub against your big toe or any part of your ankle. This allows your feet to expand when you exercise. And don't forget about socks! If they are too small, they can squash your toes just as much as tight shoes can.

Don't try on new shoes if your feet are hot – they may be swollen. And remember that loose shoes are bad for your feet, too. Clenching the toes to keep them on can strain the muscles in your feet.

Walking and exercising barefoot can be good for your feet. Air can circulate around them and they can move freely. It also builds up the layers of small muscles, and this helps prevent collapsed or flat feet.

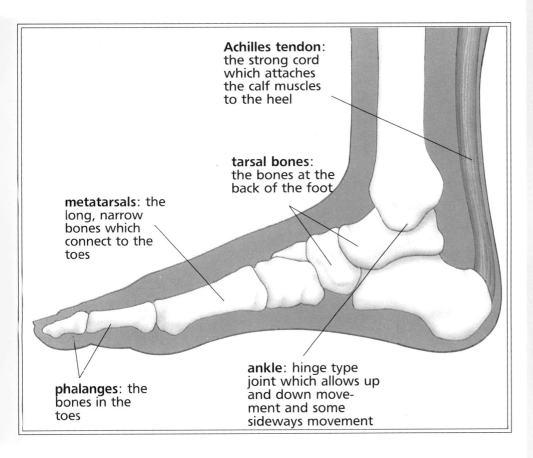

Achilles tendon: the strong cord which attaches the calf muscles to the heel

tarsal bones: the bones at the back of the foot

metatarsals: the long, narrow bones which connect to the toes

phalanges: the bones in the toes

ankle: hinge type joint which allows up and down movement and some sideways movement

Your feet are in danger

Your feet have to support your body and maintain it in a state of balance. They also have to be rigid enough to withstand pressure caused by your body movements – these forces can be very large indeed. The feet, helped by other mechanisms in the body, also act as shock absorbers. They prevent the rest of your body from being jolted when you walk, run or jump. In order to perform these tasks your feet have to be flexible and resilient.

Some people have flat feet, when the foot's arch collapses so that the sole is almost flat. Remedial exercises to strengthen the muscle can be helpful.

Like other parts of your body, feet can be damaged by over-use and shock. Muscles and ligaments can be strained, and bones fractured. Wearing shoes gives good protection to your feet. Not only do shoes keep your feet warm, and protect your soles from sharp objects but they also help to support the structure of your feet. This means that they are less likely to be injured from impact and jarring.

If your shoes are too small or fit badly, they will be uncomfortable. Badly fitting shoes can also eventually lead to permanent damage and disability. Your feet grow slowly. Consequently, badly fitting shoes can damage your feet gradually. You may not even notice the damage until after the fact.

Your muscles

"Show us your muscles!" someone is bound to call out when they see you exercising. But muscles aren't just the obvious big, beefy biceps. They are the parts of your body that help you move and there are over 600 of them. Everyone has muscles, arranged around the boney frame of the skeleton.

Strength is an important component of overall fitness. Training for strength is just as appropriate for girls as boys.

It's possible for both sexes to improve their muscle strength before puberty. But young people have low levels of a hormone called testosterone, so the muscles can strengthen but won't get much bigger. NEVER attempt to improve your strength by lifting heavy weights! Growing muscles and joints are very vulnerable to damage. The best strength exercises are those in which the body provides the resistance. Do sit-ups, pull-ups and press-ups. Weight training with fixed and free weights is popular with many adolescents, but it is important to learn the correct techniques to avoid injury.

Building up

Muscles are like all the other parts of your body. They thrive on exercise! Exercise makes them grow bigger so that they can work better. People with well-developed muscles not only look healthier, they are healthier. They can play games for longer periods of time without getting tired.

Good muscle control makes you stand properly and gives you a tight, flat stomach and firm limbs. If you've ever been ill for a while, and had to stay in bed, you probably felt weak when you got up. That's because you weren't using your muscles. Muscles need to be used in order to stay healthy.

All physical activity helps to build up muscle power, especially water sports. Swimming is a good exercise for building up muscular strength because it uses almost every muscle in the body. Canoeing and rowing are good for muscles in the upper body. So are exercises like press-ups.

The smallest muscle is the stapedius, which is in your ear. It is less than 0.127 centimetres long.

Muscles account for about 40% of your body weight.

HOW DO MUSCLES WORK?

Muscle fibre can contract and relax. When a muscle contracts, it shrinks and becomes thicker and more solid. Many muscles move in pairs. Each one of a muscle pair takes it in turn to contract or relax. These muscle pairs can move your bones. When a muscle attached to a bone (such as the biceps in this diagram) contracts, it pulls on the tendon and moves the bone. At the same time, the partner muscle (here, the triceps) stays relaxed, allowing the bone to move easily.

The biggest muscle is the buttock muscle, or gluteus maximus.

Isaac ('Dr Size') Nesser has biceps measuring 66.35 centimetres before he flexes them!

WHAT ARE MUSCLES?
There are two kinds of muscles – voluntary and involuntary.

Involuntary muscles
These work even when you are asleep. You don't have to think about them. The muscles in your intestines are involuntary muscles. So is the heart, which keeps beating all the time. Goose pimples appear when involuntary muscles make your hair stand on end in a cold wind.

Voluntary muscles
These are the kind of muscles you see on body builders – those bulging biceps and triceps! They are sometimes called skeletal muscles because they are attached to the bones of your skeleton with strips of tough material called tendons. Voluntary muscles usually work in pairs. You move voluntary muscles when your brain sends a message that asks another part of your body to move.

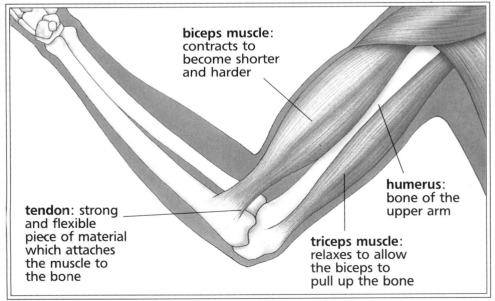

biceps muscle: contracts to become shorter and harder

humerus: bone of the upper arm

tendon: strong and flexible piece of material which attaches the muscle to the bone

triceps muscle: relaxes to allow the biceps to pull up the bone

Mighty or miniature?
Before puberty there is actually very little difference in strength between boys and girls. However, at puberty, boys show a rapid increase in muscle size and strength. This occurs mainly because levels of the male hormone testosterone increase when a boy matures.

Hormones are chemical substances produced in minute amounts in special glands in the body. There are many different hormones produced. Each has a specific and vital function such as growth or controlling development and metabolism. Metabolism is the breakdown of food in your body in order to produce energy and to build up your tissues.

One of the main effects of the hormone testosterone is to make muscles develop. Girls don't develop big, bulky muscles because their bodies don't have as much testosterone as male bodies have, but they can certainly tone up their muscles and make themselves strong and fit.

Some athletes take steroid hormones to make their muscles develop larger and faster. This is a **VERY DANGEROUS** practice and should be **AVOIDED**. These steroids can cause serious injury to the body and can interfere with normal growth and maturation. Athletes are often tested to find out if they have been using steroids. If they have, they may be banned from competing in their sport for several years.

Suppleness

When you were a baby, you were naturally supple. Your muscles, tendons and ligaments were more elastic. Babies can easily suck their toes. Young children can bend their bodies into many different positions. They don't need any extra suppleness training at all.

Many of the world's greatest gymnasts and dancers started their training when they were very young and supple – you may have seen amazing performances by some 13-year old Olympic gymnasts.

As you get older, your suppleness starts to decrease. Your muscles, ligaments and tendons lose some of their elasticity. Older adults may find they get quite stiff if they don't keep bending. But you don't have to seize up altogether! You can keep supple by doing flexing and stretching exercises. If you regularly stretch the joints and muscles, you will find that your movements will stay free and supple.

Can you still put your foot in your mouth?

Bendy benefits

Supple bodies can bend, stretch, twist and turn easily, and flexing and stretching exercises will also strengthen your muscles and make you feel relaxed. Being supple also helps you to stand and sit properly, and to have good posture.

The most obvious benefits of increasing your flexibility will be noticeable when you take part in more energetic sports and activities. In contact sports, for example, you can easily be knocked and injured. Your body will be better able to cope if you can 'roll the punches'. Flexible limbs move in a smooth and flowing way and are less brittle on impact. If you do get hurt, you will suffer fewer aches and pains.

fitness exercises

dancing

squash

swimming

karate

HOW SUPPLE ARE YOU?

Start by warming up with some gentle stretching. Once your circulation is going and your muscles have warmed up a little, put yourself to the suppleness test. You will need a tape measure and sticky tape.

Warm up
In a standing position, reach out with your arms and swing them up, down, and around. Do this gently and slowly.

Then do some jogging on the spot.

Suppleness test
1. Sit on the floor with your legs in front of you and your feet about 15 centimetres apart.

2. Mark the place where your heels touch the floor with a piece of sticky tape. Keep your heels on the tape.

3. Put the tape measure flat on the floor between your legs with the lower numbers

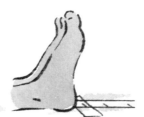

towards you. Put the 40 centimetre mark on the nearest edge of the sticky tape.

4. Slowly reach forward with both hands as far as you can and touch the tape measure.
5. Make a note of the distance. Don't bounce or jerk forward at any time.

6. Reach forward twice more and write down your longest reach.

Bendy results
50 centimetres and over: Excellent. You are supple already and must be leading an active lifestyle. Keep exercising to stay bendy!

40 to 50 centimetres: Good. You have quite a bit of flexibility. Make the most of your bendy body by enjoying different sports and activities.

Less than 40 centimetres: Fair. Your body would like to be a bit bendier. Give it a treat – try a new activity which is good for suppleness and do some gentle stretching every day.

fencing

yoga

Here are some of the sports and activities that will keep your joints supple and flexible. It's a good idea to bend and stretch before you begin any exercising. If your joints are inflexible, you can strain them if you try to push them too far.

Bones and joints

Your body is supported by a framework, or skeleton, of about 206 bones. Most people think of skeletons as hard and dry, but these are only the kind you see in science classrooms and museums! Bones in a living body are filled with a soft, fatty core called marrow which produces new blood cells. Each bone is able to bend slightly. Bones are not dead – they are living tissues.

Shaping up

Like skin, bone is constantly wearing away and repairing itself. Children's bones repair themselves at a faster pace than they wear away, and this is how they grow bigger and stronger. By the time you reach your twenties, your skeleton will be fully formed. Exercise is very good for bone building, so you can see that the most important time to exercise is when you are young!

How is your skeleton held together?

The bones of the skeleton are joined together, usually at each end. The point at which one bone joins another is called a joint. Different kinds of joints allow a variety of movements. Some joints, such as your knee, can move only forwards and backwards, while other joints, such as your shoulder, can move in many directions.

Strong, flexible strips of material support the joints and keep them in place. These are called tendons and ligaments. Tendons attach muscle to the bone around a joint. Ligaments are attached to the bone on either side of a joint. They keep the bones together, supporting them and allowing them to move at the same time. Both tendons and ligaments can be damaged if they are wrenched or over-used. Damage to a tendon is called a strain, while damage to a ligament is called a sprain.

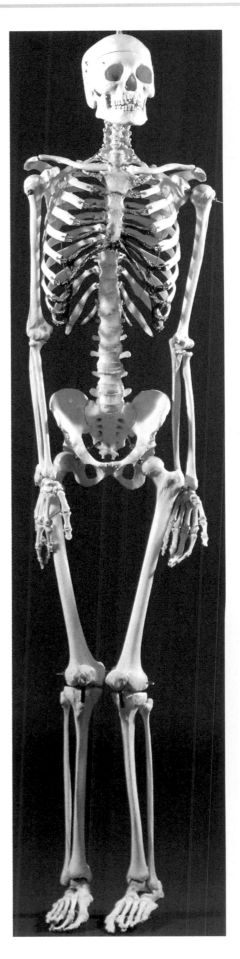

You can see clearly how the bones of this skeleton meet at different shaped joints.

DIFFERENT JOINTS

sliding or gliding joint: this joint is found where the collar bone meets the shoulder blade. It allows only a limited amount of movement.

ball and socket joint: found where the bones meet at the shoulder and hip. This kind of joint can move in all directions.

pivot joint: allows a circling movement. This kind of joint can be found at the wrist. It allows you to turn the palm of your hand upwards or downwards.

saddle joint: only found in the thumb. This unusual joint allows a forward and backward and side to side movement.

hinge joint: only moves forwards and backwards. It is found in the knees and fingers.

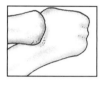

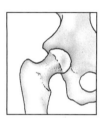

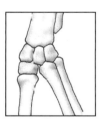

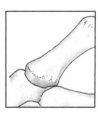

PARTS OF A JOINT

The ends of the bones in a joint are cushioned by a slippery material called cartilage. This acts as a shock absorber protecting the joint whenever it is moved by a muscle. Next to the bone and cartilage is a joint capsule containing an oily substance called synovial fluid. This helps the ends of the bones to glide smoothly past each other.

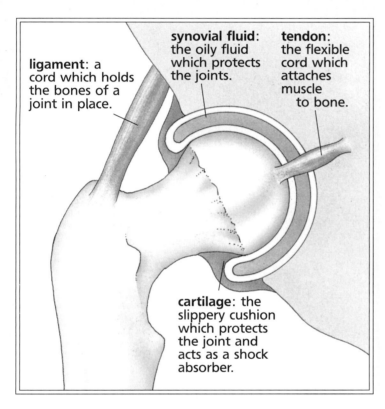

ligament: a cord which holds the bones of a joint in place.

synovial fluid: the oily fluid which protects the joints.

tendon: the flexible cord which attaches muscle to bone.

cartilage: the slippery cushion which protects the joint and acts as a shock absorber.

'Double-joints'

'Double-jointed' people have the same number of joints as everyone else, but their ligaments are longer and looser. This means they can move their bodies into positions that most other people can't stretch to.

Joint damage

All your joints are at risk when you exercise, especially those in your legs. When we move, our legs not only have to support body weight, but they also have to absorb the impact of the energy created by our muscles and spread this energy to the ground. The force in this energy can be very great. High jumpers, for example, will develop a force of more than five times their body weight in their jumping leg when they take off.

Although our joints are well able to cope with the stresses of moderate exercise, injuries can occur when the stress increases beyond this level. The knee is the joint which is injured most frequently. In fact, between a quarter and a third of all sports injuries are to the knee joints. If the game involves body contact, as in soccer and rugby, the chances of injury to the joints increases dramatically. Teams should always be made up of people of similar size, to avoid the danger of large players colliding with smaller players and injuring them.

The joints of the arms and shoulders carry a great deal of stress in activities such as pitching in baseball, javelin throwing or serving in tennis. Here a lot of force must be transmitted through the arm in a jerking or slamming motion. The stress on the arm builds up even more when the activity starts suddenly without a period of training first, or continues for a long time without enough rest periods. Injury is far more likely to happen when players are badly prepared for strenuous exercise.

45

Exercising at home

If you can't take up a sport for some reason – maybe there isn't anything on offer near you, or the time you have available doesn't match the time the sports centre is open – don't despair! You can exercise at home. There are many exercises you can do in a relatively small space. Here are just one or two to get you going. It's best to do the warming up exercises on pages 18 and 19 first!

These exercises will stretch your limbs and strengthen them. Make sure you are wearing loose, comfortable clothing and that you won't knock against anything as you move. You should do the floor exercises on a carpet or mat. Remember not to push yourself too hard or to rush through the movements. If any of your limbs starts to hurt, stop doing that exercise and move on to another.

It may seem obvious, but remember to breathe regularly and deeply when you're doing the exercises! If you let all the air out of your lungs, and then take a deep breath before you start, you'll fill your lungs full of air, making sure that plenty of oxygen reaches your blood and brain.

Squats
Stand with your feet a shoulder width apart. Slowly squat down but not too deeply. Resting your hands on your thighs, bounce up and down gently. Be careful not to put too much pressure on your knees. Do this exercise 20 times. It makes your muscles work!

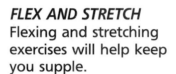

FLEX AND STRETCH
Flexing and stretching exercises will help keep you supple.

1. Stand as tall as you can with your hands stretched high over your head.

Be aware of all your muscles stretching, from your feet right up to your fingers. Feel the pull on your shoulder and stomach muscles.

Stomach lifts
Lie on your back with your hands at your sides and your knees bent. Your feet and knees should be slightly apart. Push with your feet and lift your hips as far as you can. You should feel your stomach muscles pull in. Repeat this 15 times. This one's good for the stomach and back.

Leg lifts
Lie on your back with your hands behind your head. Raise your right knee to your chest. Your left leg should be lifted off the floor. Now lift and twist your shoulders

so that your left elbow is reaching towards your right knee. Lie back and do the same with the other leg. After a while you should be able to get into a rhythm and build up some speed.

Do this exercise 10 to 15 times. Once you find your rhythm, this exercise gets your stomach muscles working and your blood pumping at a faster rate.

Leg stretch

Kneel on all fours with your hips further back than your knees. Bring one knee up to your chest. At the same time bend your head down towards your knee. Now stretch your leg backwards and raise your head, so that your spine is stretched. Next, bend your knee again

and keeping it bent slowly move your leg sideways. Your knee should be level with your arm, and outside it. Hold this position for a few seconds, then

stretch your leg backwards again. Finally, bring your leg up to your chest and back down to a kneeling position.

Repeat the whole exercise with your other leg. Do this exercise five times with each leg. Use this exercise to stretch and work your thighs and buttocks.

Now reach down and try and touch your toes. Keep your legs straight or bend your knees slightly.

Make this a slow, flowing movement. Never jerk or bounce downwards to try and reach further. Repeat five times. This stretch is good for your arms, back and shoulders.

Can you feel the muscles pull at the back of your legs? It's good for them, too!

2. Sit with your knees bending outwards and hold on to your ankles. The soles of your feet should be touching. Feel the stretch in the inner thighs.

Lean forwards as far as you can without straining and hold this position for four or five seconds.

Repeat the exercise five times. This movement stretches your back and inner thighs.

Curl-ups

Lie on the floor on your back with your knees bent and your arms by your sides. Curl up slowly by raising the top half of your body, keeping your arms straight out in front of

you, until your elbows touch the tops of your knees. Repeat 10 to 15 times. This is a good exercise for tightening up the stomach, strengthening the back and improving your posture.

Lean-backs

Kneel upright on the floor with your arms by your sides. Lean backwards and raise your arms until they are pointing straight ahead. Hold this position for three or four seconds. Repeat 10 to 15 times. Can you feel the

muscles pulling at the front of your thighs? This exercise will strengthen them.

What is co-ordination?

Co-ordination enables you to move your body in sequence. This means that your movements flow smoothly one after the other. Walking is a co-ordinated movement. When you walk you move both legs and bend your knees and ankles, but not all at the same time! Co-ordination is all to do with moving the different parts of your body in the right order at the right time.

The message system

All over your body, in your skin and attached to all your muscles, you have special cells called nerves. Together, we call the nerves the nervous system. It carries messages to your brain. These tell your brain what position you are in, whether you are hot or cold and if you feel any pain. Nerves carrying information to and from the brain travel through the spinal cord. This main communication route is inside your spine, which runs up the centre of your back and neck.

The brain sorts out the information and sends messages back through the nervous system. This is rather like a very complicated telephone exchange system, with the brain as an operator, controlling all the calls that go through the system. The brain can send instructions to parts of the body to make them move. These instructions include details of how, where and when the movement should happen.

Co-ordination and exercise

There are two parts of the nervous system that carry messages about how to move. These are the motor system and the sensory system. The motor system controls movement of your muscles. The sensory system carries all the information from the five senses: sight, hearing, taste, smell and touch.

HOW THE NERVOUS SYSTEM WORKS

The nervous system consists of the brain, spinal cord and nerves.

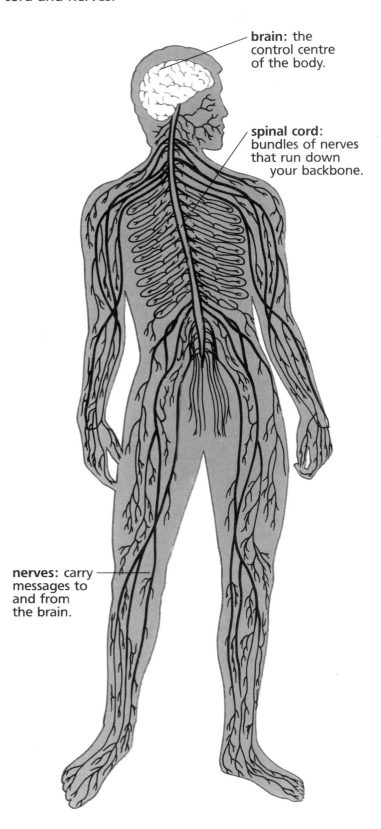

brain: the control centre of the body.

spinal cord: bundles of nerves that run down your backbone.

nerves: carry messages to and from the brain.

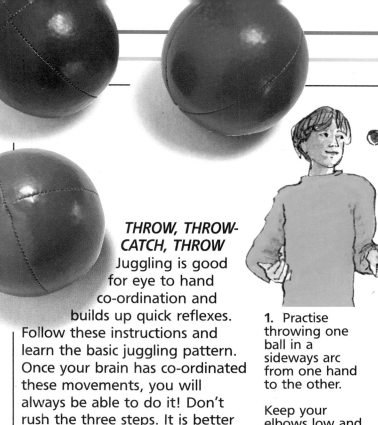

THROW, THROW-CATCH, THROW

Juggling is good for eye to hand co-ordination and builds up quick reflexes. Follow these instructions and learn the basic juggling pattern. Once your brain has co-ordinated these movements, you will always be able to do it! Don't rush the three steps. It is better to feel really confident with each one before you move on. You need three small balls or bean bags of equal weight.

1. Practise throwing one ball in a sideways arc from one hand to the other.

Keep your elbows low and relaxed. Change over every so often so you throw with each hand.

2. Now take two balls, one in each hand. Imagine a square box shape in front of you with the top side at eye level.

Throw one ball and then the other to the opposite top corner of the box.

3. Take two balls in one hand and the third ball in the other hand.

Throw one of the two balls first, then the single, then the third. Keep aiming for those imaginary top corners.

The time to throw the second ball is when the first reaches that imaginary corner.

This should be a throw, throw-catch, catch rhythm. Don't worry about trying to catch the balls at first.

Concentrate on the throw and your reflexes will start to make the catch response. With practice, you will start to make a flowing throw, throw, throw rhythm.

Happy juggling!

Reflexes

To be good at many sports, you need to develop reflexes. A reflex is a very quick response by the muscles to messages from the nerve cells. It happens so fast that it seems as if you haven't thought about the movement at all. In fact, scientists have shown that the fastest messages passed by the nervous system can travel at speeds of 288 kilometres per hour. Some people have naturally quicker reflexes than others, but all reflex action improves with practice. This is because the brain is able to learn from past experience and store the knowledge to use next time. Here are some sports good for reflexes and hand-eye co-ordination.

archery

fencing

table tennis

tennis

baseball

Keeping your balance

Tightrope walkers, gymnasts, and stilt walkers, unicyclists and bare-back riders all have something in common. All these acrobats have good balance. A sense of balance isn't only needed by acrobats, however. Everyone needs a sense of balance just to stand on their feet, or even to sit on a chair. If you didn't have a sense of balance, you'd keep falling over. You need to train your body to do what you want it to do. Once it is trained you don't have to give it a second thought.

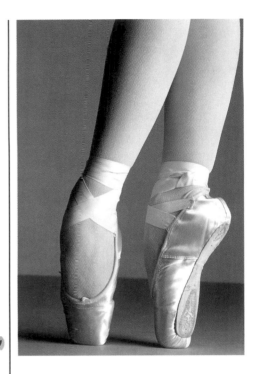

A ballerina achieves perfect balance on her toes.

Body balancing

Some sports and activities take special balancing skills, which you have to learn. This takes a lot of practice – just as a toddler practises how to walk and run. But when you have finally learned to balance in the right way, it feels like your body has switched on to 'automatic pilot'. You can cycle or do handstands without having to think about it.

Turning a half hoop on the skateboard

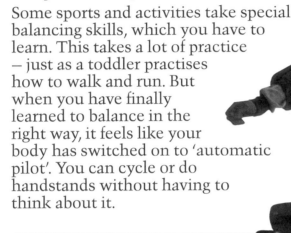

A gymnast performs a difficult balancing act on the bars.

SPORTS AND ACTIVITIES THAT NEED BALANCE

Part of the secret of balancing is knowing what it feels like. If you can get a friend to hold your ankles while you do some handstands, your body will soon recognize what needs to be done.

Gymnastics
Beam work takes a lot of concentration and practice.

Ballet dancing
You have to train very hard to be able to do the complicated movements or to hold positions.

Skating
Roller skating and ice skating are two separate skills. Blades have a different balance point from the four wheels of a roller skate.

Surfing, water skiing
It is even harder to balance if the watery surface underneath you is moving as well!

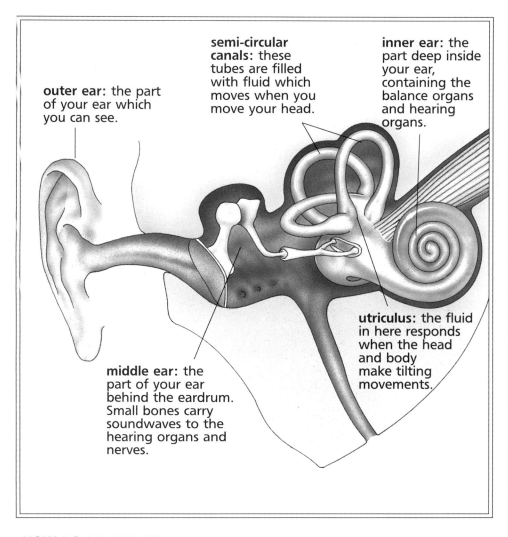

outer ear: the part of your ear which you can see.

semi-circular canals: these tubes are filled with fluid which moves when you move your head.

inner ear: the part deep inside your ear, containing the balance organs and hearing organs.

utriculus: the fluid in here responds when the head and body make tilting movements.

middle ear: the part of your ear behind the eardrum. Small bones carry soundwaves to the hearing organs and nerves.

HOW DO I BALANCE?

The part of your body that controls balance is deep inside each ear. In the inner ear, there is a tiny bundle of semi-circular tubes, or canals, attached to a pouch called the utriculus. This looks a bit like a curled up octopus. The utriculus is filled with fluid.

You have three minute semi-circular tubes filled with fluid in each ear. One detects up-and-down movements, one detects forward movements and the third detects sideways, or lateral, movements.

Every time you move, the fluid in the utriculus moves as well. The movement makes the sensitive fibres inside the tubes send messages to the brain. The brain tells the body to move in whatever way is needed to balance again.

The messages the eyes send to the brain also help you to balance. Seeing how near or far away things are helps you to judge the right position for your body. You can test this out by turning round and round with your eyes open. Stop and see how it feels. Now do it again with your eyes closed. You will feel more off-balance the second time!

Training for perfect balance

Acrobats have to do a lot of training before they can confidently balance on a high wire. Good balance requires great strength, suppleness and agility. Muscles have to be trained to react quickly to a shift in balance.

When your body is perfectly balanced, you say that it is in equilibrium. Imagine being pulled up by a string from the top of your head. Then imagine a line running down through your body, from your head downwards. This is your centre of gravity. When this is perfectly balanced, and you remain still, you should not fall over. However, in practice, it is not easy. Your muscles twitch, your centre of gravity changes, and you sway a little.

It's often easier to balance when you are moving. Trying to stand still on ice-skates or on a bicycle is very difficult. But once you are moving, the momentum carries you along.

There are several exercises you can do to improve your balance. You could try some high hopping on one leg, about 20 hops with each leg. If you walk along a narrow beam on the ground, you will find that holding your arms out to the side, or holding a long pole, will help you keep your balance. Try holding a pole across the back of your shoulders with both hands. Then squat down, and twist to touch the floor with each end of the pole in turn. Do this 15 times each side.

Pains and problems

The best way to avoid any problems when you exercise is to take things gently and to listen to the messages from your body. If an exercise hurts to start with, stop and allow time to recover. You can't always avoid accidents, though, and some problems are quite common. Here are a few personal experiences.

"A couple of months ago, I fell off my bike and really hurt myself. I was covered in bruises, cut my head and scraped both my knees. Even though it's all healed up, I feel nervous about riding again."
Clio

Expert comment: Taking a tumble from a bicycle or skateboard can shake you up, especially if you are going at speed. It sounds as if you weren't wearing protective clothing. Knee and elbow pads, wrist guards, a helmet and gloves could have saved you a lot of suffering! So, kit yourself out and as soon as you can get back on your bike. Think about the fun cycling gives you. It's also one of the best exercises there is!

"I tripped and hurt my ankle during a tennis game. I thought I had strained it but the doctor said it was a sprain. Is this the same thing?"
Louise

Expert comment: Strains happen when muscles are stretched or torn. A sprain is when a ligament is wrenched or torn. Sprains are usually caused by stumbling and forcing the joint to bend in an awkward way. The treatment for both injuries is the same. Use a cold compress to reduce the swelling, then support the injured area with an elastic bandage. You must rest the area for as long as it takes to heal. Keeping the sprained or strained arm or leg elevated helps to reduce pain and swelling. Sprained ankles are one of the most common sports injuries.

"A flying ball hit me on the head when I was playing baseball in the park. I think I passed out for a split second. I had a mild headache and a lump, but otherwise I felt fine. My friend's dad rushed me off to the doctor even though I was OK. I thought he would send me straight home – instead I ended up staying in hospital overnight! Why did everyone make such a fuss?"
Mehmet

Expert comment: You must always see a doctor after losing consciousness from a knock on the head – even if it's only for a second – or if you feel sick or dizzy afterwards without actually passing out. It is quite routine for your doctor to send you into to hospital for 24 hours. This is to make sure you haven't got concussion. Concussion is an injury to the body – usually the brain – caused by a blow. It's not worth taking a risk with anything as precious as your brain!

"My brother loves playing rugby. He dislocated his shoulder a long time ago, and now he has done it again! Is this because it hadn't healed properly?"
Ricki

Expert comment: In a very physical sport like rugby, players often crash into each other in the excitement of the game. Dislocation happens when a joint is forced out of place. The shoulder joint is the joint most often dislocated. This is because the 'socket' part of the bone where the ball of the arm bone fits is quite shallow. Once this has happened, a joint can be prone to dislocating again. Dislocations heal quite quickly though.

WARNING

You should never try and put a bone back into place with this type of injury. Always get medical treatment.

"Because I was late, I had to miss lunch before rushing out to meet my friends at the pool. We had to stand in line for ages in the entrance hall, which was very hot. I suddenly felt sick and weak. The next thing I knew, I was on the floor and someone said I had fainted. Why did this happen? Is it serious?"
Ruth

Expert comment: No, it's not serious. People who faint usually recover very quickly without side effects. Fainting is caused when not enough blood reaches the brain. Skipping meals and standing for too long in a hot atmosphere are the most common reasons for fainting – you did both of these! If you ever feel faint again, sit down and lean forward. Put your head between your knees and take a few deep breaths – you will soon feel better.

"Recently my feet have been really itchy and I've noticed that there are small blisters and cracked skin between my toes. They look awful and feel very uncomfortable. What can I do about it?"
Kim

Expert comment: You have one of the most common infections that active people can get – athlete's foot. This is actually a fungal infection which lives on moist skin. It is passed from person to person in swimming pools, showers, or places where you go barefoot. You have probably picked it up from someone else. But you could have got it from wearing tight shoes, so first of all, stop wearing any tight shoes. If you get your feet wet, make sure you dry them thoroughly, especially between your toes. You should be able to buy a special powder for athlete's foot at a pharmacy. Dust this onto your dry feet once a day.

Coping with special conditions

You might think illness would prevent someone from being really fit. Not true! Regular exercise not only helps people who suffer from special conditions like asthma and diabetes, it can also help reduce the risk of developing health troubles later in life, particularly those common killers like heart disease, strokes and high blood pressure.

Aerobic activities such as swimming, dancing and cycling tend to be the best kind of exercise for people with a health problem.

Asthma

An asthma attack makes it difficult to breathe. Your chest feels tight, and you cough and wheeze. You may gasp for air. Asthma is a condition caused by a narrowing of the small bronchial tubes in your lungs. This means that air cannot easily get into the lungs. Asthma is often caused by an allergic reaction to something. Breathing in dust, pollen or fumes may bring on an attack, so can being tired or under stress.

Asthma is usually treated with drugs, and sufferers often carry around small inhalers which spray medication into the lungs when necessary.

Adrian Moorhouse fact file
1964 born in Bradford, UK
1979 selected for English Youth team
1980 selected for British Senior team
1984 Olympic Games (Los Angeles, USA) Finalist 100m breaststroke
1985 European Championships (Bulgaria) Gold 100m breaststroke (World Record)
1988 Olympic Games (Seoul, South Korea) Gold 100m breaststroke
1989 European Championships (Germany) Gold 100m breaststroke (World Record)
1990 Commonwealth Games (New Zealand) Gold 100m breaststroke (equal World Record)
1992 Olympic Games (Barcelona, Spain) Finalist 100m breaststroke
Awarded MBE for services to swimming

Adrian Moorhouse, MBE

This is the story of a British Olympic swimmer who triumphed over asthma to come out on top.

"I've had asthma since I was very young and bronchial asthma was my particular 'variety'. I was given every opportunity of following almost any sport. But I found it hard to run a lap of the track without being badly out of breath. I found that swimming didn't affect me like this.

Since I was eight I was winning local championships and breaking school records. It's quite hard to explain my condition really, regarding swimming, because I was never as bad as some of my friends. However, quite occasionally it would knock me out. Even now if I get a bad cold it goes on to my chest and that's training gone for a week, but when I'm really fit I don't usually have any problems.

I really owe the fact that I kept up swimming to a specialist I saw when I was about 12. I was having problems with athletics and he told me to keep on swimming training as it would do me the most good. I don't know how much of his advice was true medically – but at that time it was psychologically the best thing that could have happened to me. I kept training hard, and even if it got bad I thought that it was doing me some good. I don't know if I grew out of my condition, or if the training helped to make me breathe easier – but now I don't have many problems.

I don't think that asthma has interfered with my ambition at all, because I haven't let it. I just kept on training. I suppose it made me more determined, because at school I was never going to get on the athletics team or the rugby team. I just

Asthma did not stop Adrian Moorhouse becoming an Olympic medallist.

had to prove that I could do something as well as the other kids – swimming was the way to do it."

Diabetes mellitus

People suffering from diabetes are unable to control the levels of a sugar called glucose in their blood. The bodies of some diabetics do not produce enough insulin, which is the hormone which controls our blood sugar levels. As a result these people have daily injections of insulin. Other diabetics are unable to use the insulin their bodies produce. Exercising removes glucose from the blood and this helps to control diabetes. Diabetics are at higher risk of becoming overweight and developing problems with their heart and circulation. Exercise helps to prevent heart disease and control weight so it is particularly good for diabetics.

One problem facing diabetics during exercise is the possibility of hypoglycaemia. This occurs when blood sugar falls below normal levels and it causes hunger, dizziness, weakness and fainting. It can be prevented by eating an extra carbohydrate snack, such as cereal or sandwiches, one or two hours before exercise, to make sure blood sugar levels are high enough.

Heart trouble

Although the possibility of developing heart trouble may seem a long way off, the truth is that what you do to your body in your teens affects your health when you are older. Research shows that large numbers of teenagers, especially in western countries, are already in trouble. They eat a diet high in animal fats and cholesterol, and don't take enough exercise. Exercise and a healthy diet both help to control body fat and lower the fat content of the blood.

High blood pressure

The same research has shown that many teenagers eat far too much salt in their food. Salty snacks are particularly bad. Overuse of salt can lead to high blood pressure. High blood pressure occurs when the blood puts too much pressure on the blood vessels as it circulates round the body. This, in turn, leads to heart attacks, kidney failure and strokes. Under medical supervision, regular aerobic exercise is ideal for people with high blood pressure as the exercise can lower and help control blood pressure.

The most popular sports

Some sports are played all around the world. Sometimes different versions of similar sports have developed in many different countries. Bowling is one of these.

In some countries, a bowl is rolled down a wooden lane to knock down nine or ten pins, while in others the bowl is rolled as close as possible to a small ball called a jack. Often countries play the same sport, but have slightly different rules, which can cause all sorts of confusion! Gradually, as more countries started to play sports, international associations were set up to make sure competing teams played using the same rules and with the same equipment. This means that teams from all parts of the world can meet up to play matches of a particular sport without any problems.

Here are some of the top favourites:

Soccer crazy

Soccer is the most popular sport in the world. It is played in more than 140 countries. The earliest known form of soccer was called Tsu Chu and was played in China in the third century BC. In the United Kingdom, it is known as Association Football. The game as it is played today developed in England, and the first proper set of rules was drawn up by the Football Association, when it was founded in 1863. The Association met in Cambridge, England, so these rules are called the Cambridge rules. In 1904, the Fédération Internationale de Football Association (FIFA) was born and soccer fever took over the world!

All the countries marked on this globe rate soccer as their number one sport.

Basketball

Basketball was invented in 1891 in the United States of America by a gym teacher called James Naismith. This exciting game spread like wildfire and is now one of the most popular sports in the world. The country with the most participants is China, where millions of players enjoy this fast and furious game.

The Harlem Globetrotters from the United States of America are one of the most famous basketball teams in history. Their games mix comedy, music, and highly skilled basketball.

Wilt 'The Stilt' Chamberlain scored a record 31,419 points in the American National Basketball Association matches between 1959 and 1973. At over 216 centimetres tall, he was only about 80 centimetres shorter than the basket!

Bowls

Bowling is one of the oldest sports in the world. In different forms, it is enjoyed nearly everywhere. Boule, boccie, klootschien, skittles and ninepins are all kinds of bowls. Ten-pin bowling is the most popular version of bowls. There are about 64 million regular players in the United States of America alone.

Road bowling is played in Ireland with iron balls along public roads. In this sport players try to roll balls set distances in the least number of throws.
Road bowling is played in only two other countries – Germany and The Netherlands. There it's called klootschien.

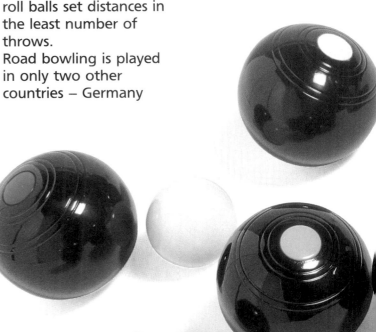

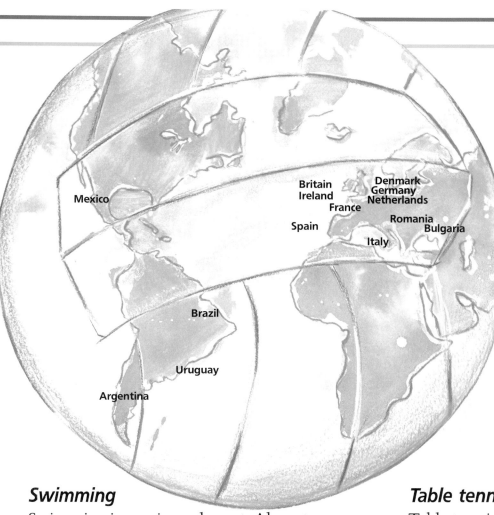

Mexico

Britain
Ireland
France

Denmark
Germany
Netherlands

Spain

Romania
Bulgaria

Italy

Brazil

Uruguay

Argentina

Swimming

Swimming is a universal sport. Almost everyone loves playing with water, and playing in it is even more fun!

15-year-old Galina Prozumenshchikova was the first Russian to win an Olympic gold medal for swimming. She may also hold the world record for the longest name of any Olympic champion!

Karen Muir from South Africa is the youngest world record holder in any sport. She was just 12 years old when she broke the record for the 100 metres backstroke.

The world's largest swimming pool, in Casablanca, Morocco, measures 470 metres by 75 metres.

Table tennis

Table tennis is the most popular racquet sport in the world. It was invented in England in the late 1800s, when it was called ping-pong. Since then, it has achieved world-wide popularity. Hungary produced the world's best players in the 1920s and 1930s. In more recent years, Japan and China have led the world in this game of lightning reflexes. Many villages and cities in China have public stone slabs set up for ping-pang-chiu, or ping-pong.

Joy Foster was the youngest ever table tennis champion. She was only 8 years old when she won the Jamaican singles and mixed doubles titles with her teammate in 1958.

Exercise for the disabled

More and more people who suffer from disabilities are taking up a sport and the exercises needed to succeed in it. Exercise for the disabled emphasises how much each person is capable of achieving, rather than concentrating on the difficulties which their disability might cause.

Fitness is for everyone, and numerous organizations and activities exist to make sure no one has to be left out because of disabilities. The equipment just has to be adapted slightly. Disabled people can and do take part in activities ranging from outdoor pursuits to exciting ball games. In fact, the sky is the limit for people who want to train seriously and become champions.

No matter what their type or level of disability, people take part in vigorous physical activity and sports for many reasons. They may wish to get fitter, to have fun, push themselves to reach a goal, or just be with friends.

Snooker players need great concentration

Skiing gives you a great sense of speed

Basketball players move about the court at great speed

Archery strengthens arms and shoulders

This javelin thrower gathers all his strength for the throw

58

Water-skiiers need a good sense of balance

SPORT FOR ALL
Whatever the organization or competition, people with disabilities are usually classed by their level or type of disability.

The different types of disability are:

1. Physical disabilities, where people have problems moving their bodies and are often in wheelchairs.

2. Sensory disabilities, where problems are to do with hearing or sight loss.

3. Mental disabilities, where a person's intelligence is affected by damage to the brain.

A person who is disabled can choose to take part in almost any exercise, although some exercises have to be changed slightly to make the exercise available. These changes alter the rules, of course, but they still allow events to offer a good and equal contest.

PHYSICAL DISABILITIES
Some people with physical disabilities have difficulty moving their bodies, and they may be in wheelchairs. Wheelchair basketball and marathons are popular options for the sports-minded physically disabled. Swimming, track and field, and horseback riding are other possibilities for those not restricted to wheelchairs.

People with physical disabilities can also compete successfully with able-bodied competitors at international level. In the Commonwealth Games, in 1982, one of the New Zealand archery team was physically disabled. And in Victoria, Canada, the venue for the Commonwealth Games of 1994, both the disabled and the able-bodied will compete in their own events at the same Games for the first time ever.

Even when restricted to a wheelchair, people with physical disabilities are capable of achieving outstanding performances. In the marathon, the world record for finishing the 41 kilometre race in a wheelchair is under 1 hour 40 minutes for men and under 2 hours for women. This is a much faster speed than foot runners have achieved. The fastest men have only just gone below 2 hours 10 minutes!

SENSORY DISABILITIES
Sensory disabilities include problems such as hearing or sight loss. Nearly every sports activity and exercise is open to people who cannot see or who cannot hear. Some adjustments may be necessary. In track athletic events, for example, a blind racer has a guide-runner who runs alongside. The system works well. Of course, the guide-runner has to be a very good runner to keep up with the actual competitor. In the longer races, such as the 1,500 metres, this could mean completing the course in under four minutes!

MENTAL DISABILITIES
Mental disabilities include those in which a person's intelligence is affected by damage to the brain. The Special Olympics is the best-known event organized for people with mental disabilities. A whole range of activities takes place, including soccer, swimming, softball, gymnastics, basketball and volleyball.

At the international level, more than 90 countries participate in Special Olympic summer and winter games, which are held alternately every two years.

An important aspect of the Special Olympics is that anyone who can perform a sport or activity successfully can take part with everyone else. This is known as integration.

Sports round-up

All around the world, people play sports for fun, to compete with each other, or simply to keep fit. Many countries have their own national sports, while some games are unique to just one country in the world. However, all sports can be divided into different groups. Here's a round-up of some of those groups with details of one sport found in each category.

Athletics

The marathon long distance race commemorates a Greek soldier who is said to have run 40 kilometres from Marathon to Athens in 490 BC. He brought news that the Athenian army had beaten the Persians at the battle of Marathon.

The modern race is run over a distance of 42.2 kilometres. The extra distance was added in 1908, when the British organizers of the Olympic Games wanted to start the race at Windsor Castle and finish it in front of the royal box at White City stadium in London!

Animal sports

The toughest race in the world is the Iditarod Trail. Dogs pull sleds from Anchorage to Nome, in Alaska, USA – a distance of 1,688 kilometres. It commemorates a disaster in 1925 when there was a diphtheria epidemic. The only way to get a life saving drug to the diphtheria sufferers was by sled.

Target sports

Archery is a very old sport. From prehistoric times, shooting with bows and arrows was important in warfare and hunting. The Ancient Greeks and Egyptians practised archery for fun. A modern bow can propel an arrow more than 777 metres at up to 65 metres per second.

Wheels

Roller skates were invented by a Belgian named Joseph Merlin in 1760. They were not a success! Merlin skated into a room full of people and crashed into a mirror.

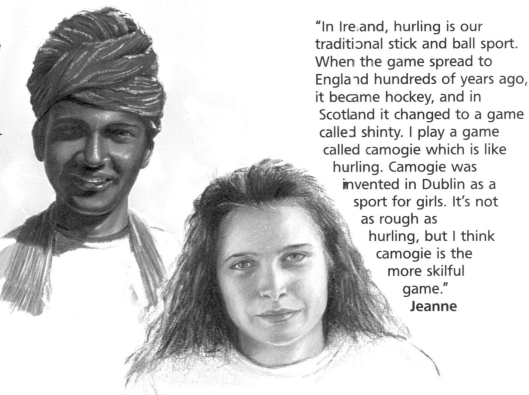

MY FAVOURITE SPORT

"In Pakistan we play a game called gilli danda. Any number of people can play on any open space and there are no firm rules. We don't play in competitions – it's all for fun. It is a batting and fielding game with a big stick called a danda which is used to hit a little stick called a gilli. When the batters are running they must hold their breath and chant which makes it a lot harder!"
Adri

"In Ireland, hurling is our traditional stick and ball sport. When the game spread to England hundreds of years ago, it became hockey, and in Scotland it changed to a game called shinty. I play a game called camogie which is like hurling. Camogie was invented in Dublin as a sport for girls. It's not as rough as hurling, but I think camogie is the more skilful game."
Jeanne

Combat sports

Sumo wrestling is a very popular sport in Japan. Extremely heavy men who can move fast take part. The heaviest wrestler ever is Salevaa Fuali Atisnoe from Hawaii, who weighed 252 kilograms in 1988.

Court sports

Pelota, or jai alai, is the fastest ball game in the world. A pelota ball has been recorded travelling at about 300 kilometres per hour.

Stick and ball sports

Lacrosse is derived from a game called baggataway, played by Iroquois Indians in North America. Sometimes more than 1,000 players took part. The goals were miles apart and games could last three days.

Team Sports

Rugby is traditionally thought to have started in November 1823 when William Webb Ellis, a pupil at Rugby School, in England, picked up the ball and ran with it during a game of soccer. The oval ball used by rugby players was adopted because it's easier to throw and catch.

Water sports

Racing highly decorated boats called dragon boats was a popular sport in imperial China. Today, Hong Kong and Singapore stage annual dragon boat races which are attended by large, enthusiastic crowds. The highly decorated boats are rowed over a course of 640 metres by teams of 20 paddlers, one steersman and one drummer.

Winter sports

The longest ski race in the world is the Vasa Race. It commemorates the time in 1521 when Gustav Vasa fled 85 kilometres from Mora to Sälen in Sweden. He was overtaken by scouts on skis, who persuaded him to return. He did, and became king of Sweden!

Target ball sports

Ten-pin bowling started in Germany as a game with nine pins called Heidenwerfen which means 'knock down pagans'. It was taken to America in the early 1600s. In 1841 nine-pin bowling was banned in Connecticut, USA, and other states soon followed. The tenth pin was added to avoid the ban by a change of name!

"Baseball is the favourite game in the United States. To us it is part of our life and a sport that is special to America. Even the smallest village in most parts of the United States has a baseball team and thousands of people go to watch the big American League games."
Daniel

"Kabaddi is a national sport in India. Two teams play a kind of 'tag' game. A 'raider' from one team has to touch people in the other team saying 'kabaddi-kabaddi-kabaddi' without stopping. Raiders are out of the game if they pause for breath or get caught."
Mina

Know your body

Your body is a marvellous machine. Understanding how to keep it in good working order by exercising it properly will help keep it in shape for the rest of your life. Try this quiz to test your body knowledge.

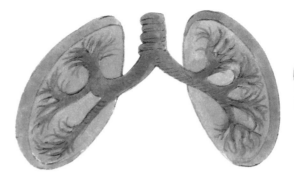
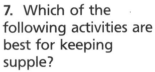

1. What is the aerobic system?

☐ **a.** An exercise video, record or tape
☑ **b.** Oxygen and carbon dioxide
☐ **c.** The heart, lungs and blood circulation

2. The 'happy hormones' that are released during exercise are called:

☐ **a.** Endorphins
☐ **b.** Morphine
☐ **c.** Dolphins

3. Which of the following is a kind of joint?

☑ **a.** Ball and socket
☐ **b.** Bat and ball
☐ **c.** Hinge and bracket

4. The two kinds of fibre in muscles are called:

☐ **a.** Long fuse and short fuse
☐ **b.** Slow twitch and fast twitch
☐ **c.** Relax and contract

5. What should you do if you feel faint?

☐ **a.** Drink some water and loosen your clothes
☐ **b.** Take a deep breath and walk around
☐ **c.** Sit down, lean forward and put your head between your knees

6. A balanced diet should include:

☐ **a.** Calories, fibre and sugar
☐ **b.** Carbohydrates, protein and fat
☐ **c.** Cereals, caffeine and glucose

7. Which of the following activities are best for keeping supple?

☐ **a.** Yoga, gymnastics and karate
☐ **b.** Rowing, horse-riding and jogging
☐ **c.** Walking, water-skiing and wind-surfing

True **False**

☐ ☐ **1.** To help your bones to grow you must take regular exercise.

☐ ☐ **2.** You must exercise at least three times a week for 20 minutes to keep healthy.

☐ ☐ **3.** Weight-lifting is a good exercise for young people.

☐ ☐ **4.** You should always eat a good meal before exercising.

☐ ☐ **5.** Skipping is a good aerobic exercise.

☐ ☐ **6.** You build up stamina by eating fresh fruit.

True **False**

☐ ☐ **7.** Double-jointed people have twice as many joints.

☐ ☐ **8.** It is dangerous for people with disabilities to exercise.

☐ ☐ **9.** You must always do a warming up routine before exercise.

☐ ☐ **10.** Exercise relieves stress.

HOW DID YOU SCORE?

Give yourself one point for each correct answer. Check your body score:

13 to 17 points: You are well on the way to a healthy, active lifestyle.

8 to 12 points: You won't let a few wrong leads slow you down. You already know where you're going. Don't give up!

Under 8 points: Exercise your brain and read this book! And how about a little exercise for the rest of you? You don't want to look like a lumpy sack, do you?

Answers:

1. **c** Read the section on **Aerobic exercise** on pages 30-31.
2. **a** Read the section on **Exercise for your mind** on pages 10-11.
3. **a** Read the section on **Bones and joints** on pages 44-45.
4. **b** Read the section on **Strength** on pages 36-37.
5. **c** Read the section on **Pains and problems** on pages 52-53.
6. **b** Read the section on **Getting energy** on pages 26-27.
7. **a** Read the section on **Suppleness** on pages 42-43.

True or false:

1. True. Read the section on **Bones and joints** on pages 44-45.
2. True. Read the section on **How active are you?** on pages 8-9.
3. False. Read the sections on **Strength** and on **Your muscles** on pages 36-37 and 40-41.
4. False. Read the section on **Getting energy** on pages 26-27.
5. True. Read the section on **Aerobic exercise** on page 30-31.
6. False. Read the section on **Stamina** on pages 28-29.
7. False. Read the section on **Bones and joints** on pages 44-45.
8. False. Read the section on **Exercise for the disabled** on pages 58-59.
9. True. Read the section on **Warming up and cooling down** on pages 18-19.
10. True. Read the section on **Exercise for your mind** on pages 10-11.

63

HELPLINES

Here's a list of organizations you could contact in case you'd like to find out more about some of the things discussed in this chapter. Whichever part of the world you live in, there are organizations that can answer your questions. These organizations will be happy to give you useful information and advice.

Australia
Australian Red Cross
Young People's Health Service

India
Bombay Deaf and Dumb Institution
Tata Memorial Hospital, Parel (cancer)

Malaysia
Rersatuan Bulan Sabit, Merah
(Red Cross Society)
General health concerns

Philippines
Health Action Information Network
Philippine Dental Association

UK
British Dental Association
British Red Cross
Cancer Research Campaign
Health Education Authority

You should be able to find the telephone numbers in your local telephone directory or by phoning directory enquiries.

2

LOOKING GOOD

A young person's guide to body care

When you were young, your parents or other adults looked after you. They kept you clean and washed your hair. They cared for you when you were not well, and tried to make sure you didn't hurt yourself. As you get older, you have to take on this responsibility yourself. You have to look after your own body – it's the only one you've got, and it has to last you all your life! So find out in this chapter how to make the most of your body.

How do you see yourself?

As you grow up, many changes take place in your body, and they're not always the ones you want! This is the time when your hair may always look oily or you might be getting pimples on your face. On the other hand, you may feel quite happy about your appearance, about getting taller or losing puppy fat and feeling more confident.

We all know that the kind of person you are is more important than the way you look. But we all still want to look good! You owe it to yourself to look after yourself.

This book will explore your changing appearance, from your head to your toes. You'll learn how certain parts of your body function and how this can affect the way you look and feel. You will also find answers to any questions or problems you might have about your changing body. And there's plenty of advice on how to stay healthy and look good, both inside your body and on the outside.

The first step to looking and feeling good is getting to know yourself. Most of us have three similar, but separate, images of ourselves – how we think we look, how we would like to look, and how we believe other people see us.

How do you feel about yourself?

The way you feel about yourself shows! If you stand huddled in a corner of a room, worried that someone might notice that you are too fat or too thin, the chances are people will wonder what's wrong with you! But if you feel confident in yourself, you will be able to face the world without worrying about what you look like.

You can influence the way other people see you too. If you walk tall and greet people with a smile, they'll almost certainly be attracted by your outward show of confidence and friendliness.

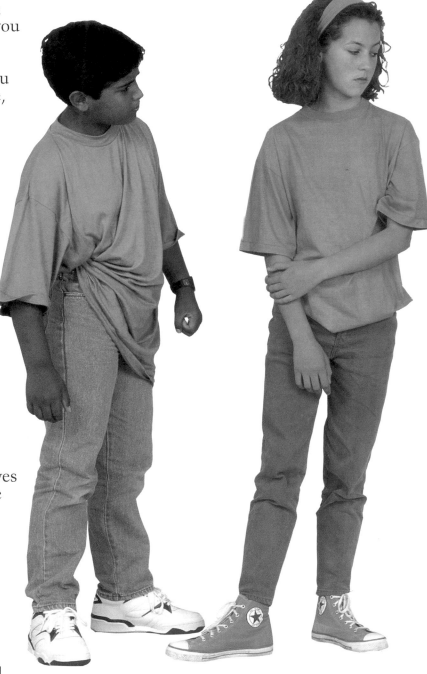

How you'd like to look

Don't spend time being jealous of models. Remember that they have the help of lighting, make-up and all sorts of professional tricks to make them look the way they do. If you really want to change the way you look, be realistic about what you can achieve. You can't change your height or the shape of your face, but you can look after your skin and your hair.

You may have a false idea of how you look – others may see you very differently.

Be positive!

Start by taking a long look at yourself, preferably in a full length mirror. Then name at least two of your good points. You may have large eyes, glossy hair or clear skin. Everybody has got something to feel pleased about.

Try to remember these good points whenever you're feeling unsure about your appearance. It will help you feel better about yourself. Then take some steps to help yourself look and feel better. The first ones are easy – you're probably doing them already. If not, you can't do better than to start right now. Eat plenty of fresh fruit and vegetables, get enough fresh air, exercise and sleep, and read on. You'll find plenty more tips in the rest of the book.

Looking after yourself doesn't have to take a lot of time, or a lot of money. If you do look after yourself, though, you won't regret it!

Why not concentrate on your good points instead of worrying about your faults?

How others see you

Remember that other people are far more likely to remember your cheerful personality than the fact that you had a spot on your nose the day you saw them. Try to give yourself the benefit of the doubt! After all, the whole you is a combination of your inner and outer selves. What you see in the mirror is only part of the truth!

The shape of your body

Your height and the shape of your body are inherited from your parents. If they are tall and thin, it's likely that you will be tall and thin, too. There are over five billion people on this planet, and it's doubtful if any two of them are precisely identical. That's more than five billion differently shaped bodies – tall, small, fat and thin – happy to be the shape they are – or, deeply unhappy about it!

Some people are large with big feet and broad shoulders. This usually means that their body is built around a larger bone structure, or skeleton, rather than that they are fat. On the opposite end of the scale are those people with small frames built on a delicate skeleton. These people sometimes find life hard when they are teenagers, because they look younger than all their friends.

Readers' views

"I've got a small, fairly slim body but large hips. I think trousers make me look fat, so I wear loose dresses most of the time."
Alexia

"I'm into the body-building bit. My shoulders are broad and I'm developing my muscles – but I still feel my legs are too short."
Pete

What is metabolism?

Apart from the problems, or benefits, inherited from your parents, the shape of your body will also depend on your metabolism. Metabolism is the word which describes the process in which your body changes food into energy. Some people have a faster metabolism than others.

The amount of food you eat and your rate of metabolism can both affect the shape of your body and your weight. People who are thin and wiry often have the fastest rate of metabolism. They can eat as much as they like and still not put on any extra weight. People with a more rounded figure usually have a slower rate of metabolism. Their bodies take longer to change food into energy and any extra food is stored as fat.

We come in every possible mix of shape, size and appearance.

"My body hasn't got any curves and everyone calls me a bean pole. I can put up with this right now, though. I'm pretty good at athletics and swimming."
Sue

"I've got quite a short body and very long legs. Everything seems to be growing at a different rate. I look really gangly."
Cliff

"I've got the biggest feet in my class! It's impossible to buy a pair of decent shoes when you've got feet as big as mine!"
Pauline

Exercise

Your lifestyle is very important in determining your shape. If you don't take much exercise, you won't need as much food as somebody who rushes about all day. Any food you eat which is surplus to your energy needs will be stored as fat.

Of course, you can control your weight by watching the amount you eat and how much exercise you get. And different exercises can work on different parts of your body slowly, to change or firm up your shape. But don't get too obsessed with your weight! Going on a diet to try and force your weight down, or even starving yourself, is both dangerous and unhealthy. Obviously, if you're sick, you're not going to look good nor feel at your best. Recognize that as long as your body is still growing, your weight will go up and down. It may not settle at a steady weight until you are in your early twenties.

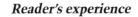

Reader's experience

"I have always been taller than everyone else in my class. It was great when I was a kid, but now I'm in my teens, I'm not so sure. My body's filling out and I look far more grown up than any of my friends.

People tell me I'm lucky to look older than I really am. They say people will treat me like an adult and I'll be able to get away with things. Trouble is, it works the other way sometimes. No one will believe me when I ask for a child's fare on the bus. Some of the kids at school tease me. They say I look as old as the teachers, and by the time I get to the teachers' age I'll look like an old woman.

Eventually, I told my Mum about all this and, of course, she said it was nonsense! She told me that everyone develops at a different rate, starting from when they are babies. Babies don't all walk at the same time, so why should everyone grow up at the same age.

She said everyone in my family had been a fast developer and to use it as an advantage and not to worry about it. She's right. Being tall is really useful when you want to see over people's heads. And because I look older, people expect me to act older and be wiser. My friends tend to ask me for advice about things, even though I'm actually younger than most of them!"
Robin

Your skin

Skin covers every part of your body. It's a tough, waterproof wrapping, which is elastic enough to allow you to move in every direction. Its most important job is protection. Skin protects your body from such things as heat, cold, wind, dirt and germs.

New layers of skin are constantly growing inside your body. They gradually move to the surface and replace the top layers of older skin which are being continually rubbed and scratched off. You are shedding up to a million dead skin cells every day!

Your skin also is a great revealer of what's going on inside your body. It will react if you are in poor health, or if you're cold or feverish. It will also give you away when you're emotionally upset, particularly when you are embarrassed!

Your skin as a thermometer

The normal temperature of the inside of your body is around 37 degrees Celsius. If you heat up too much, or get too cold, your body can't function properly and you become ill. That's why it's so important that your body temperature stays more or less the same all the time. It's your skin that controls your temperature. If you are cold, your skin forms little bumps which some people call goose pimples. The hairs on your skin stand up straight, trapping a layer of air next to the surface of the skin. Your body warms the air, and it keeps you warm. The blood vessels near the surface tighten, to stop the blood losing heat. But when you are hot, the blood vessels widen to push heat to the surface, and your body loses heat, and sweat, through the pores. The sweat evaporates, cooling the skin and blood.

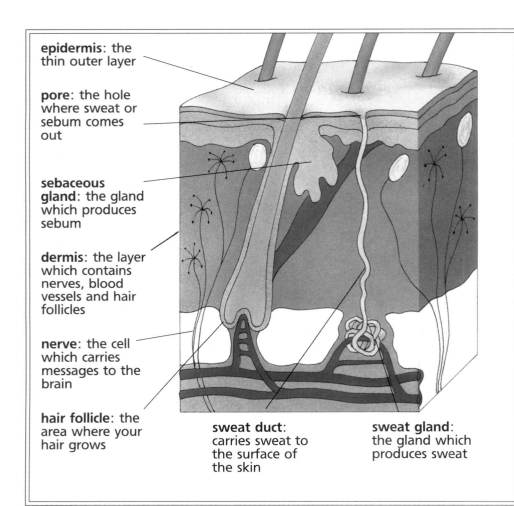

epidermis: the thin outer layer

pore: the hole where sweat or sebum comes out

sebaceous gland: the gland which produces sebum

dermis: the layer which contains nerves, blood vessels and hair follicles

nerve: the cell which carries messages to the brain

hair follicle: the area where your hair grows

sweat duct: carries sweat to the surface of the skin

sweat gland: the gland which produces sweat

WHAT IS SKIN MADE OF?

Skin is made of three layers. The surface, protective layer is made up of dead skin cells and is called the epidermis. The epidermis contains a special protein called keratin which is very tough. This layer is thickest on places where the body needs protection, such as the soles of the feet. There are tiny holes in your epidermis, called pores. These allow liquids from inside your skin to escape.

The next layer, the dermis, contains tiny blood vessels which carry blood to the skin. It also contains nerves which transport messages to the brain. These messages tell your brain what you are feeling and touching. They also relay messages of pain and temperature.

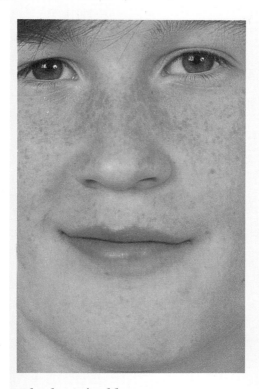

This boy's freckles spread in a band across his face.

The dermis also includes sweat glands, which produce sweat, and hair follicles, where hair grows. Next to the hair follicles are the sebaceous glands. These produce an oil called sebum which coats your hairs and skin and keeps them supple and waterproof.

The third layer is called the subcutaneous layer and it is made of fat. This layer of fat pads the muscles, bones and internal organs and protects them. The subcutaneous layer helps to keep you warm. Also, the fat is a store of energy which can be burned off when you need it.

Skin blemishes

The epidermis contains granules of a colouring pigment called melanin. Melanin is what gives your skin its colour. Most people's skin is not a uniform colour. There are often darker spots or patches on it.

Freckles are small patches of melanin that become darker when they are exposed to sunlight. People can have freckles all over their bodies, though you often only notice the freckles on the face. Many people think freckles are very attractive, and some people even paint them on!

People who have freckles are usually quite fair-skinned, and they should be careful to protect themselves from over-exposure to strong sunlight.

Moles are also patches of melanin, but are larger and darker than freckles. They may be flat or raised, and sometimes have hair growing out of them. Moles are not usually removed, unless they spoil a person's looks, or are rubbed and irritated by clothing. If a mole bleeds, or changes in colour, size or shape, you should immediately ask the advice of a doctor.

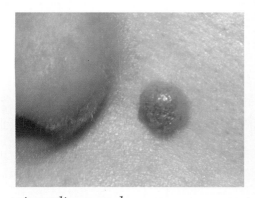

An ordinary mole close to the nose.

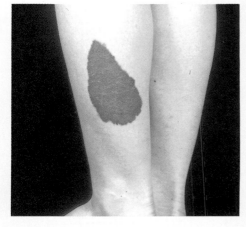

A large birthmark on the leg.

A birthmark is a skin blemish that a person is born with. Some moles are birthmarks. Other birthmarks are caused by a cluster of blood vessels just below the surface of the skin, making a raised red or purple mark. Most of these birthmarks grow during a baby's first year, but then decrease in size, and many disappear altogether.

A port-wine stain is a dark red, flat birthmark that does not disappear. It may grow with the rest of the person's body. These stains can sometimes be removed surgically, or masked with cosmetics. Some people aren't bothered by their birthmarks, and leave them alone.

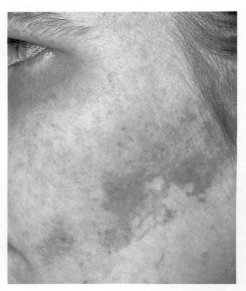

A mottled port-wine stain on the side of the face.

Caring for your skin

Your skin has to work hard to perform all those functions which are vital to your health. The least you can do in return is to look after it. This requires treatment both inside and out. Eating plenty of fresh fruit and vegetables, getting regular exercise and lots of fresh air and sleep are all important if you want healthy skin. Not everyone is born with perfect skin, but if you take good care of the skin you have, you'll look and feel better for it.

The golden rule

Keep it clean! Each day, your skin faces dirt, germs and all sorts of nasty things in the outside world. You need to wash these away. Washing prevents any infections developing and gets rid of all the grease and dead skin cells that build up. A daily wash should be enough for most of your body. But you should always make sure that your hands are clean by washing them several times a day, specially after going to the toilet and before eating.

Cleaning your face may need special care. The skin on your face is thinner and more delicate than the rest of your skin. It dries out quickly, because it's exposed to the elements all day. Don't wash it more than twice a day since this may irritate your skin and cause more problems. If you have black skin, check that cleansers do not contain resorcinol, which can cause skin to mottle.

STEAMING

To give your skin a deep clean, fill a large bowl with hot water from the tap. The water shouldn't be boiling. Cover your head and the bowl with a towel, then lower your face over the steam, keeping it at least 30 centimetres above the bowl.

Remember, steam can burn, so test the distance with your hand before-hand. After about 10 minutes, you'll find that the steam has opened the pores of your skin, leaving it clean and elastic. Take off the towel, wash your face really well, and splash it with cold water. This will close the pores again.

cleansing

steaming

SOAP

Washing with soap and water is an easy way of cleaning your face. But some harsh soaps can wash away the natural oils that keep your skin supple and waterproof, leaving it feeling 'tight'. Choose a gentle soap and make sure you rinse off all the lather.

CLEANSERS

Cleansers contain a mixture of oil and water. They are gentler on the skin of your face than soap and are particulary helpful to people with dry skin. Massage a little cleanser onto your face and neck with clean fingers, cotton wool or a tissue. Wipe the cleanser off thoroughly.

FACE SCRUB

Face scrubs are very fine, gritty cleansers that you rub gently on your face. They take skin cleansing a step further. Not only do they get rid of the dirt, but they scratch off all the dead skin cells as well. This process is called exfoliation. It leaves your face feeling smooth and fresh. Treat your face gently, though – your skin should feel fresh and tingly after a face scrub, not red and sore. You should use a moisturiser after giving yourself a face scrub.

> **WARNING**
> Never clean your face this way more than once a week. If you feel extra grubby in between, a brisk wash with a sponge or a face cloth will have a similar effect. You should also note that giving yourself a face scrub can stimulate the sebaceous glands, making your skin more oily.

moisturising

MOISTURISER

Moisturisers are creams which you apply to those areas of your face and neck that feel especially dry or tight after washing. These creams help trap natural moisture in. You also need to use a moisturiser if you are going out in the hot sun, or in the wind or rain because all of these dry skin out. Boys should use a moisturiser after shaving.

toning

TONERS

A skin toner is usually made up of diluted alcohol mixed with water and a thick liquid called glycerine. You can use it after cleansing your face, to take off any last traces of dirt or grease. Soak a piece of clean cotton wool with toner and pat it gently over your face and neck. It should leave your face feeling fresh and tingly. Toners are best for people with oily skin.

DIFFERENT TYPES OF SKIN

Most skin falls into one of three categories, depending on how much or how little sebum the sebaceous glands produce.

Dry skin

Dry skin doesn't contain enough sebum. It is very sensitive to the Sun, and needs to be moisturised regularly.

Oily skin

Oily skin produces too much sebum. It often has an oily sheen and becomes greasy soon after washing. The oiliest area is the panel down the central part of the forehead, the nose and the chin. This is where the most sebaceous glands are located. People with oily skin are likely to get more spots, but won't get wrinkles so quickly!

Combination skin

This type of skin is a combination of oily and dry skin. It normally produces greasy patches of skin down the centre of the face and on the chin and nose. The remainder of the skin on the face will be dry. If you have combination skin, you may need to use two different sorts of cleansers and moisturisers.

Skin problems

It would be wonderful to have perfect skin, and to keep it perfect all the time. But no matter how well it's looked after, your skin will normally cause you problems during your teens. The two hormones progesterone and testosterone are part of the body's chemistry. In your teens, these hormones are particularly active as your body changes and matures. During this period, the hormone levels increase, and this increase makes the sebaceous glands produce higher than normal levels of sebum. If too much sebum is produced, the pores become blocked and acne appears. This is probably the number one problem amongst teenagers.

There are ways of reducing the problem. Firstly, you must make sure that your face is thoroughly cleaned every day. Just wash your face well, or follow the cleansing routine on pages 72 and 73. Do not squeeze or pick pimples. If you do, it will almost inevitably cause infection and may even leave scars. Also, never touch your face unless you have clean fingers.

There are lots of creams and lotions you can buy to help solve the problem of acne. Don't buy anything too harsh – it may roughen your skin. Your skin will react by producing more oil, and this will cause more acne. If you have bad acne, talk to your doctor, who should be able to prescribe a treatment to clear it up.

Concealing pimples

You can disguise pimples temporarily by using a special kind of make-up. It is called concealer, and it is tinted to match your skin colour. Some brands of concealer are medicated so that they do not aggravate spots. Concealer covers your pores, and does not let your skin breathe, so remember to wash it off thoroughly at night.

Even with careful washing, not everyone is lucky enough to have perfect skin.

Acne

The sebum from a sebaceous gland normally drains into a hair follicle, and then out through an open pore to the surface of the skin. If the pore becomes blocked, the oil can not drain out. The blocked pore forms a blackhead or a whitehead. Sometimes bacteria breed in the trapped oil, making inflamed red spots. This is acne.

In severe cases of acne, the spots can spread all over the face and neck. It is thought that the sebaceous duct may actually break open, allowing oil and bacteria into the skin tissue around the spot. This causes bad inflammation. Acne can leave the face permanently scarred.

Severe acne should always be treated by a doctor. There are various methods of treatment, including antibiotic tablets, ultraviolet light, hormones and antibiotic creams. These lotions reduce the bacteria on the skin and help prevent pimples from forming. There is no evidence that diet can help in clearing acne. Many sufferers find that their acne is better in the summer when they are out in the sun, but sun protection should be used.

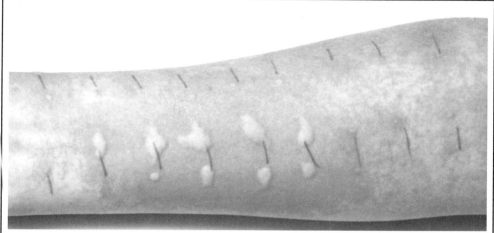

This arm is being tested for allergic reactions to different substances.

ALLERGIES

Allergic reactions can show up as rashes or dry patches of skin. These often occur on the face. They may be due to a certain type of food, or to some sort of cosmetic that you have put on your skin. Hot baths, chocolate, strawberries, detergent and perfume are all known to cause allergies.

You might be allergic to certain types of make-up. The most common allergic reaction is to eye make-up. Either steer clear of the brand that is causing problems, or look for make-up that is labelled hypo-allergenic. This means that the product is less likely to irritate your skin.

Blackheads and whiteheads

The two most common forms of skin complaints are blackheads and whiteheads. Blackheads are caused by an excess of sebum in the pores. As the sebum reaches the surface of your skin it hardens to a small, dark head. You can reduce blackheads yourself by steaming your face. Hold your face about 30 centimetres above a bowl of hot water from the tap and cover your head with a towel. The steam will cause your pores to open. You can then very gently nudge the blackhead out with your fingertips. Make sure your fingers are clean, or the pore will become infected.

Whiteheads start off as small sweat spots. Pressure builds up under your skin and a painful, white lump appears. A whitehead is a plug of sebum that has not been exposed to the air because it is covered with a layer of keratin from the surrounding skin.

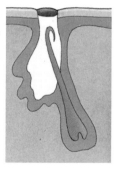

The yellow area shows how infection builds up beneath a blackhead.

Blackheads form in clogged pores and soon become inflamed.

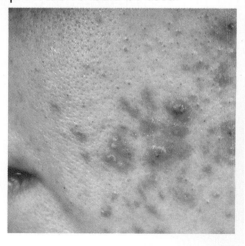

Sun and skin

Almost everyone has a substance called melanin inside their skin, produced by special cells in the dermis. Melanin gives the skin its colour. In sunshine, melanin builds up and the skin becomes darker. This protects the skin from harmful rays of the sun. Melanin can take a few days to build up and come to the surface of the skin. You should always protect your skin during this period and when you are in the sun for any length of time. You should in any case avoid being out in the sun when it's at its hottest, between about 12 noon and 3 pm. Even if you are used to the sun, you can still get burned.

Hidden hazards

You need to remember that water, sand and snow reflect the sun, and it's easy to get sunburned by reflected sunlight. You may sometimes not be aware of the sun's strength if the wind is blowing and cooling your skin. And if you're high in the mountains, beware! The thin atmosphere at high altitudes lets more of the harmful rays of the sun through to the earth.

Sunblock

Sunblocks are special creams which protect your skin from burning in the strong rays of the sun. The sun product usually carries a SPF number. This stands for Sun Protection Factor and it indicates how much longer you can stay in the sun without burning more than you normally might. The SPF sunblock protects you from UVB rays, the ones that cause burning. UVA rays are those that cause your skin to age and wrinkle, and this can start when you are young. Sun damage can be seen on people as young as 20. So delay wrinkles – think long-term and protect your skin now!

Another good reason for using sunblock is that it can protect you from skin cancer. Sunblock comes in lots of different strengths, but it's best to choose the strongest protection, just to make sure you're safe.

You can buy sunblock in some great colours.

KEEP FRESH
It's marvellous to step out of a shower or bath feeling as if you're a new person. Somehow, you just feel healthier when your skin and hair are clean and smelling fresh. Your body especially needs this refreshment when you've been out in the sun all day. Here are some products you can use after a day in the sun.

Talcum powder
Most talcum powders are scented, so you will end up smelling good after a bath. They also help cool your skin.

Foot spray and foot powder
If you suffer from sweaty or smelly feet, foot sprays and foot powders will help dry your feet and cover up the odour.

Body lotion
Body lotion is a moisturiser which you can use on your whole body. It will make your skin feel and smell good. Rub it onto patches of dry skin, such as your knees or elbows. Special body lotions called after-sun lotions will help soothe your skin after sunbathing.

Deodorants and anti-perspirants

Sweating is your body's natural way to cool down. There are two and a half million sweat glands in the skin of your body. There are a great many sweat glands under your arms which is why you sweat more there than on other parts of your body.

Surprisingly, sweat has no smell of its own. It's the stale bacteria left on the surface of your skin when the sweat dries that cause an unpleasant smell called body odour. The problem with body odour is that people who suffer from it are often incapable of smelling it on themselves! If you suspect you have a sweat problem, consider using either a deodorant or an anti-perspirant.

What is the difference between deodorants and anti-perspirants? Deodorants do not stop you sweating, but they do contain chemicals which neutralize the smell. Anti-perspirants, on the other hand, dry out the sweat glands, so that less sweat is produced.

Choose and use with care

You can buy both products in stick form, as a roll-on or in a spray can. Sprays can be strong and can cause inflammation on sensitive skins. Never use deodorants or anti-perspirants on inflamed or broken skin, or immediately after shaving your armpits.

Deodorants and anti-perspirants are available in stick, spray or roll-on form.

The danger of the sun

Sunlight is good for skin. It helps in the production of vitamin D, which activates the calcium needed for growing bones. In sunshine, the pigment melanin builds up to protect the skin. Black or brown-skinned people rarely suffer from sun-related skin diseases because they are protected by the high level of melanin in their skin. But too much strong sunlight can be dangerous for fair people. This results in painful sunburn when the skin feels sore and may blister. It can also cause sickness and fever. People with sunburn should get into the shade as quickly as possible, and cool the skin down with cold water. The treatment for sunburn is the same as that for any other burn.

Exposure to the ultraviolet rays of the sun is the main cause of skin cancer, a disease which is on the increase in fair-skinned people, as they travel more frequently to hotter countries to enjoy a holiday in the sun.

Skin cancer is a disease of the skin cells, particularly those that form the deepest layer of the surface of our skin, the epidermis. These cells are called basal cells and almost all skin cancers attack here.

The first sign of skin cancer is a small lump on the skin which may bleed or develop a crust. It never seems to heal. Sometimes a red spot or lump appears which is also scaly or crusty. Almost all skin cancers of the basal cells can be cured with medical help, if they are treated early.

Make-up

Fashions in make-up change all the time, as do the colours. At the moment the fashionable face is a natural face, with just a light hint of make-up to enhance certain features. When you are young, it's wise to make this your approach. Don't use lots of make-up trying to change your looks. Use a little, wisely, and bring out the best in your face.

First of all consider your face in a mirror. Decide what shape it is, and what your best features are. These are the ones you can emphasise by using the right make-up. Stick to subtle colours while you experiment. Also use softer shades during the day. At night, especially if you're going to a party, you can have more fun with dramatic colours!

Before you start, make sure that your face is clean and free from grease, and put on some moisturiser. Wear a hair band to keep your hair off your face.

Foundation

This is a skin-coloured cream which you can use all over your face to cover up any blemishes or uneven colour in your complexion. Smooth foundation into your face with fingertips or a pad, taking care to spread it evenly. You don't need to put foundation on your neck, which is mostly in shadow.

Remember that your complexion is at its best when you are young. It has its own healthy glow. Foundations cover this up! It is best to use a light water-based foundation which is as close as possible in colour to your own skin. Or just use a concealer to hide any blemishes.

Face powder

This is a loose, skin-coloured powder. You can use it over foundation to stop your skin from looking too shiny. Dust it over the foundation using a very light sprinkling.

Blusher

Blusher is red or pink coloured powder. It can be used on the cheek bones to give your face a little colour and to make your cheek bones stand out. The powder varieties which you put on with a brush are best. Apply a soft blotch of colour in a triangle over your cheekbones.

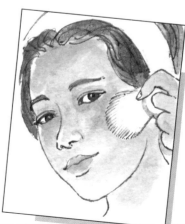

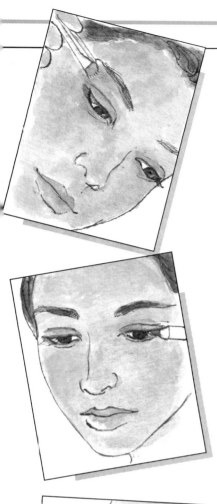

Eye shadow
You can use this coloured powder to shade your eyelids. You can mix different shades or colours. If you have deep-set eyes, use a light shade. You can even find glittery highlighter to wear over eye shadow for a party look.

Eyeliner
The easiest eyeliner to use is a soft coloured pencil. Use it to draw a thin line around the eye. This makes the eyes look bigger and more dramatic. Don't share eyeliner as you can easily spread eye infections.

Mascara
Mascara is a thick liquid which you can paint on your eyelashes to colour them and make them thicker. You can buy bright colours such as blue and purple, but for every-day use choose black or brown mascara. Don't share mascara with anyone else, as you can easily spread eye infections.

Lip colour
This long-lasting cream usually comes in shades of red or brown. Use a colour near to your own lip colour. Don't put too much lipstick on or it will just smudge. You can use a lip brush for a softer look.

Taking it off
However much or little make-up you use, you must clean it off at night. If you leave make-up on your face, it can block the pores and cause spots and blackheads. Remove it thoroughly with a cleansing cream. Massage the cream into your face and then wipe it off with cotton wool. Use a toner afterwards to remove the last traces of make-up. Read the section on **Caring for your skin** on pages 72 and 73 for more information.

To remove eye make-up, use baby oil or a very mild cream. Dab a little onto a piece of cotton wool and very gently wipe the eyes until the make-up is off. You can buy special eye make-up remover, but it is expensive.

Your hair

If you want to make a statement about yourself, your hair is the part of you which is easiest to change. You can grow it or crop it, wash it or neglect it, colour it pink or plait it into a hundred braids. You can do something different with it every day.

There are thousands of individual hairs growing on your head – somewhere between 100,000 and 150,000 of them in all! They will create a dense, thick mass or a thin, fine veil, depending on just how many hairs you have. Each hair grows about 1.25 centimetres every month, and drops out after three years.

Your hair is either curly, wavy, or straight. This depends on the shape of the root from which the hair grows. A smooth root makes straight hair while a curved root makes curly hair.

WHAT IS HAIR?

The strand of hair that we actually see, called the hair shaft, is completely dead. It is made of a form of protein called keratin. It forms scales which, if the hair is in good condition, overlap each other to form a smooth layer.

The live part of the hair grows from a tiny pocket, called a follicle, which is found just below the surface of the skin. Hair grows fast – about one centimetre a month.

Like the sebaceous glands elsewhere on your body, the pores on your head also create the natural oil called sebum. Each hair is coated with sebum and this keeps it smooth and shiny.

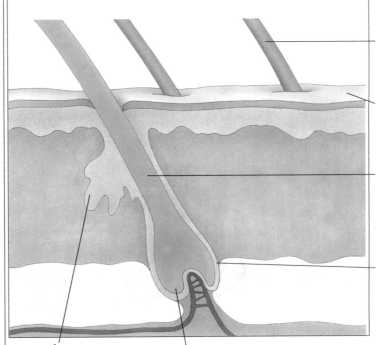

shaft: the hair that grows above the skin

scalp: the surface of your head

melanin: the substance which determines the colour of your hair

follicle: the root from which each hair grows

sebaceous gland: the gland which produces the sebum which coats and protects your hair

papilla: the base of the hair follicle, responsible for continuing growth

Everyone's hair is slightly different.

An enlarged picture of a hair, showing the overlapping scales of keratin.

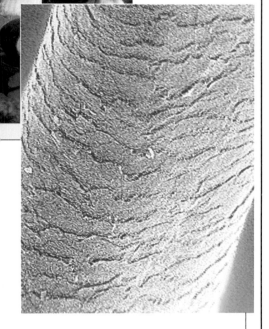

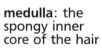

medulla: the spongy inner core of the hair

cortex: the layer which causes the strength, thickness and flexibility of your hair. It contains melanin.

cuticle: a transparent layer of tiny overlapping scales of keratin

DIFFERENT TYPES OF HAIR

Greasy hair

If your sebaceous glands produce too much sebum, you'll have greasy hair. Your hair may also become oilier when you are ill or when you are worried about something. If your skin is greasy, you are likely to have greasy hair as well. If so, it's best not to stimulate the sebaceous glands, or they will produce even more sebum. This means trying not to play with your hair or rub your scalp too often.

Dry hair

If your scalp produces too little sebum, your hair may feel dry and lifeless. This type of hair can look dull and brittle and it sometimes feels rough to touch. You'll find that washing removes what little sebum there is, so you should use a mild shampoo and not wash your hair too often. You can also use a special conditioner for dry hair.

Normal hair

Normal hair has a natural shine and is smooth to touch. If you're lucky enough to have normal hair, take care of it — shampoo and condition it regularly.

HAIR PROBLEMS

Split ends

If you have long or dry hair, the ends may start to fray or split. If you frequently use a hair drier, you are more likely to have split ends.

To prevent this, have your hair trimmed by a hairdresser regularly. Try to reduce the amount of heat you use on your hair. Use a good conditioner, too.

Dandruff

Like the skin on the rest of your body, the skin on your scalp is constantly renewing itself and shedding dead cells. If you have a dry scalp, these dead cells can build up and get caught in your hair causing dandruff.

If you suffer from dandruff, make sure you take time to massage your scalp when you wash your hair, to get a good circulation of blood to the surface skin. You can use a special anti-dandruff shampoo, but take care as some can be harsh on a scalp.

Head lice

Head lice are tiny insects that live on people's scalps. They like to live on clean hair, so it's no shame to catch them. They are a common complaint.

The first sign you'll notice is itching. If you look carefully, you'll see tiny eggs sticking to the hair close to the skin. If you have lice, you will need to buy a special lotion or shampoo from the pharmacy, and a very fine comb to comb out the eggs.

A magnified picture of a split end.

Looking after your hair

Unfortunately, we live in a grimy world and however hard we try to keep our hair clean, it can become coated with dirt and dust in a matter of days. Obviously, the easiest way to deal with dirty hair is to shampoo it clean whenever you think it needs it. For most people, this is about twice a week.

Shampoo

There are lots of different shampoos in the shops and it's easy to be confused by the variety of colours and smells! But all shampoos are made up of just three essential ingredients – water, a substance which dissolves oil and dirt, and another which makes the shampoo foam. Shampoo also contains perfume and colouring to make it look and smell attractive.

So how do you choose which shampoo to buy? Look for one which suits your hair type – dry, greasy, normal or, if you have dandruff, problem hair. If you wash your hair often, it is best to choose a mild shampoo for frequent use.

Most people tend to use too much shampoo on their hair. A small amount is enough. In fact, if you have dry hair, it's a good idea to water down your shampoo. Rub the shampoo into your hair until it foams. Remember to massage your scalp, too. Then rinse your hair well to make sure all the shampoo is washed out. Your hair and scalp can get used to one type of shampoo or conditioner and after a while they might not work so well. So change your type of shampoo every couple of months.

Drying your hair

Letting your hair dry naturally in the heat of the sun or in a warm room is the easiest and best way to dry it. But most people don't have time for this – they dry and style their hair using a hair drier. If you use a hair drier, always dry your hair as much as you can with a towel before you start drying.

Hair is weakest when it is wet, and blowing hot air directly at soaking-wet hair can cause damage. You can change the heat settings on most hair driers and it's best to use the lowest setting. Hold the hair drier at least 15 centimetres away from your head and keep moving it around. This will make sure that your hair dries evenly, without causing damage to one spot by overheating.

For short hair styles, try finger drying. This involves pushing your fingers through your hair and lifting and styling it as you use your hair drier. With curly or layered hair, you can try scrunch drying to give it a bulkier look. Hold a handful of wet hair tightly bunched up in your hand as you dry it.

CHECKLIST FOR THE BEST RESULTS

1. Don't use too much shampoo.

2. Use a conditioner suitable for your hair type.

3. Rinse your hair thoroughly.

4. Dry your hair gently with a towel before using a hair drier.

5. Don't rub your hair too vigorously when it is wet, as it is at its weakest.

6. Comb through your hair with a wide-toothed comb.

Brushes and combs

Brushing or combing your hair will help to remove dust and dirt. It also helps to spread the oil from your scalp down through the hair and keeps it looking shiny. When you brush or comb tangles out, work in sections from the bottom up using downwards strokes.

Choose a brush with soft, rounded bristles. Sharp bristles can hurt your scalp or tear at the rough cuticles of each hair. Your comb should have widely spaced teeth with blunt ends to avoid scalp and hair damage.

Combs based on the traditional African comb are best for tight curly hair. Wooden ones splinter and cause hair to break. They are also unhygienic. Use plastic ones with wide teeth for wet or tangled hair, and less wide for styling. Make sure you wash your brushes and combs regularly.

CONDITIONERS

Each hair is coated with tiny scales of protein. (Read more about this on pages 80 and 81.) If your hair is dry or damaged, the scales are ruffled, giving your hair a dull, rough look. Conditioners smooth the scales down by coating each strand with a fine film of oil. This keeps your hair shiny. Massage a small amount of conditioner into your hair after shampooing and rinse it out thoroughly.

DEEP CONDITIONING TREATMENTS

These are strong conditioners for very dry or damaged hair. They need to be left on for longer than an ordinary conditioner so after applying, wrap a towel around your head. Leave the conditioner on for about 10 to 15 minutes. Then rinse your hair thoroughly with warm water.

HOT OIL TREATMENTS

Hot oil treatments seal each hair and prevent moisture evaporating. They are especially good for dry hair. You can buy almond oil or hot oil treatments from a pharmacy. Massage the oil into your hair. For the best results, sleep with the oil on your hair. In the morning, shampoo your hair and rinse it thoroughly.

Hair treatments

Caring for your hair should be part of your daily routine. A good hair cut makes life easier – you can get up, wash and style your hair and go out quickly.

When you have more time, creating different styles for different moods, or to suit different activities can be fun. You can slick your hair tight to your scalp if you want to look sleek and confident. You can hold it back with a headband if you want to look casual and sporty.

Gel can stop your hair falling in your eyes.

Hair gel comes in different colours, but won't colour your hair.

Holding your style

Once you've decided on your hair style, you'll want to be sure that it will last for a while. There are many products on the market that will help. Most of these products are sprayed or rubbed on the hair, and stiffen as they dry. Some are very strong, and won't let a single hair fall out of place. Others have a lighter hold, and just help give your hair bounce.

Mousse

Mousse is a foamy substance. It is not as strong as hair gel, and won't hold your hair in a particular style. It is good for giving limp hair a bit of lift, and for controlling curly hair. Mousse usually comes in a can. Squirt a small amount into the palm of your hand, and massage it through damp hair.

Hair gel

Hair gel is a jelly-like substance. Gels work best on short or layered hair. Massage a small amount of hair gel into wet hair. Style your hair and then let it dry naturally. Some hair gels will make your dry hair look wet! Make sure you brush the hair gel out each night, or it will make your hair very dry. You may also need to wash your hair more frequently if you use gel.

Hair spray

Hair spray is a mist of fine droplets. It is used on dry hair to hold a style. Hair spray comes in a can. Never hold the can too close to your hair – 30 centimetres is about right. Keep the spray away from your eyes. And always brush hair spray off at night. If possible, get a can that uses a pump action, not CFC gases.

COLOURING YOUR HAIR

There are three kinds of natural colour. Blondes are people with light, yellow coloured hair. Brunettes have brown or black hair and, and obviously, redheads have red hair. There are many shades of each of these main colours and you can change to almost any of them by colouring your hair. First, work out how long you want to live with the colour. Then you can decide which of the following treatments is right for you:

Temporary colour rinses
Temporary rinses coat the surface of your hair with colour. They come in shampoo form, and are washed on. They only last until the next shampoo, when the colour will disappear.

PLAITING

This is the oldest and best known African style although it can be adapted to all kinds of hair. It's especially useful for busy people, who won't need to unwind the plaits for up to two months. Plaiting should never be done too tightly as this can pull out hair. The plaited hair is shampooed in the normal way, but don't rub too hard as the plaits can undo. Since you can't comb your hair, it's best to massage the scalp gently every day.

Most people need help with plaiting their hair.

PERMING

Hair is washed and cut, and rolled onto special perm rollers. Perming solution is then applied. This lotion penetrates the cortex of the hair and breaks down the bonds so they can be reshaped into curls. It is very important to time this process correctly, as over-permed hair easily becomes frizzy or even breaks. Different lotions can give you tight or loose curls. Perms last for between three and five months.

RELAXERS

Relaxing hair has become a popular way of transforming naturally curly hair, especially the hair of many Black people, into different styles. Relaxing hair simply means straightening it out.

Relaxing is done using the chemical solution sodium hydroxide, also known as lye. The chemical loosens the hair cuticle causing it to swell. It then penetrates the inner cortex layer of each hair where it straightens out the keratin chain.

Fine hair takes about eight minutes to straighten using a mild product. Thicker, denser hair requires a stronger product and takes about fifteen minutes. The solution must not be left on the hair for longer than directed since this may damage both your hair and your scalp.

Semi-permanent colorants

Semi-permanent colorants last from four to six washes. Shampoo the colorant into your hair, and leave it on for 20 to 40 minutes, as directed on the package, before rinsing it out.

Vegetable dyes

Vegetable dyes such as henna are better for your hair than chemical dyes. Mix the powder to a paste with warm water. Apply the paste and leave it on your hair for 30 to 60 minutes. Then rinse off thoroughly.

Permanent tints

Changing your hair colour permanently is quite a drastic step. Permanent tints contain chemicals which change the structure of hair, so it will definitely look and feel different afterwards. When new growth appears at the hair roots, it will be the colour of your natural hair. Be prepared to start colouring again!

Bleaches

Bleach is made of a chemical called hydrogen peroxide. It takes the colour out of the hair, so it's the only way for brunettes to become blondes! Never try to bleach your hair at home – this is a job for a professional hairdresser. If you do have your hair bleached, remember to use conditioning treatments regularly. As with other permanent tints, you'll find your hair's natural colour will show through as it grows.

Shaving

Mostly for boys!

You might be able to get away with being lazy about looking after your body but there's one bit you can't ignore. You have to deal with the fluff growing on your cheeks, chin and upper lip. Even if you want to grow a beard, you'll have to shave for a few years until the hair becomes thick and coarse enough. This means you still have to come to grips with shaving.

Shaving is a daily chore, and might seem boring. But think how good it is for your face! All that grimacing and face twisting keeps the face muscles in trim. Also, the razor blade removes dead skin cells as well as hair. So you can end up with a really smooth, fresh face.

There are two ways to shave, wet shaving and dry shaving. Your choice may depend on what equipment you can get or just on which method best suits you.

WET SHAVING
Equipment needed: razor with blade, shaving cream, gel or stick, shaving brush, sponge or flannel, warm water, towel, mirror in a good light!

1. Wash your face with warm water. This softens the skin, and the blade of the razor will slide over your face more easily.

2. Cover your face with shaving cream or soapy foam from a shaving stick. If you're using a stick, whip up a good lather with a shaving brush first.

3. Start by shaving the side of your face. Pull the skin downwards to stretch it, and make short, downward strokes with the razor. Rinse the blade every few strokes to remove the foam and hairs clogging the blade.

4. When you've finished, rinse your face thoroughly with plenty of cold water to close the pores.

SPECIAL NOTE
Razor blades go blunt quickly. When this happens, they will stop giving a close shave and leave your face sore, so check the blade before you shave.

Aftershave
Whether you shave wet or dry, you might like to splash some aftershave lotion on your face after your shave. This will leave your face feeling fresh. If you find that a liquid aftershave is too strong and makes your face sting, try using an aftershave cream, or a moisturiser instead.

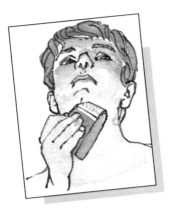

DRY SHAVING
Equipment needed: electric razor, either battery operated or with a lead for mains electricity.

1. Wash your face with warm water.

2. Make sure your skin is completely dry.

3. Switch the razor on, and run it over your face. Be firm, but don't press too hard.

4. When you've finished shaving, pat your skin with an aftershave lotion or cream.

SPECIAL NOTE
You will need to clean all the hair from the inside of the razor each time you use it. A small brush is normally provided for this.

Readers' views

"I was really bad at shaving when I started! I had to go off to school with half a dozen cuts on my cheek and neck. Now I give myself lots of time, so I make a better job of it."
Touson

"My Dad gave me an electric razor which runs off a battery. It's handy because I can use it wherever I am."
Steve

"My friends shave, and think I'm just being lazy. But I've grown a beard because it suits me. My friends don't realise that you still need to spend time on a beard, trimming and taking care of it."
Mark

"It didn't take me long to grow a moustache, although it's a bit tricky shaving around it. I think it makes me look older and more sophisticated."
Ronan

Reader's experience

"Everybody in my class started to shave long before I did. Even kids younger than me had some sort of hair or fluff on their face. Every day, I looked in the mirror to see if I'd grown any hair, and every day my face was as smooth as a baby's. I was fed up with getting teased. People were saying that I would never be able to shave.

In the end, I got so upset I decided to talk to my Dad. He was very helpful. He said I was lucky. He told me that shaving is a chore I'll have to do for the rest of my life so I may as well enjoy the time off! He also said that he hadn't started to shave until he'd been quite a bit older than his friends.

So I stopped worrying about it and soon the first hairs appeared. I'm pleased I'm shaving now, even if I do have to do it every day. Talking to Dad made me realize that everybody's different. It's nothing to do with being a 'he-man'. Your body just does things in its own time."
Jake

Body hair for girls

When you were young, you probably didn't give a thought to the hair on your body, because it was probably very fine and soft. However, during puberty you'll notice hair growing underneath your arms and on your pubic area for the first time.

As girls approach their teens, the hair on their bodies becomes darker and coarser. Underarm hair is particularly coarse. The hair on your legs, your arms and your face might also become a littler darker.

Hair grows on certain parts of your body as a protection. This is completely natural, and there is no medical or hygienic reason why you should remove it. However some women like to remove the hair on their face or body. There are several ways to do this but remember that after most methods of hair removal, the hair may grow back slightly thicker and darker than before. You may prefer to try bleaching, which takes the colour out of the hair so that it is not so noticeable but does not remove it.

SHAVING

Shaving with a razor is a quick and easy way of removing hair. Always lather the area with soap, and shave in downward movements. Shaving is strictly for underarms and legs. Make sure your razor is really sharp, otherwise it will pull the hair instead of cutting it.

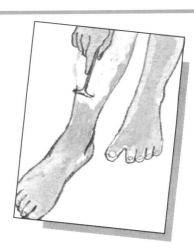

If you use an electric razor, you don't have to use soap at all.

This chart shows which hair-removal methods are suitable for different parts of the body

	shaving	plucking	creams	electrolysis	waxing	bleaching
Upper lip			✓	✓		✓
Chin			✓	✓		✓
Eyebrows		✓		✓		
Nipples		✓		✓		
Legs	✓	✓	✓		✓	
Abdomen			✓	✓	✓	
Bikini area	✓		✓	✓	✓	
Underarms	✓		✓	✓		

PLUCKING

You can pluck out hair with a pair of tweezers. You have to grasp each hair individually and tweak it out. Plucking is cheap, but it takes a long time and can be painful. It is best only to pluck your eyebrows.

HAIR REMOVAL CREAMS

These creams dissolve the hair at the root so that they can be washed away with the cream. The cream takes 5 to 10 minutes to work and the hairs don't grow back for about a week.

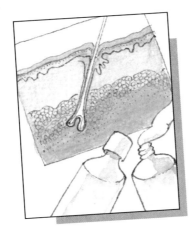

ELECTROLYSIS

Electrolysis is the most permanent method of removing hair. But it's also expensive, and has to be done by a trained technician. An electric needle is used to destroy the root of the hair. When the hair grows back, it is weaker than it was before.

WAXING

It is best to go to a beauty salon if you want to try this method. Warm wax is smeared over the hair and then ripped off. It can be painful, but all the hairs are ripped out at the root. Your legs are left silky smooth and the hairs won't grow back for at least a month. If you want to wax your legs at home, you can buy wax kits from a pharmacy. They can be messy, so make sure you read the instructions carefully before you begin.

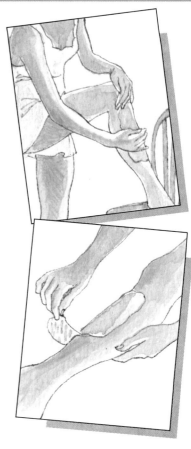

BLEACHING

Bleaching is useful if your hair is dark, but fine and soft. You should follow the manufacturer's instructions carefully. Special facial bleach should be used for your face, though it's advisable to test it on your skin first, to make sure the bleach does not irritate your skin.

Your eyes

Your eyes are two of the most delicate organs in your body, so they need looking after. But don't worry! Your body has its own efficient method of protecting them. When you shut your eyes, your eyelids form a waterproof, air-tight shield. They will snap shut at any loud noise or sudden movement. Every time you blink, you spread a wet film over the surface of the eye. Count how often you blink. Most people blink about once every five seconds, without even knowing they're doing it.

Eyelashes and eyebrows are there to protect your eyes, too. They help to keep out specks of dust, and dirt — even insects.

Tears

Tears are drops of clear, salty liquid which protect and cleanse your eyes. They are produced naturally to flush out a speck of dust, or to protect the eye from acids or strong fumes. You can see how well they work when fumes from a chopped onion hit the surface of your eyes — the eyes water immediately.

Tears come from special glands called lacrimal glands, found under the skin in the outer corner of your eyes. Tears wash over the eye when they are needed, then drain away through tiny tubes called lacrimal ducts in the inner corner of your eye and into your nose. That's why your nose runs when you cry!

Crying

Nobody knows why we cry. It's a natural reaction to different kinds of stress. We cry when we're sad, we cry when we're hurt. We cry when we're very angry or frustrated. And have you seen people with tears of laughter rolling down their cheeks? These tears are emotional tears. They are a safety valve, and leave us feeling relieved and refreshed.

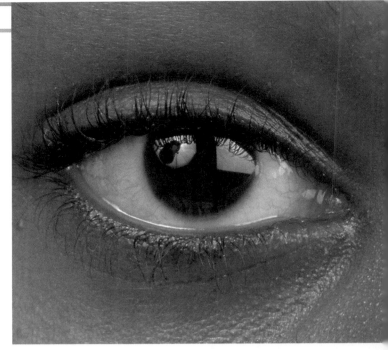

Your eyelids are a natural protective barrier for your eyes.

HOW YOUR EYES WORK

Light enters your eyes through the pupil. This small, black, circular part of the eye, is able to control how much light is let in. Watch your pupil in a mirror while you shine a light near your face. You'll see the pupil become smaller, allowing less light into your eye and protecting it from the glare.

Light passes through the lens, which changes shape according to the distance of the object you are looking at. It is round and thick when focusing on close objects and long and thin when focusing on distant objects.

Once light has been focused by the lens, it passes to the retina, the layer at the back of your eye. All the parts of the eye bend the light so that it will fall on the retina at one point, called the focus point. This makes sure the image you see is clear and not blurred.

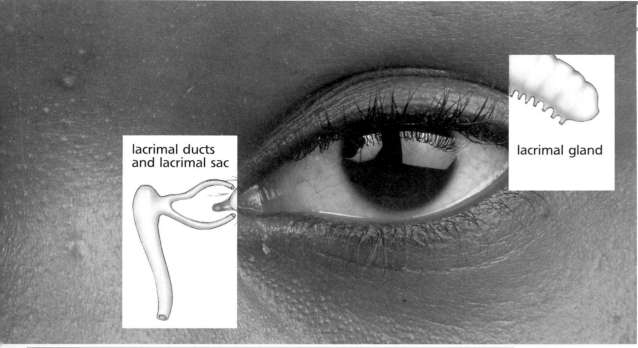

lacrimal ducts and lacrimal sac

lacrimal gland

Tears are produced by the lacrimal gland, then drain through the lacrimal ducts.

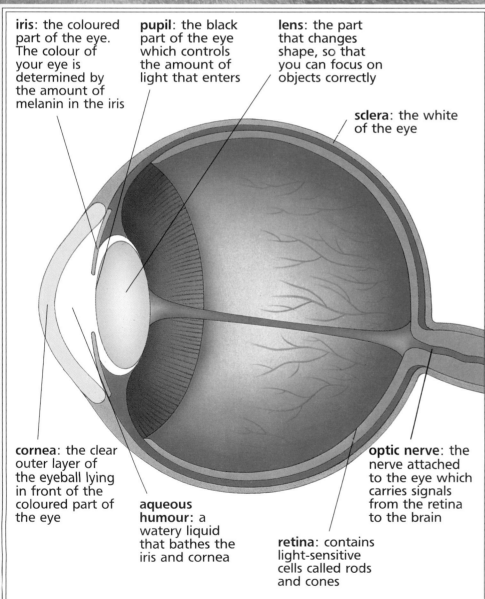

iris: the coloured part of the eye. The colour of your eye is determined by the amount of melanin in the iris

pupil: the black part of the eye which controls the amount of light that enters

lens: the part that changes shape, so that you can focus on objects correctly

sclera: the white of the eye

cornea: the clear outer layer of the eyeball lying in front of the coloured part of the eye

aqueous humour: a watery liquid that bathes the iris and cornea

retina: contains light-sensitive cells called rods and cones

optic nerve: the nerve attached to the eye which carries signals from the retina to the brain

rod and cone cells

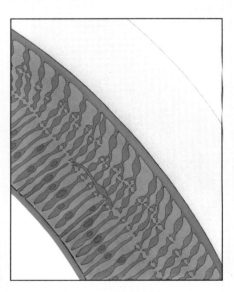

Your retina contains two types of sensitive cells. Rod cells are sensitive to light, while cone cells are sensitive to colour. The rod and cone cells send messages to your brain along special links called nerves. Your brain then puts the messages together to form an image and work out what it is you are looking at.

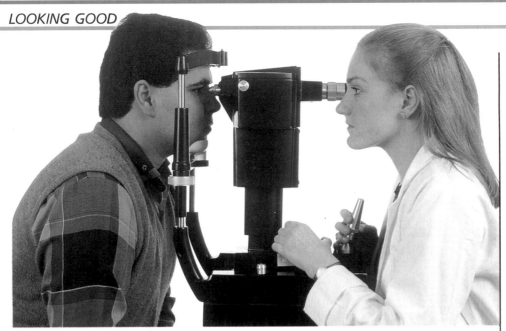

Eye tests

It's best to have your vision tested by an ophthalmologist every few years, even if you don't wear glasses at the moment. The test will show up any problems before they get too serious. If your eyes feel sore or tired, go and have them checked. If you are already wearing glasses or contact lenses, you will need to visit the ophthalmologist regularly.

The ophthalmologist will ask you to attempt tests for long sight, short sight, colour blindness and your ability to focus. If you do have problems with your eyesight, the optician will guide you as you choose glasses or contact lenses.

CHOOSING GLASSES

Nowadays, glasses are made in a whole range of fashionable designs with every possible shape and shade of frame to choose from. But before you choose your glasses, there are a few things to bear in mind.

Choose frames that are strong and that will last. If you have lightweight frames, you will need to treat your glasses with extraordinary care!

SHORT SIGHT

If you have short sight, you can see things best when they are close up. Objects at a distance appear blurred. Short-sightedness occurs because light entering the eye meets at a focus point before it reaches the retina. The image is not properly focused when it hits the retina and the brain receives a picture which is blurred.

LONG SIGHT

People who suffer from long sight can see things clearly at a distance, but objects close up are fuzzy. The light coming into the eye doesn't actually meet at a focus point before it falls on the retina. Again, the brain sees a picture which is out of focus.

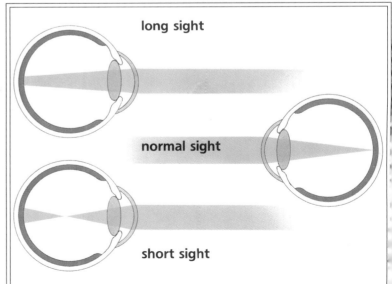

long sight

normal sight

short sight

Look at the shape of your face before deciding which frames to buy. If you have a small face, don't hide it with a huge pair of frames. Your glasses should be in proportion with your whole body, not just your face. So, when you choose the frames, try and take a look at yourself in a full length mirror.

Don't choose a pair of glasses that keep slipping. These will be uncomfortable to wear and you will have to keep clenching your face to try to keep them on.

Glasses can be fun. But before you settle for a pair of outrageous frames, remember you may be wearing your glasses most of the time. They have to look right with your school wear as well as your party clothes.

Don't be rushed into buying a pair of glasses that are someone else's choice. Your glasses are personal to you and only you can tell if they meet all your requirements.

Make sure your glasses don't lie too heavily on the top of your nose. You should hardly feel that you have glasses on at all.

Contact lenses

Many people do not like wearing glasses or find them impractical for activities such as sports and dancing. For them, contact lenses are ideal. Contact lenses are worn on the part of the eye called the cornea. They can correct short or long sight and can be used to disguise unsightly or damaged eyes. Some people even use them to change their eye colour. There are two main types of contact lenses, soft lenses and rigid, or hard, lenses. Your optician will help you decide which type of lens is most suitable by taking into account your prescription and lifestyle.

Soft lenses
Soft lenses are soft and pliable because they contain water. If a soft lens is left out of its storage solution in air it will dry up and become brittle. This does not happen when the lens is on the eye because the tears in your eye keep it moist. Soft lenses can tear easily unless handled carefully.

A soft lens drapes over the whole cornea and extends a few millimetres onto the white of the eye. It only moves very slightly with blinking and is comfortable as soon as it is inserted because the eyelids cannot feel it.

Rigid lenses
Most rigid lenses are made from gas permeable material which looks and feels like perspex. They often are called 'gas permeable lenses'. Rigid lenses are smaller than soft lenses and are moved around the

cornea with each blink. This movement pumps fresh tears under the lens, supplying the cornea with oxygen and keeping it healthy. Rigid lenses are not comfortable when first worn because the eyelids have to get used to the movement of the lens. It usually takes a few weeks to get used to them, by which time they can feel just as comfortable as soft lenses.

Care
Your eyes are very precious, and by wearing lenses you risk infections and other complications which may damage them. To minimise the risk it is **very** important to care for your lenses properly and to have regular check-ups. There are a few golden rules to follow:

ALWAYS wash your hands before handling lenses.

ALWAYS clean lenses on removal.

ALWAYS disinfect lenses overnight to kill germs.

ALWAYS keep the lens case clean.

ALWAYS remove the lens if your eye becomes painful or red and seek advice.

It is not advisable to wear any type of contact lens overnight as this increases the risk of infection and other complications.

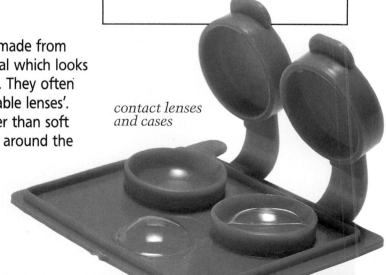

contact lenses and cases

Eye problems

Many people have more problems with their eyes than with any other part of their bodies. You can have an eye problem, such as colour blindness, from the day you are born. Some problems may occur when you are tired or stressed. Bloodshot eyes is one of these. Some problems, for example, glaucoma, may only develop as you get older.

Eyes are extremely sensitive and delicate organs. People may sometimes need to protect them by wearing goggles, for instance when they're swimming, or working with machinery or in a dusty atmosphere. You can't avoid all eye problems, but if you treat your eyes well, you'll be giving them the best possible chance.

Relaxing with old, cold teabags can ease puffiness.

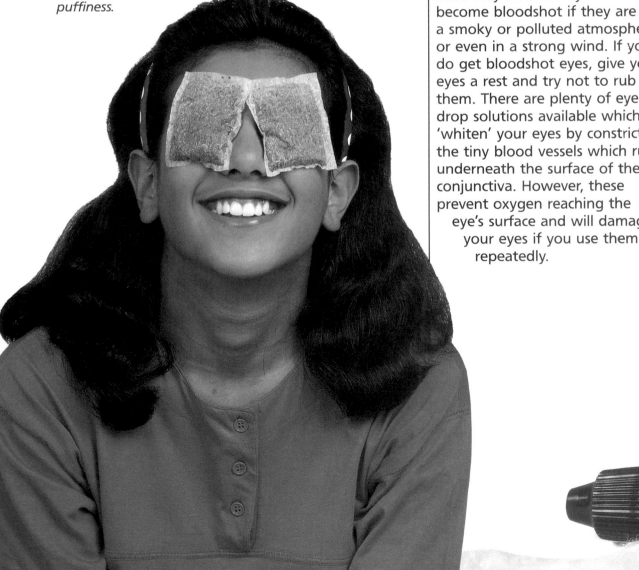

TIRED EYES

When you are tired, your eyes may start to feel gritty and ache. This sometimes happens if you have been reading for a long time. It helps to make sure that light is coming from behind you and is falling on the book. If you face the glare of direct sunlight or electric light, you will have to screw up your eyes and this will make them tired and sore. When you are reading, give your eyes a rest every 10 to 15 minutes by closing them for a minute or two to ease the strain.

Tired eyes feel gritty and painful.

BLOODSHOT EYES

When the whites of your eyes look red and sore, we say that they are bloodshot. This normally just means that your eyes are tired or irritated. Some people have very sensitive eyes which become bloodshot if they are in a smoky or polluted atmosphere, or even in a strong wind. If you do get bloodshot eyes, give your eyes a rest and try not to rub them. There are plenty of eye drop solutions available which 'whiten' your eyes by constricting the tiny blood vessels which run underneath the surface of the conjunctiva. However, these prevent oxygen reaching the eye's surface and will damage your eyes if you use them repeatedly.

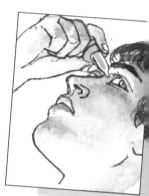

Put eyedrops in the inner corner of the eye.

PUFFINESS

If you're over-tired or suffering from a cold, hayfever or an allergy, you might find that your eyes become puffy and tender. Before taking any action, make sure you're getting enough sleep and eating properly. You can cool your eyes by covering them for a few minutes with cold tea bags or slices of cucumber.

COLOUR BLINDNESS

Colour blindness occurs almost always in males. If you are colour blind, you will have difficulty telling the difference between certain colours. It is most common to confuse red and green. This can cause problems when driving if you can't distinguish red and green traffic lights. Colour blindness may happen because the cells sensitive to colour in the retina do not develop properly or are damaged.

You are born with colour blindness and there is no treatment. However, many people don't even realize they are colour blind because it doesn't affect their life too seriously.

SQUINT

If someone has normal eyesight, both eyes focus on the same thing at the same time. If you have a squint or lazy eye, each eye looks in a slightly different direction. Squints are usually due to a problem with your eye muscles. Usually it is only one eye which is looking the wrong way. There are several different treatments which doctors may recommend. Sometimes a squint can be cured by exercising the weaker eye, or by covering one eye to make the other work harder.

STIES

A stye is an infection which forms in the small glands of the eyelid. Usually, a sore red lump forms, but sometimes the whole eyelid swells up and becomes tender. You are more likely to suffer from sties if you are ill, tired or generally run-down. Don't squeeze the stye. Sponge it gently with warm water, which you must first boil and then leave to cool. Then dab on some antiseptic cream, as advised by your doctor. Most sties will heal themselves in a few days, but if not it's best to see a doctor.

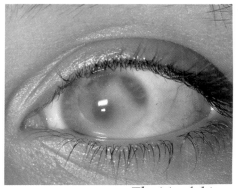

The iris of this glaucoma sufferer has turned cloudy

GLAUCOMA

Glaucoma is caused when excess fluid builds up inside the eye. This puts pressure on the eye lens and optic nerve and can cause blindness. Glaucoma usually develops in middle age, but it can also happen suddenly in much younger people. It is a condition that can run in families. Glaucoma sufferers may see rainbow rings around lights and have pain in their eyes and forehead. If you think you may have glaucoma, it is important to get urgent medical advice.

CONJUNCTIVITIS

Conjunctivitis is a swelling or inflammation of a part of your eye covering, called the conjunctiva. This is the membrane, or layer of tissue, which lines the undersurface of your eyelid and covers the white part of your eyeball. Conjunctivitis can be caused sometimes by an infection or by an allergy or irritation. The result will be eyes which are watery, red and sore. Try sponging your eyes gently with warm water, which you must first boil and then leave to cool. You should also see your doctor who will normally prescribe an antibiotic ointment or drops.

A colour blind person might use these crayons to colour a red rose green!

95

Your ears

When you are listening to music, you're actually just hearing vibrations, or sound waves, which are passing through the air. Your ears are acting as receivers, picking up the sound waves and passing the information relayed by them to your brain. Your brain then sets to work to interpret the sounds you are listening to.

There are three main parts to your ear – the outer, the middle and the inner ear. Your outer ear is made up of the ear flap, the ear canal and the ear drum. The only visible part is the ear flap at the side of your head.

Caring for your ears

There is a natural sticky substance inside your ears, called ear wax. This is produced by glands in the ear canal and it's there to protect your ears from dirt and dust. Sometimes, the ear wax can build up and harden inside the ear canal. This can cause temporary hearing loss and you may want to go to a doctor to have your ears washed out and the wax removed.

You do not need to clean inside your ears. When you need to, just wash the outside visible part. Never insert anything into the ears, as you can easily damage them by poking something inside them.

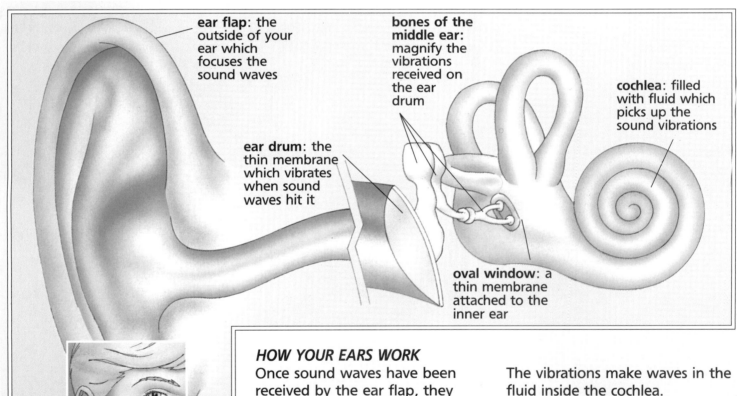

ear flap: the outside of your ear which focuses the sound waves

bones of the middle ear: magnify the vibrations received on the ear drum

cochlea: filled with fluid which picks up the sound vibrations

ear drum: the thin membrane which vibrates when sound waves hit it

oval window: a thin membrane attached to the inner ear

Your inner ear is very close to your eye!

HOW YOUR EARS WORK

Once sound waves have been received by the ear flap, they travel down a hollow tube called the ear canal to your ear drum. This is made up of a thin piece of skin called a membrane. Sound waves hit this delicate membrane making it vibrate. These vibrations then travel across the tiny bones in your middle ear to the cochlea in your inner ear.

The vibrations make waves in the fluid inside the cochlea.
Inside the cochlea there are thousands of sensitive hairs. As the fluid passes over the hairs, it stirs the nerve endings of the ear. The nerves carry the sound messages to your brain. Then it's your brain's job to make sense of it all and tell you what you're hearing.

Expert's view

The dangers of noise

The ear is a vulnerable organ. Many people do not realize that partial, or even total deafness can be caused when the eardrum is damaged by noise. Repeated loud sounds are the most common cause and it is unlikely that a single noise will cause permanent deafness.

Sound is measured in units called decibels. The sound of a person whispering is about 20 decibels, a telephone ringing is 70 decibels and a noisy motorcycle is 90 decibels. Repeated exposure to noise above 120 decibels can damage the organ of hearing, called the organ of Corti, which lies deep inside the cochlea. Damage to the organ of Corti cannot be repaired. A rock band playing live may measure more than 130 decibels.

The first symptom of noise damage is a buzzing or ringing in the ears when the noise stops. This usually disappears after a few days. However, if you are regularly exposed to noise which has this effect on your ears, you should protect your hearing with ear plugs or ear guards.

Many people use headphones or personal stereos so that they can listen to music without disturbing those around them. But damage to the ears can occur if the sound is turned up too high. So keep the volume as low as possible if you are listening to a personal stereo for a long time. Remember, deafness is permanent!

Pierced ears

When you have your ears pierced, a tiny hole is punched in the earlobe, the fleshy lump at the base of the ear. Your earlobe is mostly made of fat and luckily there are very few nerves to feel pain. Most jewellers or beauticians can pierce ears. It is very important that you only have your ears pierced by a licensed operator. Sterile equipment must be used, as infections can easily be passed on if the equipment is not sterile.

People with pierced ears have a tiny hole in their earlobe.

Ear piercing doesn't damage your ears, but the hole can become infected. If this happens, you should bathe the holes with antiseptic twice a day, until they are healed, or if the infection persists, see your doctor. It's best to rotate your earrings once or twice a day to prevent scabs forming.

When you first have your ears pierced, you will be given gold or stainless steel earrings. Many people are allergic to other types of metal which can cause a rash. If this is the case, it is best to wear hypoallergenic earrings. In a few weeks, when the holes in your ears are fully healed, you can remove the first earrings and wear others.

DIFFERENT KINDS OF EARRINGS
There are three main kinds of earrings:

Studs
Studs are small earrings attached to a thin shaft which goes through the hole in your ear and is secured with a butterfly.

Dangly
These are the long kind of earrings! It's best not to wear these when you're exercising – they may get caught on something and tear your earlobe.

Clip-ons
You don't need to have your ears pierced to wear earrings. You can wear clip-on earrings!

97

Hands and nails

Your hands are among the most useful parts of your body, as well as being one of your most expressive features – just think how often you've used your hands today. Because they often face harsh treatment, hands need extra care to keep them looking good.

Try to protect your hands whenever possible. this means wearing rubber gloves when you do the washing-up! Make sure you dry your hands well if they have been in water. Most importantly, apply plenty of moisturizing cream.

Hand problems

Chilblains and chapped skin are two problems you might suffer from if you live in a colder climate. Chilblains are painful, itchy swellings, usually on the fingers or toes. Chapped skin is skin which is cracked and red. Both are caused by exposure to cold weather.

To prevent these complaints, wear gloves when you are outdoors and try not to expose your hands to extreme changes in temperature.

Exercise your fingers or toes with some gentle stretching, and allow them to warm up gradually at room temperature. Try not to rub or massage them because you will aggravate the inflamed skin tissue.

Nails

Nails grow quite quickly – fingernails grow about three millimetres each month, toenails more slowly. Each nail takes about three months to grow from the root to the tip.

While you can't do anything about the shape of your hands, you can change the condition of your nails. If you keep them in good shape with a regular manicure, healthy nails and cuticles will make your whole hand look more attractive. If your nails seem brittle, massage in cuticle cream daily before you go to sleep. Ease cuticles back off the nail gently and never push them with sharp, metal objects. Don't try and grow long nails unless they are naturally strong.

A WEEKLY MANICURE
If you follow these five easy steps, you can keep your hands and nails in good condition. It won't take long, so try it once a week.

First, lay out everything you will need – a pair of nail scissors or nail clippers, an emery board, a bowl of warm soapy water, cotton wool buds and hand cream.

1. Wash your hands thoroughly, using the same sort of soap that you would use on your face.

2. Use a nail brush to remove dirt from behind your nails. If there are any stains or hard patches on your hands, rub them gently with a rough cloth or emery board.

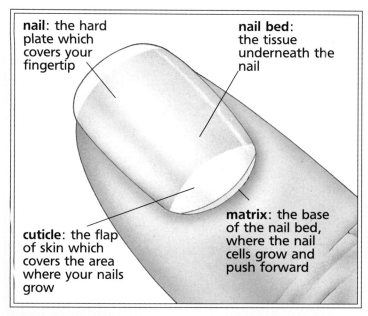

nail: the hard plate which covers your fingertip

nail bed: the tissue underneath the nail

cuticle: the flap of skin which covers the area where your nails grow

matrix: the base of the nail bed, where the nail cells grow and push forward

WHAT IS A NAIL?

A nail is the hard tissue that protects the surface of the tips of your fingers and toes. It is made of a protein called keratin. The part of the nail that you can see is dead. The living part grows from the nail bed, or matrix, inside your finger. The matrix is protected by a flap of skin called the cuticle.

Nail problems

If your nails chip or break easily then you're probably giving them too much rough treatment. And remember – your nails, like your hair, are indicators of your general state of health.

Chipped nails and small white flecks or ridges on the surface of your nail can be signs that you aren't eating a balanced diet or that you are in poor health. A mineral called calcium will help to strengthen your nails. Calcium is found in meat, milk, cheese, eggs and fish and is essential for strong bones and nails.

Biting your nails

There is only one cure for nail biting and that is to stop! It's a nervous habit which results in painful, sore fingers. To help break this habit you can buy evil tasting lotions to paint on your nails, but you'll need to renew the coating each time you wash.

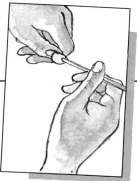

5. Dry your hands well and rub in a little hand cream or moisturiser. Very gently push back the cuticle with a cotton wool bud.

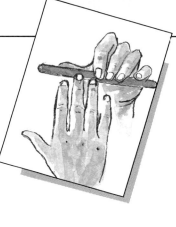

3. Trim your nails to the required length, cutting them in a slight curve.

You might want to file your nails gently with an emery board to get rid of the rough edges. Always file in one direction only.

4. Soak your finger tips in the bowl of warm water for about five minutes. This will soften the skin and the cuticles.

Your feet

Your feet carry the full weight of your body and they keep you upright. They also do all the walking — an average of 15,000 steps a day! So you can see why it is so important to look after them. If you take care now, you are far less likely to suffer from unhealthy feet when you get older. Many foot problems are caused by wearing shoes which don't fit well.

Looking after your feet

Wash your feet every day. Use a nail brush to remove dirt from your toenails and a pumice stone to get rid of hard skin. Always dry your feet thoroughly, taking extra care to dry between the toes. Dust them with a little talcum powder to help keep them dry and cool. If possible, try not to wear the same kinds of shoes day in, day out. Your feet need a change. And if you've had a particularly tiring day, sit with your feet propped up for ten minutes. The rest will do them good.

BUYING SHOES

When you buy a new pair of shoes, check that they don't rub against your big toe, or cut into the side or back of your ankle.

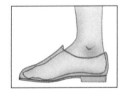

Shoes should fit snugly across the widest part of your foot, without pinching.

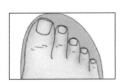

If new shoes are too loose, you will find yourself clenching your toes to keep them on. This strains the muscles in your feet and can result in corns and calluses.

Don't try on new shoes after you have been walking a lot, as your feet may be hot and swollen. You could end up with the wrong size.

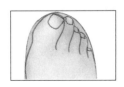

FOOT PROBLEMS

Smelly feet

The soles of your feet have more sweat glands than any other part of your body, so it's no wonder that your feet can get smelly! Give them a regular airing by walking around barefoot as often as possible. Don't wear trainers for too long, as they make your feet very hot and sweaty. If your feet perspire heavily, change your socks frequently. Cotton socks are the most absorbent and keep your feet drier. If you do have smelly feet, wash your feet every day and dry them thoroughly. Use a little talcum powder or foot spray to help keep them dry.

Plantar warts

Plantar warts, which are also known as verrucae, are warts which occur on the soles of your feet. They are caused by a virus which you can catch from someone else, particularly if you are barefoot. They eventually disappear by themselves, but if they are causing large or painful lumps you should go to a doctor or chiropodist to remove them.

Blisters

Blisters are painful water-filled bumps. They swell up in a few hours wherever something hard rubs against your foot.
To treat a blister, wash your foot gently with soap and water. Smooth on a little antiseptic and protect the blister by covering it with a gauze dressing. Don't break the blister, as this will make it more likely to become infected.

Ingrowing toenails

Ingrowing toenails are nails which have grown into the skin of your toe. This can happen if you wear shoes or socks that are too restricting. The pressure on your toes forces the toenail to bend over. Ingrowing toenails can be very painful and may need to be treated by a foot doctor, or chiropodist.

Try and avoid the problem completely by making sure your shoes fit correctly and cutting your toe nails regularly. You should cut them straight across. Cutting in a curve actually encourages ingrowing toenails.

Athlete's foot

Athlete's foot is a fungal infection that grows between your toes, making the skin itchy, white and flaky. You can catch this infection in public places where you walk barefoot, such as changing rooms or swimming pools. Always wash and thoroughly dry your feet if you visit such places. If you do catch athlete's foot, you can treat it yourself with special foot powder or cream from a pharmacy, but you might like to confirm the diagnosis with your doctor.

athlete's foot

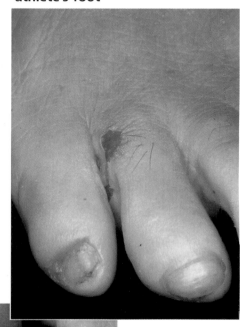

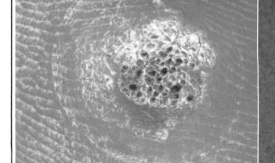

plantar wart

ingrowing toenail

Caring for teeth

Don't ignore your teeth! Neglected teeth decay, fall out and have to be replaced by false ones. It's not just your teeth that need attention – problems with your gums can cause just as much damage in your mouth.

Visiting the dentist

Get into the habit of visiting your dentist for a check-up every six months. Your dentist will be able to spot any possible tooth problems at an early stage and prevent them becoming painful or serious.

Brushing your teeth

Any particles of food left on your teeth will encourage bacteria. A thin film of food particles and bacteria called plaque can soon cover your teeth and start the process of tooth decay. Brushing your teeth helps clean away plaque.

Remember to brush all three surfaces of your teeth – the back, front and biting surfaces. Brush downwards on the upper teeth and upwards on the lower teeth. Use small, circular, movements on the biting surfaces. Use a toothbrush with soft bristles and a small head which can reach into the corners of your mouth and which won't be too hard on your gums.

The gums can suffer too if you don't clean your teeth properly. Healthy gums are pink and moist. If your gums look red and swollen, it means you should be extra careful to clean the areas where your gums meet your teeth.

Flossing your teeth

Dental floss is special thread which you pull through the gaps between your teeth. This removes any food particles which may be stuck there. To floss, wrap a length of floss about 40 centimetres long around each middle finger. Guide the floss between two teeth and pull it up and down, cleaning the sides of both teeth and the areas around the gum line.

You can buy waxed or unwaxed dental floss. Choose whichever is more comfortable for you.

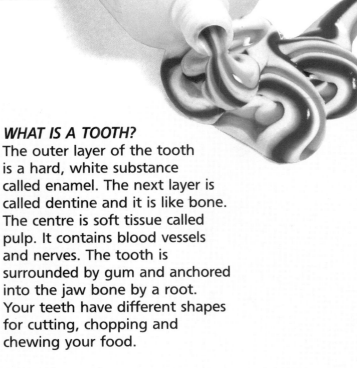

WHAT IS A TOOTH?
The outer layer of the tooth is a hard, white substance called enamel. The next layer is called dentine and it is like bone. The centre is soft tissue called pulp. It contains blood vessels and nerves. The tooth is surrounded by gum and anchored into the jaw bone by a root. Your teeth have different shapes for cutting, chopping and chewing your food.

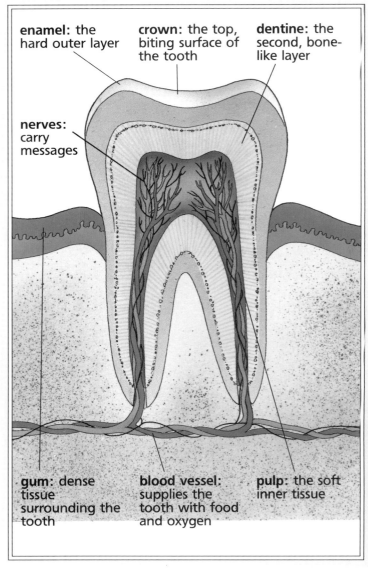

enamel: the hard outer layer

crown: the top, biting surface of the tooth

dentine: the second, bone-like layer

nerves: carry messages

gum: dense tissue surrounding the tooth

blood vessel: supplies the tooth with food and oxygen

pulp: the soft inner tissue

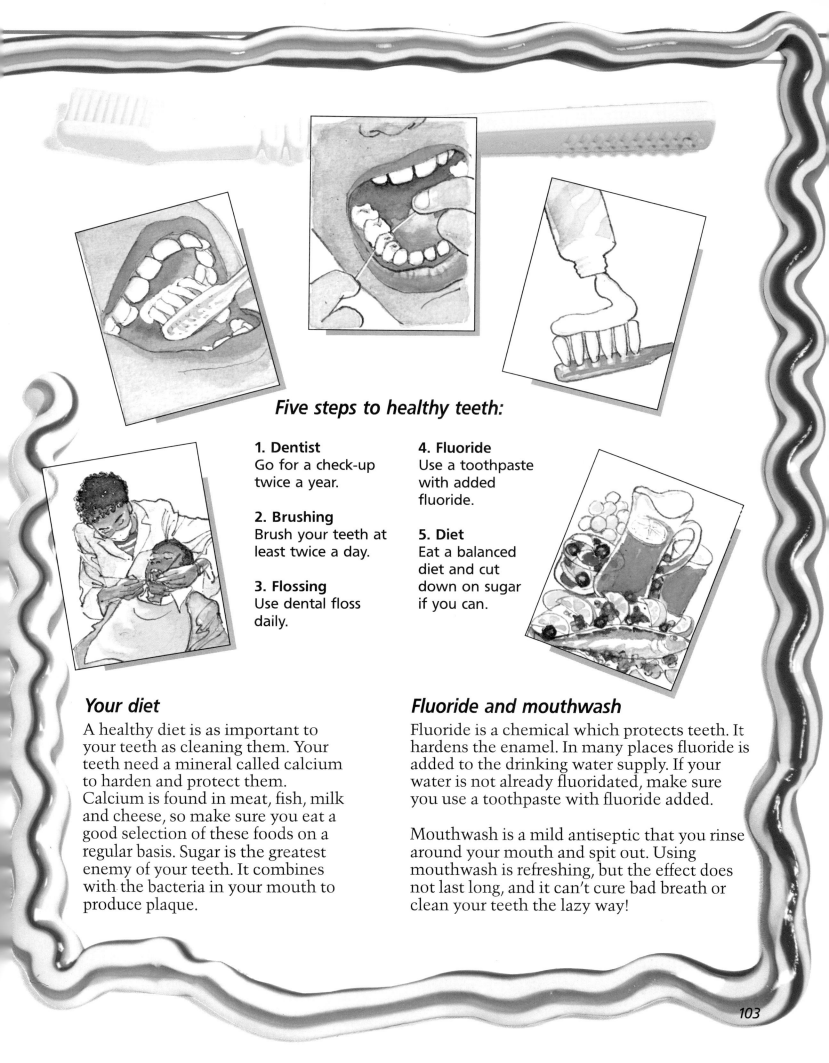

Five steps to healthy teeth:

1. Dentist
Go for a check-up twice a year.

2. Brushing
Brush your teeth at least twice a day.

3. Flossing
Use dental floss daily.

4. Fluoride
Use a toothpaste with added fluoride.

5. Diet
Eat a balanced diet and cut down on sugar if you can.

Your diet

A healthy diet is as important to your teeth as cleaning them. Your teeth need a mineral called calcium to harden and protect them. Calcium is found in meat, fish, milk and cheese, so make sure you eat a good selection of these foods on a regular basis. Sugar is the greatest enemy of your teeth. It combines with the bacteria in your mouth to produce plaque.

Fluoride and mouthwash

Fluoride is a chemical which protects teeth. It hardens the enamel. In many places fluoride is added to the drinking water supply. If your water is not already fluoridated, make sure you use a toothpaste with fluoride added.

Mouthwash is a mild antiseptic that you rinse around your mouth and spit out. Using mouthwash is refreshing, but the effect does not last long, and it can't cure bad breath or clean your teeth the lazy way!

Teeth problems

Tooth decay and gum disease are the two most common tooth problems. But both can be avoided if you look after your teeth properly. Remember the formula? Go for regular dental check-ups, clean your teeth at least twice a day, and eat a well-balanced diet.

Sometimes, the dentist will X-ray your teeth to check if there are any signs of internal decay. X-rays are also used to examine wisdom teeth and check whether they are growing correctly.

Plaque

If plaque is not removed, it will start to eat into your tooth, through the enamel and into the dentine. Eventually, the decay reaches the nerves inside the pulp and you feel pain. Your dentist will be able to find any holes in your teeth at your check up and give you a filling.

Plaque can be removed with regular brushing and flossing. The biting surfaces of your back teeth tend to decay more easily than your front teeth because they have small pits in the surface which can trap food, so make sure you clean these well. You can buy a special brush to do this job.

Gum disease

Your gums hold your teeth in place. If your gums are unhealthy, they may become weak and eventually your teeth will fall out. If your gums bleed when you clean your teeth, it is an early warning of possible infection or disease.

Plaque is the main cause of gum disease. When plaque builds up between the teeth and gums, it makes the gums red and irritated. Again, regular brushing and flossing are the best ways to avoid gum disease.

Tartar

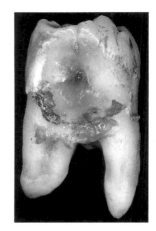

You can see the ring of brown tartar on this extracted tooth.

Tartar is a very hard substance. It is made from plaque which you have left on your teeth and which has hardened. If it is allowed to stay on your teeth, it can cause gum disease. Dentists remove tartar by chipping it away from the surface of the tooth. They will do this as part of your check-up routine. You shouldn't have too many problems with tartar if you clean your teeth regularly.

FILLINGS

If there is any decay in a tooth, the dentist will probably want to block the hole, to stop the infection from spreading. First of all, you may need an injection to numb the part of your mouth which needs attention. The effect of this will wear off after a few hours.

The dentist will dig the decay out of your tooth, using a high-speed drill. Your tooth will then be filled, probably with a special metal made of silver, copper and tin, called amalgam. When the filling has hardened, any rough edges are smoothed off.

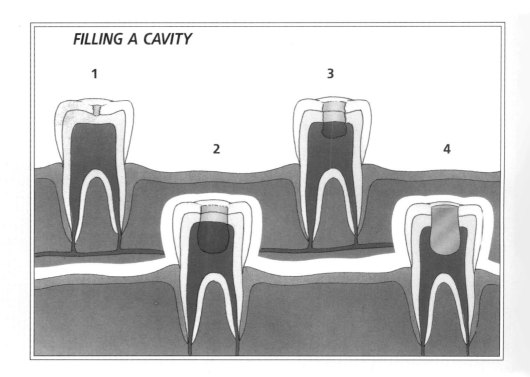

FILLING A CAVITY

1

2

3

4

Braces for teeth

Straight teeth look great and make it easier for you to chew properly. The teeth are not only easier to clean but if they meet together properly are likely to last longer and put less strain on the jaw joints. Unfortunately, many people have teeth that are crowded or crooked. In some people the top teeth stick out a lot. Orthodontic treatment can be used to straighten them.

The treatment people need varies from person to person. If there is not enough room for all the adult teeth, it is sometimes necessary to extract some of them so that they can be straightened. Usually some sort of appliance will be fitted to the teeth. Wearing one of these 'braces' involves a bit of effort, but most people find they cope quite happily with them and are certainly glad they went to the bother of getting their teeth straightened.

1. Tooth decay on the crown penetrating the enamel and dentine.

2. Serious decay penetrating the pulp if the decay is left unchecked.

3. Cavity drilled out by dentist.

4. Amalgam filling in the cavity.

Your dentist may also give your teeth a final polish using some toothpaste and a high-speed brush. If this is done every six months or so, you teeth will stay looking good.

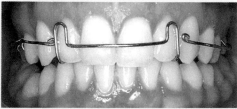
Removable brace

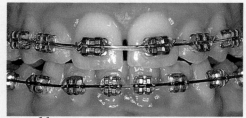
Fixed brace

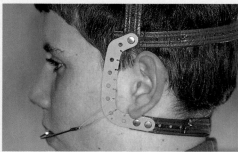
Headgear

There are three main types of braces.

1. Removable braces can be taken out of the mouth for cleaning but apart from this generally have to be worn all the time. They usually have a plastic plate which fits into the mouth and are held in position by clips on the teeth. Springs and wires gently move the teeth into the right place.

2. Fixed braces are made of metal pads glued to the teeth with special cement. Putting them on doesn't hurt at all, and taking them off is almost as easy. Thin wires pass between the metal attachments and move the teeth to the correct position. This type of brace is usually used for people with very crooked teeth that can't be straightened with removable braces.

3. Functional appliances are for people whose top teeth stick out a long way. This kind of brace has upper and lower removable parts which are glued together. This makes the brace a little bulky, but people soon get used to it. Sometimes the orthodontist will ask patients to wear a brace outside the mouth called headgear. It is usually worn just in bed at night or sometimes in the evening, too.

When treatment with the braces is finished, your orthodontist will usually ask you to wear a retainer. This is a very simple removable brace which holds the newly straightened teeth in the correct position. This is important because the gum and bone around the teeth are very soft at this stage and need to be given time to toughen up so that the teeth will not move back to the position they started in.

Orthodontic treatment usually starts when most of the adult teeth have come through. This is usually between 10 and 14 years of age, although it can start either before or after this. The length of time people have to wear braces varies from person to person but usually treatment with a fixed brace will take about eighteen months. During this time you will have to visit the orthodontist every four to six weeks to get the brace adjusted.

Of course, wearing a brace makes it more difficult to keep the teeth clean. It is important that if you do have a brace you spend a bit longer brushing your teeth, and brush a little bit harder than usual. You should also avoid sweets or fizzy drinks.

Your back

Your back supports the weight of your head, your chest and your hips. And it has to stay upright! Your backbone, or spine, is the most important part of your body's 'scaffolding' – your skeleton. To have a strong, straight, flexible back, every muscle, ligament, and vertebra in your spine must be in line and working smoothly together. This is a complicated process which can go wrong, causing back problems. People of all ages can suffer from back problems, many of which happen because too much strain is put on the back.

It is very easy to strain your back. You can strain it by stretching your muscles or ligaments in a way which they aren't used to. Sudden, awkward movements or lifting or carrying something very heavy can all cause a bad back strain. If you do damage your back like this, the muscles or ligaments will be sore for a few days. Rest is the best cure, but if the pain persists you should see a doctor. Remember that your back is a delicate structure, and try to avoid straining it by taking care of your spine.

This young gymnast has an extremely flexible spine.

YOUR SPINE

Your spine is your back's main support. It is made of 33 small bones called vertebrae which are stacked one on top of another in five groups. There are 7 neck vertebrae, 12 chest vertebrae and 5 lower back vertebrae. Then come 5 vertebrae that are fused together, and lastly 4 fused vertebrae that form the coccyx. The vertebrae protect nerves inside the spine. Pads of tissue called discs separate the vertebrae. The vertebrae are held together by special cords called ligaments. Muscles also run up and down the spine, producing movement. Some muscles extend up to the skull so that the head is supported.

HOW TO AVOID BACK STRAIN

1. The best way to look after your back is to be aware of how you use it. Make sure that you bend your knees when you are leaning over or picking up a heavy object.

Bending your knees eases the pressure on your spine. The right way to pick up an object is to bend your knees, then slowly straighten them as you lift, keeping your back as straight as possible.

2. Never hunch your shoulders when you are carrying a weight. The weight of the object adds to the pressure on your spine.

3. Bend your knees slightly instead. This means that your arms and legs take the weight of the object instead of your spine.

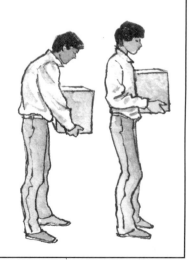

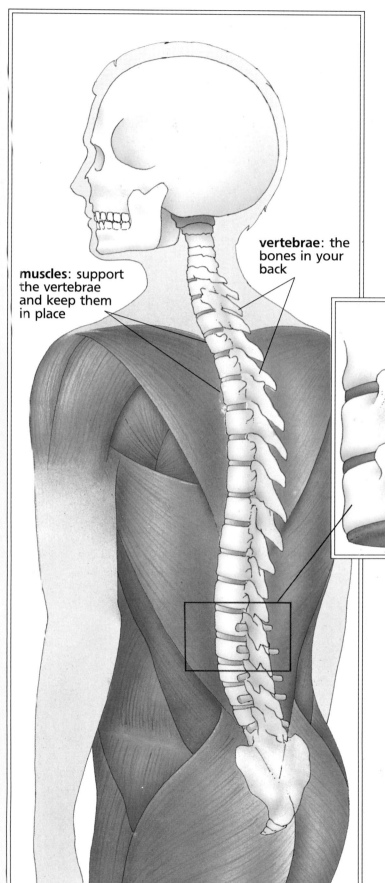

muscles: support the vertebrae and keep them in place

vertebrae: the bones in your back

Slipped discs

The discs between vertebrae are made of a strong rubbery material called cartilage. They separate and cushion the vertebrae. If one of the discs is stretched or pushed out of position, you will suffer from a slipped disc. It is usually one of the discs in the lower back that slips out, because this is the part of your back that takes most of the strain when you are lifting or carrying.

A slipped disc in the neck is also fairly common. This is usually caused by a sudden twist of the head.

discs: fleshy pads which protect and pad your vertebrae

When you are young, the discs are rubbery and flexible. But as you get older, the soft centres of the discs get harder and more brittle. That's when slipped discs are more likely to happen. A slipped disc can be very painful. Once the disc is out of place, it puts pressure on the nerve endings in the spine. The pain can be felt all along the nerve, which runs from your lower back, down the back of your leg and even as far as the sole of your foot. If you have this kind of pain, you should see a doctor.

If the pain from a slipped disc is not too severe, the doctor will prescribe painkillers and advise the patient to rest so as to move the spine as little as possible. In severe cases, the patient may have to go into hospital for treatment or even surgery to remove the disc completely.

Posture

Posture is the way that you hold your body. It can tell people more about you than you think! If you're tired or depressed, you may find yourself standing with your shoulders hunched and your body slumped. But if you walk tall and hold your head up high, you radiate self-confidence without having to say a word! As well as looking better, your body is functioning better, too. You are giving your organs room to work, rather than squashing them.

Think about your posture whenever you can. Are you sitting with your back straight or are you slouching in your chair? Remember that your body gets used to the positions you use most frequently, so bad habits now can decide your posture in the future. So stop and take time to look at the way you stand now.

How do you stand?

Try examining your posture in front of a full length mirror. Be critical! Imagine that you have a piece of string attached to the top of your head and somebody is pulling it gently upwards. This will help you keep your neck straight and hold your head high. Check your shoulders from a side view. Do they look rounded and hunched forward? Pull them back and push your chest out. You will find that your back will automatically straighten. Make sure that your hips are directly above your feet, not leaning backwards or forwards. Are you standing with your stomach sticking out? Tilt your pelvis forward and tuck your bottom in. Your stomach will look flatter. Your feet should be hip-width apart, with your body weight carried evenly on both feet. Now that's good posture!

Other positions

Good posture applies to sitting and moving as well as standing. The rule is more or less the same, though. You need to make sure your weight is evenly distributed over your centre of gravity.

BACK EXERCISES
Exercise your back regularly to strengthen the muscles and improve your posture.

1. Sit on the floor with your legs crossed. Put your arms above your head and stretch upwards, moving from your hips. Stretch and relax in this way about 10 times.

2. Kneel on all fours. Drop your head down and, at the same time, arch your back. Then look up again and relax your back. Repeat 5 times.

3. Lie on your back. Bend your knees and bring them into your chest. Hug your knees with your hands and lift your head and shoulders to touch your knees. Rock gently a few times.

4. Kneel with your bottom on your feet. Bend forward, turn your head sideways and rest it on your knees. Place your arms, palms up, by your sides. Relax.

BALANCING A GLASS
About 100 years ago, young ladies were taught to dance with a glass of water on their heads! If their posture was good, the glass didn't fall off. A bit extreme!

What about this exercise? Try walking round the room with a book on your head. It's quite difficult but very effective. You'll find you have to glide along very smoothly with a very straight spine.

Scoliosis

Scoliosis is a side-to-side curvature of the spine. In a person with scoliosis, the spine appears curved when viewed from the front. A normal spine appears straight when viewed from the front.

Scoliosis most often appears in childhood or the early teens. It affects more girls than boys. Many schools test all students from the ages of 10 to 15 for scoliosis. Symptoms include unlevel hips or shoulders, a prominent shoulder blade, or a hump on the back.

Many people have some degree of scoliosis, but only a few need treatment. In mild cases, a doctor simply checks the spine regularly to make sure the condition doesn't worsen. Moderate cases are often corrected by wearing a back brace and doing special exercises. Severe cases may require surgery. If untreated, these cases can lead to deformity that may interfere with the proper functioning of the heart, lungs and nervous system.

Rest and relaxation

Did you know that we spend a third of our lives asleep? But you're not wasting time when you're asleep. Every living creature needs sleep, to recharge their bodies with energy before another busy day. Nobody really understands all about sleep and why we need it. But it is known that there are at least two centres in our brains which control sleeping. One triggers off the actual act of falling asleep and the other keeps you asleep. When you're asleep, you are completely relaxed, and your heartbeat and breathing rate slow down.

The average person needs about eight hours of sleep each night. When you are a teenager and your body is growing, you need more sleep than usual. Your body needs more time to rebuild cells and tissues.

If you don't get enough sleep, you may become clumsy and find it difficult to think straight. Excitement, stress, exercise, poor diet and nervousness can all affect your sleep pattern, making you sleep more or less than you usually do. People who are depressed or worried often need more sleep, but may have difficulty getting to sleep, and staying asleep.

Preparing for better sleep

If you've had plenty of exercise during the day, by night-time you will feel physically tired and ready to sleep. But for a good night's sleep, both your body and your brain have to need to rest. Some people find it difficult to relax. They rush around all day. Then, when they finally come to sit down or to go to bed, they find their brain is still too busy to let them relax.

It is possible to train yourself to relax so that you can easily drift into a refreshing sleep. Before going to bed, it can be relaxing to read a few pages of a book, listen to the radio or watch television – as long as you're not watching a horror movie! Try having a warm bath or drinking a hot drink – but choose a herbal tea rather than coffee.

Leave a window open. You'll sleep better if your bedroom is well aired. If your body feels tense, concentrate on relaxing every part of it. Start with your head and neck and relax all your muscles. Then relax all the parts of your body, one after the other, until you feel calm and sleepy. Sweet dreams!

Reader's experience

"I went through a period of not being able to sleep at nights. At first it was just annoying. I turned my light on, read books, even did some of my homework until I finally dropped off. Then I began to get really worried about how much sleep I was losing and how tired I felt during the day. I used to dread going to bed, because I knew I wouldn't be able to sleep. My parents, teachers and friends all noticed I was tired. They tried to help me by telling me to relax or read a book, but nothing worked.

Eventually, my Mum took me to the doctor. I thought the doctor would think that I was silly and wasting her time, but she didn't. She told me that a lot of people my age have difficulty in getting to sleep, especially if they are worried about something like exams. When I thought about it, I was worried by my exams. She said the first thing to do was to stop worrying about it, as that made it worse. She told me to pretend that I didn't mind if I couldn't get to sleep. Then she said that I could always catch up by having a nap when I got back from school. My exams are over now and my sleeping has got better. Also I've realized that I don't need as much sleep as some people, so I've stopped worrying about it."
Pablo

DIFFERENT KINDS OF SLEEP
The time you are asleep is divided into two types of sleep. One is called Rapid Eye Movement sleep (REM) and the other type is called non-REM sleep.

Non-REM sleep is the deepest sleep. During non-REM sleep, the heart rate slows down, breathing becomes slower and the body temperature becomes one degree cooler. The metabolic rate gets slower, too.

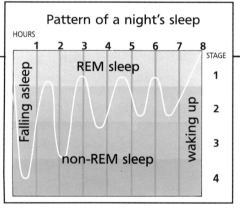

Pattern of a night's sleep

REM sleep lasts for about 20 minutes at a stretch and occurs four or five times during the night. Your eyes move around quickly under your eyelids and your heart rate speeds up. This is the time when you dream.

Meditation and massage

Meditation is an effective way of completely relaxing the body and freeing the mind from anxiety and worry. With a bit of practice, a person can use meditation to enter a state of deep stillness, similar to that between sleep and waking. Breathing and heart rate are slow and even, the mind is calm and still, and you are only dimly aware of your surroundings.

Always prepare yourself for meditation by sitting comfortably upright in a quiet spot where you will not be interrupted. Close your eyes, breathe deeply for a few minutes and relax. Then you can either repeat a word or phrase that you like, or concentrate on your breathing for about 20 minutes, or until you are fully relaxed.

Massage is relaxing and good for your body, too. Ask a friend to give you a massage, and give them one in return. Oil, cream or talcum powder helps the hands to glide smoothly over the skin. With fingers closed and hands stretched out, use firm, even strokes, always in the direction of the heart. Using the heel of your hand, knead certain areas, such as legs, back and upper chest. On knots of tension in the shoulders or back, press with the pad of your thumb or forefinger and rotate slightly for 10 to 15 seconds. Release slowly and follow with gliding strokes. Massage is relaxing to give as well as to take.

Clean is healthy

You probably already keep yourself clean enough to always smell good. Keeping clean also keeps you healthy. But you can't always be sure that your environment is as clean as you are.

Certain illnesses can be caused by tiny organisms called viruses and bacteria. Whilst some forms of these can be helpful, and normally thrive harmlessly in your body, others can be highly dangerous and make you sick. You can find out how this happens on pages 114 and 115. You can't help becoming sick sometimes, but you can steer clear of problems if you know what to look out for. Bacteria and viruses spread in lots of different ways. Here are some to watch out for.

WATER

Infection can spread very fast if it's in the water supply. Diseases such as hepatitis, cholera and typhoid can be caught by drinking contaminated water. The water that comes out of taps should be safe to drink because it is normally cleaned, purified and tested before it reaches you.

Drinking water can become dirty if the waste products from sewers leak into the water supply. In some countries, chemicals used in farming are allowed to leak into the rivers. Obviously, it's difficult to purify water completely – some chemicals may be left.

In some countries, you can't trust tap water. People have to boil water to make sure it's completely clean before they drink it. Others prefer to drink bottled spring water. This is water that comes from springs deep underground, so it's unlikely to be dirty or contaminated.

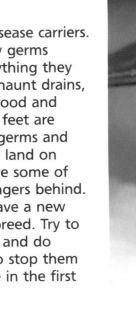

FLIES

Flies are first class disease carriers. Their hairy feet carry germs gathered from everything they land on. Since they haunt drains, sewers and rotting food and rubbish heaps, their feet are often covered with germs and bacteria. When they land on your food, they leave some of their bacteria passengers behind. The bacteria then have a new place to grow and breed. Try to keep them off food and do whatever you can to stop them entering your house in the first place.

Scientists test the drinking water at a water purification plant in East Africa.

Bottled water is pure, but it can be expensive!

Flies carry bacteria, which can cause disease.

FOOD

Stomach upsets or, even worse, food poisoning, are usually caused by eating bad meat or fish. Never leave meat or fish uncovered, especially if you live in a hot country. Fresh food should not be stored for too long, even if it is kept in a fridge. Unopened tinned food can be kept for a long time, but once the can is opened, the contents should be emptied out and eaten as soon as possible.

Mould will grow on fresh food if it is kept too long.

Fruit and vegetables are often sprayed with special chemicals called fertilizers and pesticides to make them grow faster and bigger and to kill pests. Traces of these chemicals can remain on the produce even after it is harvested, so it's important to wash all fresh fruit and vegetables before you eat them. Before preparing or cooking food, make sure you wash your hands.

COUGHS, COLDS AND SNEEZES

Some diseases are passed from person to person. One of these is the common cold. This is caused by a very infectious virus for which there is still no cure. You pass on the virus when you sneeze or cough by spreading a fine spray of saliva from your mouth. If you're suffering from a cold, this spray is packed with germs. If someone else breathes it in, they are very likely to catch your cold. Colds are often spread when an infected person touches someone else with a hand which carries germs from the nose or mouth. If you have been near someone with a cold, it's wise to wash your hands. And never share eating or drinking utensils.

It's not easy to avoid spreading your cold around! You can try your best by keeping your distance from other people, and covering your mouth and nose with your hand when you sneeze or cough.

GERMS AND DISEASE SPREAD BY FAECES

Faeces are the solid matter that leaves your body when you go to the toilet. Diseases such as hepatitis or salmonella can be caught from germs in faeces, so you should always wash your hands after you have been to the lavatory.

SCRATCHES AND CUTS

Scratches and cuts become infected if not covered. Wash your hands before touching the wound. Clean it gently with soap and water, and cover it with a plaster until it has healed.

Fighting infection

There are a lot of illnesses caused by bacteria and viruses that attack the cells in your body. Many of these bacteria and viruses never get a chance to infect your body at all. They are prevented by your body's natural defences.

Invasion force

So how do bacteria and viruses attack the human body? They can invade your body in different ways. When someone coughs or sneezes, viruses or bacteria can shoot out of their mouth and nose at amazing speed. When you breathe in the viruses or bacteria, a body invasion begins. Bacteria can also get in through a cut in your skin.

Once they are inside your body, the bacteria start to attack the healthy cells. The bacteria multiply, and this makes you feel ill. When a virus gets into your body, it attaches itself to a healthy cell. Then it works its way inside the cell, where it multiplies hundreds of times. These new viruses then infect more cells.

The immune system

No body's defence mechanism is perfect. If none of your natural defences have worked against an invasion of bacteria or viruses, special cells in your blood take over the fight. These cells are part of your immune system. Your immune system involves different kinds of cell. White blood cells called B cells release chemicals called antibodies. The antibodies stick to the invading bacteria, clumping them together. The clumps are then surrounded and destroyed by bigger cells called phagocytes. Other cells called T cells attack and destroy viruses in the body.

The immune system is designed to recognize the invading viruses or bacteria it has dealt with before. If you had mumps when you were young, your immune system made antibodies specifically designed to attack the mumps virus. So if the mumps virus invades your body again, your immune system knows how to tackle it. The virus is destroyed before it can make you ill. That's why you seldom get an illness like mumps twice.

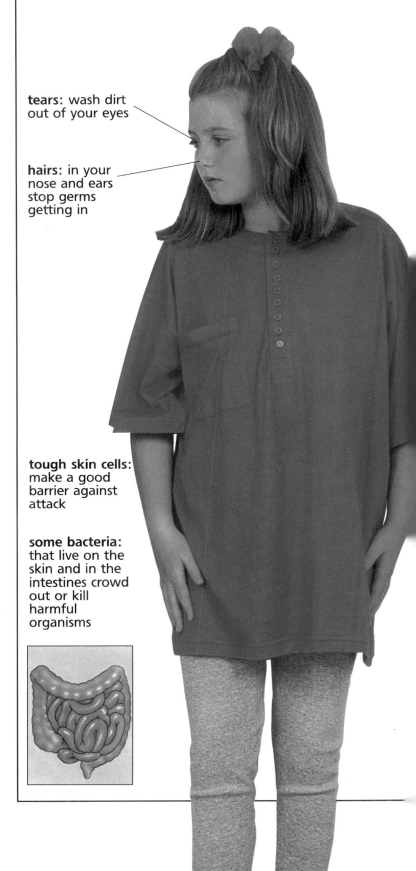

NATURAL DEFENCES

This diagram shows some of the parts of your body that help to fight infection and keep you well

tears: wash dirt out of your eyes

hairs: in your nose and ears stop germs getting in

tough skin cells: make a good barrier against attack

some bacteria: that live on the skin and in the intestines crowd out or kill harmful organisms

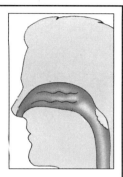

adenoids and tonsils: produce cells that fight infection

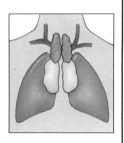

thymus gland: produces cells that fight infection

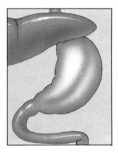

stomach juice: contains many chemicals that fight disease

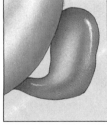

spleen: produces cells that fight infection

Immunization

Many diseases can be prevented by immunization, or vaccination. Immunization makes the body immune to a particular disease, by causing it to produce antibodies. If the body is later exposed to the harmful bacteria or viruses, the antibodies recognize and destroy them before they have time to cause illness.

When people are given a vaccination, a small amount of a harmful bacterium or virus is injected into the body. The bacterium or virus can be dead, or live, but in a very weak form. In both cases, the vaccine is chemically treated, and the amount injected is very small, so the vaccine does not usually make you feel ill. A single dose of some vaccine gives life-long immunity against a disease. Others need to be strengthened by one or more booster doses.

Doctors recommend that children be vaccinated against some illnesses when they are quite young. Other vaccines are given only if people are going to parts of the world where a particular disease is common.

Thanks to immunization and other public health methods, diseases like smallpox have disappeared. If everyone in the world could be vaccinated against such diseases as cholera, tuberculosis and tetanus, these diseases might disappear too. For some diseases, doctors have not yet been able to find an effective vaccine. AIDS is probably the most dangerous of these. The search for a vaccine against this terrible disease goes on.

Treatments

Bacterial infections can be treated by drugs called antibiotics. A doctor will normally give you a course of antibiotics which will last for one to two weeks. Even if you feel better after a day or two, you must finish the course. If you don't do this, the infection may come back.

You can't treat viral illnesses with antibiotics. Some viruses can change shape, so that the antibodies do not recognize them and can't destroy them. Influenza and cold viruses act like this, which is why we get these illnesses more than once. For most viral infections, you can only relieve the symptoms, then rest and let your body recover.

If you eat a healthy diet with lots of fresh fruit and vegetables, and get regular exercise, you are doing your best for your body. You are keeping it strong and well and you should have no problem fighting off most infections that come your way.

Immunization forces the body to produce antibodies to protect against a particular disease.

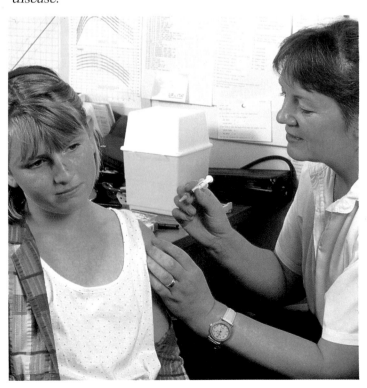

Going to hospital

When people are sick or are injured in a minor way, they usually just need to rest and check with a doctor that everything is OK. But sometimes, if things are a bit more serious, they need to visit a hospital. Hospitals can seem like pretty scary places. But not if you know the ropes. Here are some personal experiences that might help you feel easier about a hospital visit.

"A few days ago I had a very sore throat. When I went to the doctor he said that I had tonsillitis and that I needed to have my tonsils removed. Now I have to go into hospital and I'm more scared of that than of the tonsillitis. Is this normal?"
Laura

Expert comment: Yes. Most people who have never been into hospital find the idea unpleasant. But hospital staff are trained to be helpful. They know how you feel. All you need to take with you to hospital is a small case containing your nightclothes and a dressing-gown, your washbag and some books or magazines to read while you recover from your operation. When you enter the hospital, go to reception. The staff there will book you in, just as if you are going in to a hotel. Then a nurse takes you to a ward, where a bed is already made and waiting for you. You rest in this bed until the

operation. The doctor will visit you here and talk to you about the operation. The nurse may take some blood to do tests. You can always contact the nurse by pressing a button located by your bed. After the operation you are watched carefully and made as comfortable as possible. Your friends and family can visit you. So there's really no reason to be scared of the hospital.

"My friend cut herself badly the other day and had to go to the emergency department of our local hospital. My dad says there aren't enough staff in these departments and people have to wait far too long. Is this true?"
Julian

Expert comment: No. Emergency rooms are set up to cope with the unexpected and they must operate differently to other wards because they deal with emergencies. Someone seriously injured must be treated straight away. So less serious problems may have to wait. Nurses and doctors in the emergency room work as quickly as they can. They have little time to talk, so may seem unfriendly. If you need treatment quickly, go to the emergency room. Be prepared to wait until you can be seen by the doctors. If your injury is life threatening then you will be dealt with immediately.

"When I broke my leg, I had to stay in bed in hospital. It was so boring. I had to lie with my leg up in the air, with weights attached to it. Why couldn't I just have it in a plaster cast and come home? That's what my brother did when he broke his leg."
Dominic

Expert comment: You probably broke the femur in your upper leg. If you break one of the bones in your lower leg, as your brother probably did, it's quite easy to hold the broken ends in place with a splint, until the bones knit together. The plaster cast often covers the knee and ankle so that the leg can't move very much. When the plaster is set hard, it's possible for you to walk about, because the cast is taking the strain. But with a break in the femur, it's much harder to stop you moving your leg, and the bones won't heal properly unless they are kept in position. So you had to stay in bed. The weights hanging from cords above your bed pulled on your leg and kept the two parts of the broken bone in the right position until they healed.

"I broke my arm recently, and noticed that the technician who took the X-ray of my arm went out of the room while the machine was on. Is this because X-rays are dangerous? After all they are a type of radiation."
Leo

Expert comment: X-rays are used in a field of medicine called radiology. They produce a photograph of bones or tissue under the skin. X-rays are given by doctors called radiologists. An X-ray is a type of radiation, and radiation can harm living tissue. The amount of radiation you absorb when you are given an X-ray is too small to be harmful to you, and is restricted to the area the radiologist wants to look at. But if radiologists absorbed this amount of radiation every time they gave a patient an X-ray, they could be harmed. So radiologists have to take special care not to over-expose themselves to X-rays.

"I am having an operation next month, and I have been told I'll have to have a general anaesthetic. The doctor says it's quite safe, but I don't like the idea of being unconscious. I might never wake up! How safe are anaesthetics?"
Kirsty

Expert comment: The chance of anything going wrong when an anaesthetic is used is very small. Anaesthetics are given by doctors who are specially trained in their use. They are called anaesthetists. Their job is to supervise the use of drugs for the relief of pain during surgery. Anaesthetics may be injected, swallowed or inhaled. Most operations could not be done without anaesthetics as they greatly reduce the physical shock and emotional stress of the operation. Also, they give doctors time to perform the operation safely. So relax and treat the anaesthetist as a friend.

First aid

What would you do if you were present at an accident at home or at school? You may think this will never happen to you. But it could, and you should be prepared. If you know a little about first aid treatment, you will be able to help swiftly and calmly.

When treating any injury, it is important to remember that everything must be clean. You should wash your hands before dealing with cuts and bruises or stings, and use antiseptic and sterile dressings. Sterile dressings have been specially cleaned so that they are absolutely free of germs.

You don't normally need to call a doctor for minor accidents, such as cuts and bruises. But if you think an accident is serious, do call a doctor. It might save someone's life.

A first aid kit

Every home should have a first aid kit. You can buy a ready-packed kit from a pharmacy – check the contents to make sure it has all you need before you buy. Or you can make up your own kit.

Here is information about how to deal with some common injuries:

EMERGENCY EQUIPMENT
It's a good idea to keep a first aid kit at home, in the car, and to take one when you go on holiday, too.

A first aid kit should contain:

A small pair of scissors

A pair of tweezers

A tube or bottle of antiseptic lotion

At least 12 sterilized dressings of assorted sizes

A reel of adhesive plaster

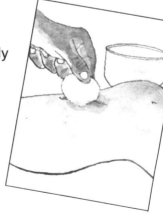

NOSEBLEED
Some people get nosebleeds quite often. This can happen if they have high blood pressure or blow their nose too hard. Also, picking or scratching inside the nose can cause bleeding.

1. Support the patient in a sitting position with the head tilted slightly forward.

2. Ask the patient to breathe through the mouth.

3. Pinch the soft pad at the top of their nose for about ten minutes.

4. The blood will clot and the bleeding will stop. The patient should not blow the nose for a few hours in case bleeding starts again.

CUTS
A cut which is bleeding heavily should be treated quickly. If the person has been cut by something dirty, they should go to a doctor, as they may need to have an anti-tetanus injection to prevent infection.

1. Wash your hands and if possible, put on surgical gloves.

2. Then wash the cut with soap, gently removing any grit or dirt.

3. Cover it with a dressing or a bandage. Take the patient to a doctor if necessary.

A packet of sterilized absorbent cotton wool

A triangular bandage to use as a sling

A packet of safety pins

A few pairs of surgical gloves

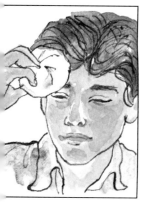

BRUISES

A bruise is caused by bleeding which is trapped beneath unbroken skin. Bruises are usually caused by a fall or a blow.

1. Apply a cold compress – a flannel or a towel soaked in cold water, or a bag of ice.

2. Call a doctor if the casualty has bruised very easily without any obvious reason.

ANIMAL BITES

Animal bites can be serious, especially if there is a chance the animal has rabies. Rabies can be deadly in a person if left untreated. If there's a chance the animal may have rabies, seek medical help. The person may need to have anti-rabies injections.

1. Calm down the patient.

2. Clean the wound with soap and running water. Wash it from the middle outwards.

3. Apply a dressing and a bandage if it needs one.

4. In the case of dog bite, try to find out if the dog has been vaccinated for rabies.

BLEEDING

You might be surprised at how much blood can come from a small cut or wound. But the bleeding will eventually stop. The body naturally forms scabs and blood clots to stop the bleeding. Bleeding can be controlled by pressing on arterial bleeding above the cut or wound.

1. Cover the cut with a pad or bandage and press down hard on the wound with your fingers for 5-15 minutes.

2. If the wound is large, squeeze the two sides gently together and seek medical help.

SNAKE BITES

Some snakes are poisonous and the bite may be dangerous.

1. Calm down the patient.

2. Wash the snake's poison, or venom, from the wound.

3. Find medical help as soon as possible.

INSECT STINGS

1. An insect sting usually looks like a thin splinter. If it is visible, remove it with a pair of tweezers.

2. Don't let the patient scratch the sting, as this can cause infection.

3. Get immediate medical help if the patient develops swelling in the mouth or tongue, or if there is difficulty in breathing. This may be a symptom of hives, a severe allergic condition to stings.

4. Find out if the patient has a history of allergy to insect stings. Some people carry special instructions and supplies with them, or wear an emergency bracelet containing relevant personal information.

More first aid

First aid may save somebody's life, and can prevent a condition getting worse. Always get medical advice if you're not sure about something. You will need some knowledge of first aid to deal with these situations, too.

FAINTS

People may faint from shock or from being in a hot and stuffy atmosphere. A faint is caused by less blood than usual travelling to the brain for a short time. There is usually some warning before the person faints. They may go pale and complain of dizziness.

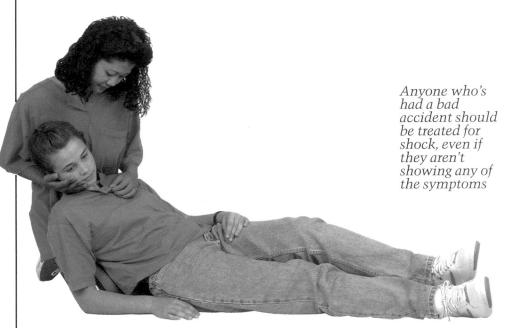

Anyone who's had a bad accident should be treated for shock, even if they aren't showing any of the symptoms

1. Take the patient out into the fresh air if possible.

2. Sit them down and put their head between their legs. This lets the blood flow back into the head.

3. If the person has already fainted, raise their legs onto a chair or low table and loosen any tight clothing, especially any things around their neck.

4. The patient should come out of the faint in a very short time. Give them small sips of cold water and reassure them.

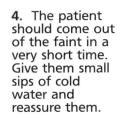

5. If the patient is unconscious for more than three minutes, get medical help.

SHOCK

Anyone who gets involved in an accident will usually be upset, even if they are not hurt badly. They may go pale, shake and feel faint. This is often called shock.

Reassure the patient, make them lie down for at least 10 minutes and keep them warm. Give them sips of cold water if they are awake, and when they have fully recovered, a cup of something hot and sweet.

There's also a more serious kind of shock. This is when a person's body has a bad reaction to something, such as an insect sting or the injection of a drug. Their blood pressure falls, and their breathing becomes wheezy. Their throat may swell up, making it difficult to breathe. This kind of shock needs emergency medical treatment.

ELECTRIC SHOCKS

Electric shocks are caused by an electric current passing through the body. Electric shocks can be slight or very severe depending on the amount of electricity the patient has been in contact with.

If the patient has had a shock from a mains cable, electric railway line or an industrial electric supply, you should seek immediate medical help. If they are still lying on the cable you must not touch them. These electric currents are very strong and will still be turned on. If you touch the patient, you could get a severe shock as well. Get help from the emergency services immediately.

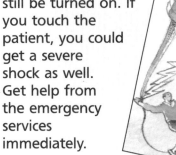

BURNS

A burn or scald can be very severe. Burns are caused by the sun, direct heat or exposure to chemicals. Scalds are caused by hot water or hot oil.

1. Cool the area of the burn by holding it in cold water for at least 10 minutes. If this is not possible, keep pouring cold water over the burn area.

2. Remove bracelets or rings, as the burned area will start to swell.

3. Clothing soaked in boiling water should be carefully removed but do not attempt to remove any clothing that is sticking to a burn.

4. Do not apply grease or ointment, as this will stick to the burn.

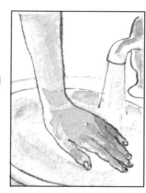

5. Give the patient sips of cold water.

6. Get medical help as soon as possible.

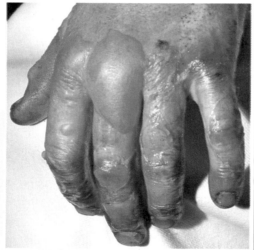

A burn can make your skin blister

Sometimes the shock may be caused by a domestic appliance. If this is the case:

1. Turn the electricity off by turning off the switch or taking out the plug.

2. If possible, push the person away from the source of electricity, using anything dry made of rubber, cloth or wood. Electricity cannot flow through these materials, so you won't get an electric shock.

3. Seek medical help as soon as possible even though the patient may not appear to be badly injured.

SPRAINS

Sprains are caused by wrenching or tearing the ligaments, which are the tissues connected to a joint. A sprained ligament can produce swelling, and can be very painful.

1. Rest and support the injured part in the most comfortable position.

2. Apply a cold compress to the joint.

3. If you think a bone may be broken or damaged, call medical help.

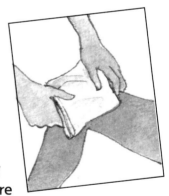

STRAINS

Strains are caused by over-stretching a muscle. They often happen during vigorous exercise if the body hasn't been warmed up properly. Strains are generally less serious than sprains.

1. Place the patient in the most comfortable position.

2. Apply a cold compress to the injured muscle.

3. The patient should treat the injured muscle gently for a few days.

Are you looking good?

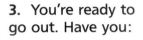
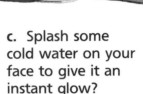

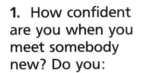

1. How confident are you when you meet somebody new? Do you:

a. Smile, shake their hand, take down their address and do a song and dance routine?
b. Bemuse them with your brightest smile whilst looking deeply into their eyes?
c. Keep your focus well and truly on the floor?

2. When you look in the mirror, do you feel:

a. You're the most wonderful person in the whole world?
b. Very pleased with what you see?
c. Pleased, but you don't like your nose much, or your smile, and your hair's not looking too good today?

3. You're ready to go out. Have you:

a. Soaked yourself in bubbles and washed and ironed your outfit?
b. Done all the right things in the right order and are feeling fairly self righteous?
c. Run your fingers through your hair and eaten a piece of chewing gum to freshen your breath?

4. You want your skin to look glowing and healthy, so do you:

a. Spend as much money as you can afford and a fair amount that you can't on creams and lotions?
b. Eat a good healthy and balanced diet, with lots of fresh fruit and vegetables?

c. Splash some cold water on your face to give it an instant glow?

5. It's that important day, and guess what, you've got a huge pimple on your face! Do you:

a. Throw a tantrum?
b. Put a dab of cream on it and use a concealer stick to cover it as best you can?
c. Not go out?

6. You overhear somebody saying you smell. Do you:

a. Boast about your special, very personal brand of 'eau de moi', and hope you can get away with it?
b. Have a shower and splash on some deodorant?
c. Change your shirt?

7. You've got toothache! Do you:

a. Rush to the dentist and ask for immediate treatment?
b. Make an appointment with your dentist to have a filling, and meanwhile keep an extra special eye on the food you eat?
c. Put up with the pain and hope that the offending tooth will soon fall out?

8. Your eyes feel pink and sore. Do you:

a. Convince yourself that you've got a dreadful disease?
b. Bathe them with water and make sure you have a good night's sleep?
c. Hide behind a pair of dark glasses?

9. You've seen some shoes you really want to buy, but they are a size too small for you, so do you:

a. Buy them because you think you can stretch them – and live with the blisters meanwhile?
b. Buy a different pair which you don't want really as much but which are the right size?
c. Cut the toes out?

10. You want to look taller. Do you:

a. Buy a pair of boots with thick soles and heels?
b. Stand up straight and walk tall with confidence?
c. Hang around with people smaller than you?

11. You are having trouble getting to sleep at nights. Do you:

a. Go to a hypnotist?
b. Have a hot bath and relax a little before you go to bed?
c. Stay up really late, until you can't keep your eyes open?

12. You have been invited to a smart, party which you suspect will be very 'chic'! Do you:

a. Take an intensive course of confidence building lessons?
b. Sit down, take a deep breath and write a list of all your good points?
c. Go with a confident friend who you can hide behind all night?

HOW DID YOU SCORE?

Mostly as
You really want to look and feel good, don't you? And you'll go to any extremes to get there! Calm down a bit, and think before you act. Remember you're young and healthy, and you don't have to spend lots of money to look good.

Mostly bs
You seem to have got the balance right – well done! You're beginning to use your head to look after the rest of you.

Mostly cs
You know what you want to look like, and you know how you would like to feel, but you take the easiest option whenever you can. Sometimes, you end up doing yourself more harm than good. Relax and have a bit more confidence and if you're not sure what to do, read through this book again.

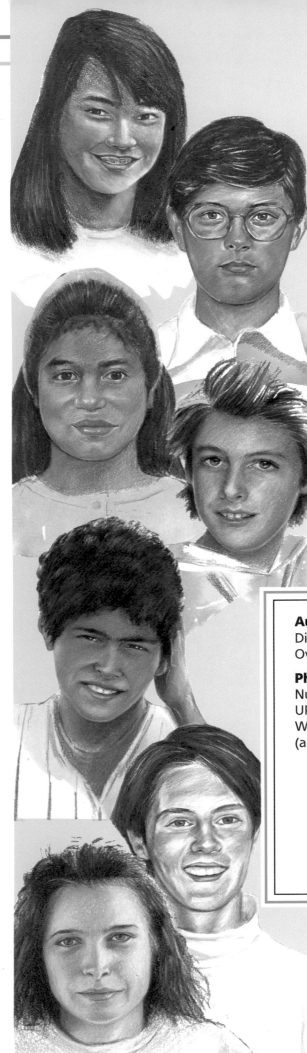

HELPLINES

*Here's a list of organizations you could contact
in case you'd like to find out more about some of
the things discussed in this chapter. Whichever
part of the world you live in, there are
organizations that can answer your questions.
These organizations will be happy to give you
useful information and advice.*

Australia
Diabetes Australia
Overeaters Anonymous

Philippines
Nutrition Center
UP Philippine General Hospital,
Ward 21, Taft Avenue, Manila
(anorexia, bulimia)

UK
Anorexia and Bulimia Nervosa
Association
British Diabetic Association
Health Education Authority

*You should be able to find the telephone numbers
in your local telephone directory or by phoning
directory enquiries.*

3

EATING WELL

A young person's guide to nutrition

You are what you eat! The food you put into your body is used to make your body function, and keep healthy. People eat in different ways. Some people like to eat lots of small snacks throughout the day, others prefer two or three larger meals. Whichever way you eat, it's good to know about the food you're putting into your body, and what it's doing for you.

Different foods around the world

Wherever you live in the world, you'll have your favourite things to eat. Some foods may come from a traditional dish eaten in your own part of the world, and based on a crop that your country grows easily – a staple food such as corn or rice. But others such as chips, pizza or ice-cream sundaes may be new arrivals in your part of the world. They have become popular dishes all over the world and are part of what we can call our international diet.

"I can eat popcorn all day. I like popping it at home and pouring extra butter on it as it puffs up."
Gloria

INTERNATIONAL FAVOURITES
There's a huge variety of cooking traditions in different countries around the world. Here are a few – just some of the local dishes that use mainly home produced ingredients. How many do you recognize?

Britain: fish and chips, Lancashire hot-pot, sandwiches.

China: fried rice, prawn omelette, red bean pancake.

France: moules marinière, quiche Lorraine, crepes.

India: gobi dhal, naan bread, curries.

"In India we blend dry-roasted spices with oil and yoghurt to flavour meats and vegetables. It's delicious."
Smita

"In the West Indies we cook the roots of the yam, which is like a sweet potato. Yam fritters are super!"
Errol

"Dim sum all day long –
and loads of them.
That'll do me."
Sam

A Muslim family enjoy meatballs, riceballs and grilled fish.

Israel: potato latkes, felafel.

Italy: pizza, lasagne, risotto,
spaghetti bolognaise.

Japan: sukiyaki, sushi.

Mexico: tortillas, enchiladas.

Russia: bortsch, blinis.

Spain: paella, gazpacho.

Turkey: imam bayildi, kebabs
and dolmas.

USA: hamburgers, waffles.

Food goes round the world

How does a dish that originated in one country spread around the world? It can happen in several ways. When immigrants arrive in a new country they often introduce food dishes from their original homeland, even if it is difficult to get all the ingredients. Their neighbours see something new that looks good, and try it – and the recipe spreads!

People who travel abroad also get the chance to try new dishes. After two weeks of delicious pasta for example, or genuine Mexican enchiladas, who can blame them for wanting more when they return home?

Round the world in a basket

Next time you're buying food, take time to find out where it comes from. Labels and packaging have the country from which the food originated printed on them. Fruit and vegetables are often labelled – Jamaican bananas, or Chilean grapes. Coffee can come from many countries, such as Brazil or Kenya, and tea usually comes from India or Sri Lanka. Most countries in the world are represented on your grocery store shelves. Food is truly international.

"In Greece, we eat lots of fresh crunchy vegetables. I dip them in a yoghurt sauce called tzatsiki or in a paste of chickpea known as hummus!"
Sophie

Balanced diet

Everyone follows a diet. Your diet probably isn't anything special. Diet is simply the name given to everything you eat. You probably get a varied diet, with different things to eat every day. But however much you like eggs, you'd soon get very tired of them if you ate nothing else. To make sure you grow well and stay healthy, you need to know what to eat across a whole variety of foods, and how much of each is best for you.

What's in a diet?

Although there are hundreds, even thousands of different foods, they all fall into just a few categories. Each category provides different kinds of nutrients that your body can use. The three most important kinds of nutrients are protein, carbohydrate and fat. These nutrients provide energy and are vital to a healthy body. Put the right amounts of nutrients on one side of a balance and you'll get the right measure of growth and health on the other.

Choosing the right balance

You can easily find out whether you're on the right dietary track. Look at the list on the next page. It shows a range of food with the amount of protein, carbohydrate and fat in a 100 gram serving of each. Choose what you'd like to eat from the list.

When you've written down everything you might eat in a day, add up the total amount of protein, carbohydrate and protein in all the food, and draw a bar chart like the one on the right.

Remember, if you choose toast and spread butter or margarine on it, you must add this fat to your list. The same applies to rice which has been fried instead of boiled. You will need to add in a serving of butter or oil. If you're particularly hungry, you might want an extra large portion. If you do, double the gram count listed. If you normally eat small helpings, halve the number given for that item.

MEET THE NUTRIENTS

Protein is an important nutrient. It is used by your body to form the cell tissue that helps you grow. It also repairs and replaces parts of your body which wear out. Large amounts of protein are found in meat, fish, nuts, eggs, cheese, milk, and dried peas and beans. Smaller amounts are found in cereals such as bread and rice.

Carbohydrate foods provide the fuel your body needs to give you plenty of energy to live, work and play. Starches are carbohydrates. They are found in bread, potatoes, cereals, rice and pasta. Sugars are also carbohydrates. These occur naturally in many fruits, and refined sugar is added to many foods such as cakes and soft drinks.

Fats give you energy just as proteins and carbohydrates do. They also help to build the cells that make up your body. Some fats are easily recognizable. You find them as cooking oil, butter, ghee, margarine or lard. But the fat in many foods is not always obvious. Nuts, biscuits, sausages and cheese all contain fats.

YOUR DAILY DIET

You need to eat around 2,100-2,800 calories a day if your body is going to stay working, growing, repairing itself and looking good. Those calories should come from 60-75 grams of protein, 65-85 grams of fat, and 310-385 grams of carbohydrate.

You can read more about calories on pages 154 and 155.

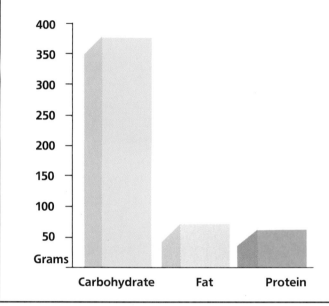

Bar chart (Grams): Carbohydrate ~375, Fat ~70, Protein ~60

Scientists say that the ideal diet should contain 12 percent protein, 58 percent carbohydrate and 30 percent fat.

fat
protein
carbohydrate

(100g)	Protein (g)	Carbohydrate (g)	Fat (g)
Apples	—	12	—
Baked beans	6	17	1
Beefburger (fried)	18	6	16
Biscuits (sweet)	5	66	30
Bread — white	8	53	2
Bread — wholemeal	9	47	2
Butter	—	—	82
Carrots (boiled)	1	4	—
Cheese (hard)	25	10	35
Chips (fried)	4	38	9
Chocolate	9	54	37
Corned beef	27	—	12
Crisps	6	50	38
Eggs (boiled)	12	—	11
Lamb	29	—	13
Lettuce	1	0	—
Lentils (boiled)	7	18	—
Milk — whole	3	4	3
Milk — semi skimmed	3	5	1
Oranges	1	8	—
Peanuts	28	8	49
Pears	—	13	—
Peas (boiled)	5	7	—
Potatoes (boiled)	2	19	—
Rice (boiled)	2	30	—
Spaghetti	10	84	1
Toast (white)	9	64	2
Yoghurt (natural)	5	5	2

How did you do?

Now comes the moment of truth. Be honest! How does the diet you've chosen match up to the scientists' recommendations? If you're on the mark, well done. If you're way out, keep reading this book! How much fuel for energy would your daily choice have given you? Too much fat won't help you at all — it will just be stored around your waist! Too little carbohydrate will leave you feeling tired. If you're not getting enough protein, your hair and skin might not look so good. Work out how to adjust what you eat to fall in with the recommendations.

In many countries, the information printed on packaged food lists what nutrients the food contains. Out of interest, take a look at some of the labels on food in your store cupboard, to see just what you're eating.

A meal in a meal

Whatever and wherever you eat, you'll know that most meals contain bits and pieces of a variety of foods. Look at any recipe book and you'll see a whole list of ingredients which you must mix together to create a single dish. Nutritionists who study the content of our food believe that we need to eat a whole variety of foods to get a balanced, health-giving diet. As you know, there are three main groups of nutrients – proteins, carbohydrates and fats. We also need to eat foods from a further two groups, the vitamins and minerals. These nutrients can be found in many different foods.

	Group 1: Proteins – meat, poultry, fish, eggs, dried lentils, beans and peas, nuts, cheese, milk.
	Group 2: Carbohydrates – breakfast cereals, bread, flour, rice, pasta, potatoes and yams.
	Group 3: Fat – butter, ghee, margarine, vegetable oil, hard cheese, cream, meat fat.
	Group 4: Vitamins – fruit, vegetables, eggs, milk, meat, fish.
	Group 5: Minerals – milk, yoghurt, cheese, vegetables, nuts, meat, wholemeal bread, fish, dried fruit.

Spaghetti bolognaise

It's interesting to analyse a dish and find out how many nutritional groups you've sampled.

Let's take a dish of spaghetti bolognaise with a sprinkling of grated cheese on top.

Group 2
pasta gives you carbohydrate.

Group 1
meat and cheese give you protein.

tomatoes

minced beef

cheese

Group 3
cheese gives
you fat.

Group 4
meat, tomatoes and
onions give you vitamins.

Group 5
tomatoes, cheese and
meat give you minerals.

The perfect mixture

So the Italian dish spaghetti bolognaise stands
up quite well! It provides some food from every
group in just one meal. Just think how easy it
will be to eat from every group in the course of
one day. Break down your next meal using this
grouping system. How many groups have you
eaten from? Eat something from each group
every day – that's the way to stay fit
and healthy.

pasta

onions

Body-building proteins

About 16.5 percent of the body of an adult male is made up of protein.

Proteins are one of the three important types of nutrients that our bodies need. The word protein comes from a Greek word meaning "I am first". And this is true. After water, every cell in your body is made up of more protein than anything else. In fact, you are made up of more than 15 percent protein!

Until you are about 18 years old, your body grows by growing new cells. Then, over every seven year period of your adult life, every cell in your body, except those in your brain and teeth, will die and be replaced by a new cell. And what does your body need to perform this amazing growth and replacement job? Body-building protein, of course!

We find the protein we need in certain kinds of foods. There are two kinds of proteins:
Animal proteins are found in meat, fish, cheese, eggs and milk.
Vegetable proteins are found in the seeds of plants – peas, beans and other pulses, cereals like rice and bread, and nuts.

Proteins in your body

So what exactly do proteins do for your body? Scientists have discovered that proteins are made up of substances called amino acids. You can read more about amino acids on the next page. Proteins help you to grow. Some proteins carry chemicals around the body. Some proteins, called enzymes, bring chemicals together to trigger essential reactions, and are a vital part of your digestive system. Some of your hormones are proteins.

Food 100 g	Grams of protein
Milk	3
Peas	5
Baked beans	6
Flour, wholemeal	9
Eggs	12
White fish	18
Mackerel	20
Cheese, hard	25
Beef	26
Peanuts	28
Soya beans	34

PROTEIN CONTENT OF SOME FOODS

Some foods contain far more protein than others. This table shows how many grams of protein there are in 100 grams of each of the foods.

You need about 60-75 grams of protein a day to carry out an efficient job of building and repairing the cells in your body. If you eat more protein than you need for growing and repairing, the spare amount is broken down and used for energy. Choose a variety of sources of protein in your diet, including animal and vegetable proteins.

Vegetarians and proteins

If you're a vegetarian, you'll need to plan carefully how to work out your dietary balancing act. For example, you will need to mix nuts or cereals with the protein you get from peas or beans. This way you will get enough of the essential amino acids which are found in both types of food. For more on this see the article on being a vegetarian on pages 166 and 167.

Some nuts and beans are cheaper than meat, and often contain more protein.

VOTE FOR SOYA!

Look at the chart again. You can see that soya beans are one of the best sources of protein available. There's more protein gram for gram in soya beans than in lean beef. Here are some other interesting facts about this bean:

The soya bean was first grown at least 3,000 years ago in China, where it is still so highly regarded that it has names like 'Great Treasure', 'Brings happiness', 'Yellow Jewel' and 'Heaven's Bird'.

It grows well in poor soils and helps to improve the soil by supporting colonies of micro-organisms which add nitrogen to the ground.

It is very productive. China could feed a quarter of the world's population if it were to use just one tenth of its arable land for growing beans.

Soya beans are versatile! Foods derived from them include soya bean sprouts, steamed green beans, roasted nuts, milk, soya sauce, miso (a fermented paste), flour and oil.

Soya beans can be crushed and the juice turned into tofu, or bean curd which can be used as another source of protein.

Soya beans can even be used to make a food called textured vegetable protein, or TVP for short. This can be made to look and taste like meat, but it contains less fat, provides fibre – and it's often cheaper too!

A hen's egg is an excellent source of protein, providing all eight of the essential amino acids our body needs.

Amino acids are essential

Amino acids are the basic building blocks from which proteins are made. Proteins eaten in foods such as meat and cheese are digested and broken down into amino acids. These amino acids are absorbed into the bloodstream and used to build up the specific proteins which the body needs.

There are 20 amino acids and eight of these are called the 'essential' amino acids. They must be eaten in foods because the body is unable to make them. The remaining 12 amino acids can be made in the liver from the eight essential ones.

Babies, children and adolescents need amino acids for growth. Everyone needs them throughout life for the building and repair of body tissues. The proteins in the body are constantly renewed – a few are broken down and replaced each day with new amino acids. This means that protein is constantly needed although the amount needed each day varies at different stages of life. Children need extra protein for growth, and pregnant women need more to nourish the baby growing inside their bodies.

The body does not store excess amino acids. These are used to make glucose, or they are broken down in the liver. This produces urea which is passed out, or excreted, by the kidneys. The more protein we eat, the more urea is produced.

Carbohydrates

Carbohydrate is one of the three main nutrients necessary for good health. Foods containing carbohydrates supply three things, – sugars, starches and fibre – which don't really look as though they belong together. Foods containing sugar and starch provide us with our main sources of energy. Foods containing fibre help us to get rid of any waste products.

About 1.5 percent of an adult male body consists of carbohydrates.

Where do carbohydrates come from?

The surprising answer is that carbohydrates come from plants! We eat the plants directly, or we eat products which come from animals that have eaten plants.

Here are the sources of the three kinds of carbohydrates: sugar, starch and fibre.

Sugar
The sugar you put on the table comes from sugar cane or sugar beets. Natural sugars are also found in milk and fruit. Sugar is very easy to digest and will give you energy. But it will give you nothing else and should be eaten in moderate amounts! Read more about this on pages 136 and 137.

Starch
Starch is found in flour, bread, potatoes, root vegetables, rice, beans, peas and yams. It is an important source of energy. Your body digests many starches slowly, which means that it is able to supply you with long-lasting energy and stamina. When starch is digested by your body it turns into a form of sugar called glucose.

Fibre
Fibre comes from fruits, cereals and vegetables. Humans cannot digest most of it, although animals can. However, we need to eat some of this fibre, or roughage, as it helps our bodies to bind up and dispose of the remains of all the other things we eat.

GROWING CARBOHYDRATES

Just like you, plants need to feed and grow in order to stay healthy. But unlike you, plants make their own nutrients. To do this, they absorb water and minerals which they get from the ground through their roots. Plants also take in light energy from the Sun through their leaves. This occurs in a process called photosynthesis. Plants use carbon dioxide from the air to combine the water, minerals and light energy to make nutrients. The nutrients are stored in the plant as starch, which is a kind of carbohydrate, that animals and people can eat.

CARBOHYDRATE COUNT

Here's a list showing you how much sugar and starch carbohydrate there is in 100 grams of some foods.

Food 100g	Sugar g	Starch g
Baked beans	6	9
Bananas	16	3
Chocolate biscuits	43	24
Cornflakes	7	78
Honey	76	0
Ice cream	19	1
Meat	0	0
Milk	4	0
Oranges	26	0
Potatoes (boiled)	1	17
Rice	trace	31
Sugar	100	0
Tomato ketchup	23	1
White bread	3	46
Yams (boiled)	trace	29

Staple cereals

Crops such as wheat, oats and barley that are turned into flour are a staple part of most people's diets. Think of all the varieties of bread, pastry and pastas there are. Rice and maize, sometimes called sweet corn, provide the basis for meals in many countries. You'll find a lot of rice in Asian dishes, while many Africans rely on a diet of maize.

These crops are cereals. They help fill you up but don't provide much taste on their own or supply all of the essential nutrients that help to give you a healthy diet. Usually vegetables and fruits, and eggs, dairy products, meat, fish or nuts are added to these basics, both to boost their nutritional value and to make them tastier.

Nutritious rice

Rice is the main food for half of the world's population, and is the second most important food on our planet after wheat. It needs a warm climate to grow and most kinds of rice are planted in paddy fields which are flooded with water after planting.

Rice contains very little fat and a large amount of starchy carbohydrate. It has slightly less protein than other cereal grains, but the protein in rice is of higher quality. Rice also provides fibre, minerals and B vitamins.

After harvesting, the rice grains are removed from their stalks by threshing. The grains are protected inside a tough, fibrous husk which is usually removed in a mechanical rice mill. Almost the whole of the rice grain itself is made up of starch – called the endosperm. This is covered with bran and outer layers of the husk, which is where much of the vitamin content is found. However, in milling, most of these outer layers are lost, and white or 'polished' rice is left. Highly refined white rice can be almost completely lacking in vitamins.

More recently, a way of producing white rice has been found that helps to keep in the vitamins. The rice grains, still with their husks on, are partly cooked by steaming or boiling in water. This means that the woody husks can be more easily removed before milling. It also means that the vitamins in the outer layers of the grains are carried through into the endosperm, before the husks are removed.

A disease called beri-beri used to be common in all countries where rice is the main food. It is caused by a lack of thiamin (one of the B vitamins). But parboiling rice is a simple way to preserve the levels of thiamin in the milled rice and protect people against the disease.

Brown rice is almost the whole grain – just a little of the bran is removed with the inedible husk. Brown rice is higher in protein, fibre, vitamins and minerals than any kind of polished rice. It also has a better flavour and texture!

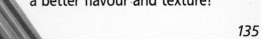

Watch out for sugars

One hundred years ago, the average European ate about two kilos of sugar a year. Nowadays, most people in Europe and the United States eat about 50 kilos of sugar a year! This is far too much. In Britain, for example, half a kilo of sugar is bought for each person to consume each week. As if that isn't bad enough, British people eat almost twice that amount when you add together all the sugar that's put in cakes, biscuits, sweets, chocolate and some drinks.

Sugar in disguise

Sugar sneaks into foods which we consider savoury like tomato ketchup, tomato soup and baked beans. If you look on the labels of many processed foods – even cheeseburgers and sausages – you'll see sugar listed as an ingredient. You soon begin to realize that sugar is almost everywhere.

The trouble is, sugar is almost always called something else! Watch out on food labels for anything which ends in -ose – you can be sure it's a form of sugar. The main ones are shown in the chart below.

Sugar as a food

Your body changes the carbohydrates you eat into glucose, no matter what they started out as. But it's far healthier for you to get your glucose from starch and fibre than from straight sugar. This is because it takes time to digest starch, and foods that provide starch and fibre help to fill you up.

So what does sugar give you? It gives you sugar! That's all. It is quickly absorbed into your blood, and the glucose quickly reaches every part of your body to be used as energy. It would be great to think that by eating plenty of sugary things you'd have the energy to leap about all day, but it's not necessarily so! All foods provide energy, and if you eat more sugar than you need the spare amount can't be used up. It gets stored as body fat.

	Sugar	Where you'll find it
	Glucose (or dextrose)	occurs naturally in fruit and vegetable juices. It's also a natural sugar found in the blood of living animals – including humans! Glucose sugars are used in many foods like jam, sweets and drinks.
	Fructose	found in some fruit and vegetables, and especially in honey. It's the sweetest sugar there is.
	Lactose	only found in milk, including human milk.
	Maltose	a combination of other sugars which is produced from grain. It's often used for making malt brewed drinks.
	Sucrose	comes from sugar cane and sugar beet. There's also a small amount in carrots and a few types of fruits. The sugar you use in cooking or add to tea or coffee is pure sucrose.

PROBLEM SUGAR

There are two main problems with eating too much sugar.

Tooth decay

Sugar is one of the worst things for teeth, especially if you have a lot of sugary drinks and snacks. Bacteria combines with sugar in your mouth to form plaque. Plaque contains acids that will eat holes in your teeth, so eating sugar causes tooth decay!

Too much weight

Adding sugar to foods makes it easier to eat more, because our taste buds enjoy it so much. Sugary foods that don't contain many other nutrients or fibre don't fill you up so easily. You eat more – and more. You don't feel full, but any extra glucose is stored as body fat. You add on the kilos.

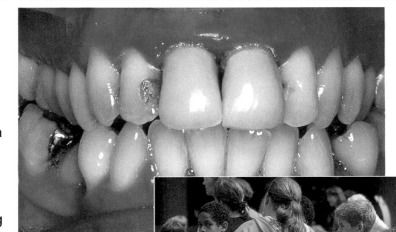

Sugar which is left as a deposit on your teeth makes your teeth decay.

People can be fat for various reasons, but all obesity will result in health problems.

A glass of ordinary cola contains about 5 teaspoonfuls of sugar.

Cut down now!

It is not necessary to go to extremes and cut out sugar completely – that would be almost impossible. But you can re-educate your taste buds! If you have become used to eating sweet things, don't worry. There are several things you can do to reduce the amount of sugar you eat and drink. You can halve the amount of sugar used in recipes. This works for most things except jam or meringues. You can choose low calorie drinks or unsweetened fruit juices. If you do put sugar in tea or coffee, cut down a little at a time. If sweets are irresistible, try to eat them at the end of a meal, or at a time when you can brush your teeth immediately afterwards. That will help stop the rot!

Field of wheat.

Fibre

Fibre is one part of our diet that we cannot do without. In fact, many of us do not eat enough although it is found in many foods. We should try to eat at least 30 grams of fibre a day.

Fibre is only found in foods which grow from the ground, such as cereals, rice, beans, vegetables and fruits. There are two forms of dietary fibre. Soluble fibre is digested by the bacteria in the large intestine. It is the soluble fibres which slow down the absorption of glucose into the blood, which is especially helpful for people with diabetes. Then there is insoluble fibre. An example of insoluble fibre is cellulose, which is found in all plant cells. Insoluble fibre isn't digested. It adds bulk and holds water in the bowel, making bowel motions soft and easier to pass from the body. This means that you won't get constipation if you eat enough insoluble fibre, providing you are drinking adequate fluids.

Filling fibre

Diets which contain plenty of fibre tend to be more satisfying. They are also often low in calories. A diet which is high in fibre takes longer to chew. All those grains and seeds keep your jaw working for longer, so you're less likely to ask for another helping. If you're watching your weight, fibre is great!

THE FIBRE LEAGUE
Fibre is found in many sorts of food. The figures show how many grams of fibre there are in each 100 grams of the listed foods.

Cereals 100g	g
Wheat bran	44
Soya flour	14.3
Wholemeal flour	9.6
Brown flour	7.5
Brown rice	5.5
Maize	4.7
White flour	3.0
White rice	0.8

Fruits 100g	g
Dried dates	8.7
Raisins	6.8
Cranberries	4.2
Bananas	3.4
Strawberries	3.2
Apples	2.0
Oranges	1.5
Pineapple	1.2

Nuts 100g	g
Almonds	14.3
Fresh coconut	13.6
Brazil	9.0
Peanuts	8.1
Hazel	6.1

Pulses 100g	g
Peas (frozen)	12.0
Haricot beans	7.4
Baked beans	7.3
Peas (canned)	6.3
Lentils (split)	3.7
Broad beans	3.4
Runner beans	3.4

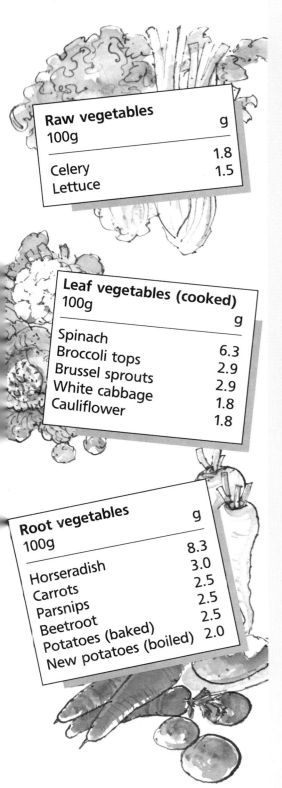

Raw vegetables 100g	g
Celery	1.8
Lettuce	1.5

Leaf vegetables (cooked) 100g	g
Spinach	6.3
Broccoli tops	2.9
Brussel sprouts	2.9
White cabbage	1.8
Cauliflower	1.8

Root vegetables 100g	g
Horseradish	8.3
Carrots	3.0
Parsnips	2.5
Beetroot	2.5
Potatoes (baked)	2.5
New potatoes (boiled)	2.0

FOOD LABELS

In many countries, you'll be able to find out how much fibre is contained in a food by looking at its packaging. Become fibre-conscious!

More fibre facts

Fibre is not a single substance but a group of substances. It is found only in plant foods and is made up of the parts of plants that the human digestive system is mostly not able to break down. Fibre helps other kinds of food and waste material to pass quickly through the digestive system. It slows down the taking in, or absorption, of sugar into the blood, which is helpful for people suffering from the disease called diabetes. It also helps to lower cholesterol levels.

Scientists have carried out tests to compare the diets of different countries and have found that high-fibre diets seem to protect people against diseases of the large intestine, such as cancer.

In countries where the average amount of fibre in the diet is low, people have been advised to eat more fibre. For example, in Europe and North America, the average amount of fibre eaten is 20-25 grams per day and people are told they should eat at least 30 grams for a healthy diet. In Africa and Asia, fibre intake ranges between 50 and 150 grams per day.

More fibre can be taken in by eating wholegrain cereals instead of refined ones, and more green vegetables, nuts and grains. It is important to include different types of fibre in the diet. It is also important to eat high-fibre foods in their natural state, such as whole grains, rather than fibre that has been separated from its natural source, such as bran.

There are two main types of fibre – soluble and insoluble. Soluble fibre includes gels and pectins and is found in foods such as oats, apples and some vegetables. It is this type of fibre which slows the absorption of sugar into the blood. Soluble fibre also helps to lower high levels of cholesterol in the blood. Insoluble fibre includes cellulose and is found in wholegrain cereals, such as wheat and brown rice. It helps in getting rid of waste material and helps to prevent constipation and other bowel disorders.

A diet like this contains plenty of fibre.

Facts on fat

Fat, as you know, is one of the three most important nutrients, along with proteins and carbohydrates. We all need a proportion of fat in our diets. You'll have no difficulty eating enough fat. It is everywhere! Dairy products like whole milk, cheese and butter contain fat. The same goes for meat, nuts, sauces, puddings, biscuits, chocolates and cooking fats – and that's just a start. Different types of fat are found in some fish and vegetable oils like soya, corn and sunflower oils.

About 15 percent of the body of an adult male is fat.

What are fats?

Fats and oils are actually the same thing. They contain the same basic substances. However, the term 'fat' is used to describe substances that are solid at room temperature, while 'oil' is used to describe substances that are liquid at room temperature.

And what do fats do for you? Fats are a rich source of energy. One gram of fat will provide you with twice as much energy as one gram of protein or one gram of carbohydrate. Fats also contain the important vitamins A, D and E. Fats help these vitamins to be used properly by your body. Fats help you to feel full. This is because you digest fat slowly, so it stays in your stomach for a long time.

Fat in the body helps you to keep warm, too. Some fat is stored under the skin and around other parts of your body. Some of this fat can be converted into energy when your body needs it.

A NATURAL DIFFERENCE

It is natural for women to have more fat on their bodies than men. This seems to be nature's way of protecting them so that if there is a shortage of food, women will survive by using their store of body fat to sustain them while they produce and rear children. A young woman's body weight may include about 20-30 percent fat. By comparison a young man's body weight will be about 10-15 percent fat.

The acid test

Fat is made up of substances called fatty acids and glycerol, a thick liquid. We manufacture some fatty acids in our bodies but others must be obtained from the foods we eat. These are called essential fatty acids and are important for resisting infection, for growth, and for keeping skin healthy. Here are some of the fatty acids we need to take in from food.

Saturated fats

You may come across the terms 'saturated' and 'unsaturated' fat, or even 'monounsaturated' and 'polyunsaturated' fat. These words tell us something about the chemistry of these fats – the way different fats are made up.

Saturated fats mostly come from animals. They are found in lard, suet, butter and meat, as well as in coconut and palm oil. Unsaturated fats are found in most vegetable oils like olive oil, corn oil, sunflower oil and soya bean oil, and in nuts and seeds.

Type of fatty acid	Found in
Linoleic acid	sunflower oil, corn oil, safflower oil
Alpha linolenic acid	rape seed oil
Gamma linolenic acid	evening primrose oil, borage oil, blackcurrant seed oil
Arachidonic acid	liver, brain and offal
EPA	fish oil
DHA	fish oil

Basically, unsaturates are healthy, saturates are not! Consuming large amounts of saturated fat is thought to increase the amount of cholesterol in the blood. Find out more about this on page 143. The message is – choose unsaturates whenever you can.

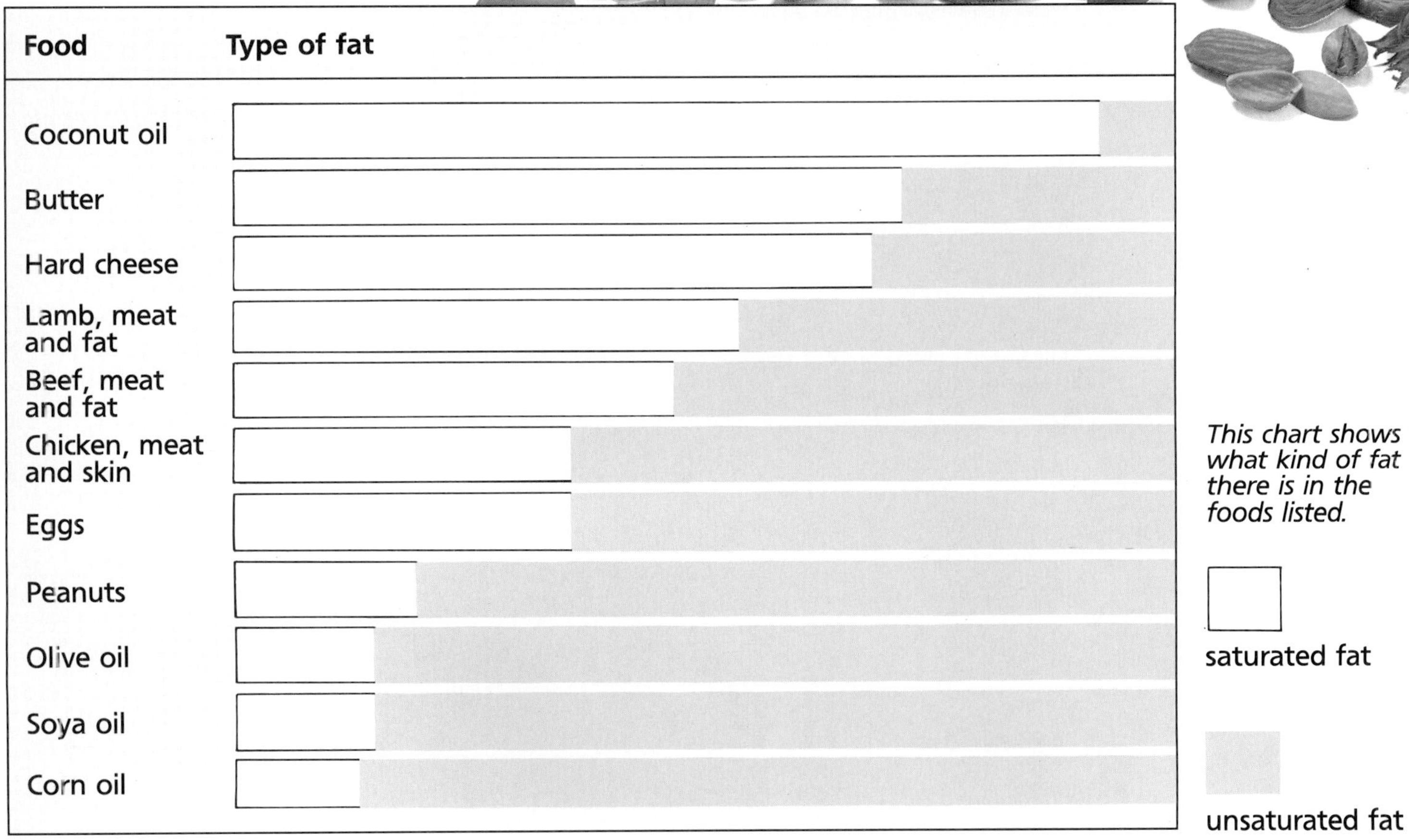

Food	Type of fat
Coconut oil	
Butter	
Hard cheese	
Lamb, meat and fat	
Beef, meat and fat	
Chicken, meat and skin	
Eggs	
Peanuts	
Olive oil	
Soya oil	
Corn oil	

This chart shows what kind of fat there is in the foods listed.

□ saturated fat

▨ unsaturated fat

Excess fat

If you have ever spilled some melted butter or oil, you'll know that a little fat goes a long way, especially if you have to clear it up! The same goes for the fat content in your diet. A little should go a long way because of the problems caused by eating too much.

The first problem with fat is that it is full of calories – and if you take in too many calories, your body doesn't use them up but stores them as body fat. And being overweight makes you feel uncomfortable, as well as making you feel tired. You can find out more about calories on pages 154 and 155.

Every 500 grams of extra fat on your body means that your heart has to push blood through over 300 more kilometres of capillaries! And that puts a lot of extra strain on it.

The next problem is that deposits of fat can build up in arteries, preventing the blood from flowing properly. This can lead to serious heart problems. The Expert's view on the next page tells you more about this.

Are you a centimetre cheater?

Some parts of your body are more likely to store fat than others. A lot depends on your shape and whether you're a boy or a girl. The two places where it's often easy to spot extra fat are just above your waist and at the top of your arm, just below your armpit.

If you think that you're carrying too much fat, try this test on those two areas of your body.

With your thumb and forefinger try to pinch as much flesh you can. If you can pinch a thickness of more than 2 centimetres, you should think carefully about how much you're eating. And no, before you ask, it's not relaxed muscle! It's fat! This test works for everyone, whatever their age, so get other people to try it out too and compare notes.

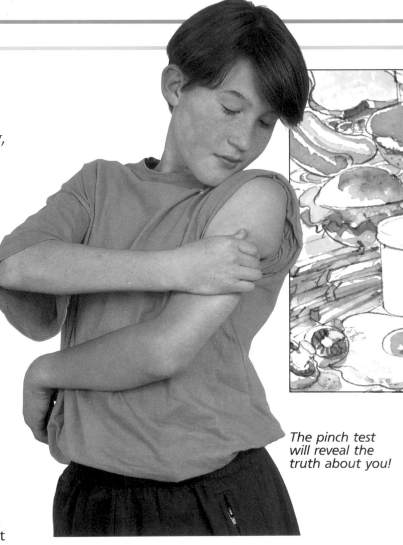

The pinch test will reveal the truth about you!

Cutting down

It is not necessary to cut out fat completely from your diet. This would be unhealthy. But it's easy to keep a check on the amount you eat. It's not difficult to spread your butter thinly, or to choose grilled food instead of fatty fried food.

Also, there are low fat alternatives to many foods which are normally high in fat. Take a half litre of milk. This is the fat content for three different kinds:

whole milk	half-fat or semi-skimmed milk	skimmed milk
22 grams	11 grams	1 gram

Which should you be choosing to keep the fat in your diet at a healthy level?

Food (average serving)	grams of fat per serving
Potatoes (boiled or baked)	0.1
Low fat yoghurt	0.3
Low fat spread	4
Fish fingers (grilled)	6
Butter or margarine	8
Chapati	10
Milkshake	10
Double cream	13
Small bar chocolate	15
Cheeseburger	15
Thin-cut french fries	17
Hard cheese	19
Steak (grilled)	20
Bacon (grilled)	20
Sausages (grilled)	21
Paratha	22
Bacon (fried)	25
Samosa	26

A FAT DIET!

The chart above shows the amount of fat in grams contained in an average serving of some popular foods.
You saw on page 129 that the ideal fat intake for the day should be between 65 and 85 grams. You can see how easily you could reach that limit if you ate a few samosas and a bar of chocolate.

Cholesterol

Cholesterol is a fatty substance which is found in body tissues. It is an important part of the membrane, or covering of cells. Cholesterol is used to make hormones, vitamin D and bile acids which help in the digestion of fats. It is made in the body, mainly by the liver. Cholesterol is also taken into the body in animal foods such as eggs, meat, dairy foods and shellfish.

Cholesterol is carried round the body through the arteries. If there is more cholesterol than the tissues need, the excess may be left as a deposit on the walls of the arteries. As the excess cholesterol builds up, the arteries become thicker and harder and less blood can flow through them. The heart has to work harder to push blood around the body. In time this extra effort strains the muscles of the heart and weakens it.

The higher the level of cholesterol circulating in the blood, the greater the risk of heart disease. Unfortunately this is not just a problem for adults, but for young people too. Your arteries can start to thicken in your teens.

Surprisingly, a high level of cholesterol in the diet is not the main reason for high levels of cholesterol in the blood. When cholesterol is present in the diet, the body makes less of its own cholesterol. On the other hand, when too little cholesterol is absorbed from food, the body makes more. It is the level of saturated fat in the diet that can cause problems. A high intake of saturated fats leads to high levels of blood cholesterol.

Eating less saturated fat can help to reduce blood cholesterol. Other helpful changes to make in the diet are to eat more fibre and to choose to eat unsaturated fats, such as corn oil.

These diagrams show how fatty deposits build up in a coronary artery.

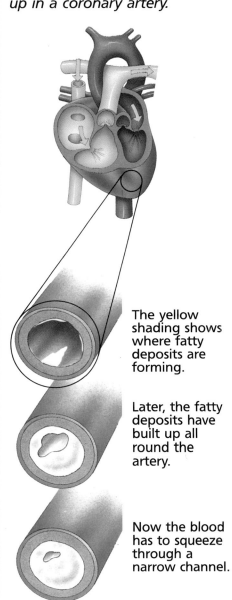

The yellow shading shows where fatty deposits are forming.

Later, the fatty deposits have built up all round the artery.

Now the blood has to squeeze through a narrow channel.

Vital vitamins

Vitamins really are vital! You must have them in your diet to be healthy. There are 13 different kinds and each one has its own particular contribution to make. Some vitamins help give you healthy eyes, others contribute to strong teeth. Certain vitamins act as transformers so that your body can use minerals more efficiently. Some vitamins help your body to attack infection.

About 1 percent of the body of an adult male consists of vitamins.

Water and fat-soluble vitamins

Vitamins are divided into two groups, fat-soluble and water-soluble. Vitamins A, D, E, and K dissolve in fat. Vitamins B and C dissolve in water. The important fact to remember is that your body can store fat-soluble vitamins for longer than it can store water-soluble ones. A balanced diet should enable you to maintain the right level of both kinds of vitamin.

Daily intake

We only need small amounts of each vitamin, but they are all important. If you're a vegetarian, be careful that you get enough vitamins, especially those from the B group.

Some people swallow pills and mixtures known as 'vitamin supplements'. This isn't necessary if you are eating well. It is better, and more economical, to get your vitamins from a healthy diet. In fact, too much of some vitamins can make you ill. There's a famous case of some Arctic explorers who ate polar bear's liver. They became ill because the liver contained 100 times more vitamin A than they were able to digest.

Vitamin deficiency problems

Rickets

Rickets comes from taking in too little vitamin D because of a poor diet or lack of sunshine on the skin. Children suffering from malnutrition are likely to be early victims of rickets. The bones in their legs become so weak that they bend under the weight of the child's body.

Scurvy

Scurvy is a disease you get from not eating enough vitamin C. This disease was first diagnosed back in the 1500s. Sailors on long sea voyages became lethargic. Their wounds would not heal, old wounds sometimes opened up again, and their teeth fell out. Then a Scottish doctor discovered that by eating lemons and limes the illness could be eliminated.

Beri-beri

Nearly 100 years ago, a scientist noticed that chickens fed only on scraps of white rice started to look tired and showed little energy to peck properly. They kept dropping their food. When the same chickens were also fed the outsides of the rice – the husks – their condition improved. We now know that the chickens were suffering from a disease called beri-beri. They weren't getting enough thiamin, one of the B vitamins, which is found in rice husks. Today, this vitamin is recognized as important to good health and it's often added to breakfast cereals and to white bread by the makers. It is present in some meats and cereals.

VITAMINS

Here's a table of vitamins you need, where they are found and how they benefit you.

What they're called	Where they're found	What they do
A (retinol)	Liver, butter, milk, egg yolk, fish oils, enriched margarine	Helps the growth of healthy skin and eyes.
B Thiamin (B_1) Riboflavin (B_2)	Yeast, wholegrain, cereal, liver, pork. Milk, cheese, yeast, green vegetables	Helps your body to transform food into energy. Helps your body cells use oxygen.
Niacin (nicotinic acid)	Liver, yeast, whole grains, milk, eggs, fruit and vegetables	Essential to keep your cells working.
B_6 (pyridoxine)	Most vegetables, yeast, fish, meat	Needed for healthy teeth, gums and red blood cells.
B_{12} (cyanocobalamin)	Animal products	Essential for the development of red blood cells.
Biotin	Most fresh vegetables, egg yolk, nuts, liver, kidney	Keeps the circulatory system and the skin healthy.
Pantothenic acid	Eggs, broccoli, nuts	Helps change your fats, carbohydrates and other substances into energy.
Folic acid	Asparagus, spinach, broccoli, liver, yeast	Helps cell formation, especially red blood cells. It may prevent certain kinds of anaemia.
C (ascorbic acid)	Oranges, blackcurrants, rosehip, citrus fruit, strawberries, broccoli, green peppers, tomatoes, potatoes	Keeps the skin, bones, teeth and muscles healthy. It also helps fight infections.
D (cholecalciferol)	Butter, milk, eggs, oily fish, enriched margarine. Sunshine on the skin helps in the production of vitamin D	Helps develop strong bones and white teeth. It also helps your body to make good use of calcium and phosphorus.
E (tocopherol)	Vegetable oils, nuts, wholegrain cereals and leafy vegetables	Helps keep your blood and other body cells healthy.
K (menadione)	Green vegetables, soya beans, tomatoes, honey, bran, egg yolk, wheatgerm	Helps maintain healthy blood.

Mainly minerals

You may have thought that minerals were found in rocks and metals. You're right, they are! Not all the minerals we eat come from metals, though. Minerals are substances that have never been alive and that have a particular chemical composition. Only one percent of the total nutrition our bodies need comes from minerals, but that one percent is so important you wouldn't last long without it! Minerals provide the nutrients that help your blood form, and your teeth and bones to grow. They also get your muscles and nerves moving.

There are about fifteen minerals that your body takes from food. Some, which are known as trace elements, have exotic names like chromium, molybdenum and selenium. You only need minute quantities of these as too much could be very dangerous.

About 6 percent of the body of an adult male consists of minerals.

Important minerals

If you eat a wide range of foods, you'll be in no danger of running short of the minerals you need. However, there are three minerals you may like to check on to make sure you are getting enough. These are calcium, iron and zinc.

Calcium
Calcium is contained in milk, cheese, yoghurt, tofu, some leafy green vegetables, and nuts. This mineral helps your blood clot properly. It helps build strong teeth and bones and, together with phosphorous, it contributes to the easy movement of your muscles and to the sensitive feel of your nerves.

Iron
Iron is found in liver, kidney, meat, cereals, enriched bread and some kinds of flour. And wait for the good news – there is also some in chocolate. Iron helps give your blood its rich red colour. The iron-rich blood cells carry oxygen from your lungs to your body to help it function and repair itself.

Zinc
Zinc is found in beans, lentils and meat. It has a vital role in the human body, and plays a part in control of the body's metabolism. It's also important for growth, for helping wounds to heal and for sexual development.

Mounds of salt are left when the sea water evaporates.

...and the rest

Other minerals are needed in small quantities but are also essential in your diet.

Potassium is supplied by fruit, vegetables and meat. It plays an important part in the body's process of changing food into energy. It also works with sodium to control the normal flow of water in the body's cells.

Iodine is found in fish, and is sometimes added to salt. It controls the way in which energy is released from food in the body.

Fluorine is found in tea, sea fish and drinking water. It helps to build strong teeth.

You also need even smaller quantities of the trace elements chlorine, chromium, copper, magnesium, manganese, molybdenum, phosphorus and selenium.

Tasty sodium

Eating salt is the way that most of us get our supplies of the mineral sodium. You need some sodium to replace the salt that you lose when you sweat. And some is needed to help balance the fluids in the body, and to keep the nerves functioning properly. But most people eat much more salt than they need. Salt can be harmful to some people, and they may develop high blood pressure if they sprinkle salt too liberally on their food.

It's worth re-educating your taste-buds to having less salt on your food. You might be quite surprised by how tasty some foods are in their natural state.

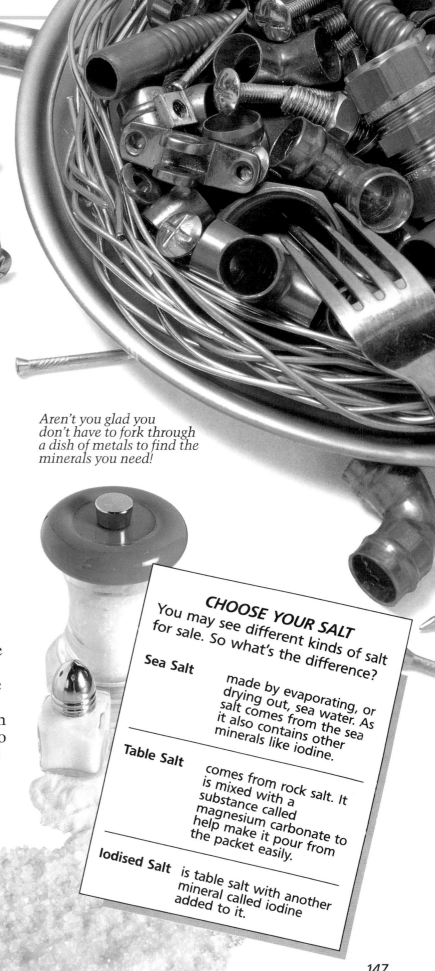

Aren't you glad you don't have to fork through a dish of metals to find the minerals you need!

CHOOSE YOUR SALT

You may see different kinds of salt for sale. So what's the difference?

Sea Salt
made by evaporating, or drying out, sea water. As salt comes from the sea it also contains other minerals like iodine.

Table Salt
comes from rock salt. It is mixed with a substance called magnesium carbonate to help make it pour from the packet easily.

Iodised Salt is table salt with another mineral called iodine added to it.

Water is vital

Your life depends on water. If you were to lose more than approximately ten percent of the water in your body, you wouldn't live very long. In fact, people are made up mostly of water! About 75 percent of a baby's weight is water. This changes to between 60 and 65 percent of the weight of an adult man.

Every living thing needs to keep its water at around its normal level all the time. A person can live without food for many weeks, but can't survive for more than about seven days without water.

Why does your body need so much water? Surprisingly, every part of you has to have water in order to work. About two thirds of the water in your body is kept in your cells. The other third travels round your body in your blood and other fluids.

As a teenager, you may be as much as 70 percent water. You take water into your body whenever you eat or drink. This water then becomes trapped inside your body by your skin, which acts like a waterproof bag. If you didn't have skin, the sun and air would dehydrate your body, and you would start to shrivel up like a prune!

The body of an adult male is about 60 percent water.

Losing water

Although you take water in and retain a great deal, you also lose about two litres from your body every day. You lose it when you breathe. You can see this if you live in a cold country, when you can see the water forming a small cloud of vapour when you breathe out. You lose water when you sweat. When you get hot, water is released through your pores as sweat, and evaporates on your skin. This helps to keep you cool. If you live in a particularly hot country, you lose a lot of water this way. And you also lose water in urine. Each day you lose about a litre of water when you urinate.

Putting water back

If your body needs so much water to work properly and if you lose two litres a day breathing, sweating, and urinating, it's obviously very important to replace that liquid. If you don't, you will feel dry, thirsty and weak. Salt will build up in your blood and you will eventually put strain on your heart. Also if you've been exercising, or working very hard, you will probably feel even thirstier. Thirst is a signal that your body needs water – so take a drink!

Water is good for you

To replace the water your body is losing, you should drink at least one litre of water a day. You can do this simply by drinking tap water. Use the cold tap. Let it run for several minutes to get rid of the stagnant water which has been lying in the water pipes.

It is possible to get a filter which can be fitted to your cold tap. This will extract harmful substances. You might plan to get one of these if your tap water doesn't taste too good.

Both tap water and bottled mineral water are good for you. They contain tiny quantities of minerals like calcium, potassium and magnesium, all of which your body needs.

OTHER LIQUID INTAKE

You can also take in the essential one litre of water a day as drinks like fruit juice, cola or milk. But be aware of the other ingredients in your drink. Many drinks have added artificial flavours. Coffee, tea and some soft drinks contain a stimulant called caffeine which is not very good for you. Also, many drinks contain a surprising amount of sugar. Just look how many grams of added sugar there are in each 100 gram serving of these drinks.

Drink (100g)	calories	added sugar (g)
Cola	34	8.8
Cola (diet)	1	0
Cream soda	24	6.4
Lemonade	22	5.7
Orange squash	30	7.0
Milk (semi-skimmed)	48	0
Tap water	0	0
Mineral water	0	0

EATING WATER

If you drink a litre of water a day and need to replace two litres, where does that extra litre come from? It comes from the food you eat. Nearly every food contains water, sometimes in surprising amounts. Just look at the water content of these foods!

Food	Water content
Cucumber	99%
Carrots	90%
Oranges	86%
Eggs	75%
Cottage cheese	75%
Bread	39%
Hard cheese	37%

Digestion

Your body's digestive system is a super-efficient machine! It's like the ultimate food processor. Each section has its own task to do. First, the food must be broken down so that your body can make use of it. Your bloodstream carries the nutrients off to different parts of your body. And waste materials need to be disposed of.

The digestive system consists of several organs. The alimentary canal is the tube that leads from the mouth down to the anus. The stomach and the small intestine produce digestive juice, and so do the salivary glands, gall bladder and pancreas.

An apple a day

You can see how the digestive process works by looking at what happens when you bite off a piece of apple.

In the mouth

Here's where it all starts. Your teeth break up the apple. Glands in your mouth produce saliva, which mixes with the apple and starts the digestive process. It makes the apple easy to swallow, too. Your tongue helps to roll the food into a ball – and down it goes to the next section.

In the oesophagus

The ball of apple is pushed into the oesophagus. This is a length of tube running from the back of your throat to your stomach. Muscles in the oesophagus move with a wave-like action to push food down to your stomach. It takes about ten seconds for each wave to travel from top to bottom of your oesophagus.

In the stomach

Your stomach is a bag of muscle, shaped rather like the letter J. At each end is a valve called a sphincter that opens and closes the entrance and exit to the stomach. As you eat and fill up your stomach, the walls stretch and expand. For between 2 and 5 hours, your stomach muscles churn up the apple, mixing it with gastric juices which are secreted by glands in the stomach wall. Each day your stomach produces about three litres of gastric juices.

The gastric juices are mostly made up of a mixture of an enzyme called pepsin and hydrochloric acid. This juice starts to break down the apple into a sludge-like substance called chyme.

In the small intestine

The chyme leaves your stomach and travels down a long tube called the small intestine. This is where the nutrients in the chyme pass through the walls of the small intestine into the surrounding blood vessels. The nutrients are carried off as molecules in your bloodstream. The waste materials carry on to the next stage.

In the large intestine

This is where the fibre contained in the apple peel plays an important function. Fibre can't be broken down in the small intestine, so it ends up here as roughage. Bacteria in the large intestine digest the soluble fibre, but the cellulose in the apple peel is insoluble. It carries water and other waste material along with it. The waste fibre goes to the bowel and is passed out of the body as faeces.

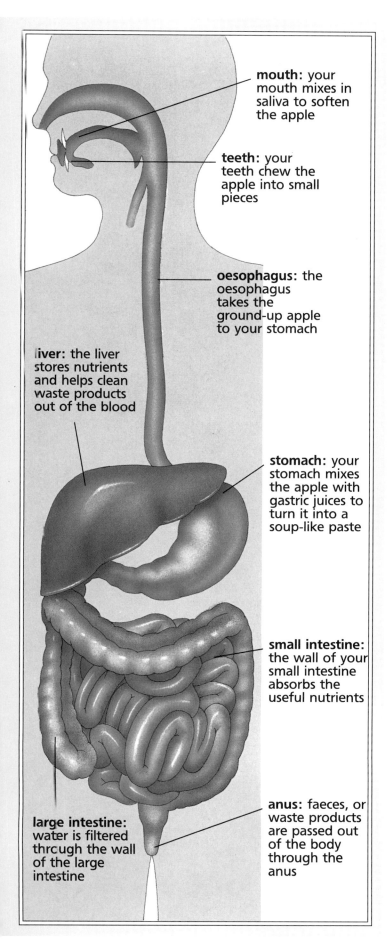

mouth: your mouth mixes in saliva to soften the apple

teeth: your teeth chew the apple into small pieces

oesophagus: the oesophagus takes the ground-up apple to your stomach

liver: the liver stores nutrients and helps clean waste products out of the blood

stomach: your stomach mixes the apple with gastric juices to turn it into a soup-like paste

small intestine: the wall of your small intestine absorbs the useful nutrients

anus: faeces, or waste products are passed out of the body through the anus

large intestine: water is filtered through the wall of the large intestine

When things go wrong

Indigestion

Indigestion can be a painful burning spasm near the top of your stomach. It happens when the valve between your oesophagus and your stomach doesn't, or can't, close off properly. Indigestion can also be caused by a build up of acidic gastric juices in the stomach or by eating too much, or too fast and swallowing air, which makes you feel bloated.

Vomiting

If you over-eat, or eat something that has 'gone off', your body swings into defensive mode. It needs to get rid of that food that's upsetting it. Muscles in your stomach squeeze together, and the sphincter at the end of your stomach stays shut. The food has got to go somewhere so it travels back up your oesophagus and out of your mouth as vomit.

Constipation

Food can stay in your digestive system for a week, or even longer. Many people feel they have to open their bowels every day, but this is not necessarily so. Some people feel comfortable if they pass faeces only two or three times a week. If you can't easily get rid of faeces, you may well be constipated. It seems that severe constipation is more of a problem for girls and women than for males. Hormones may be a cause, since constipation regularly appears to be worse around the time of menstruation.

Taking laxatives to cure constipation is not a good idea. Prevention is much better than cure, so make sure you eat plenty of fibre, drink plenty of fluids, and exercise to stimulate the muscles of the large intestine.

Irritable bowel syndrome

There are several different symptoms of this disorder. You may have a pain in the abdomen, or constipation or diarrhoea, and may be tired or depressed. It may develop when you are under some kind of emotional stress, or may be the result of an allergic reaction. This problem is usually solved by additional fibre in the diet, and maybe some medication to reduce the irritation in the bowel.

Spreading it around

Proteins, carbohydrates, fats – we know the kinds of nutrients the body needs. They are used to provide energy and to help your body grow and work properly. But how does your body store these nutrients until they are needed? And how do they go to the right place?

Think of your body as a supermarket. A vehicle transports the nutrients to the store. The goods are then put into the loading bay. When they're ready, the goods are taken to the different aisles to be stacked up, ready to be collected. The vehicle is your blood, the loading bay is your liver. The rest of your body is the aisles.

First, the goods have to be processed in the digestion factory.

Carbohydrates

When you digest your food, carbohydrates are changed into a type of sugar called glucose. This is now ready to be dealt with by the supermarket.

Fats

Fat contains twice as much energy as the same weight of carbohydrates. When you digest fat, it breaks down into fatty acids and glycerol which can be processed by the supermarket body.

Proteins

Proteins are broken down in your intestine into substances called amino acids. Then these amino acids are carried to your liver in the bloodstream. Once they're in the loading bay liver, they go their different ways, ready to perform different functions.

Your body is a fascinating piece of machinery. It's amazing to think that it can figure out what to do with all these nutrients without you even realising it's all happening. Think how much is going on inside you just while you're reading this book.

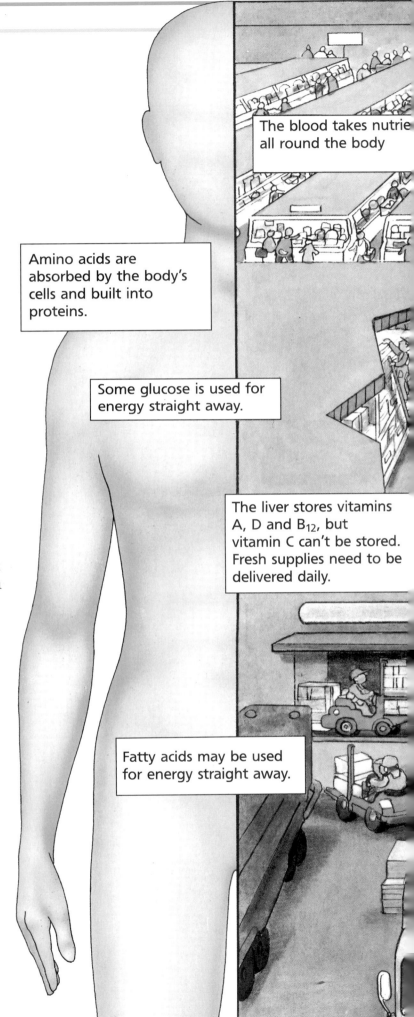

The blood takes nutrie[nts] all round the body

Amino acids are absorbed by the body's cells and built into proteins.

Some glucose is used for energy straight away.

The liver stores vitamins A, D and B_{12}, but vitamin C can't be stored. Fresh supplies need to be delivered daily.

Fatty acids may be used for energy straight away.

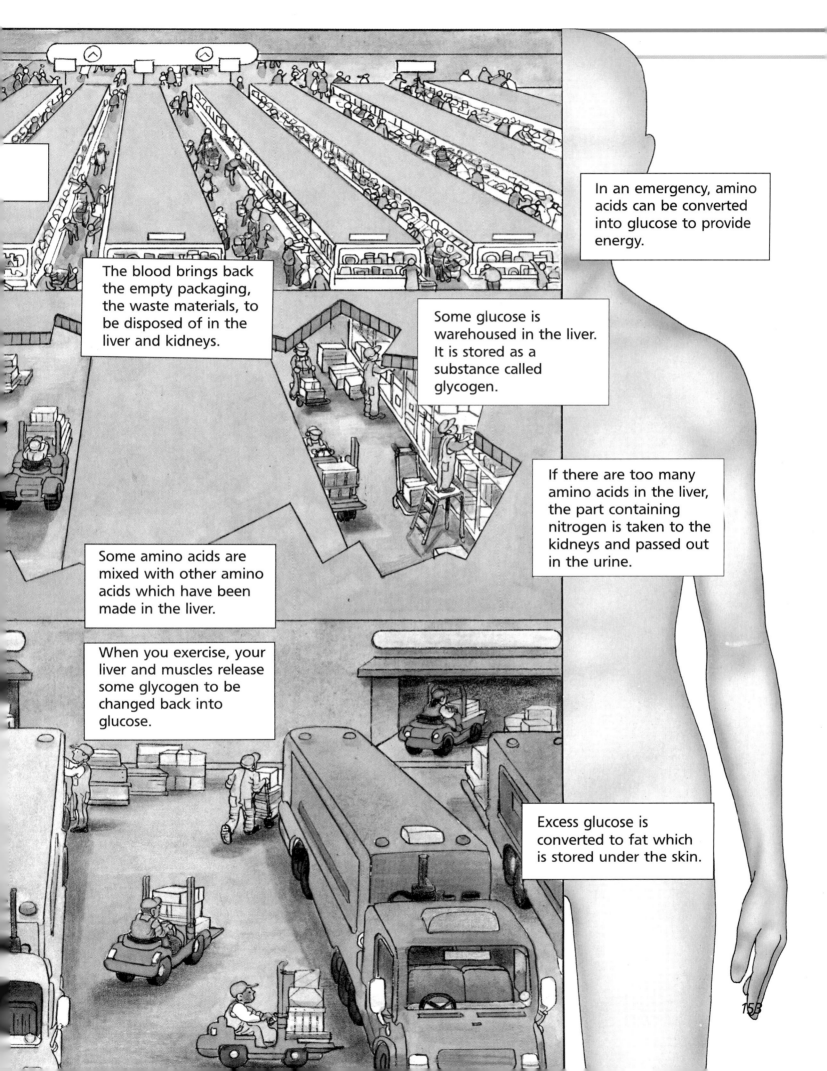

Energise!

Energy is the power you need to make your body work – whether you're sleeping peacefully or climbing a mountain! To energise means to supply your body with energy, and you do this by eating. Food is your body's fuel. But you need to make sure you put the right fuel in – after all, you wouldn't try to run a car on orange juice!

A car has a petrol tank that can be filled with a certain amount of fuel. When this has been used, the tank needs to be filled up. But your body is different. It can be filled with more fuel than it needs and can go on working for some time after the last intake of fuel. This is because your body can store fuel in the form of fat.

Burning it up

The energy in food can be measured in calories or kilojoules. You can find out more about this in the Expert's view on the opposite page. Some nutrients produce more energy than others.

1 gram of protein	1 gram of carbohydrate	1 gram of fat
• • • •		
produces 4 calories	produces 4 calories	produces 9 calories

You can see fat has a higher energy value per gram than protein or carbohydrate – it's a good food to eat for energy. But it's also the easiest nutrient for your body to store as fat. Be warned!

HOW FAST DOES IT GO? *Different activities burn up calories faster than others. These charts show how long you'd have to do the activities listed, in order to burn up the calories in the food.*

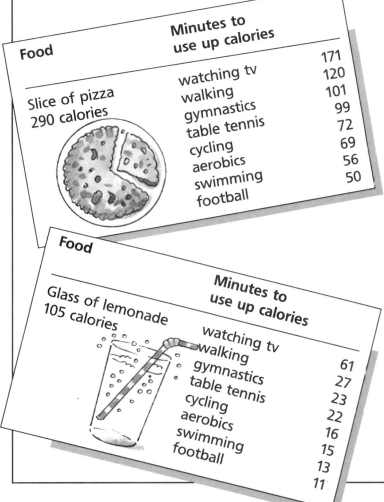

Food	Minutes to use up calories
Slice of pizza 290 calories	
watching tv	171
walking	120
gymnastics	101
table tennis	99
cycling	72
aerobics	69
swimming	56
football	50

Food	Minutes to use up calories
Glass of lemonade 105 calories	
watching tv	61
walking	27
gymnastics	23
table tennis	22
cycling	16
aerobics	15
swimming	13
football	11

Fuelling your framework

Scientists have worked out that a healthy young person who takes regular exercise needs to take in about 2,100-2,800 calories a day. You need part of this intake just to keep your heart beating, keep your lungs breathing and keep all your body tissues functioning. If you ask your body to take on extra work – like walking, running or swimming, it will need more energy, and so use up more calories.

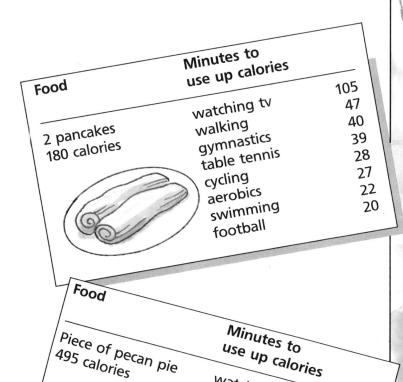

Food	Minutes to use up calories	
2 pancakes 180 calories	watching tv	105
	walking	47
	gymnastics	40
	table tennis	39
	cycling	28
	aerobics	27
	swimming	22
	football	20

Food	Minutes to use up calories	
Piece of pecan pie 495 calories	watching tv	291
	walking	130
	gymnastics	110
	table tennis	107
	cycling	78
	aerobics	75
	swimming	61
	football	55

The physics of energy

The food you eat is converted by your body into a form that the body can use. We say that the food is converted to energy.

As a useful way of measuring how much food we need, scientists can measure how much potential energy there is in different foods. This kind of measurement does not make any distinction between energy from fat, protein or carbohydrate.

To measure the energy given out by a food, the food is burned in a special strong steel chamber which is filled with oxygen. The chamber is surrounded by a jacket filled with water. As the food burns, it heats up the water in the jacket. The temperature of the water can then be measured to see how much heat energy the food has given out. The heat energy produced by the food is measured in calories.

Scientifically, a calorie is the amount of energy needed to raise the temperature of one gram of water by one degree Celsius. This is the measurement used to calculate heat energy in physics. Food calories are really kilocalories, or 1,000 heat calories.

Another unit used for measuring heat energy is the joule, which got its name from the British physicist, James P. Joule. A joule is equivalent to about 0.24 calories. One joule of energy per second is needed to pass one ampere of electric current through one ohm of resistance. A kilojoule is a unit of 1,000 joules.

Your metabolism

It's not fair! Some people can eat whatever they like and stay thin. Others feel that they only have to think about a wedge of chocolate cake, and they put on weight!

Why is this? Why can two people eat the same food and end up being such different shapes? The answer lies in their metabolism.

Energy from food

Metabolism is the word given to the sum of all the different processes that go on in the cells of your body. That includes the process of converting food into energy that your body can use. The speed of metabolism varies from person to person, and is called the metabolic rate. Your metabolic rate can be measured by how much oxygen you take in, or how much carbon dioxide you give off.

Quick or slow?

Someone with a slow rate of metabolism converts food into energy slowly. They are likely to store food on their body as fat. A high rate of metabolism is just the opposite. Food is converted into energy quickly, and doesn't need to be stored. People with a high rate of metabolism are often the ones who can eat what they like without a second thought, though they still need to eat a balanced diet to stay healthy.

Changing your metabolism

While there are people whose rate of metabolism is fixed at one extreme or another, most people fall somewhere in between. However, everyone is born with a particular metabolic rate which they can't change. However they can do one thing to ensure they burn up more calories.

Exercise, of any kind, will increase your metabolic rate and helps you to use up energy. Whether you're walking the dog or playing football regularly, using your body will speed up your metabolism. The more fat you burn off your body, and the less weight you carry round, the better your metabolism will function.

food

Your heating system

Have you ever noticed that your body heat increases after you've eaten a meal? That's because digesting and absorbing food uses up energy, increasing the metabolic rate and producing body heat. This process is called thermogenesis. It is usually slim people who burn off most calories this way. But some people with a slow rate of metabolism also have a very efficient thermogen system.

Metabolism

A high metabolic rate converts food to energy not fat.

energy

Metabolism is the term used for all the chemical and physical processes that continually take place in the body to keep it alive and healthy. Metabolism includes the processes of producing energy from digested food, storing excess nutrients and preparing waste material. It also includes the building up of proteins needed by the tissues from amino acids.

Metabolism produces heat which allows the body to stay at a constant temperature. It also allows the functions of the internal organs and muscles to carry on. These include the beating of the heart, breathing and the working of the nervous system.

Any form of regular exercise, such as jogging, helps to increase your metabolic rate.

To carry out all these processes, metabolism needs energy, which is measured in calories. The amount of energy used up is known as the metabolic rate.

The basal metabolic rate, or BMR for short, is the amount of energy needed by the body just to stay alive. It does not include any energy needed for physical activity, like walking or swimming, or the energy that is needed to digest food. The BMR is measured when the body is lying down at complete rest, after a 12-hour fast. The total amount of air breathed out from the lungs is measured over a period of 20 to 30 minutes and the level of oxygen in this air is taken. The BMR is worked out from these measurements.

The BMR varies from one person to another. It depends mainly on how much lean tissue — muscles and internal organs — a person has in their body. The more lean tissue they have, the higher their BMR. Females are usually lighter in weight than males, and have less lean tissue and more body fat. For this reason, the BMR is usually 10 per cent lower in females than in males. It also varies at different stages of life. For example, in relation to their body size, babies and growing children have a high metabolic rate. The amount of lean tissue usually becomes less with age, so elderly people have a lower BMR than younger adults.

Equally, a slim person may feel the cold less than a fat one. Although a chunky person may look well-insulated against the cold, you may find that person shivering when the temperature drops. That's because their metabolism isn't burning enough calories to keep their body heat up. A thin person with good thermogenesis will make more body heat. Their own personal central heating will keep them warm.

Weight and growth

When you step on to a set of scales, you read your weight in kilos. You may have seen the kind of chart that tells you what the ideal weight for someone of your height should be. These charts give you a weight to aim for. But the scales don't tell you what kind of figure you should have to achieve these ideals. How do you know if you are too fat, too thin or just right?

Here are two charts showing you the average weights and heights of boys and girls. But what is average? Charts like these are worked out by taking the weight and height of thousands of young people, adding together the measurements and dividing the total weight and height by the number of people measured. The average weight doesn't mean that this is the weight you should be. Your weight won't settle down until you are in your twenties. Muscle weighs more than fat, so the weighing machine is not always an accurate way of finding out if you have too much fat.

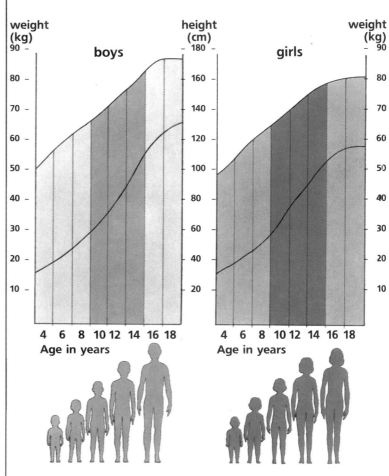

ARE YOU AVERAGE?
These graphs show the average height and weight of boys and girls. Remember that everyone is different, and people don't all grow at the same rate.

Growing taller

Have you grown a lot recently? If you are in the middle of a growth spurt, your weight might be lower than average for your height. Perhaps you've shot up in height recently. Your limbs are gangly and you seem very skinny. You're underweight because you haven't yet built up the muscles to go with your new shape.

Make sure you eat lots of protein while your body is growing, and keep exercising to help the muscle grow firm and strong. Give your body another year to settle down before you check the chart again.

Growth spurts

At the start of puberty, hormones trigger a sudden burst of growth. Hormones are chemical substances produced by glands in your body. One of their vital functions is to control growth.

In girls, the growth spurt usually starts before they start to develop sexually, while boys have often already started to develop before the growth spurt begins. Many girls start their growth spurt when they are 10 or 11, and boys at 12 or 13. This means that for a while, girls tend to be taller than boys. Boys can grow by between 7 and 12 centimetres in a single year, and girls from 6 to 11 centimetres.

Not all parts of your body grow at the same rate. You will find that your feet and hands grow first. You might need several new pairs of shoes in a year. Then your arms and legs grow longer. Lastly, the rest of your body grows. The shape of your body also changes, with girls developing wider hips, and boys' shoulders becoming broader.

How old you are when you start your growth spurt makes no difference to your final adult height. Your final adult height depends largely on how tall the members of your family are. Growth spurts do not usually last for more than a year or two. Afterwards, you grow more slowly until you reach your adult height at the age of about 19. All this rapid growth means that you might get more tired and hungry than usual. Make sure that you have enough rest, and plenty of good food.

BODY SHAPE

You only have to look around to see that there are as many different body shapes as there are people. Scientists have identified three main body shapes. Most people are a mixture of the three. On the right are the three basic shapes.

Scientists use a scale from 1 to 7 to evaluate how much of each basic shape a person has. Four-four-four means an absolute average of each!

Whatever shape you are, you will have inherited that shape, and you will not be able to alter it dramatically. All you can do is keep it in good condition.

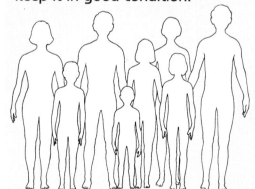

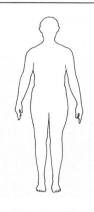

1. Endomorph
An endomorph is well rounded, with a heavy build and plenty of body fat. They often have large internal organs.

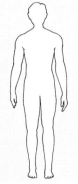

2. Mesomorph
A mesomorph has a classic athlete's body, with a broad chest and well muscled arms and legs. They have little body fat.

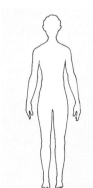

3. Ectomorph
An ectomorph is thin and angular. Ectomorphs don't carry much muscle or fat. They are often tall.

Does perfection exist?

Remember that there's no such thing as the perfect shape. 'Perfection' is all to do with current fashion, and fashions come and go. A couple of centuries ago in Europe, it was considered very fashionable to be plump and curvy. This is still so in some parts of the world. In the next European fashion phase, women went through agonies squeezing their waists into tight corsets, despite the fact that this often damaged the organs inside their bodies. There's no need for you to go to extremes. If your body is fit and healthy, and your posture and confidence carry this off to good effect, it will look attractive whatever its shape.

Getting it right

Are you one of those people who look at their bodies and worry that they are too fat or too thin, too short or too tall, too straight or too curvy? If so, you're not alone! A lot of people aren't satisfied with their shape. You can't work miracles by changing your diet, but eating well can make your body feel good.

Weight worries

You don't need to lose weight unless you have so much extra fat on your body that there's a risk that you could strain your heart. If you think you are a little bit overweight, think about what you're eating. How many portions of chips or pieces of cake do you eat every week, how many fizzy drinks do you drink? You may find by cutting down on foods like this, you'll soon take off that extra kilo. If you're really worried about your weight, talk to your doctor about it.

Weighing too little can be bad for you, too. You risk picking up infections, and you may feel weak and tired because you aren't eating enough to give you the energy you need.

Read what the expert answer is to some readers' questions on dieting.

"I sometimes think I'm too fat, but other people always say I look just right for my height. How can I tell who's right?"
Charlie

Expert comment: The answer is that there is no hard and fast rule which says "now you are overweight". Get to know your body and its ideal shape, study the section on your weight on page 158 and use the weight chart as a very rough guide. This will help you determine if your body is carrying extra weight. If you're heavier than average but your body's all muscle, there's no need to worry! Concentrate on being healthy and worry less about what you weigh.

"I went on a diet last year and lost weight. I still want to lose a kilo, and I've been trying extra hard. I've been really good, but I just can't lose it. Why is this?"
Alexia

Expert comment: You may not realize that dieting slows down your metabolic rate. So each time you diet you need to consume fewer and fewer calories before your body starts to shed fat. Make sure you exercise as well as dieting. Exercise should increase your metabolic rate again, so that extra kilo should just burn off!

"I'm really tempted to go on a diet, but I've heard that dieting can be dangerous. Is this true?"
Rory

Expert comment: Yes, it can. For example, there are people who think they should be thinner, even though they are thin already. They diet until they are dangerously thin and become ill. These people are suffering from the slimmers' disease, anorexia nervosa, which you can find out more about in the section on eating problems on page 162. If you are dedicated to starting a diet, make sure it is a sound one. Talk it through carefully with an adult first. Set a goal for your weight loss and set aside a reasonable amount of time to achieve it, so that you lose weight slowly. Combine exercise with the diet so you speed up your metabolic rate. If you're careful, and you really need to lose weight, the only problem you should have in following a sensible diet is will power!

"I want to lose weight, but I love food! Whenever I sit down to eat a meal, all my will power goes and I eat as much as I always do. Will it help if I eat something sweet before a meal so that I'm not so hungry?"
Terry

Expert comment: Sweets do kill your appetite because they raise the blood sugar level and your body thinks it's been fed. But, an hour later, your blood sugar level has dropped and you'll be hungry again. And if you've missed the chance of a well-balanced, filling meal, you'll probably end up eating unhealthy snacks instead. Try to eat smaller portions, but enjoy your meals!

"My friend wants to lose weight in time for a party next weekend. I said she'd have no chance, but she's sure she can do it by going on a crash diet. What is a crash diet?"
Tina

Expert comment: People go on crash diets when they want to lose weight fast. They cut down drastically on the amount of food they eat for a week or so and usually lose some weight. But most of this weight is lost as water, so they put it on again very quickly. Crash diets are a shock to the system – they're not a good way to control your body weight. Severe crash diets cause loss of muscle, which is later put back on as fat. If your friend really wants to take off weight, she should take it slowly, eating plenty of fruit and vegetables, and cutting down on snacks and sweets.

Special cases

Imagine all the fats, proteins, sugars, starches, vitamins and minerals in your body as a team who are always working to keep your body active and healthy. A successful team like this depends on everyone working together. When some of that team are missing, things can start to go wrong.

Malnutrition

Someone suffering from malnutrition has an incomplete team of nutrients. Malnutrition is bad nutrition. It is a problem caused by eating too little, or from eating too many of the wrong things. If you ate nothing but doughnuts you'd soon be suffering from malnutrition, because you wouldn't be supplying your body with the protein and vitamins it needs. Over a period of time, malnutrition causes ill-health, and even death.

Starving your system

When someone starves, it means that the body is deprived of the material and energy it needs to grow and stay fit. When that happens, the only alternative is for it to use up what is already there. The body starts first on the stored fat. When all the fat is used up, it moves on to use energy in the muscles. When the muscles start to weaken, a person becomes lethargic and less able to resist infection. The body cells stop repairing and replacing themselves and all the body processes slow down – until they eventually stop altogether. Starvation takes a long time. The body has to be deprived of nutrients for about 60 or 70 days before death occurs.

Anorexia nervosa and bulimia

Some people, particularly teenage girls, become obsessed with trying to gain the kind of 'ideal' figure they see on TV and in advertisements. Some diet so much that they end up with an illness called anorexia nervosa. Anorexics become afraid of eating any food, in case it makes them put on weight. They make excuses not to eat. They manage to reduce their weight by vomiting, taking laxatives and taking excessive exercise. They get thinner and thinner. They can't stop. Even when they are painfully thin, anorexics still believe they're fat.

There are serious side effects of becoming anorexic. Sufferers' blood pressure falls, their heartbeat slows down, their hair falls out, their periods stop (or fail to start), and soft, downy hair may grow on their bodies.

Bulimia is another eating disorder. Bulimics eat huge amounts of food at one go – they binge. But they avoid getting fat by vomiting or by taking large doses of laxatives, which can damage their bodies.

Anorexia and bulimia aren't just physical illnesses. They are caused by mental problems, which need careful psychological treatment. If you think you are anorexic or bulimic, you should ask for help straight away. You could save your own life.

Beating bulimia

"When I was 14, I went to a girls' boarding school. It was there that my friends and I developed a preoccupation with food. We bought bagfuls of brownies and gobbled them down. We stuffed ourselves with peanut butter and bacon sandwiches.

I remember one year when we studied Roman civilization, we came across a footnote explaining how the Romans made a practice of retreating to a room known as the vomitorium during their feasts. After vomiting, they would return to the feast and start all over again. "Aha," we thought, "here's a way to have our cake and **not** eat it too!" It gave us a heady sense of being in control. We barely seemed to notice that the more we vomited ourselves into emptiness, the more we needed to eat. I didn't understand for a long time that the act of vomiting causes a sudden drop in blood sugar which, in turn, produces a craving for more food. We had no idea that what we were playing with was anything but harmless. For some, this starve/binge/vomit cycle proves fatal. For several of us at my school, it was the beginning of a nightmarish addiction that would undermine our lives for decades to come – an addiction as dangerous as alcohol or drugs and perhaps as difficult to beat.

When I was in London many years later, I was fortunate enough to meet a wonderful doctor. Until I met this doctor, no one had ever explained that there were other ways of losing weight besides starvation diets. If only I had known what I was doing to myself! If I had only understood twenty years ago the futility of trying to fit oneself into a mould. It was as if I was thinking of myself as a product rather than a person. I had yet to learn that the most satisfying way of life comes from making the most of what you really are."

Jane Fonda is an American film actress. She has appeared in about 35 films, of which she has also produced several. Jane Fonda has devised fitness and workout programmes and tapes that have become very popular. She also holds strong opinions on politics and has campaigned energetically for the causes she believes in.

A medical diet

Diabetes is a very common disease. In fact, it's possible to have diabetes and not know it. No one knows what causes this disease, although doctors know that there are some hereditary factors.

Symptoms of diabetes are excessive thirst and excessive urination. The body of a diabetic is not very efficient at using sugar, so sugar builds up in the blood. Some of this sugar comes out of the body in the urine, some stays in the body and makes the sufferer ill. A hormone called insulin enables healthy bodies to use and store sugar. Diabetics who do not have enough insulin to process the sugar in the blood have to inject daily doses of insulin to do the job.

As well as some diabetics taking daily insulin, all diabetics must follow a careful diet. They have to balance the amount of fat, carbohydrate and protein they eat, and need to make sure their meals are at regular times. If they are not careful, their blood sugar may become too low, and they become dizzy, shaky and weak. If this happens they must quickly eat some sugar or drink orange juice to increase the blood sugar level. It works almost instantly. Diabetics usually carry something sweet around with them in case of emergencies.

An apple will give you vitamin C and some fibre.

A peanut butter sandwich is a high protein snack.

Hamburgers are very quick to make.

Fast food

You rush back home with only half an hour to eat, wash and change, and be ready to go out again. So what can you eat? There's no time to chop and cook and prepare a proper meal. It has to be 'fast food'!

Fast food is any food that you purchase in a ready, or nearly ready, state. You might buy it from a take-away, or eat it in snack bar. You can buy it from a van in the street, from the kiosk at the railway station or even from a slot machine. A lot of the food you'll find in the supermarket is 'fast', too. Think of the pre-cooked or frozen meals that are ready to eat after five minutes in the microwave.

Good and quick

There's no reason why fast food can't be as nutritious and healthy as any other food. The food you can buy in fast food restaurants isn't necessarily any worse for you than food prepared at home. You could choose a baked potato with grated cheese, or a Chinese take-away. A pizza topped with meat, vegetables and cheese is full of goodness. And a sandwich made with wholemeal bread, filled with tuna and cucumber, makes a delicious snack.

Fast versus junk

So why does fast food have a bad reputation? The reason is that so much of the fast food you can buy is highly processed. It is often high in fat and low in fibre, and short of valuable vitamins and minerals. This so-called 'junk' food contains too much of the wrong things, and too little of the right ones. It won't do you much good, but then it won't do you much harm either, provided that you don't eat it all the time.

If you chose to eat nothing but hamburgers, fried chicken or fries, you'd undoubtedly invite moans about eating junk food. But even worse, and more 'junky', are the foods that are laden with sugar, salt and fat. They include cakes, sweets, ices, sweet biscuits, fizzy drinks and bags of crisps.

Milkshakes contain a lot of sugar and fat.

You'll be doing your body a favour if you don't eat too many french fries.

Nature's fast food store

Fast food can turn up just about anywhere. If you think of it as food which is instantly ready to eat, then fast food can just as well be an apple picked from a tree, or a handful of blackberries or strawberries. How about a banana, an orange, a kiwi fruit, a piece of cheese, a carton of yoghurt, a slice of water melon, or a piece of pitta bread? All of these are healthy foods – and fast foods too.

The quickest, fastest, and most convenient food is milk. It's almost the most perfect food too. There's more protein in half a litre of milk than in 100 grams of meat. Now no-one could describe milk as 'junk' food, could they? But it's certainly fast.

It's your choice

It may sometimes seem easier to make the 'wrong' choice, and go for the most convenient option. There are burger bars round every corner and bars of chocolate at every supermarket checkout. You can kill your appetite in one go with a carton of french fries. But Nature's fast food store can also cope with most of your orders. What's more, the food is quite cheap, much healthier than junk food – and it doesn't create a lot of litter!

A glass of cool milk is a great drink.

Why be vegetarian?

Vegetarian is the word that describes people who do not eat meat. Maybe you don't eat meat already, or perhaps you have friends who don't.

There are several reasons why people become vegetarian. Some people believe that it is wrong to eat animals or animal products for moral reasons. They are put off by certain forms of rearing animals for food, such as battery farming and intensive farming. Many people start on the path to vegetarianism by cutting out one or two types of meat, such as red meat and meat products. Eventually, as they get used to eating more meals based on vegetable protein, they may cut out other meats. They may cut out all other animal products, too.

Some people live in places where it is very difficult to get meat. If the agricultural land in that region is not suitable for raising animals, meat will be very expensive to buy. The local people will probably eat mainly cereals, vegetables and fruit.

Religious and cultural rules are another reason why many people adopt a vegetarian diet. The Coptic Church of Ethiopia, for example, forbids the eating of meat on more than 200 days in the year. Jainism, which is a very ancient religion in India, teaches a reverence for all life. The strictest Jainists will not even eat root vegetables, or eat or drink at night, in case they kill an insect by mistake.

These turkeys have been intensively reared.

Beef cattle are sometimes kept in a very confined space.

People of the Jain religion vow never to kill any living thing.

OTHER REASONS FOR BEING VEGETARIAN

Ecology
Some people believe that meat-eating makes inefficient use of food supplies. Without adding in the cost of labour and machinery, four hectares of land could provide enough soya protein for 61 people. Or it could provide wheat protein for 24 people, or maize for 10. But if the land were used for cattle rearing, it would provide meat protein for only two people.

Soya protein 61 people

Wheat protein 24 people

The vegetarian diet

People who don't eat meat or animal products are known as vegetarian. There are different types of vegetarian diet, depending on which animal foods are excluded:

Ovo-lacto-vegetarians do not eat meat or fish, but do drink milk and eat dairy foods and eggs.

Lacto-vegetarians leave out eggs, meat and fish from their diet, but include milk and dairy foods.

Ovo-vegetarians do not drink milk or eat dairy foods, meat or fish. They do eat eggs.

Fruitarians eat only raw fruit, nuts, cereals and seeds.

Vegans do not eat any foods of animal origin – even honey.

Vegetarians have to be especially careful to eat a balanced diet. Animal protein, in other words, meat, fish, dairy foods and eggs, contains all the essential amino acids in amounts that the body needs. However, plant proteins, from foods such as grains, nuts, seeds and legumes, do not usually contain enough of one or more of the essential amino acids.

By putting two plant foods together at one meal – for example, beans (a legume) with wheat (a grain) – the right balance of amino acids can be obtained. The right combination of foods results in complete protein.

These are the ways different plant proteins can be combined:

grain + legume – eg beans on toast

grain + nuts – eg nut rissoles with brown rice

seeds + legume – eg hummus made from tahini paste (sesame seeds) and chick peas.

Adding milk or eggs improves the quality of plant proteins:
cheese + grain – eg macaroni cheese

milk + legume – eg lentil lasagne

eggs + grain – eg eggs on toast

So it is possible for vegetarians to eat enough protein without too much difficulty. What is harder is to ensure that they get enough vitamins and minerals.

Vegetarians must be particularly careful to take in enough iron. Meat provides a unique form of iron, called haem iron. This is more easily absorbed into the body than iron found in plant foods. People who choose not to eat meat must ensure that they get enough iron from other foods. Dried fruits, legumes, eggs and fortified breakfast cereals all contain iron. Vitamin C helps the body to absorb iron, so a glass of orange juice with a meal, or a piece of fresh fruit eaten afterwards is a good idea.

Obviously in a world where half the population is under fed, there are good, practical reasons for 'growing' crops not animals.

Maize protein
10 people

Meat protein
2 people

Health

The vegetarian diet is high in fibre and starchy carbohydrates. This is excellent for your health. But meat is high in protein, iron, zinc and B vitamins so if you stop eating meat, you must ensure you get enough of these nutrients from other sources. Nuts and soya beans are protein-rich foods, lentils and dried fruits provide iron, and cereals provide B vitamins.

Food allergies

A food allergy is a reaction to something you have eaten. Most of the time you are protected by your immune system, but some foods, often proteins, cannot be contained by this. An allergy is usually mild and affects only the skin, but some may affect your breathing. Some allergies are inherited. You might have had allergies to many things when you were small – you probably don't even remember these, but ask your parents. They will certainly remember if one particular food made you sick! Young children tend to grow out of allergies before they're three, but others can last a lifetime.

Many people suffer from allergies to foods. Sometimes they don't even realize an allergy exists because they avoid a particular food which they don't like, or which they know upsets them.

Eczema, which is a skin disorder, and asthma which affects breathing, are two common allergic reactions. Another is migraine. This is a very severe headache which may be accompanied by disturbances in your eyesight, like seeing flashing lights or experiencing double vision, even by tingling sensations or dizziness. Migraine sufferers can experience sickness and they cannot bear strong lights or loud noise. Some migraines seem to be caused by a reaction to foods such as cheese, chocolate, red wine and smoked or salted meat.

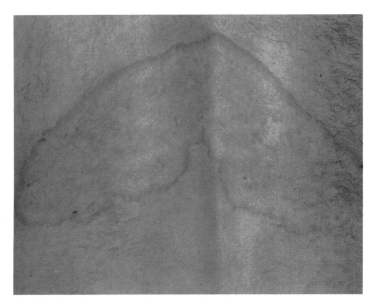

Immediate reaction

Allergic reactions usually start within a few minutes of eating the problem food. Signs to look out for are tingling in the mouth or throat, vomiting, pain or burning sensation in the stomach, difficulty in breathing and runny eyes.

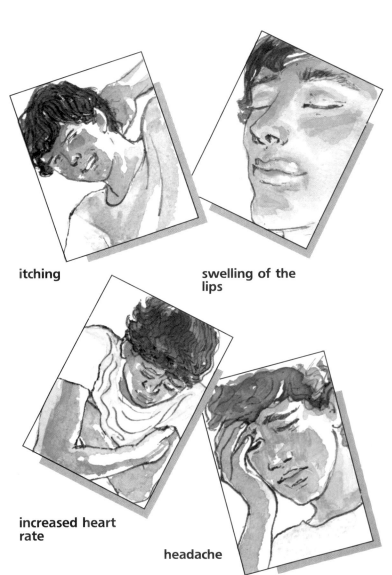

itching

swelling of the lips

increased heart rate

headache

Delayed reaction

Some allergic reactions start a few hours after you have eaten the food, and can include diarrhoea, a feeling of being bloated, constipation and a severe headache.

A rash like this may be caused by fish, eggs, berries or nuts

Identify the culprit!

Eczema and asthma have many different causes, not all of them related to food. People can be allergic to dust, to mites and animal fur or to anything else in the environment. It's essential to find out what's causing a problem before giving up a favourite food.

Treatment of an allergy involves avoiding the food that triggers off the reaction. But sufferers may have trouble in identifying which of the many thousands of ingredients in a food is the culprit. A proper diagnosis is essential. No-one should attempt self-diagnosis or spend money on 'allergy clinics' until they have seen a doctor for advice.

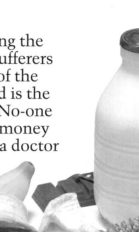

Some common causes

A reaction to shellfish is one of the most common of these problem foods. People are also frequently allergic to eggs, milk, soya, coffee, tea, chocolate, bananas, oranges, strawberries, yeast extract or cheese. These can all bring on allergy symptoms.

An allergy to one protein – gluten – is also common, affecting about one in two thousand people. Gluten is found in wheat, barley and rye. The number of foods which contain gluten is vast. It includes breakfast cereals, porridge, pancakes, cakes, pasta, pizza, buns, and bread, in fact, the list is almost endless. Staple crops containing gluten are also added to many processed foods, as well as being eaten in their natural form.

If you think that cow's milk is causing you problems, consult your doctor. Some people find goat's or ewe's milk does not upset them. But soya milk isn't necessarily a good alternative as many people are allergic to that as well.

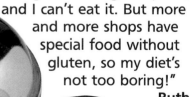

Reader's experience

"I was quite ill a few years ago. I was constantly short of breath, I had terrible cramps in my muscles, and a swollen stomach. I thought it was dairy products that were disagreeing with me, so I stopped eating them. But I went on feeling really bloated and uncomfortable.

At first the doctor wasn't sure what was wrong with me, but then she decided to do an allergy test. She found out that I was allergic to gluten. Now I have to avoid all the foods which contain gluten. That means no bread, no pasta, no cakes. It's quite difficult – especially when all my friends are eating something like pizza, and I can't eat it. But more and more shops have special food without gluten, so my diet's not too boring!"

Ruth

Food additives

"Waiter, waiter, there's a fly in my soup..."
"Don't shout so loudly, Sir, or everyone will want one."

Unlike the fly above, many substances are deliberately added during the preparation of food. These substances are called additives. Although you've probably heard people say that additives are unnecessary, it would be difficult to produce manufactured food without them. They help food taste and smell good, stay fresher and, when used as processing aids, they also help liquid or solid foods to stay that way.

Some additives, like salt and spices, are quite natural. Others are man-made chemicals. In fact, most of the prepared food we eat, such as oven-ready meals, canned food and anything that comes in a packet, wouldn't be edible by the time they reached our shelves if additives were not added.

Additive arguments

There are many arguments about the use of additives. They centre around three main questions. Are they really safe, are they effective, and are they really necessary? Individual countries and groups of consumers, like the EC or USA, have their own lists of what is and what is not considered acceptable and safe. Many natural products, like vitamin C, also known as ascorbic acid, will appear on a list of additives – and no one can dispute the benefit that has on our health. But other additives may be harmful.

FOR OR AGAINST?

Al is in favour of additives.

Here are his arguments to support their use.

"Adding additives means that we can buy foods from far away so we get more variety in our diet."

"They keep food prices down because foods with additives can be made in bulk and stored."

"They help food to last longer by preventing it from going bad as quickly as it might in its natural state."

"They help give us healthier alternatives to traditional foods, for instance low fat spread as opposed to butter, or diet drinks instead of sugar-laden ones."

"Without the addition of permitted colours, margarine would look grey! Colouring makes food look more appetizing."

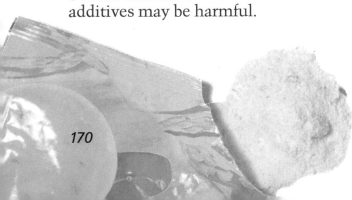

Jenny is against the use of additives.

This is her case.

"Some additives can be bad for your health. The sweetener cyclamate, which is 30 times sweeter than sugar, was banned in the UK and the USA because it was feared it might cause cancer."

"Some young people have an unpleasant reaction to additives like tartrazine – a yellow colouring."

"Additives can be used to disguise second-rate food by introducing colourings and flavourings."

"Foods can be filled with air and water, giving a false impression of how much food you're actually getting for your money."

WHAT DO ADDITIVES DO?

Anti-caking agents
These stop dry foods like flour and sugar from going lumpy.

Anti-oxidants
Anti-oxidants are used to stop a process called oxidising. Fat goes rancid and fruit juices turn brown when they are exposed to the air, but anti-oxidants prevent this.

Colourings
These are added to give colour. Some are natural like yellow saffron, or paprika which is red. Sometimes colouring is added to suggest that a food contains an ingredient. Some orange coloured fizzy drinks may have no real orange in them at all!

E additives
In Europe, there's a long list of additives that has been approved by the European Community. Manufacturers have to list any additives on food labels, and identify them with what's called their E number. If you see an ingredient listed as E-something, you'll know that the EC has given it the OK.

Emulsifiers and stabilizers
Emulsifiers make it possible to mix oil and water, as in the case of low fat spreads and mayonnaise. Stabilizers, used in the same foods, stop the emulsified mixture from separating back into its original components.

Flavour enhancers
One of the most common flavour enhancers is monosodium glutamate, or MSG. This is used in hundreds of processed foods to make them taste better. Glutamate occurs naturally in our bodies and is found in plentiful quantities in soya beans.

Flavourings
Many flavourings are natural. Citrus oil comes from lemons and gives a lemon flavour to food. But some flavourings are man-made.

Preservatives
Preservatives help to keep food fresh longer. Chemicals such as sorbic acid and saltpetre are used for this. You can find out about other methods of preserving food on the next pages.

Sweeteners
Sweeteners are probably the most tested group of food additives. There have been fears that some sweeteners cause illness, but until there's firm proof either way, many remain in use. Saccharin and aspartame are artificial sweeteners that enable many processed foods to be called 'low calorie' by reducing or doing away with sugar. They're around 200 times sweeter than sugar – so you don't need very much. These artificial sweeteners can also be a good alternative for diabetics who can't tolerate sugar in their diet.

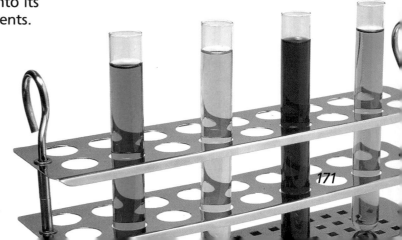

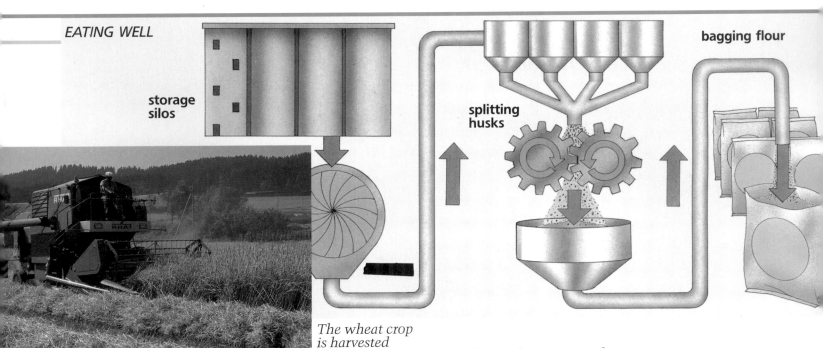

storage
silos

splitting
husks

bagging flour

The wheat crop is harvested using a combine harvester.

Change means process!

A lot of the food we eat has been processed in some way. Maybe you think that doesn't sound too healthy. When you hear the word processed, you probably think of additives, preservatives and plastic supermarket packaging. You might think it's better to eat natural, unprocessed foods.

But wait a minute. Think about digging your fork into a whole, un-gutted fish, or trying to spread milk on a pile of wheat grains! These foods need to be processed in order to transform them into something you can actually eat — a fillet of fish, butter and bread.

Processing is just a way of describing how food is prepared so that it is ready to cook and eat. Processing can also improve the food in some way, and make it taste better or keep longer. But does processing make the food any less natural or healthy? That really depends on how many additives are put in, and how much of the original goodness is left. There's no reason why processed food shouldn't be just as healthy as unprocessed food.

Let's look at cereals

Cereal crops are the seeds of grasses grown for food. When a cereal grows well in an area, it often becomes a major part of the diet of the people living there. It becomes a staple food. But cereals are more often eaten in their processed state than in their natural form.

Important cereals around the world are shown in the chart below.

Cereal	Area where staple food
Wheat	All over the world
Maize	South America, Africa
Rice	China, India, Pakistan, North and South America, Italy
Millet	China, India, Russia, West Africa
Rye	Northern Europe, Asia, North America
Oats	Northern Europe, North America
Barley	Northern Europe, Canada, Spain

FROM WHEAT TO BREAD

Bread is one of the most important foods we know. It can be made from several kinds of cereal grain once these have been processed into flour. Most bread is made from flour which comes from wheat grain.

The grain is harvested from the field, separated from its outer husk and cleaned to remove dust and soil. Sometimes it is also treated with chemicals at this point, to ensure that the grain stays fresh and does not get damp or go mouldy. The next part of the process depends on whether the flour will be white or wholemeal.

White flour

White flour has to go through several stages of processing. At the mill, the grain is ground between rollers. These strip off another layer of grain – the bran – and crush the remaining grain into flour. This process is called milling. The wheat germ – the part of the grain where the seed grows – is also removed. Millers may enrich the flour by adding iron and vitamins to it.

Wholemeal flour

Wholemeal flour needs less processing. The whole of the grain is crushed and used, including the bran and the wheat germ. Nothing is taken away, which means that it is more natural, and better for you. By retaining the bran and wheat germ, the wheat holds valuable fibre, protein, fat and some vitamins. Its nutty flavour is delicious, too!

baking

Processed into
bread, cakes, pasta
breakfast cereals, salad dressing, vegetable oil, corn meal, popcorn
savoury and sweet dishes, breakfast cereal, flour, wine
flatbreads, porridge, and used like rice
crispbread, black rye bread, rye whisky, gin
biscuits, cookies, breakfast cereals
soup, beer, whisky

Organic produce

Many farmers spray chemicals on crops to destroy pests and weeds, and add chemicals to grain after it has been harvested. Some scientists and farmers think this is wrong. They believe the chemicals, which are sometimes poisonous, stay in the fruit and vegetables. In other words, these people favour organic farming, farming without using any artificial chemicals. Other people argue that we are being tricked into paying high prices for organic food when there is no real evidence that the chemicals are dangerous.

Whatever you feel about organic food, organic farming is certainly better for the environment and kinder to animals. Organically reared animals are not given drugs to force them to grow quicker or larger than normal, while other methods of rearing animals do use drugs for these purposes. But in the end, it's for you to decide whether organic food is worth the extra price you have to pay.

Keep it fresh!

The availability of fresh natural produce is one of the bonuses of living in today's world. At any time of the year you may be able to eat kiwi fruit from New Zealand, oranges from Florida and pineapples from the Pacific. Fresh natural produce is extremely good for you, because it's full of the nutrients you need.

Many people buy some fresh foods daily, like bread or milk, but others we like to buy in advance, and store the food until we need them. If you do store fresh food for any length of time, there's a chance that it will go bad. You will soon know when this has happened – it will start to smell bad and you may even see mould growing on it. Most deterioration is caused by the natural ageing of the food itself or by microbes, including moulds and bacteria. The toxins, or poisons, produced by some bacteria can cause food poisoning, so it's important not to let the bacteria develop in the food in the first place.

The solutions

You already know that additives and preservatives are used to keep processed foods in good condition. But what about fresh food? There are different ways of preserving fresh food. Some change the taste and texture of the food a great deal, while others keep it nearly as fresh as the day it was picked or packaged.

Machines fill these bottles at great speed.

Pickling

Onions, eggs, herring, walnuts, vegetables and citrus fruits are examples of food that can be pickled. Food is kept in a preservative like acetic acid, which is found naturally as vinegar or wine. This kills off micro-organisms. Jam is 'pickled' too – but using sugar as the preservative instead.

Bottling

Bottling is done in the same way as canning – the difference lies in the container, which is made of glass.

Drying

Foods that can be dried include fruits, vegetables, herbs, spices, pasta, fish and meat. Drying uses heat to remove water from food. This makes it difficult for the microbes to grow. It destroys most of the vitamins in the food, but doesn't affect the proteins.

Smoking

Foods that can be smoked include ham, bacon, cheese, fish, and bananas. Smoking usually involves soaking the food in salt solution – the salt stops the microbes breeding. Then the food is dried in hot smoke made by burning wood shavings. The smoke leaves some chemicals on the food which the microbes don't like either.

Watch out, though – some food sold today with a smoky flavour hasn't been smoked! It's been treated with chemicals such as pyroligneous acid, and won't last any longer than fresh food.

Encapsulating or Vacuum Packing

Most kinds of food can be treated this way. The food is sterilised by heating it, then it is placed in a sterile, sealed container.

No air comes in contact with the food, and no moisture can touch it, so the food can be kept for long periods of time without refrigeration.

These pies have not been cooked before freezing.

Freezing

A large number of foods can be frozen. Freezing stops microbes working. The colder it is, the longer the food will last. Freezing is good for keeping ready cooked meals and prepared food.

Some vitamins and minerals are destroyed when food is frozen but, generally, freezing preserves nutrients well. Frozen peas and other vegetables can contain more Vitamin C than those bought from a market or those stored at home for a while. This is because frozen vegetables are blanched – put in boiling water for a few moments or two – almost as soon as they are picked. This preserves all the vitamin C in the vegetables at that moment.

Canning

Cans are used to preserve vegetables, fruit, fish, meat – in fact almost anything. The food is first cleaned, cut and prepared. Machines

Large cans are filled with strawberries.

then fill cans with raw food. The cans are sealed, then heated to destroy microbes. More nutrients are lost in canning than in freezing, but canned food lasts much longer than frozen food.

Sterilisation – or UHT

This process is used for milk, cream, and some yoghurts. By using ultra high temperatures (UHT), all micro-organisms are destroyed but the flavour of the milk may be changed.

Pasteurisation

Pasteurisation is a method of preservation often used to treat milk. The milk is heated to a temperature which will destroy bacteria but preserve nutrients.

Irradiation

Irradiation exposes food to low doses of radiation. Radiation kills bacteria and insects and stops seeds from sprouting. Many people are concerned about the health and safety aspects of irradiation and it is not yet widely used.

Food in store

In many parts of the world, it's possible to buy fresh food every day – fish straight off the fishing boats, and fruit and vegetables brought from the farm to the market stalls. But some foods have to be stored. Perhaps it's cheaper to buy more than you need and store the rest to use later. Or maybe you live in a part of the world where it's hard to get food. If your home is isolated by snow drifts, you want to know that you have enough food to live on until the snow thaws and you can get to the market again.

In-store storage

Food you buy in a supermarket is usually pre-packaged in some way. You buy things in cans or cartons, bottles or plastic bags, in paper bags or shrink-wrapped. Food is packaged for many good reasons. Packaging protects the food and stops it getting damaged. It preserves it or makes it easier to handle. The packaging can be printed with information about what's inside, and the manufacturer can use it to advertise the product.

Home storage

When you get your food home, you need to store it properly to keep it in the best possible condition. You may like to check the temperature inside your fridge. The ideal temperature is between 0 and 5 degrees Celsius. This picture gives you some tips on how to store your food.

Never eat food after the 'use by' or 'best before' date has passed.

Keep shelves and cupboards clean. This will help stop insects and vermin from setting up home or helping themselves to a free feast!

Onions make potatoes go bad more quickly if they are touching.

Apples and carrots kept together can make the carrots taste bitter.

Cover up food to stop flies walking all over it.

Some fruits like lemons and grapefruit contain a lot of acid. If you store them in aluminium foil the acid will start to eat away at the foil until the aluminium dissolves! Even a tomato-topped pizza will do the same!

Some foods lose their flavour quite quickly. Things like tea, coffee, dried fruit, herbs and spices should be eaten within six months of purchase. Even if you haven't opened the packet during this time, the contents will have deteriorated.

Use cans in the order you buy them. Eat within a year of purchase.

Keep all food out of direct sunlight as it can destroy vitamins A and C, and some B vitamins.

Food kept in the fridge should be covered up. This will stop it drying out.

Keep raw and cooked food on separate shelves.

Don't store anything in an opened can. This is really important with tomatoes as the acid in them can start to break down the surface of the can. When this happens the metal from the tin gets into the food – and you eat it!

Peaches and nectarines can start to grow mould very quickly. They should be stored in the fridge to slow down any growth.

Potatoes should be stored away from sunlight or they will turn green. The green is a mild poison called solanine.

If you don't keep milk in the fridge, it will go sour.

Keep raw meat on the bottom shelf of the fridge, in case it drips.

Bananas should be kept in a cool, dark place. They go brown in a fridge.

Lettuce keeps longer in a moist plastic bag in the bottom of the fridge.

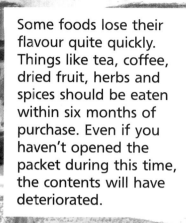

What's cooking?

From the North Pole to the South Pole, and from Siberia to the Society Islands, people cook their food, in other words, they apply heat to it. Cooking can be done by using a simple method like packing a food around hot stones, or at the other extreme by using an advanced technological product, like a microwave cooker.

Many kinds of food do require cooking. Some food, like meat or eggs or flour are hard, if not impossible, to digest in their raw state. They certainly taste less good, although some people enjoy steak tartare, which is a plate of raw minced beef with a raw egg in the middle.

Some foods must be cooked or they will make you ill. For example, tapioca is a form of a root called cassava. In its natural state it is full of a poisonous juice. It has to be prepared by washing, drying and cooking, when it turns into a delicious and nutritious food. Cooking also destroys many of the microbes in food that might otherwise be harmful.

HOW DO YOU LIKE YOUR POTATOES?

It's amazing how the nutritional content of food can change with different cooking methods. A potato can be a highly nutritious source of fibre, vitamins and minerals, but badly treated, it won't do you much more good than eating mashed paper! Potatoes provide vitamins C, B_6, B_1 and folic acid, and the mineral potassium. They provide a little protein, too.

Many of the vitamins and nutrients in potatoes lie just under the skin. So if you boil potatoes in their skin, they'll retain many of these nutrients.

Baked potatoes do not lose much vitamin C. As long as you don't smother the potato with butter, this is healthy eating!

COOKING SYSTEMS
You can cook your food in many different ways.

Baking
Food is cooked by the dry heat of an oven. Many flour-based foods, like bread and cakes are baked. Some meat dishes, like casseroles, can be baked, also fruits and vegetables like apples and potatoes.

Boiling
This is a common way of cooking vegetables and fruit. They are heated in boiling water in a saucepan.

Frying
Small pieces of food are cooked in fat in a long handled pan over a source of heat. Frying adds calories to food, because as it cooks, the food absorbs some of the fat.

Shallow frying
Food is cooked in a small amount of fat. Bacon and eggs are fried by this method.

Stir frying
Food is cut into very small pieces and cooked at extremely high temperatures in very little fat. The food must be stirred all the time to prevent burning.

Chipped potatoes, or french fries are very high in fat and calories, but do contain some vitamins from the cooking oil.

When you peel a potato, you take away more than 25 percent of its protein, and when you boil it, most of the vitamin C is lost in the water.

Mashed potato has to be eaten straight away. If the potato is left in the air, nearly all the vitamin C is lost. If you reheat mashed potato, the remaining vitamin C is lost, too.

HANDY HINTS FOR HEALTHY COOKING

Wash and boil vegetables in large pieces as there are fewer surfaces from which nutrients can be lost.

Cook vegetables in a small amount of water, using a pan with a tightly fitting lid.

Place vegetables in boiling water so they will take less time to cook and fewer nutrients will be destroyed.

Save the water in which vegetables have been cooked and use it to make soup, sauces or gravy.

Choose lean cuts of meat and trim off visible fat to cut down the amount of saturated fat.

Grilling is preferable to frying, as the food's fat content is reduced and not increased.

Stir frying retains nutrients in vegetables, as they are cooked quickly without water.

Grilling

Small, tender pieces of meat, fish, and some vegetables can be grilled. The food is placed on a rack, very close to a source of heat either above or below the food. The food must be turned so that both sides are cooked. Barbecuing is a form of grilling.

Microwave

Food in a microwave oven is cooked by short radio waves. The waves move through the food, making it heat up from inside. Food cooks very quickly in a microwave oven.

Roasting

Roasting is a form of baking. It usually describes the way a piece of meat is cooked. Roasting meat is usually placed in a pan and left uncovered in the oven to cook.

Simmering

Foods which are simmered are heated in water that is kept just below boiling point. Eggs can be simmered, also combinations of egg and milk, like custard. Meat may be cooked this way (this is also called stewing or braising) and vegetables of the pea and bean family.

Steaming

The food is put on a rack in a saucepan. A little water is added – not enough to reach the rack. The lid is put on, the water heats and the food cooks in the steam from the boiling water. Steaming is the best way of cooking vegetables if you want to keep the nutrients!

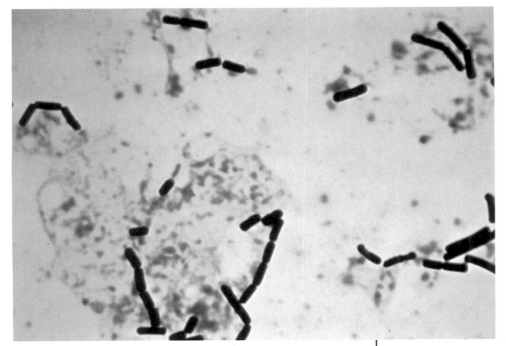

DANGEROUS BACTERIA
The bacteria shown here are the ones most likely to cause food poisoning.

Clostridium botulinum

This is the most dangerous of all the bacteria. About 200 grams of the toxin would be enough to kill the entire population of the world! These bacteria grow where there is no oxygen and a low quantity of acid, and can be found in badly canned food. In such conditions the bacteria produce a toxin which, if eaten, gives you a food poisoning called botulism. When food is canned, it is heated to temperatures that destroy the bacteria. Botulism is extremely rare, but you should avoid cans which are damaged in any way.

The toxins from clostridium botulinum can be fatal.

Fancy some poisoning?

Perhaps you have been unlucky enough to have experienced food poisoning. You'll know how ill you can feel when you suffer bouts of vomiting and diarrhoea. Food poisoning is a very unpleasant experience for anyone. But for babies or old people, or people who are already suffering from illness, food poisoning is not just unpleasant, it can be very serious indeed.

Food poisoning is caused by some types of bacteria. Bacteria are one form of microscopic creatures called microbes. Some kinds of bacteria are helpful. Others can make you ill if they multiply inside you, or if you eat the poisons or toxins they produce. Bacteria need four things in order to grow.

They need food. They grow specially well on meat, poultry, fish and dairy products. They need warmth. They prefer a cosy 37°C – which just happens to be your body temperature – but they'll make do with anything between 5°C and 63°C. They need moisture. Only a little is enough! They need time. Bacteria multiply at amazing speed. If you use a dirty knife to introduce a hundred salmonella bacteria onto a piece of chicken, those hundred microbes can multiply to 26 million within a few hours.

Escherichia Coli, or E.Coli

This is often the cause of diarrhoea in travellers. These bacteria inhabit the large bowel without any harmful effects to the host. The problems start when the bacteria get out. When Escherichia Coli is transferred to someone else, through faecal contamination of food or by flies or bad hygiene, it causes havoc. The way to avoid Escherichia Coli is to make sure that you have clean hands when you are handling food. In parts of the world where hygiene is poor, avoid raw foods and tapwater and peel or cook fruit and vegetables.

Salmonella

This is one of the most common causes of food poisoning. It is found in sewage, so it is most important to wash your hands after you have been to the toilet. Salmonella is also found in raw milk, meat and eggs.

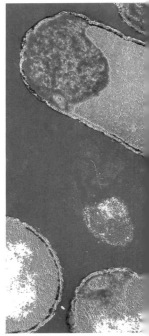

Many E. Coli bacteria live in your intestine.

Salmonella bacteria are destroyed by cooking.

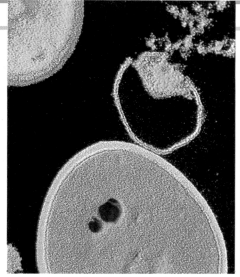

This empty bacterium is being destroyed by antibiotics.

Staphylococcus

These bacteria can be found in infected cuts, boils and sores. They can pass into food and produce poisons which act on the stomach and intestines.

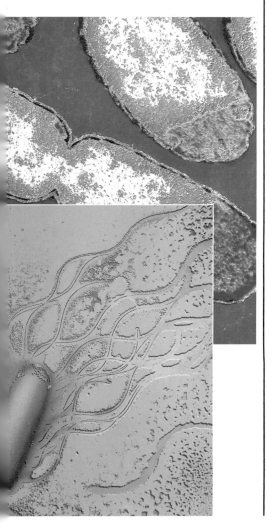

You may not realize that it's not just food which can poison you – there are other hazards in your kitchen which could make you just as ill.

Lead

Don't drink water from the tap if it comes through a lead pipe. Lead is a poisonous metal which can damage your red blood cells and brain cells. It builds up in your body, doing more and more damage.

Moulds

Don't eat nuts that are discoloured, decayed or obviously bad because they might contain a mould that could make you very ill. The mould produces poisons called aflatoxins. Similar moulds can grow on cereals too. If these cereals are fed to animals, the mould can be transferred to humans via meat and cheese.

The mould on these strawberries would probably not harm you.

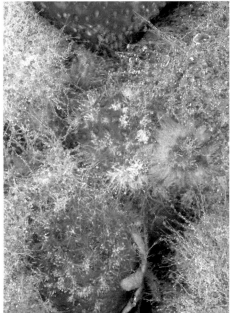

Cracked equipment

Cracks in pots and pans and wooden spoons provide a good place for bacteria to grow. The bacteria easily transfer onto your food. It's best to avoid using broken or cracked equipment when you're cooking.

Pets

Pets carry parasitic worms, and spread bacteria and viruses. Don't let them anywhere near food that you're going to eat, whether it's cooked or raw.

Remember to wash your hands after playing with any animal and prepare their food well away from human food.

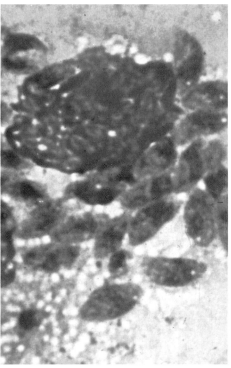

The parasite toxoplasma gondii is carried by animals.

This looks like a horrendous list. But if you take care and keep everything in the kitchen really clean, you should be able to avoid most dangers.

Are you an eating expert?

Do you think you know all there is to know about food? Try our true/false quiz, and then our memory quiz, and test yourself to find out.

TRUE OR FALSE?

True	False
☐	☐ **1.** You'll only get fat if you eat a lot of fat.
☐	☐ **2.** Everybody needs to eat meat.
☐	☐ **3.** An apple a day keeps the doctor away.
☐	☐ **4.** Chocolate is better for your teeth than toffee.
☐	☐ **5.** Fat people are lazy.
☐	☐ **6.** Milk contains many of the nutrients you need.
☐	☐ **7.** Diets are just for people who want to lose weight.
☐	☐ **8.** You should never eat chips.
☐	☐ **9.** Wholemeal bread is better for you than white.
☐	☐ **10.** You should always leave the table feeling hungry.

True	False
☐	☐ **11.** There's less calcium in skimmed milk than in full cream milk.
☐	☐ **12.** There's sugar added to tins of baked beans.
☐	☐ **13.** Old vegetables are just as good as fresh ones.
☐	☐ **14.** If an egg floats in water it's fresh.
☐	☐ **15.** Yoghurt is good for you.
☐	☐ **16.** Reducing cholesterol in your diet will reduce cholesterol in your blood.
☐	☐ **17.** There is no goodness in white flour.
☐	☐ **18.** Liver and eggs are rich in iron.
☐	☐ **19.** An apple a day is better for you than an orange if you want plenty of vitamin C.
☐	☐ **20.** Sugar is the main cause of tooth decay.

STRETCH YOUR MEMORY!

1. Which plants provide oil?

2. Can you match up the parts to the body?
- ☐ large intestine
- ☐ stomach
- ☐ anus
- ☐ oesophagus
- ☐ liver
- ☐ small intestine

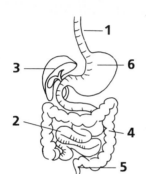

3. You've invited three new friends round to your house for a meal. They tell you they're vegetarians. Sammy is a vegan, Hashti is a lacto-vegetarian and Jo is an ovo-lacto-vegetarian. What foods do you have to avoid?

4. It's easy to get food poisoning. You only need four things to make bacteria grow. What are they?

5. How can food be preserved?

Answers:

1. False.
2. False. Vegetarians don't!
3. False. An apple is a healthy snack, but you need more than this to stay fit!
4. True.
5. False.
6. True.
7. False.
8. False. Never say never! Chips are OK – in moderation.
9. True. Wholemeal bread contains a good proportion of the fibre you need. White bread has had some removed.
10. False. Leaving the table feeling hungry is a sure way of wanting to fill that hole with fat, salt or sugar rich snacks.
11. False. There is slightly more calcium in skimmed milk.
12. True.
13. False.
14. False.
15. True.
16. False. To reduce blood cholesterol, you need to eat less saturated fat.
17. False.
18. True.
19. False.
20. True.

STRETCH YOUR MEMORY:

1. Oil can be made from olives, sunflower seeds, soya beans, cotton seed, rapeseed, palm kernel, coconut, peanut and almonds.
2. **1** oesophagus
   2 small intestine
   3 liver
   4 large intestine
   5 anus
   6 stomach
3. For Sammy: no animal food at all, not even milk.
   For Hashti: avoid meat, fish and eggs, but can eat milk and cheese and other dairy products.
   For Jo: she will eat milk, eggs and dairy products, but not meat or fish.
4. Food, warmth (a cosy 37°C of body warmth is ideal), moisture (just a little) and time (a couple of hours is generally enough).
5. Methods of preserving food are drying, smoking, pickling, canning, freezing, vacuum packing, sterilizing, pasteurising, irradiating.

HOW DID YOU SCORE?

Score one point for each correct answer. Where there is more than one answer to a question, score a point for each correct answer.

over 25 points: You should be proud of yourself. You're heading for a healthy life!

15 to 24 points: Almost there. You're off to a great start and with a little more effort, you'll be a real eating expert.

Under 15 points: Either you've started this book at the back, or you've got some way to go. Keep trying though, a healthy body is worth it in the end!

183

HELPLINES

Here's a list of organizations you could contact in case you'd like to find out more about some of the things discussed in this chapter. Whichever part of the world you live in, there are organizations that can answer your questions. These organizations will be happy to give you useful information and advice.

Australia
Salvo Youth Line
Alateen

India
Narcotics Anonymous
Samaritans

Malaysia
Drug abuse hotline
Child abuse hotline

Philippines
DARE Foundation
(drug dependency)
Multidisciplinary Child and
Adolescent Unit
(emotional problems)

Singapore
Samaritans
Singapore Anti-Narcotic
Association
Tinklefriend Hotline

South Africa
SA National Council for
Alcoholism and Drug
Dependence

UK
Alcoholics Anon
Childline
Drugline
Rape Crisis Centre
Samaritans

You should be able to find the telephone numbers in your local telephone directory or by phoning directory enquiries.

4

THOUGHTS & FEELINGS

A young person's guide to emotions

As you get older, you may find yourself looking at life in a different way. You'll gradually be taking more responsibility for your own life. You'll feel many different emotions, your relationships with friends and family may change. No one can guarantee that everything in your life will always go your way, but having a positive attitude will help you to get through the tough times, and enable you to enjoy the good times too.

Changing lives

As you say goodbye to childhood and begin the exciting trek into young adulthood, your feelings will change and you'll experience new emotions. This is an exhilarating time. Growing up is all about learning to make choices – choices about your lifestyle, about your friends, and about yourself. You'll find that you want to put your life together in the way you choose and not the way someone else chooses for you. You may want to reorganize the elements of the great jigsaw puzzle of life in your own way.

The most important thing to remember is that everybody has to go through these changes. You're not on your own. Everyone grows up. Every adult has been an adolescent once.

Who is grown up?

You don't physically change from a child to an adult at a predetermined age. Puberty begins when your own body clock tells it to. But at what age do you become a young adult mentally?

Actually, this depends on many things. You may be the oldest in your family and so used to leading the way for the other children. Perhaps you feel more grown-up than other people of your own age. You may even feel impatient with your classmates for being immature or juvenile, and prefer friends who are older than yourself. If you're a middle child, you have to work out whether you're willing or able to take more responsibility, or whether you feel safe being second in line. If you're the youngest, you will have older brothers and sisters from whom you can pick up ideas and information. So you may be quite mature for your age anyway. On the other hand, your family might always treat you as the baby.

So you can see that there's no one age when you'll be grown up. You probably know some grown-up ten year olds and some childish 25 year olds! You'll grow up at your own pace.

IN THE EYES OF THE LAW
When does the law say you are a young adult and not a child? The society in which you live decides the official grown-up age. In many countries, it is 18. At that age you can vote in a political election, get married without your parents' consent – and pay taxes!

Reading through

Thoughts and Feelings is divided into four sections. Each one deals with part of the great puzzle of life. The first section looks at you – the individual. The first part will help you to find out more about yourself. You probably think you know yourself quite well already. But it's important that you get to know and to like yourself as much as possible. It's important to be proud of yourself and to know what you're capable of. Many young people go through a period when they question the rules set by their families and by society. You'll find suggestions in the book about how to deal with some of the questions and problems that might arise.

The second section discusses your family and the way your relationship with them changes as you grow up. When you're very young, your family is probably the most important influence in your life. But as you get older, your ideas may change. Things you accepted when you were younger may become issues you want to challenge when you are an adult.

Life isn't always smooth; there will be problems to overcome. So there are sections in this book specifically written to deal with them. There is a section on parent separation and divorce. There is also a discussion about loss, death and grief. These are important subjects – but subjects some societies try to avoid. Sooner or later, though, everyone must face them, so it's best to know what can happen and how you might feel.

The third section concerns friends and close acquaintances, and how you relate to them. Naturally, your friends will be very important to you. Some of the friendships you make when you're a teenager may even last for the rest of your life. You can read here about these different types of friendship, including those with people of your own age – your peer group. There are also sections giving you the facts on alcohol, tobacco and drug abuse. As you reach puberty, you begin to discover that you have sexual feelings as well as emotional feelings. So there are pages to help you deal with boyfriends and girlfriends, love and sexual relationships.

The last section discusses many of the new emotions you might feel as you grow up. You may, for instance, find you're very moody – happy one moment and sad the next. You can find out in this section how to handle these moods, how to allow yourself to make mistakes through shyness or lack of confidence and how to learn from these mistakes.

You'll also find out how to recognize feelings of uncertainty, anger, jealousy, depression and boredom and how to cope with them. For example, you may be taking exams at school and experiencing stress and pressure for the first time. How do you cope? The rest of this section looks to the future – your job, your role in society, how you feel about the world – your future in a big, wide, exciting world.

Who am I?

When you're a teenager, it's not only your physical body that's changing, your thoughts and feelings are changing as well. You'll be experiencing new and different emotions and these will all influence how you feel mentally and emotionally. You might feel you just want to rewrite the entire rule book on how to live with the world, your family, your friends and, especially, yourself.

Some people find that adolescence is a time of tremendous ups and downs. Your mood can swing from one of ecstasy to one of gloom all in the same morning. But as you'll find out, your hormones can be held partly responsible for these mood swings. You may find you keep changing your mind as well. One day, you'll be quite sure about something, and the next day, you'll wonder how you could ever have thought that way.

Whatever happens, it's important that you stay positive about yourself. After all, everyone's entitled to their own opinion, and that includes you. Remember that each day makes you a little older and, more importantly, each new experience in life makes you a little wiser.

In the family

When you're a child, people keep telling you how much you resemble some other member of your family. You'll be told that you're round-shouldered like your mother, or knock-kneed like your father, or that you have your grandmother's nose. People will go on making these comparisons as you get older. Of course you have inherited features and mannerisms from your parents, but now's the time to define you. You're an individual and unique person. No two people have exactly the same combination of features and feelings. Even identical twins are different, though people can't always see the difference.

So start identifying the special qualities that make you feel good about yourself and getting rid of some of those you don't like. Get into the habit and you'll probably go on doing this all through your adult life.

You are both an individual, and a member of your family.

Influences in your life

All through your childhood, your family was the most important influence on you. You learned from your parents how to behave. You learned how to get on with other people. You learned what was right and what was wrong. You didn't question this influence. You accepted it. It's part of growing up.

But you gradually become aware that other people have different ideas. Maybe you like some of these ideas. Other people – adults, your friends or people you see and admire on

WHAT SORT OF PERSON ARE YOU?

When you're feeling especially confused about who you are, it might be a good time to ask yourself a few simple questions.

What do you most like about yourself?
What makes you happiest?
What pleases you?
What makes you angry?
What excites you?
What bores you?
How do you like to spend your spare time?

Who are you?

Some questions are a little more complicated. For instance, a group of friends may be talking about a television programme which they all enjoy. Do you agree with them because you genuinely enjoy the programme too, or because you don't want to be different? Do you even disagree just to be contrary or to draw attention to yourself?

Answering these questions honestly can be hard. But there is no point in fooling yourself. Finding out what you think enables you to establish your own individual points of view. As you grow to know yourself better, you will also discover your limitations. You could make a list of all the things you'd like to do in your life. You'll realize that there are probably some things that you cannot do and will never do. Coming to terms with this is particularly important. But remember, it's up to you to choose what you want out of life. It's up to you to decide whether or not you develop your own special talents.

What do you like?

television and in magazines – will probably begin to influence the way you think. There's nothing wrong with listening to or even imitating people you admire.

But don't forget you've a mind of your own, you'll need to discover some things for yourself, as well as gathering information and ideas from all these different sources and images. It's up to you to choose which values you take from your family and friends and, of course, which values you reject.

Self-esteem

Self-esteem means knowing and valuing yourself. It means understanding and knowing your worth. You have a place in your family and in society. Most likely, you will have grown up in an environment which offered security and support. But if your childhood has been difficult, you may find yourself having to trust your own judgement at an early age, rather than relying on your family. You may or may not be a genius, you may or may not be very talented or a great achiever – but be comfortable with what you are. Self-esteem is not conceit. If you have a realistic sense of your own worth, you'll be confident, and able to make a contribution when you want to.

Self-esteem affects the way you do things, from simple tasks, like asking for something in a shop, to more complicated issues like dealing with authority. It helps you decide what you want out of life, and how to work towards it.

Thinking for yourself

There is a difference between taking advice about something and believing everything you are told. If you're not sure about something, it's easy to be influenced by another person's opinion. This doesn't mean that you shouldn't listen to people. But it does mean that you must listen and then work out your own responses. Don't be afraid to question. It shows you are thinking for yourself.

Sticking to your guns

There is nothing wrong with saying no to people when you mean no. And you don't have to feel guilty! Sometimes you have to do things that you don't want to do. Sometimes you may do things you don't agree with simply to please others. But you shouldn't have to. Be proud to stand up for your beliefs. When you've made your decision, you'll feel much better. Whatever they may say, your friends will admire you for sticking with the decisions you've made.

Taking criticism

Your self-esteem can be easily hurt when you are criticized. Try to decide whether you deserve that criticism or not. For example, you are told off at school for not handing your work in on time. This may be your fault – you knew that work had to be done but you didn't get round to doing it. Accept that you're at fault and resolve to do better next time.

There may be occasions on the other hand, when people criticize you and it's not your fault. This is much harder to take. Perhaps you couldn't get your work done on time because somebody was ill in your family and you had to spend time looking after them. Explain your situation or you will feel angry and resentful. Some criticism, however, is purely spiteful. This is a kind of bullying. If this happens to you, try to tell an adult you trust what has happened. You don't have to put up with this sort of unkindness.

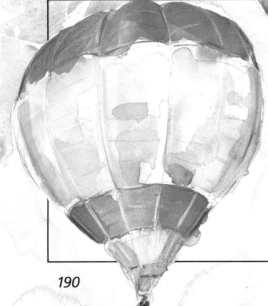

Reader's experience

"My friends all wanted to go up in a hot air balloon. So when Ben's father fixed it for us, they all got really excited. But I felt worried, because I'm really scared of heights, and knew I couldn't face it. Everyone crowded round me, teasing me and calling me all kinds of names. I felt dreadful about it.

Then I put my foot down. I said I wasn't going up, and I didn't care what they thought of me. End of story. Everyone calmed down then, and didn't tease me any more. But I went along on the morning of the flight, and I took some great photographs of the lift-off."
David

Saying what you mean

Sometimes people find it difficult to say what they mean, especially if they're talking about an emotional subject. Maybe they're not clear about what they feel, or perhaps they have several ideas at once and haven't taken time to work out which should come first.

To build up your self-esteem you need to sort out your thoughts and place a value on each of them. That way you begin to get a complete picture of what you want to say and in what order you want to say it. This will help you feel more confident.

Think clearly

When you have something important to say, that something may become lost if you don't know how to communicate properly. Communication skills can be learned. Decide what you want to say then focus on the most important part of the statement and say this first. Don't repeat yourself and don't feel it's necessary to add to your statement with other, weaker ideas. Then wait for a reaction. Listen to what others have to say. Don't interrupt even if you feel like it. Use this time to think about your answer.

Speak clearly

Know your audience. Find the right moment to speak out. For example, don't ask a special favour of your parents when you know they are busy. Wait until they have time to listen so they can give you all their attention.

It's best if you don't slump in a chair when you're talking – even if it does seem laid back. And look people directly in the eye when you're making a point. You're more likely to get your point across if you do. The secret is to be direct and to seem confident.

Your expressions and gestures often mirror the way you feel.

PRESENTING AN OPINION

What do you want to say? Organize your facts and your arguments.

Try and pick the right moment to speak. Good timing can make all the difference to the impact of what you want to say.

It's best to look alert and pleasant, even if you don't feel it. You'll find it easier to win people over with a smile.

Listen to any reply.

Speak clearly but not loudly.

Try to disagree without being disagreeable.

Facts are not the same as opinions. You need facts to back up your opinion and win an argument. Facts are not 'woolly'.

Bring up further arguments if you have to.

If you're asking for something and don't get it, wait a while and try again.

If you're expressing an opinion that no one agrees with, admit they have a right to a different point of view. Agree to differ and accept the situation.

Avoid using sweeping statements, for example, "Nobody I know comes in at 8 o'clock at night". There probably are people you know who do. Sweeping statements are too easy to argue against.

Working out values

What do you believe in? What do you think is right and what do you think is wrong? As you grow up you need to sort out your own views and opinions about things, but you will find from time to time that others don't necessarily share them. You will probably find that the first disagreements come from your own family.

Rebel in the home

As you become a young adult you may sometimes begin to question your parents' ideas, instead of just accepting that they're right as you did when you were small. In other words you'll begin to rebel.

Questioning your parents' values is part of the process of growing up. So far, your parents have been your undisputed guides through life. They have given you a moral code to live by and they'll probably go on doing that. But perhaps you are starting to find out you don't agree with some of their views any longer.

Temper tantrums seldom work

You don't always have to verbalize your rebellious feelings. Perhaps there's a certain rule in your household on which your parents will never give way. It's probably a waste of energy to shout and make a fuss about it. This only antagonizes people and makes them more resolved not to budge. Instead, go for a long walk and shout at the trees! Swim some lengths, or kick a ball around. Strenuous exercise relieves the tension and helps to calm you down.

Many teenagers question some of their parents' values.

Violent action often causes more problems than it solves.

NEGOTIATE
If you find adults sometimes make rules you disagree with, it's best not to rant and rave in protest. That will only convince them they were right to set limits in the first place. Try to negotiate a new rule which they are still comfortable with. You might be able to agree a trial period. If you stick to the rules, you might be able to gain new privileges.

Rebel in society

Every country has laws. These are important since they govern how we act towards each other. They provide discipline within the society which, because of our human nature, we need! Without them we would live in a chaotic world. We all feel more comfortable when we know we can act within certain limits.

At the simplest level, it makes sense to have rules about driving on the roads or people would be crashing into each other all the time! However, there are other rules that are not written down but are still understood. These are social rules, sometimes called social values. Each one of us has to make a personal decision as to whether these rules apply to us or not and we have to understand what the consequences may be if we disobey them.

Tolerance is a virtue

In our world of many cultures, races and religions, we need to be especially tolerant of other people's ideas and beliefs.

As you grow older, you will begin to discover more about the unwritten rules that govern our lives. You may not like everything you see and hear around you but if you want to be part of your society you have to be tolerant of its rules. Many people have very strong opinions about what is right or wrong with the world. You too may feel strongly about the way things are done. You might want to join in and fight for improvement, or argue strongly against a change that you believe can only bring bad results. There is nothing wrong with that. It is the way you try and change things that is important.

You can be absolutely certain that you will meet many people in your life who hold very different opinions and beliefs from your own. You will find some of these fascinating. Others you will accept because everyone is entitled to a point of view. Some you will find almost impossible to accept. It may be difficult to hold a polite conversation with someone who hunts animals if you're opposed to this kind of sport. Unfortunately you're going to come across intolerance at one time or another. Remember the rules of good argument from the previous page, try to get your more tolerant opinions heard, and forget violence. It only feeds on itself and leads to greater injustices.

GROUP ACTION

Individuals can change things in a peaceful way although it often doesn't happen overnight. Groups of individuals can bring about change even more quickly and successfully. If you feel strongly about an environmental issue, for instance, there are now lots of groups you can join. Find out as much as possible. Try and define to yourself exactly where you stand on each issue.

On the other hand, you won't get it right all the time, so don't be afraid to re-evaluate your position. Sticking to a particular line 'right or wrong' is called dogma and can be counter-productive.

Understand your parents

WE WERE YOUNG

Believe it or not, your parents can be your best friends, and they'll be very pleased that you're growing up. They'll enjoy being able to hold adult conversations with you, as well as going out with you in the evening. However as you grow up, relationships within your family will necessarily change. The adults will continue to love and look after you, but the relationship will become much more one between equals.

If you do have a problem, try talking about it with one of your parents. You may think they aren't as flexible as you are, but just try them. Ask them about how they felt when they were teenagers. Of course, times were different but human nature isn't. They probably experienced many of the same feelings you're having now. By remembering some of their experiences, they'll very likely find it easier to understand how you're feeling. Remember that people go on developing all their lives. And that includes your parents.

Unfortunately, there are parents who don't seem able to relate to their children at all. If you feel your parents really don't understand you, try to talk to somebody else about it.

You may find one parent easier to get on with than the other. Many people do. You may get on better with the parent who's the same sex as you, or with the one who's the opposite sex. Everyone's different.

The generation gap

The difference between your philosophy and way of life and your parents' is often referred to as the generation gap. Your parents experienced this gap too – with your grandparents! Wherever you come from, the way your parents live and the way you want to live may be different. Times are changing fast.

You may think your parents are really old. But try to think about them as ordinary people, not just as your mother or father. They have good days and bad days too. Sometimes parents are under all sorts of pressures. They may worry about money, or if they're a single parent, they

194

may be lonely. There may be an elderly or sick relative in your family who needs to be taken care of. Or they may be worried about getting old themselves and what that will mean to them and you. Your parents are also having to deal with a world that is changing faster than it did when they were young.

Learn to get on

Mother, father, brothers and sisters – they can all get on your nerves from time to time, just as you can get on theirs. Have you ever felt that you don't want your father to pick you up from a party because you think your friends might laugh at the way he dresses? Do you find your mother's loud voice gives you the shivers? And what about you? Have you ever asked your parents personal questions in a public place? Or divulged a family secret by mistake? The members of a family can embarrass each other in all sorts of different ways, without meaning to. But if you're sensitive to each other's feelings, you'll be able to avoid upsetting each other too badly.

A parent often worries their children are the only ones who want to do things they don't approve of. Help your parent to see that it isn't true. Introduce them to your friends and show them that you all want similar things. Talk to other people's parents and see how they react. Introduce your parents to other people's parents. It can be an eye-opener – for everyone.

A parent is a parent is a ...

Remember, parents can never stop being parents, whatever age they are. Your grandparents are probably still fussing over your parents. Respecting your parents is a sign of maturity. You don't have to agree with everything they say, but you should respect them for their views.

You may think your parents won't ever change themselves or their lives, but some parents embark on a new career as their children grow up. A mother may want to pick up her old career again and concentrate on activities outside the home. Are you mature enough to cope? You will undoubtedly be called on to share more of the routine responsibilities of running the home. Your parent will have lots to think about and won't want to be spending all their time worrying about you. They will need to trust you more than ever.

Strict parents

Some adults can be difficult to live with and you may long for the day you will be able to leave home and find real independence. The rules that exist in your family are your parents' way of ensuring that you appreciate the responsibilities of being an adult. Your parents feel that the way you behave at home will teach you how to behave in the outside world. They may follow a strict moral code, perhaps as part of their religion. If this is the case, they will expect you to observe the same moral code. In some ways, you will find life easier than those young people who are allowed to do anything – at least you know where the boundaries are. And remember, if you do want to change things, think before you act. Never lie or deceive your parents. They would far rather hear the truth from you than not know what is going on.

Getting your way

Understanding a parent is a two-way process. If your parents are open and reasonable with you, you owe it to them to be open and reasonable with them. On a practical level, that means telling them where you're going, who you're going with, and what time you'll be back. Just think how worried you'd be if your mother or father went off without telling you what they were up to.

What's the best action to take if you want to do something that you think a parent will disapprove of? First of all, work out why you think they'll disapprove. Can you think of any reasons why you should be allowed to do whatever it is? If you can present a carefully worked out argument in your favour, you're doing well.

Talk things over with friends or brothers and sisters. Has anyone been in a similar situation? How did they deal with it? If you treat your parents in an honest and straightforward way, their response is bound to be more reasonable. If you antagonize them, your job will be made much harder.

195

When parents separate

In many countries and communities, divorce or separation is becoming a familiar family crisis. Although it's the parents who divorce, it may be just as hard, if not harder, for the children to cope with the break-up.

It's desperately difficult living in a home where there is tension and quarrelling. You may not know what it is all about. At first, you may think your parents are quarrelling about you, especially if you hear your name mentioned. In addition, your parents may be trying hard to protect you by pretending nothing is wrong, which means you are trying to read signs and undercurrents without really understanding what is happening. If your parents are clearly not going to discuss things openly, you may need to talk to a relative or friend. The uncertainty at this time, as to whether your parents will stay together or live apart, can be very hard to cope with.

One reason they may find it hard to talk to you is because they themselves don't really know what will happen. You may want the quarrelling to stop and everything to get back to normal. But you may have to accept that the separation of your parents is the best solution.

Some people can't discuss their problems without arguing.

Feelings about divorce

Many children feel guilty when their parents split up. They feel that somehow it was their fault. Perhaps if they had been better behaved at school their parents would still be together. But of course this isn't so. Parents separate because they just cannot work out a way of getting along together any more. It may not be the fault of either parent – they may simply have grown apart. The mature thing therefore is to accept that they can't force their relationship back into its former close friendship. Separation may be the best solution.

Some families manage to get through a crisis with minimum upset to everybody. You may well find that nothing much changes when your parents separate. In fact, you may feel relieved that you don't have to witness your parents arguing any more. You may even live in the same house and continue to see them both. You may feel very little emotion about their troubles. However, it's natural to feel anger and resentment towards one or both parents when they upset the family home and your life. It's likely that you'll feel worried about how a single parent will manage to look after you.

You may feel that your parents don't love you as much as they used to, or wonder how your friends will react when they find out. The important thing to remember is that separation may be the only real alternative, and best for everyone concerned.

Deciding whom to live with

When people divorce, one parent usually looks after the children most of the time. Your parents should discuss with you, which of them you want to live with. This is a very difficult decision for everyone. You may feel that one of your parents needs you more than the other. Perhaps you think that you will hurt one parent by deciding not to live with them. You need to be sure that you will be allowed to see the absent parent regularly if that is what you want.

Parents who re-marry

In time, one of your parents may want to get married again. You will be invited to become part of a new family. Sometimes it's a relief when one of your parents re-marries. You are pleased to see them happy and your life will probably become more stable.

Many step-parents don't try to take the place of a mother or father but prefer to fulfil the role of a friend. Often it is more difficult to accept a step-parent when they arrive with step-brothers and-sisters. Try to remember that it is hard for your new family too and if you can at least get on with each other, life will be easier.

Your new life will be easier, of course, if you go on living in the same house and going to the same school. But this isn't always possible. Talking to a friend who has been through a similar experience will help you sort out your feelings, and help you to come to terms with your new situation. Or you could talk to an adult whose opinion you respect.

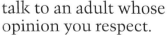

Your own room is a great place to retreat to.

Standing on your own

It is normal for teenagers to have mixed feelings about their parents. One minute you love them and the next you can't bear them. These strong feelings can be hurtful both to you and your parents but at this time of your life, you want them to realize you're no longer a child. You want to be treated as an adult.

Your parents have probably accepted your growing need to be independent since you learned to walk and they are more likely to continue encouraging and supporting you than to stop you developing. However, they may not change their attitude quite as fast as you would like them to. You may have to show them that you can be trusted with more freedom. At the same time, you may be feeling confused about just how much freedom you want. On one hand you want to be seen as independent, but on the other you may not like having to accept more responsibility.

Your own room

If it's possible, ask for a bedroom of your own. This will be your escape hole from the family and the rest of the world. It will be a place where you can play your own music, study or read, and if your parents allow, meet with your friends.

Ask if you can decorate your room and change it around a little so it has your special look and feel. However, remember why you wanted this room. Being independent also means showing maturity and respect. You are still living in your parents' home, and there is no reason why your room shouldn't be as clean and tidy as the rest of the house.

Be responsible for your own money.

Your own money

Do you get pocket money? If your parents give you a weekly allowance, you'll know something about the value of money. You probably feel you never have enough. Some teenagers manage to negotiate a larger allowance so that they can take responsibility for such things as personal clothing, presents and toiletries.

As well as your allowance, you may be earning from a weekend or spare time job. If this is the case, you might also have a bank account or a savings or deposit account. It's a good idea to save a little each week or each month. You'll be paid interest on the savings, and the total amount will grow, so that eventually you'll be able to buy something you really want.

Your own home

A lot of people feel ready to leave home when they're in their late teens. They go to college or get a job away from their home town. But leaving home isn't always a simple matter.

Have you or anyone else in your house ever had a violent row which prompts you to slam out of the family home, vowing never to come back? Unless these arguments are regular events over the same cause, you are likely to want to come back sooner or later, so try not to over-react. It's better to stay and try to sort out the problem there and then.

There's little glamour in running away. Teenage runaways may be vulnerable to all kinds of dangers and abuse. There are unscrupulous people in every city who may try to befriend young people for their own purposes. Don't run the risk of ruining your life and your future. Before you act, think carefully. Is there a friend, the parent of a friend, a relative, social worker or teacher, who could help you? Once you have explained your difficulties, you will find people ready to help you solve your family problems instead of running away from them. If by running away you are simply finding a new way of venting your anger, think again. Get rid of your anger in a more positive way.

Unfortunately, there are a few teenagers for whom life at home becomes unbearable. The only solution seems to be to leave home. If they are wise, they'll let their parents know they're safe. There are organizations in most cities that will pass on messages from young people who run away without revealing their whereabouts.

Some people think that running away will solve their problems. What do you think?

Loss

There will be times of great sadness in your life as well as happiness. When parents divorce, or when a close relative dies, everyone comes together to share their sad feelings. You may feel awful when your best friend moves away from the area. Maybe you yourself have moved recently and have had to say goodbye to all your old friends. It will take you time to understand your unhappiness, and come to terms with it.

Death of a pet

In some countries, the children of a family have grown up all their lives with a family pet – a cat or a dog perhaps – which has found a way into everyone's hearts. When your pet dies, something important is missing in your life. You need to grieve over this death. It may well be the first death you have had to encounter. Grieving is a normal process that helps to relieve the pain of losing something you love.

Death of a close relative

When somebody you know dies, you may well find yourself in a state of shock. You'll feel absolutely numb. Sometimes you can't believe it. You expect the person to walk into your life again. For some people this lasts a few weeks, for others it goes on for a great deal longer. However, after a time, it's usually possible to pick up the threads of your life, return to routine things and start seeing your friends again.

Saying goodbye

In some societies, a ritual will take place when someone is buried. Such events bring everyone together and help grieving to begin. It's a time both to say goodbye properly and to celebrate the person's life. A burial ceremony also recognizes the fact that those left behind are distressed. They need time to accept the death, called a period of mourning, after which they can start to rebuild and plan their lives again. In other societies, adults believe that children should be protected from the details of death. Some societies are afraid to talk about death at all. This can be a problem because even the youngest child knows that people don't just vanish.

At a sad time like this, it is important for the whole family to stay close together. It's somehow comforting to be with people who won't keep asking you how you're feeling. Comparing notes about what has happened and remembering the dead person together will help you to accept the loss you're experiencing.

Sometimes friends will feel embarrassed in your company. They will be upset on your behalf, but they won't know how to talk to you about your loss. Reassure them that you can cope but that you need them around you. It does help to try and keep your school and social life as normal as possible.

A funeral procession in Indonesia.

A British funeral may be a solemn occasion.

Coping with grief

Throughout our lives we learn to love people and to depend upon them. So when they die, we go through a whole series of emotions to try and make sense of what has happened.

In some societies, death is not talked about or celebrated. It is endured privately with a deep sense of loss. In such cases the first emotion will be one of shock. Those who are left behind feel helpless. They want to deny that anything has happened. This feeling may turn to anger since now they are alone – left to fend for themselves. Of course, the anger is especially strong when it is a young person who dies since it seems such a waste of a life. The anger may even be mixed with guilt as they think back to things they might have done to improve a relationship or make things happen differently. Sometimes a sense of depression takes over when it is difficult to find direction, and only as time passes, and new experiences flood in, does a feeling of growing acceptance take over.

Although grief is an emotion of the mind, all strong feelings have an effect on our bodies. Most people find that crying offers release from tension. The symptoms of grief may come in waves. At worst, there is a sense of panic which will automatically release adrenalin into the body. Grief often brings temporary indigestion and heartburn, sleeplessness, a loss of appetite, a feeling of tension in the head, and as a result of all this, irritable and jumpy behaviour.

It may be difficult to do, but keeping busy and active helps people to get over grief. Time alone doesn't heal. Only the events that fill time can do that. Any activity, particularly real exercise will reduce physical stress, since this stimulates the production of glucose and energy.

A bereaved person needs time and a great deal of understanding to get over a death. They may need to talk to a sympathetic ear. It's essential to appreciate how vital it is to allow a person to grieve and mourn.

A funeral in Thailand.

Many people form close friendships with people of the same sex.

Friends

Do you spend a lot of time with your friends? The people you make friends with when you are a teenager are very important. You may be friends with some of them for the rest of your life. Of course, not all your friends are best friends. There are people in your life with whom you are friendly, without being special friends. This outer circle of friends can be very important, too. How many people do you know by name? There may be hundreds of them, hundreds of potential friends.

You'll find lots of possible friends in a large group.

Making friends

If you want to make friends, you have to make an effort. If you sit shyly in a corner, and never say a word, people will naturally think you don't want to know them. Try smiling and saying "Hi". Learn to get involved with other people's lives and successes. Share experiences. If someone has the same tennis racquet or trainers, you could ask, "Where did you get your racquet/trainers?" And when you've made contact, make sure you listen and don't just expect to be listened to. Why not offer a new friend a piece of cake from your lunchbox. Small gestures like these can be the beginning of great friendships.

There are lots of different ways to make friends, but if you're attending school or college or a place of worship, you should find it easy to make contact with someone who shares your interests. Your friend may be a sister or a brother or somebody who lives in the same street as you at home. You can also meet people and make friends if you join societies or clubs where you all have a common interest. You may find you have different friends who share different parts of your life.

You can make good friends through sporting activities.

Little acorns

All kinds of things can bring two people together in a friendship. Often it's based on some shared activity. If you're involved in a sport or a hobby, and are enjoying the coaching, the competitions and the contact with the other club members, it's easy to find a kindred spirit who shares your enthusiasm.

Sometimes you become friends when you feel a natural sympathy with someone else. You may be drawn to someone whose personality is similar to your own, someone who's shared some of the same experiences in life. Perhaps you laugh at the same things, or maybe you both live on a houseboat. Or your friend may be someone who acts more as a guide or teacher, encouraging and daring you to venture into new ideas and experiences.

Best friends

A best friend is somebody you can talk to about anything and everything. It is someone with whom you have things in common and whose company you enjoy. There are dozens of ideas you want to talk about. You may prefer not to raise some of them with parents or with the rest of the family, but you can always talk to a friend. They're going through the same experiences and they'll find it easier to understand how you feel. Your best friend is likely to be somebody with whom you spend much of your free time. This friend will share good times and bad. This is the person you can laugh with, cry with, and share your secrets with. Teenagers have lots of private concerns — relationships with parents, self-image, or feelings about the opposite sex. A best friend can be counted on to explore these thoughts with you. A best friend is also someone you trust.

Ups and downs

Friendship isn't always easy. Your best friend may drift away from you and go off with someone else. You'll be really hurt and upset, and may take a long time to get over it. If you become interested in someone of the opposite sex, you may not spend as much time with your best friend as you used to. Friends may feel jealous and hurt. But having a girlfriend or boyfriend doesn't mean that you have to desert your other friends. Make sure you carry on seeing them. Talk to them about what is happening to you. A really good friend won't mind sharing your time with others.

Keep your friends

Some friendships don't last long. But that doesn't mean they're not good friendships. They can be just as important to you as long-term friendships. All your friends are precious, so it's worth working at friendship. You can give to friends and take from them, and any real friendship needs a good measure of both. Friends really need to be able to trust each other. You can't expect friends to stick around for ever if you keep letting them down. Even if you are busy with other things in your life, try to keep in touch with the friends you really value and let them know what you're doing. Make sure they know that you care about them.

Member of the group

Being part of a group can make life a lot easier, and a lot more fun. You may find everyone in your group shares a common language, a kind of code which only members of the group understand. There are 'in' jokes, 'in' clothes to wear, 'in' places to visit or be seen in. It feels good to fit in and conform like this, and it gives you an extra sense of security. The group makes you feel more self-confident because they accept and like you, and they ask for your advice and help. All the members of the group support each other.

Within a group of friends there are usually recognizable characters. There are the leaders, or the funny ones who crack all the jokes, or the fall guys – the ones who seem to be the butt of the jokes but can take it. And there are the easy-going members who just go along with what the others say. Does this sound like the people in your group? Do any of these characters sound like you?

Acting together

Of course, when you're a close-knit crowd, you have to work out a way of making decisions so that you're all happy about what you're going to do. Usually you manage to discuss things together and arrive at an answer together.

Peer pressure

But sometimes the decisions are made by the strongest members of the group. It is true that you have all joined the group because you generally like doing the same sorts of things, but sometimes you may find that you are involved in things that either you do not want to do or that you feel are not right. This is called peer pressure. Your peers are your equals – the friends in the group. You may feel they expect you to behave in a certain way, even though you don't really want to. People go along with the ideas for different reasons. They might totally agree, of course. But there again, they might not. They might be too frightened to object because they don't want to be thought of as weak – and most important, they don't want to be thrown out of the group.

Taking things too far

There are many ways in which peer pressure can work for the good of everyone. But there are other ways in which it definitely can't. Some people think it's more important to conform to the laws of the group than to the laws of society. Many social problems among teenagers arise when members of a group urge each other on to try drugs, smoking, drinking alcohol, or committing acts of vandalism. This kind of behaviour, known as delinquent behaviour, is always destructive to the individuals who carry it out as well as to the group and to any victims whom they hurt.

Delinquency is most common in big cities. A new set of rules takes over the 'street'. No one writes down these rules. They spring up from the needs of the group. Often poverty plays a strong part. But it is more complicated than that. People will do what they believe is best for themselves. For instance, if a young person feels it better to stay at home and earn money from selling drugs or running numbers than attending school and earning nothing, he may well stay at home, especially if there is pressure from his peers to do so. In the short term this seems like smart thinking. But in the long term it is not. Kids like this often end up as drug-addicts or down-and-outs. And at worst they risk being murdered. Making decisions like this is a serious business. It takes strength to resist peer pressure of this kind, but it's well worth the effort in the long run.

Many people get a lot of support from their group of friends.

If the members of a group get bored, they need to find something constructive to do.

Bullying

There are always bullies who will pick on children less able to defend themselves and make their life a misery. The fact that bullies have always existed is not to say the problem should be ignored. Current research shows an increasing number of teenage suicides in many countries. Some of these are caused by exam pressures, and others may be a result of emotional upsets such as excessive bullying.

Young bullies usually grow up to be adult bullies, while their victims may suffer the effects for years and years. Of course it's right to try and stop it, but what should you do?

Always remember, it's the bully who has the real problem. Bullies may be suffering from some short-lived emotional upset themselves, and want to take their hurt out on someone else. Or they may be chronic bullies who are spoiled or insecure. They may have been abused in some way, their parents may be violent, they may have been the victims of bullying themselves. They may not be able to succeed in what they do, or may simply not fit in.

Try and think of them as the victim. Walk tall and look confident even if you're not. A bully will soon get bored if you don't act scared. If you are bullied into handing over money or possessions, it's probably best to give in the first time it occurs. You will be too surprised to react well anyway, and your safety is more important than your pride.

However, take action at once to prevent it happening again. Speak to an adult you trust. Don't keep it a secret. You may well feel you want to be independent and would like to be able to tackle things without grown-up help, but parents and teachers can work together to reduce the power of the bully.

Apart from this, a bully has a serious problem and his or her anti-social behaviour is wrong. There are no innocent bystanders with this problem. Even if you are not the victim yourself, you should get involved and help those who are. Ignoring the bullying is cowardly and unfair.

Bullies prefer to pick on individuals, but they themselves may act with a group of friends. Bullying does not always mean physical violence. Verbal bullying can be just as upsetting and hurtful. Bullies pick on people for any reason at all – because they are fat, thin, spotty, shortsighted, poor at sport, good at chemistry, because their dad is out of work, or their mother is pregnant. Bullies are ignorant. They don't try to find reasons for their unkindness.

Try not to get upset. Talk with friends and with adults and work out the best way to handle any unpleasant comments. As with all bullying, the best way to retaliate is to smile back and walk away. Bullies really do lose interest after a while if a chosen victim refuses to 'play'.

The opposite sex

Some people have lots of friends of the other sex and others have few. There are many reasons why you might find it hard or easy to form this kind of friendship.

If, for example, you are the only girl in a family of brothers, you'll know a lot about boys. You'll understand how they think and the things they like to do. You'll probably meet quite a few boys simply by being around when your brothers are doing things. You should find it quite easy to form friendships and relationships with boys of your choice.

Meeting up

However, you may be somebody who has had very little contact with the opposite sex. Perhaps you go to a single sex school. Perhaps you're an only child. You may have been brought up in a family which is very protective and very strict for religious or cultural reasons about the freedom allowed to daughters, if not to sons. Don't worry. There will be plenty of time to find out about the opposite sex and form friendships and relationships with them. But what is important is that you let things happen naturally. Close friendships usually arise from routine contact with friends at school, at parties, at sporting events or through introductions by families or friends.

A friendship between a boy and a girl often arises from being involved in the same activities.

Some girls feel happier in friendships with other girls

206

Point of attraction

You may think that people are only attracted by each other's looks. This is not so. People are attracted to each other for all sorts of reasons. You may like somebody who makes you laugh, who is good at conversation or who just makes you feel that it's good to be you. This may be somebody who is popular at school or who has similar interests and values to yourself.

Remember, you don't always have to be in love with somebody of the opposite sex in order to have a special friendship with them. Young people who start having serious relationships too early may miss out on a lot of group activities. Many boys and girls are simply friends. Their relationship is more like brother and sister. To be happy and comfortable with somebody of the opposite sex, without feeling that you have to be in love with them, is a sign of increasing maturity.

Many people like going out with a group of friends. This may be the easiest way for you to start seeing a particular boy or girl you like. When you go out in a group, you don't have to worry about the evening going wrong. There is always somebody to talk to. When you're together with friends, you probably won't feel so shy. If you feel strongly about one of the members of the group, you will probably be able to do something about it in a natural, more spontaneous way.

Some boys don't take much notice of girls

Breaking up

You may find that your feelings change quite fast. You can feel very attracted to somebody and want to go out with them, but they may turn out to be not as you expected. Going out with someone should be an enjoyable experience. If you find that you're miserable in your relationship, then you are definitely going out with the wrong person. If things don't work out between you, it simply means that you are not the right people for each other. Splitting up can still be a painful experience, even if you know that the boyfriend or girlfriend was hopelessly unsuitable. This is a time of finding out about yourself and other people and learning how you react to other people and how other people react to you.

Choose for yourself

If all your friends have a girlfriend or boyfriend, you may feel you're under a lot of pressure to be the same. Do what you want to do and don't be too influenced by what your friends say. You don't have to have a close relationship to be classified as human! There's nothing wrong with not wanting to date. Perhaps you don't yet feel comfortable with people of the opposite sex and are happy having valuable close friendships with people of your own sex. You may feel more confident going around in a crowd of friends. Either way is perfectly normal. If you are happy in yourself, you are far more likely to develop rewarding relationships than somebody who feels they can't exist without a partner.

Reader's experience

"I'm in a mixed class at school and we all get on very well together. Sometimes we are split into pairs to do things. When I have a girl as my partner in that kind of situation, I'm fine. When I get out of school, though, it's a different story. I feel very nervous when I am around girls. I just don't know what to say to them, I always think they're laughing at me.

One of my friends started going out with a girl and he said he'd introduce me to her friend. He's fixed up a date now. He seems to find it easy to get on with girls. Just act like you do in class and you'll be fine, he said. So I'm going to go out with them. I feel really nervous about it. I just wish we were in a classroom situation and not out on a date."
Joseph

Kelly meets Jason at the club.

"I've never felt this way before. I must be in love!"

"But we don't really have much in common."

Falling in love

As a young person, your first encounters with love will probably be very intense and absorb a great deal of your thoughts.

Some people are in love with love. They have learned about love from television and magazines and they just can't wait to try it out for themselves. But love can take many different forms. You may love somebody who is older or younger than yourself. There is no age limit to this emotion. The feelings you have when you are 14 can be just as strong as those you have when you are an adult. However, one thing is for sure – love is a very demanding emotion.

First encounters with love

One of your first experiences of love may be an infatuation. Infatuation literally comes from the word fatuous, or foolish. It's really about allowing your passion to become so overwhelming you act foolishly, or make a fool of yourself. You might adore somebody so much that you won't be able to think about anything else. Your passion might even become an obsession.

A relationship based on infatuation is more about giving than receiving love. Objects of infatuation are usually unavailable, an older friend perhaps, or a film star. People who are infatuated with somebody can sometimes be really disappointed if their dream comes true.

Once they actually spend time with their idol, they find that all that glitters is not gold. An infatuation is a way of getting ready to handle a mature, two-way relationship. Remember that in order to love somebody, you have to love and value yourself first. Once you can begin to sort out your own feelings, you will be ready to start forming a close relationship with somebody else in the future.

What does it feel like to be in love?

When you are in love the whole world looks different. Everything is good. The weather is beautiful even if it is raining, and the most unpopular teacher at school suddenly seems bearable. You are filled with energy and happiness.

When you are in love you are aware of someone else's needs. When you make another person happy, you are happy. You and your friend like each other despite the fact that you may be completely different. You trust each other enough to reveal your emotions to each other.

As well as being physically attracted, the two of you are also best friends. You talk to each other about everything under the sun. You have fun and you laugh together.

HOW DO YOU GET OVER A BROKEN HEART?

Love is wonderful when both partners are in love with each other. But you may fall in love with somebody who doesn't love you. Or maybe you've been happy with someone but now they don't love you any more. They want to be free – maybe even to see someone else. This hurts. It's bound to. You now have to face the fear of loneliness and the anger you will feel at being left in this situation. However, there are many ways to get over an unhappy love affair.

You can cry. You can voice your anger. You can talk to someone – don't bottle it up. You can stay busy. You can write down your feelings in a diary, poem or song.

Jason can't understand what went wrong.

And you can start thinking about a new friendship.

It is important and normal to express your feelings. You have given your love to somebody and you have been rejected. You need to grieve about a lost love in order to start feeling better. Whatever the reason behind your unhappiness you have been loved and you have proved you are loveable. Now, get back out in the world, and be loved again.

Arranged marriages

In most countries, children are encouraged to make choices for themselves. This freedom extends to choosing their own friends, their own boyfriends or girlfriends, and eventually their own marriage partner. Young people meet in school, spend spare time together, and develop friendships freely. Unfortunately, there is no doubt that many choose their partners unwisely and a huge number of marriages end in unhappiness and, finally, divorce.

Not everyone has this much freedom. In India and parts of Asia and the Middle East, a more traditional arrangement is accepted. Here it is often the parents who choose a wife or husband for their child. They select carefully, trying to arrange a marriage with someone of the same age, from the same type of family and background. They take their child's good points and bad points and match them with someone else's. They know their children believe in family wisdom and will trust their decision. Children may be promised in marriage, or even married, at a very early age. After choosing a likely candidate, the parents will arrange for the two young people to meet. The first meeting usually takes place at the girl's house with both families present.

There are arguments in favour of this approach to marriage. In an arranged marriage, a lot of the hard work of understanding your partner's attitudes is already done for you. You can assume his or her approach to most things will be compatible with your own. And, in those countries where arranged marriages are normal, girls have often been kept apart from males of their age, and have not had the opportunity to meet and date boys freely. People who've had an arranged marriage don't fall in love straight away. They are not expected to be everything to each other. Their feelings for each other develop gradually as they live together.

Divorce rates among arranged marriages are low, though this does not necessarily mean that all arranged marriages are happy. The family is usually very supportive in times of trouble.

A deep problem arises where girls grow up in a society which adopts a freer and more liberal approach to dating and marriage. It is difficult for an Indian son or daughter growing up in London or San Francisco to accept that their parents will choose a marriage partner on their behalf, and expect them to meet up for the first time at the wedding.

Although Asian mothers are increasingly accepting different attitudes in their children, they naturally feel disappointed about discarding the old system. They are torn between the pride they feel in a daughter who is studying to become a lawyer and who is brimming with confidence and independence, and nostalgia for the values under which they themselves grew up and married.

Going out

Are you or any of your friends going out with a boyfriend or girlfriend? As you go through puberty, more and more people start to enjoy the special company of a particular boy or girl. Some people start going out when they are only 12 or 13, while others are quite happy going around in a group until they are 17 or so.

Many people prefer to meet friends of the other sex in a group.

What about your parents

Some people who start going out when they're quite young may find their parents need persuading before they give their permission. Your parents may want you to come home by a certain time, or they may disapprove altogether, and not allow you to go out at all. This may be hard to accept, but your parents are only trying to protect you, they're not usually being deliberately unkind or unfair. Try and think up a compromise they'll be happy with. Maybe they'd let you invite your friend around to your house.

What gets you going?

There are lots of things that can attract you to another person. Physical appearance is the most obvious one – though it's not always the most good-looking individuals you'll find attractive. You'll probably also be drawn to people who think the same way as you do, and maybe to people who dress in a similar way. Then what happens? You may first catch the other person's eye. Perhaps you'll smile. If the other person smiles back, perhaps you'll feel encouraged to start up a conversation. Your first words may not be anything special – just a superficial greeting. But if the other person seems interested, you'll soon be having a more meaningful conversation.

A close relationship can grow out of a good friendship.

Making the first move

When your parents were young, it was probably the boy who did the asking out, but now it's more acceptable for the girl to take the initiative. Some girls say their boyfriend was so shy that nothing would have happened at all if they hadn't asked him out.

If you feel nervous about asking your friend face to face, telephone instead. Give a few days warning so they can arrange transport and tell their parents. It's also helpful if you have some idea of what you're going to do. It's not very practical to turn up for ten-pin bowling dressed for a party. Try to think of interesting things to do on your date – something that you'll both enjoy. The first time you ask someone out, you may be worried she or he will turn you down. Try not to let that stop you asking. Once you've asked someone a few times, you'll find it gets easier. You'll become more confident.

Double-dating

A half-way stage between going around in a group and going out on a one-to-one basis, is to go out on a double date, with two boys and two girls. When there are four of you, you may feel comfortable socially, and you'll find the conversation won't dry up, as it sometimes can when there are only two of you and you're feeling awkward with each other on a first date.

Don't give up

If someone declines your invitation, don't get discouraged. It doesn't mean there's anything wrong with you. It may mean the person is going out with someone else, perhaps they are just not interested, or maybe you're asking good-looking and popular people who have already had lots of offers. Dating a good-looking and popular person isn't a guarantee of having a great time. It's more important that you ask yourself whether you feel really comfortable with the other person, and whether you think you'll have fun together.

There's certainly someone, somewhere, who'd like to go out with you, so don't give up. And remember, not every date has to blossom into a romance. You can go out with someone, have a great time and just be good friends.

Unpleasant encounters

There are many good things about being a teenager, such as becoming more independent. But it's difficult to come to terms with the fact that you are also more vulnerable.

Unfortunately, your new-found freedom may invite unwanted attention, even as bad as assault. You need to be able to recognize and avoid situations which may lead to danger.

Even if you live in a culture where life seems very safe, you are coming up to an age where you may well travel abroad or travel in cities where disturbing things can and do happen. You are vulnerable. You now look mature, and you are going out more often on your own. You probably won't be able to afford to take a taxi, so you may frequently travel on public transport. In the United States, one in four girls and one in ten boys will experience some kind of sexual assault as they grow up. This may seem a high proportion to teenagers living in other countries, but it's silly, and potentially dangerous, to believe that nothing bad can ever happen to you.

Sexual harassment

Sexual harassment can take lots of forms. You may find you are touched or rubbed in a sexual way when you are moving along or standing in a crowded place.

But this kind of behaviour doesn't always involve strangers. When we are young, we are used to being hugged and caressed by our parents, by relatives and by family friends. Sadly, some people may also take advantage of your trust and affection. They may love you, but still can't resist touching you. If you feel that your body is being touched and explored in an intimate way which you don't feel comfortable with, or if things are said to you which embarrass or upset you, make sure you tell someone you trust.

Remember, none of this is your fault. It is the result of someone else's problem with their own sexuality. Don't be afraid to reveal what they are doing. They need to stop this behaviour, and you need to be left alone.

Unwelcome attention

Flashers are people, usually men, who expose their genitals in public to try and shock you. If somebody exposes himself, move away quickly, join other people who may be walking nearby or try to attract attention by shouting.

Obscene phone calls can be frightening, especially if you're alone in the house. Don't ever give your name to a caller who doesn't appear to know it. The best tactic is to put the phone down and arrange for a man to answer all phone calls until the caller stops. Or report the calls to the police, who will be able to advise you about what to do.

Rape

Rape is forcing someone to have sexual intercourse against their will. A rapist is usually a man, and a rape victim is usually a woman, but not always. Boys and young men can be victims of sexual assault too. In law, a rapist enters a woman or girl with his penis, though rape can also involve other kinds of sexual assault. You may think that a rapist is a weird stranger who leaps out of bushes and attacks you. This may sometimes be the case. However, the frightening thing is that more than half of the cases of rape and sexual assault occur between people who know each other. This is known as acquaintance rape.

Rape can take place in a friend's car or at a friend's party – even in your own home. A rapist may be someone that nobody would suspect – a person who might take advantage of someone who is weaker and sexually inexperienced. It's very important that you make your position clear. If you were to say no, and you meant no, and if you were still forced into sex against your will, this would be rape, and would have to be reported. Rape should be reported to the police as soon as possible.

Clearly, you can lessen the risk of an attack from an unknown person by not walking alone on the streets at night. Make sure you lock doors when you are home alone and don't let strangers into the house at any time.

It is difficult to know what to do if you are attacked. You can carry around a rape alarm that makes a high-pitched shrieking noise. Or you may be able to scream and shout to attract help. Being fit and having some training in self defence will be valuable. You may be able to defend yourself by poking your attacker's eyes. Don't put yourself off balance, or you might be pushed over. If your attacker is completely in control, or threatening you with a weapon, it is sometimes best to try and talk. Concentrate on getting a description of the person to give to the police once you are free.

Telling your story

It's vital that you tell a sympathetic adult about any unpleasant encounter as soon as it happens or it could continue to haunt you and disturb you for many years. You may worry that people won't believe you, or that they will blame you for what happened, but this is unlikely to happen.

A rape victim will be physically and emotionally upset. You may be badly bruised and your doctor may wish to conduct certain medical tests and keep you under careful observation until you are completely healed. The psychological damage may take longer. The more you talk about this experience to people who can help you, the sooner you will get over it and be able to pick up your life and build your confidence again.

Smoking

Five out of twenty smokers will die from a smoking-relating illness.

So you've decided not to be a smoker. That's great! You'll live longer, breathe fresher air, and save yourself a bunch of money.

Some young people think that if they smoke it will make them look grown-up and cool. They may think it's a way of joining the crowd. Most young people smoke because their friends pressurize them to do so. They may be copying their parents who smoke, or other adults whom they respect. At one time, this would have been accepted as normal. But in the last 30 years attitudes about smoking have changed. Smoking is now banned in many public places so that other people don't have to breathe in smokers' choking tobacco smoke. Passive smoking, when you're breathing in someone else's tobacco smoke, can damage a person's health just like smoking can.

Remember that smokers are using a highly addictive drug, and one which is absolutely guaranteed to damage health. Smoking very quickly becomes addictive , and it is one of the hardest habits to break. Take a thousand young people who smoke 20 cigarettes a day. A quarter of them will die early from a disease caused by smoking. That's 250 lives wasted! Only six of those thousand teenagers will die in road accidents. Nothing is as dangerous as smoking.

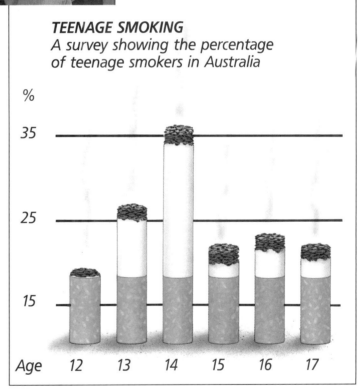

TEENAGE SMOKING
A survey showing the percentage of teenage smokers in Australia

%

35

25

15

Age   12   13   14   15   16   17

Giving up

If you already smoke, decide to stop smoking and stop today — even if you're half way through a pack. Of course this will be difficult, but your doctor can help you to quit smoking, and to stay smoke free. Don't talk about tomorrow or the future. You are in control of your own life and can do what you want today.

Smoking-related illnesses

There's no doubt that smoking damages your health. So what is it in cigarette smoke that is harmful?

A chemical called nicotine is the substance that causes addiction. It is a stimulant, and helps to cause an increase in the pulse rate and a rise in blood pressure. Other substances irritate the delicate linings of the air passages. Cigarette smoke also contains tar, which is a major factor in causing cancer and carbon monoxide, a gas that acts as a poison.

When tobacco smoke or any other irritant is breathed in to the lungs, the cells lining the air passages are stimulated to produce more mucus. The mucus traps the dirt, and is normally pushed by small hairs called cilia back up the air passages. You get rid of the mucus by blowing your nose or coughing and spitting. When cigarette smoke is inhaled, the cilia stop working, and no longer prevent the tar and nicotine in the cigarette smoke from getting into the lungs. The cilia eventually give up working altogether, making it easy for an infection to set in and harder for the body to clear the mucus.

Chronic bronchitis occurs when tar and mucus damage the air sacs in the lungs. The sufferer has a bad cough which is worse in the mornings, and may get breathless easily.

Emphysema is an illness in which the air sacs in the lungs become over-inflated as they lose their elasticity, and are no longer able to push out all the carbon dioxide gas in the lungs. This makes the sufferer feel unwell, tight in the chest and always short of breath. Smoking is the principal cause of emphysema.

Chemicals in the tar can cause certain cells in the lungs to turn into cancer cells. These multiply, destroying healthy cells in the lungs, and spreading around the body to start new cancerous growths. Lung cancer is not easy to treat, as the cancer is often not diagnosed until it is quite far advanced.

Gases in cigarette smoke increase your blood pressure and pulse rate. This can contribute to heart disease. Smokers are twice as likely to have heart trouble as nonsmokers.

Apart from lung cancer, smokers can suffer from other cancers too, such as of the mouth, tongue, cervix, larynx, bladder and pancreas. 'Smokeless' tobacco that is chewed not smoked is also harmful, causing mouth sores, damage to teeth and cancer.

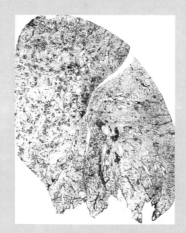

This shows what smoking can do to your lungs.

SAY NO TO TOBACCO

Far from making you look mature and attractive, the smell of smoke on your breath and clothes will put people off.

Someone who smokes 15 cigarettes a day can forget six to nine years of their life.

Nicotine is a poisonous and addictive drug.

The chances of dying of cancer of the lung or larynx, emphysema, peptic ulcers or heart disease double when you take up smoking.

You are burning a great deal of money. In many countries, cigarettes are heavily taxed.

Your skin will wrinkle faster and deeper than that of a non-smoker. Females who smoke heavily may wrinkle like a woman 20 years older in age.

Pregnant women who smoke run a high risk of damage to their unborn babies, as it makes them smaller.

Taking a drink

When you eat your dinner, what do you drink with your meal? Do you have water or juice, or maybe milk or coffee? Does anyone in the family drink beer or wine or cider? It's pleasant to have a meal and a glass of wine with friends. Maybe some of the adults in your family go to have a drink with their friends in the evening. When you were young, this is probably how you became aware of alcoholic drink. Later, you may have asked for a taste, and then a glass of your own.

Many people enjoy a social drink.

Alcohol can make you lose control.

Alcohol is a drug

If you like to share alcohol in a family setting, that's all right. But remember, alcohol is a drug. It can make you sick, and you can become addicted to it. It's a very common form of drug abuse among teenagers. Don't let anyone at a party pressure you into drinking if you don't want to, specially if you're legally under age.

You don't have to drink alcoholic drinks at all. There are lots of people who don't like the taste of alcoholic drinks, but don't dare to say so. Maybe it seems childish not to like alcohol. But you don't need to lose face. There are plenty of very sophisticated non-alcoholic drinks you can choose. Anyway, who knows whether there's any rum in that coke, or vodka in that orange?

Never drink and drive

For years we have been told not to drive after we have drunk alcohol, which weakens our senses and clouds our judgement. And yet people still do. Young people who are drunk are less likely to wear their seat belts, and are less experienced when a problem occurs. The alcohol makes them think they are brilliant drivers and can take risks without getting hurt. But more importantly they become a risk to other drivers and pedestrians – a potential killer. If they do have an accident, the alcohol in their body will make treatment of any injury more difficult. Remember, there is no way you can drink and drive safely.

Nearly half the car-related deaths in the USA are caused by drunk drivers.

ALCOHOL AND ITS EFFECTS

Alcoholic drinks are made up chiefly of water and ethanol, which is an alcohol produced by fermenting fruits, vegetables or grain. Beer is about one part ethanol to twenty parts water. Wine is stronger, and spirits are about half ethanol and half water.

Alcohol is a drug, in fact, it is a mild poison. It is absorbed quickly into the bloodstream within 4 or 10 minutes of being drunk. Absorption is slower if there's food in the stomach. Once inside the body it passes through the bloodstream to the liver where poisons are digested. But the liver can only process 28 grams of pure alcohol each hour.

Heavy drinking causes cirrhosis of the liver.

This is a small amount – just over half a glass of beer. Anything else you drink is pumped round the body while it waits its turn to enter the liver.

When alcohol reaches your brain, you may immediately feel more relaxed and light-hearted. You may feel you can do crazy things, and take stupid risks such as deciding to have unprotected sex or trying an illegal drug. It makes some people feel aggressive.

After two or three drinks, your actions are clumsy and your speech is slurred. If you over-drink, you might suffer from double vision and loss of balance, even fall unconscious. Alcohol forces water out of your body cells, and this can make you very thirsty. Drinkers may also suffer from headaches, heart flutters and tension. On average, it takes one hour for the body to get rid of the alcohol in one standard drink.

What is a standard unit of drink?

Recent reports by doctors suggest that it is sensible for adults to keep alcohol intake below 14 standard units a week. Although the law in many countries forbids the sale of alcohol to young people, up to 25 percent of fourteen year olds say that they drink alcohol on a regular basis, either in public bars or at home. Moderate drinking is unlikely to damage your health, but heavy drinking certainly will. Also, drinking alcohol is closely linked to taking stronger drugs, and this can be highly dangerous. This is because the combination of even low amounts of drugs and alcohol can prove fatal.

Coping with a hangover

When your body can't cope with the amount of alcohol you have poured into it, it protests. A hangover is a thoroughly unpleasant condition you have to endure after you've been drinking too much. You will have a headache and feel sick. A hangover reminds you that drinking too much is bad for your body.

Rest is the best cure for a hangover. Drink plenty of water and take paracetamol for the headache. And next time, ask yourself, 'Is it really worth it?'

1 standard unit is

½ pint beer or lager
½ a glass of wine
a small glass of sherry
a measure of vermouth
or an aperitif
a single measure of whisky,
gin or other spirits

Drug abuse

All medicines are drugs. You take drugs for your headache or your asthma. But you need to remember that not all drugs are medicines. Alcohol is a drug, and nicotine is a drug. There are many drugs that do you no good at all. There's nothing wrong with medicinal drugs if they're used properly. The trouble is, some people use them wrongly and make themselves ill. Most of the drugs you'll read about on these pages are illegal drugs, but some are ordinary substances that are used in the wrong way.

People take drugs because they think they make them feel better. Young people are often introduced to drug-taking by their friends. When a friend offers you a chance to have some 'fun' with drugs, and points out that everyone else is doing it, it's natural for you to wonder what it's like. Your friends may be full of stories as to how wonderful the drugs will make you feel. What they won't be telling you is how addictive the drugs are, and how many young people do lasting damage to their bodies, or eventually die from continued drug abuse each year. Many users take drugs to escape from a life that may seem too hard to bear. Drugs may seem the only answer, but they are no answer at all. They simply make the problem worse.

Side effects

Depending on the type and strength of the drug, all drug-abusers are in danger of developing side effects. Drugs can bring on confusion and frightening hallucinations and cause unbalanced emotions or more serious mental disorders. First time heroin users are sometimes violently sick. Cocaine, even in small amounts, can cause sudden death in some young people, due to heartbeat irregularities. Children born to drug-addicted parents can be badly affected.

Regular users may become constipated and girls can miss their periods. Someone who is drowsy or hallucinating, may put him or herself in danger through an accident in the home or in the street. Some drugs can slow, even stop the breathing process, and if someone overdoses accidentally they may become unconscious or even die.

drugs as medicine

Amphetamines (speed, ecstasy)
Commonly a white or brown powder but can be in pill or capsule form. Usually sniffed or injected. Makes people hyperactive, alert and irritable, but depression and difficulty with sleep can follow. Heavy use can produce feelings of persecution.

Cannabis (marijuana, pot, dope, hash, grass)
Hard, resinous material or leafy herbal mixture. Smoked in a joint or pipe, sometimes with tobacco. Distinctive herbal smell. Users may appear drunk.

Cocaine (coke)
A white powder, commonly sniffed. Can be injected or sometimes smoked. Similar effects to amphetamines but more likely to lead to dependence. Crack cocaine is a specially dangerous, highly addictive form of cocaine.

Heroin (smack, skag)
Off-white or brown powder, or black tar-like substance. Can be sniffed, injected or smoked. Produces initial alertness followed by drowsiness. Overdose can result in unconsciousness. Regular, frequent use results in dependence.

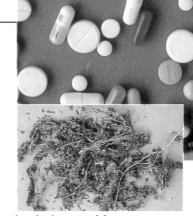

herbal cannabis

amphetamines

forms of LSD

heroin

preparing for
a lecture

LSD (acid)

Tablets or capsules (including microdot tablets) and small impregnated paper squares. Taken by mouth. Effects are totally unpredictable and may range from excitement to panic and fear.

Magic mushrooms

Types of mushroom containing a substance like LSD. Produce hilarity, over-excitement and with high doses, dream-like images.

Solvents

Solvent, or glue, sniffing describes inhaling chemicals found in a whole range of household cleaning products as well as in aerosols, glues, thinners and gases. Solvent sniffing is an addictive habit and may result in dependence. Accidents due to solvent sniffing are common and can result in death.

cocaine and crack cocaine

Tranquillisers

Prescribed tablets and capsules sometimes taken illegally for kicks. Similar effect to alcohol and increased effect when taken with alcohol.

Different drugs are available in different parts of the world. They do not always look the same.

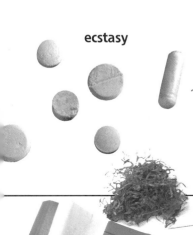

ecstasy

Getting out

People who start taking drugs are unlikely to do so for long without being found out. Symptoms of even light drug use are drowsiness, moodiness, loss of appetite and almost inevitably, a high level of deceit. First there's the evidence to hide, but second, drugs are expensive and few young people are able to find the money they need from their allowance alone.

If their parents find out, they are very likely to react badly. They are going to be frightened and worried and they will probably need advice themselves before they can start helping the abuser. Drug abusers need advice and medical treatment, to reduce any dependence. If their body is already tolerant of the drug, the withdrawal effects may take two to three weeks to wear off. This will be a difficult time.

If the abuser has not only used the drugs, but handed some out to their friends, they may well find they are in trouble with the police. First offenders are normally cautioned by the police, or fined. This could result in a criminal record, and may later prevent them getting the job they want. This is something they really don't want in their life.

Be strong

Work out ahead of time how you can resist drug experimentation. Don't be pressured into changing your mind. Try to dissuade friends from experimenting by suggesting other ways of spending time together. If you can't do this, you'll have to decide whether it is still possible for you to continue spending time with these friends. If you are worried, talk to friends, parents, teachers or counsellors.

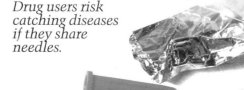

Drug users risk catching diseases if they share needles.

Someone to talk to

Have you heard the saying 'a problem shared is a problem halved'? If you keep your problems to yourself, they can seem a great deal worse than they really are. If you talk to somebody about your problem, you can come to see it in a different light. Maybe it's just arranging an emotion into words and then saying it out loud which does this. Sometimes you will find that the person you talk to can convince you that there is really nothing to worry about at all.

Problems can mount up. You may have a lot of work to do at school which is worrying you. You may have trouble at home. You may be having an argument with your brother or sister that's lasting for days. Taken on their own, all these things may not amount to very much. But when you're worrying about all of them at the same time, you can feel weighted down with cares and troubles.

Different people can help you with different problems, so if you want to share a worry, decide who would be the best person to talk to about it.

A parent

Your parents would probably like to feel that you were able to go to them with your worries. After all, they've known you all your life so they know you really well. If you can talk to a parent about your problems, they will feel pleased that you are able to take them into your confidence. And it will also help them understand what sorts of pressure you are faced with and what your life is like outside home. There may be things you take for granted that they know nothing about, or which have been puzzling them. You can fill them in.

At first, your parents may be angry and upset if you're telling them you've done something wrong. But give them time. When they realize that you need their help, and want to put things right, they'll start to think positively about what to do. Your parents may be able to deal more calmly and diplomatically with people in authority than you can. They've had more experience!

Your brothers and sisters

Your brothers and sisters have one main advantage over all your friends put together – you share the same parents! Problems with parents are often best discussed – and laughed about – with brothers and sisters.

Your relations

Your relations know all about your family. A close uncle or aunt may be the person to talk to if you are having trouble at home. Remember that they've known your parents longer than you have and have a personal store of knowledge on their strengths and weaknesses. They might just be able to give you advice on how best to get your message across.

Religious leaders

If you come from a family with a strong religious background, you will already know the leader of your church, mosque or temple. Religious leaders can help you to see your problems from a different angle. And it can be very interesting to see a church leader in a social situation. This will help you to like them as people as well as leaders, and you'll feel more at ease about approaching them with a problem.

Teachers

Your teachers know you pretty well. You may think that they only see the side of you that you show at school. But teachers are trained to see more than that and most can be very sympathetic and helpful.

Have you a problem at home? Perhaps you are not getting on with your parents or maybe your parents are not getting on with each other. It can be hard to talk directly to them about these sorts of things. Some schools have a member of the staff who is especially qualified to counsel on problems but if not, try talking to a teacher you like and respect, and see if they can offer any help.

Everyone knows that there are good teachers and 'not so good' teachers. You probably have at least one teacher in your school whom you like and respect. It may be somebody who is very different from your family. You may already have a good relationship through working in a tutorial or special class environment.

It's good to be able to confide in one of your parents.

Your friends and their parents

Most people talk to their friends about their problems. Friends of your own age are going through many of the same experiences and they will readily understand what you are talking about. Choose whom you tell your problems to with care. It must be a friend whom you can trust and whose opinion you respect, and someone who will not gossip about your business to other people.

And don't forget that if you are in need of a sympathetic adult, your friends' parents may be worth talking to. They'll probably know you already. Also, if they have a child of your age, they may already have met the problem, or one like it, and will know what to do.

And don't be misled. People your own age probably don't know much more than you do. If they say they do, they could be guessing. It's really better to seek an older, wiser ear.

Doctors

Sometimes you may feel that you have a problem that's so private, you don't want to discuss it with anybody who is close to you. It's more than likely you don't want anyone to know about it. Doctors will respect your confidentiality, and this may make it easier to talk openly to them. Doctors can be helpful even if your problem isn't strictly a medical one. And if they can't solve your problem, many of them work with counsellors or therapists who will be able to help.

Social workers and the police

At some time in your teenage years, you may come into contact with social workers or the police. This may be because you have got into trouble, or perhaps your contact with them will be through friends or family who have problems. Police officers sometimes come to give a talk in school. If they are good at their job, they will make you feel at ease and try to understand things from your point of view too. Listen and follow their advice. The authorities aren't all against you. A good police officer or social worker is there to help you, not to give you a hard time.

There are times when you have to control your temper.

All kinds of frustration

Do you feel angry sometimes? Of course you do. Everyone does. Why? Because you are afraid of something? Perhaps you are worried about an exam, or about failing at school. Fear can often be expressed as anger. Or perhaps someone you know is ill. You are angry because you feel it's unfair. You may have dropped and broken something. You may feel frustrated because you feel no one understands you, or because you can't get what you want.

When you feel frustrated like this, or when you are anxious or afraid, your body produces a hormone called adrenalin to help you to deal with the situation. But if your body has to react like this too often, you may be putting yourself under stress, resulting in tension and tiredness.

Dealing with anger

Angry feelings are OK, but you must deal with them in a mature way. That means you should always aim to lay your problems out in the open. Talk to your family or friends about them. That way, you'll relieve the pressure of anger that's building up inside you, and it's the best way of sorting out just what your problem is, and finding a solution. Your family or friends may well see just what you need to do – and help you do it.

You can't always bottle up your angry feelings. Sometimes you may need to let your anger out. You'll find that vigorous exercise is good for letting off steam. Crying will make you feel better, too. It relieves your feelings of frustration. Go for a long walk by yourself and notice the good things around you. Go to a place where you know you won't disturb anyone and have a good shout!

"There's a boy at school who has everything. He lives in an enormous house and has his own personal mini motor bike and a whole room of computer games. He's so rich that he can just go out and buy anything he wants. My brother reckons I shouldn't be envious of him, as being rich doesn't always make you happy. I don't know if I believe him though. I wouldn't mind being as rich as him!"
Adri

"When my friend is cross with me, I try not to mind. There's no point in answering back. If I do, an argument soon starts and that makes things worse. I try to walk away, or talk about something else."
Clio

"My brother used to have a terrible temper. I was quite scared of him sometimes. He stormed around the house, slamming doors and shouting at all of us for no reason at all. Then he used to go out for a long run, and would come back feeling better. But when he got into the cross country team, he seemed to change. He began to find it easier to control his temper. Now he's the coolest brother in our street!"
Gloria

"I have a younger sister of 5. I don't like her at all. She's really spoiled and gets everything she wants. Because she looks pretty and sweet, she gets all the attention, and I'm left to look after myself. My parents always say they love us equally, but it's hard to believe it sometimes. I just wish my sister would grow up quickly."
Jeanne

"My dad gets furious when he sees the amount of rubbish that people throw away every week. He reckons that at least half of it could be recycled. Last year he set up a recycling plant in our town. He said that instead of grumbling, it was better to do something positive with his anger and frustration. He's certainly done that."
Terry

223

You can feel alone even when you're not.

Lonely and shy

There is a difference between spending time alone and being lonely. You can spend time alone if you want to. You have a choice. But when you're lonely, you're alone but you don't want to be. As a teenager it's a good idea to plan your time so that you spend a certain amount of it by yourself. You need this time to sort through all the different experiences you're having, to decide how you feel about the people and the world around you.

Most people feel lonely some of the time. If your best friend goes away on holiday, you may feel unusually lonely because you're spending more time by yourself than usual. Sometimes you can feel lonely even when you are surrounded by other people. This type of loneliness hurts more because you can't understand it.

Attract or repel?

Lonely people may be people who don't like themselves very much. They think they're unattractive or they believe they are failures. They may not be very good at making friends. If you don't like yourself, it's going to be hard for other people to like you. You're not giving off a welcoming feeling and people won't feel drawn to you.

Feeling shy

Most people feel shy sometimes. Shyness stems from being unsure of yourself. You'll feel shy in an unfamiliar situation or in a new group. That's perfectly natural. You feel full of self-doubt – about what you look like and what you say. You feel that everyone is staring at you and thinking how stupid you are. You start feeling conscious of every word you utter, and every action you make seems clumsy.

Be confident

Start to be good to yourself. This doesn't means you have to be brimming with confidence all the time. Few people are. But start thinking about yourself in a positive way. Remember that you don't have to be the best at something to enjoy it. If you start liking yourself you will soon find that others will start liking what they see. If you really feel that there's nothing about you to like, try talking to somebody about it. A teacher or another adult, for example, will be able to see things in you that you may not see yourself.

When you meet someone, take the initiative, and be the first to smile. If the other person doesn't smile back, maybe they are shy or lonely too, or surprised to be noticed at all. Smile again, and try and draw a response. Once you've made the first move a few times, you'll find it gets easier.

Be a listener

Stop worrying about yourself and concentrate on the people you're with. Get back on track with the conversation. You'll probably find you have something to contribute, even if it's just a smile. A group is a mixture of those who contribute and those who receive.

Accept yourself

There's nothing wrong with being shy, though shyness may stop you making friends quite as quickly as other people do. Most people aren't shy all the time, they may just prefer to keep to themselves when they are away from home. Someone with a quiet, shy personality may be sensitive and thoughtful. Not everyone has to be brash, outgoing and extroverted, so accept yourself as you are. After all, it takes all sorts to make a world.

DO YOU FEEL SHY...?

... when you are with people in authority, for example, teachers or other people's parents? Don't over-react to your shyness by blabbering. You will be more impressive if you contribute one intelligent remark and use direct eye contact and authority in your voice.

... when you're on a date? Do you think you're reduced to a blushing and stammering pulp. Don't worry. Your new friend might be just as nervous as you.

...if you are feeling bad about yourself? You may think you don't look your best. Perhaps you feel you are wearing the wrong clothes for the occasion. When you are going out, wear something you really most comfortable in. If you're wearing tight shoes you'll be worrying more about getting blisters, than about the company.

... if you're with a group of people who are making a loud noise or are attracting attention by their strange clothes or odd behaviour? You're probably right to feel embarrassed.

SHYNESS THAT SHOWS?

Some people can look cool enough, but it can be hard to disguise shyness completely

Shyness makes you blush
Shyness makes your palms sweaty
Shyness makes your hands shake
Shyness makes your heart beat fast
Shyness makes you stammer

With confidence, you can learn to hide these tell-tale signs of shyness.

Reader's experience

"When we moved to another town I was dreading going to school because I knew how hard it would be to make new friends. Everybody seemed to know each other. My mum said I ought to join a club, but I didn't want to. After a while I got involved in the local tennis club, and I'm beginning to make some friends there, so I feel a lot better."
Clio

Mood swings

Do you sometimes feel happy one minute and sad the next? These sudden changes of mood are a very normal part of growing up.

Some of the problem might be caused by your hormones which are responsible for the physical changes you are going through.

You are changing from a child into a young adult, and new experiences are changing your view of the world. You may be excited and stimulated by what you discover. But you might also feel moody because you no longer enjoy the same things that you used to. Although you really want to grow up, you may feel sad about saying farewell to some parts of your childhood. Wasn't it great when others took responsibility for your life, when your parents were perfect, when a new toy could make your day? Things are more complicated now.

It's easy to blame the people around you for your state of mind. Perhaps you're feeling frustrated with your parents because they just don't seem to understand you any more. You may feel differently about your friends too. Some childhood friends now seem juvenile and annoying. Your mood can swing from wildly happy to desperately sad and back again.

Some days you feel everything's going your way.

GOOD MOODS
Sometimes you feel totally happy without any particular reason. You just feel that everything in the world is going your way. Of course this is great, and the more moods you have like this the better you will feel. Everyone around you will feel better too – good moods are infectious! So when you are in a good mood, make the most of it. You're clearly feeling good about yourself and your ability to cope with life, people and change.

Coping with your moods

Although you can't avoid bad moods altogether, there are ways of controlling them. First of all, don't blame yourself for being moody. Try and think back over the hours until you hit on the moment things went wrong. The reason behind your mood swing may surprise you.

For example, one afternoon somebody takes your seat on the school bus. This makes you angry and upset although it's nothing very serious. Your friends think you're silly for getting so upset about it and when you think about it seriously afterwards, you will probably admit that losing your seat wasn't the real problem at all. Perhaps it simply triggered off all kinds of other thoughts about yourself. You think it shows that nobody likes you, or that people take you for granted. It's really these feelings that are at the core of your reaction.

Think positive

Finding the reason behind your bad moods should help you do something about them. Learn to recognize moods and control them, or they might start controlling you. Positive action of some kind will make you feel better.

If you feel moody, go for a walk and take a little time to be by yourself. When you've thought things over, you may be ready to talk to somebody. Some people find physical activity helps a bad mood. Offer to clean the bathroom or wash the car. Take your aggression out on an inanimate piece of metal! Doing something quite simple and mindless for a while may make all the difference.

If there are certain people or situations that put you into a bad mood, try to avoid them. It is worth telling people how you feel and that you would rather be left alone. There's nothing worse than people who try to make you have a good time when you don't feel like it.

Observe other people's moods. It may help you to understand your own. For example, you might be out with your best friend who is usually good fun. Today, however, your best friend is moody and quiet and you are both having a rotten time. In this situation you could either decide to abandon the outing, or you could try talking to your friend and establishing what might be wrong. You have probably felt the same at some time.

Other days, you're miserable for no particular reason.

BAD, BAD, BAD!

When you are finding life difficult, you may only be able to show your frustration by being in a bad mood. Sometimes you may wake up feeling low, and you don't even know why. Nobody enjoys being in a bad mood because it can affect everything you do. When you're feeling this way try to understand the reason for it. Then decide what you're going to do about it, and do it. You'll feel a whole lot better

Emotional problems

Depression gives you a feeling of isolation.

Losing interest in life can be a sign of depression. You feel there's no reason to get through today or be excited about tomorrow. When you are depressed, you may have problems sleeping, or you may feel tired all the time. You may lose your appetite, or you may overeat. Everything looks hopeless and bleak. Your family and friends may tell you to just cheer up. They don't like to see you so unhappy. You feel angry and frustrated with yourself for not being able to snap out of it.

Depression

Feelings of rage, self-hate and anxiety kept inside, can make you very depressed. Depression isn't just a grown-up problem — nowadays more and more teenagers are suffering from real depression, often aggravated by the modern problems of drugs, alcohol, pressure with examinations, or the break-up of the family. There are physical reasons for depression as well. Sometimes a chemical imbalance in the body can cause it.

Take it seriously

Any depression that lasts longer than a few weeks should be taken seriously. Don't be discouraged from getting treatment by someone who shrugs it off as nothing and says 'You'll get over it, it's not really a problem'. This is bad advice. It is a real medical problem and should be treated as such. Effective medications are available for treating depression.

Suicide

Perhaps you have a good friend who is very depressed. Maybe this friend has mentioned to you that they would like to kill themselves. These threats of suicide should be taken seriously. Anyone who is talking about suicide needs to get medical attention immediately. Your friend needs help. If they can talk things over with you or other friends, it's a good start. But people who are seriously depressed need professional help. You must support your friend, and urge them to see their doctor.

Stress

Stress isn't always bad for the human body. In fact, we need some stress to keep us stimulated. It's when someone is under too much stress for a long time that they may suffer. When people talk about being under stress, they usually mean that they are worried. They lead busy lives and they don't have enough time to sort out their worries. When you are under stress things can go from bad to worse. You have problems piling up and you feel powerless to do anything about them.

When you're under stress, your body produces a hormone called adrenalin. This adrenalin makes your heart beat faster, and your breathing rate increases. That doesn't in itself do you any harm. But if high-level stress lasts a long time, your body can suffer a stress overload. This can result in painful physical effects, such as headaches and stomach ulcers, high blood pressure or heart attacks.

If you think you are under stress, do two things straight away. Talk to somebody about your problems and put some time into each day to relax. You need to feel that you are in charge of your life. You may need to accept that there are some things you are not able to do. Perhaps you don't have time, or perhaps some activities are taking up more time than they should. Sort out what's most important, and make decisions.

INDICATIONS OF DEPRESSION

You feel tired all the time
You wake up early in
    the morning and
    cannot get back to sleep
You can't be bothered
    to do anything
You find it hard to get
    up in the morning
Your school work begins
    to suffer
You eat too much or
    too little
You are accident prone
You find it hard to
    make decisions
You cry a lot
You feel hopeless about
    your life

INDICATIONS OF STRESS

You are bad tempered
    and snap at people
You suffer from frequent
    headaches
You suffer from
    stomach ache and
    nausea, or constant
    'butterfly' nerves in
    your stomach
You find it hard to get
    to sleep, or to wake
    early
You find it hard to
    concentrate at school
You cry a lot
You suffer from loss of
    appetite
Your appetite increases
You bite your nails

Dealing with stress

People don't all deal with stress equally well. People who are generally confident and feel they can cope with life's problems will certainly manage better than people who feel helpless. So if you can convince yourself that the problem is not as great as it seems, you'll manage better. Positive thinking really does help.

When you're worried and under stress, it helps a lot if your friends and family are supportive. This works in reverse too. If one of your friends or family members is under stress, you can be very helpful by showing that person you really care. That's the most important kind of support there is.

Live life now!

Don't wish your life away making impossible plans for your future. Grand plans are fun, but not really helpful if you can't achieve them. And don't let other people pressure you into trying to achieve things you know are not possible. You'll only worry about achieving them and that will trigger a whole host of new worries. Set yourself realistic goals, and aim to achieve them one step at a time. Remember that life is precious and you need to live in the present as well as hold onto your dreams for the future.

Some good advice for beating the blues

Get regular exercise. Physical exercise is good for the mind as well as for the body. It gives you more energy and it is a good way to work out anger. Studies show that if you exercise regularly, your body creates more beta endorphins, natural hormones that help you feel better about yourself. Also, if you are physically tired you will sleep well. Don't hold things in. Have a good cry if you can and talk to anyone who'll listen sympathetically.

It may seem difficult to do when you're down, but make a list of all the things you really enjoy in life. At first you may think there's nothing to write down. Persevere and you'll probably surprise yourself. Give yourself something to look forward to every day — little things, like visiting a good friend and having a chat, watching a favourite video or buying a good magazine.

Exam pressure

It's when you're a teenager that you have to take important exams. You are now at a crucial stage at school, studying for exams which will affect what you do in the future and what kind of future you have.

Different cultures expect different things of their students. You may feel a lot of pressure on you to succeed, both at school and at home. You may find that you are spending so much time worrying about the final exams, that you have no time for anything else. Don't let the pressure get you down. Try to give yourself time off as well as time for studying. Of course, the plus is that if you work hard at school and succeed everybody will be pleased with you and you'll be pleased with yourself.

Whether you get on well with school work or not, there will be increasing pressure on you to stay at school or college until you have achieved a recognized degree of skill, or a qualification. It's usually easier to get your qualifications while you're still at school, rather than going back to your studies after a break, though there's no reason why you can't go on attending classes until you're 90! Your education will stand you in good stead when you apply for jobs. Your exam successes are proof that you can study, can concentrate, can set goals and achieve them – and every achievement will count when you are applying for a job. This is particularly true today when there are fewer and fewer jobs available to unskilled workers. Be confident and proud of yourself if you are studying hard – don't listen to other people who may not share your serious goals.

CHECKLIST – HOW TO SURVIVE EXAM PRESSURE

Have you experienced this dreadful nightmare – you get into the examination room, turn over the paper and your mind goes a complete blank? With luck, this won't happen to you. Your teacher will probably have shown you exam papers from previous years, so that the look and type of question paper will be familiar to you.

Can you spend the afternoon before the exams playing tennis, swimming, or taking some other form of exercise? This might sound like a waste of studying time – but it's better for you than last-minute cramming. You'll sleep well, and arrive at the exam feeling rested and relaxed.

Try not to turn up for the exams too early – all the waiting around will make you more nervous.

When you study, try to take things in from day to day. This is much better than last-minute cramming. You're also far more likely to absorb facts and retain them if you study in this way. So try to keep up to date with homework and other assignments.

Some schools may teach you special exam techniques. These are usually ways of triggering your memory when you have to remember lots of facts. These techniques don't guarantee you pass exams and they don't work for everyone. Your teachers will help and guide you, but ultimately it's up to you to decide on your own way of studying and revising.

Don't even think about cheating. The consequences can be serious, and you have to live with yourself afterwards.

Steady study is better than last-minute cramming.

EXAM NERVES

It's usual to get nervous before you take an exam, even if you know you've studied hard. This nervousness shows itself in physical symptoms:

 restlessness
 being very talkative
 wanting to go to the toilet
 headaches
 stomach aches
 nausea
 sweaty hands
 racing heartbeat
 shaking hands
 dry mouth and compulsive
 swallowing

If you feel any of these things before you go into an exam, try some deep breathing. That will calm your nerves. The jitters usually go away once you've sat down and the exam has started.

Examination pressures in Japan

Juken jigoku, or examination hell, exists in Japan because nearly every 14-year-old student at junior high school wishes to continue in full-time education beyond the school leaving age of 15. But there are not enough low-cost, state-maintained senior high schools to go round, so there is competition among 14-year-old students to get into the best upper school in the locality. Indeed, the competition to pass the high school examination in Japan is so fierce that most children experience 'double schooling'. In other words, outside regular school hours, most Japanese students attend *juku* or cram school for about five hours a week in order to maximize their chances in their crucial examinations in English and mathematics.

However, once Japanese students have entered senior high school, there is only a short breathing space before *juken jigoku* starts all over again as students prepare for entrance examinations to university.

It is often claimed that excessive pressure on young people in Japanese schools results in high rates of violence, bullying and juvenile suicide. The facts clearly show, however, that this is not true. Japan may lead the world in educational achievement in science and mathematics, but it is far from being a world leader in school violence and juvenile suicide.

In fact, a recent survey showed that many young Japanese people love their studies to an extraordinary degree. One girl wrote, "I will never forget the final words of a teacher when he retired from my high school last year: Life, until death, is study." Another student wrote, "I don't think there are many students in countries other than Japan who are pushed into high school entrance exams, so I think that passing the exams is the best thing that could happen to me".

Many Japanese students work so hard they have no time for other activities.

Readers' letters

"I come from a Muslim family. I respect my parents and know what is expected of me. My family will arrange a suitable marriage for me when the time is right. I am prepared for this but I also want to make sure that I have a career. I want to be a doctor. My parents are really pleased about this – they couldn't be more proud. The problems come when I tell them that I want to join in with some of the social activities at school. At my school the two things go together. As I am the oldest in my family I feel I owe it to my younger sisters to try and change the pattern of our lives a little bit to fit in with my social life. That way it shouldn't be so hard for my sisters when they are my age."
Fatima

"My brother has this fixation about red. He has dyed every bit of clothing he owns, and has painted his room all over – bright scarlet. His friends are all just as weird in their own way. When they go around together, you can see other people shrinking away from them! I think it's all a bit silly. My brother looks like a thug, but he's a real softy at heart. He goes round to see Gran and Grandpa every week. Their neighbours all expect him to steal their pensions, but it would never enter his head. I think it's a pity he looks so weird. It gives people the wrong impression."
Jake

"Sometimes I think my parents don't care about me at all! They let me stay out late, and they don't seem to mind that I have all sorts of friends they've never met. I talked to my mum about this and she said that she wanted me to be able to express myself and learn about the world in my own way. Both she and Dad had very strict parents and they said this made them unhappy. Don't get me wrong, I like going to parties and staying up late, but I also need somebody to talk to about stuff that I can't understand. I have made a really good friend who is older than me. She's telling me more than my parents ever have."
Yvette

"There's a girl in our class who is hardly ever in school. She arrives in the morning to register, and disappears after the first lesson. She's only 14 but looks at least four years older. One day as I was coming back from a check-up at the dentist, I saw her with a group of people in a café, laughing and smoking. When I mentioned this to my friend, she said she's seen her there several times before. It's where people hang out when they've got nothing better to do. I don't know what I should do, I feel I can't tell tales on her, but she seems to be wasting such a lot. She'll never get any qualifications at this rate."
Kiki

"When I was 10, my parents told me I was adopted. That was quite a bombshell, I can tell you. I can't understand why they waited all that time before telling me. Maybe they thought I wouldn't be able to cope – that I'd hate them, that I'd always be wanting to find my real parents. I don't know. I was really upset to begin with. But when I thought about my friends' parents, I gradually came to admit that mine had always treated me straight – really honestly – they were no nicer and no meaner to me than if I'd really been their child. And I can't ask for any more than that."
Hari

"I've been going out with a nice girl, but recently she's become really clingy and possessive. I can't go anywhere or do anything without her tagging along, and it's really getting me down. I like her a lot, but don't want her round my neck all day. When I try to tell her gently and tactfully that I need space, she takes it badly, and thinks it means I don't like her any more. Dealing with other people's feelings is the hardest thing I've ever had to do in my life."
Dominic

"I sometimes wonder if it's worth bothering. However hard I try, I never seem to be the best at anything I do. My best friend is top of the class and in every sports team there is, as well as being a brilliant trumpet player. I'm always average in class, and only once got to be reserve in the football team. My dad reckons there are just a lot of bright kids in my class, and that's why I don't think I'm doing well. He says if I were in another class, I'd be up at the top for sure. I guess that makes me feel a bit better about it. Another thing that helps a lot is the fact that I've got two kid brothers who look up to me and think I'm great. They really give my ego a boost!"
Brett

Making mistakes

Oh no! You've made a mistake! Everybody makes mistakes – nobody's perfect – but can you handle it? Sometimes it is difficult to admit that you're wrong, because you feel so foolish. You wish the whole thing had never happened and you don't want to hear another word about the sorry episode.

Sometimes you'll be lucky. You can put the whole thing behind you and face the world afresh. But sometimes your mistakes linger on, then you have to face up to them and, if you can, learn by them.

Everybody makes silly mistakes sometimes. Have you ever washed a shirt with a valuable note in the pocket, or watched a car driving off with your bag sitting on the roof? The only person to suffer from these kinds of mistake is yourself.

Accepting an apology can be difficult.

Be careful

Your mistakes are far more serious when they directly affect another person. You may be the sort of person who's very impatient and who flies off the handle easily. You judge things without knowing all the facts and make all kinds of mistakes because of this. You speak before thinking. You get angry easily. You are not very patient and you haven't learned to be tolerant. If this describes you more than you care to admit, you need to take action. Try counting to ten before you lose your temper next time. Try walking away from the situation. If you do this you'll avoid a confrontation. You won't make the mistake of hurting somebody with your words, when you don't mean to.

Apologizing

Learning to say sorry is one of the most mature qualities you can acquire. It's one of those qualities everyone will admire you for because they all know how difficult it is to do. Apologizing is not a sign of weakness, so don't look at it that way. In fact, it is just the opposite – it shows you have the confidence to confront a situation and deal with it efficiently. Once you recognize you have made a mistake, try to apologize quickly. Don't make a big deal of it. Get it over with. Feelings of guilt get in the way of other things, and stay on your conscience until they are completely out of proportion. So say sorry as soon as you can. If someone apologizes to you, just accept it calmly.

Not my fault

You may find that sometimes you're expected to apologize when you don't feel you should have to. You may feel you're not completely in the wrong. Rather than getting defensive or hostile, try to talk out the problem with the other person and resolve the misunderstanding. Then put it behind you both. Holding a grudge helps no one.

LEARNING FROM YOUR MISTAKES

Growing up is all about experiencing things for the first time. It is easy to make a mistake because you are inexperienced.

If you make mistakes because you're careless, try and give more time to things. Take life more slowly. Think things out and plan how you're going to act.

If you think you might make mistakes because you feel uncertain or ignorant about something, talk about it with someone you trust. Don't act without a second opinion.

If you make mistakes because you're nervous, take a deep breath before you act. Don't panic yourself into acting on impulse or in a way which isn't really you, just because you think you must make your mark.

Concentrate on all the good things you can do, and don't dwell on things you aren't so good at. Making mistakes is all about lacking knowledge – and that's something you can work on putting right.

DON'T BLAME YOURSELF

If you blame yourself for everything that goes wrong, you'll soon begin to lose confidence in yourself.

But everybody makes mistakes. It's part of human nature. And if you can learn from where you went wrong, you'll become a wiser person.

Feeling confident

Some people seem to be born confident. They can enter a crowded room, immediately feel at home and settle down and talk to anybody. Confidence comes from believing in yourself and feeling happy. Once you're confident about what you want out of life, you can go for it.

When you're confident about yourself – how you look and how you feel – many other problems disappear. Perhaps you have to read some of your work out in front of the whole class. If you feel confident in yourself, you'll be less pre-occupied with things that don't matter – like how you look and where you're sitting – and more concerned with making the reading interesting for the rest of the class.

What can you do?

Make a list of the things you're good at and another one of the things you think you're not so good at. Do something from the first list every day. This will make you feel pleased with yourself. While you're feeling good, try something from the not so good list. The way you feel about yourself can really affect the way you do things.

However confident you are, speaking to a lot of people can be a nerve- wracking experience.

KNOW YOURSELF
Make a list of what your strong points are. You can feel proud of what you're good at.

Not so good points	Good points
tidying room	making friends
getting to sports practice on time	swimming
handwriting	staying fit
cleaning shoes	telling jokes
nail biting	eating healthy food
brushing hair	studying hard
washing dishes	organizing games
	painting

Feeling confident will show in the way you look.

Think positive

You will be surprised to find out that if you believe in yourself other people will believe in you too. Ignore all the 'don'ts' that normally guide your life and work on the 'do's'. How often does your day start with, "Don't be long in the bathroom", "Don't gobble your breakfast", "Don't forget your games gear", "Don't miss the bus". It might seem as if you're surrounded by negatives. Unfortunately it's the way many human beings think. And over the years it starts to have an impact on the way you think and behave.

Try educating yourself and those around you to positive thinking. The next time your parents send you off with "and don't get into trouble today", come back with a smiling positive – "Bye Mum, have a nice day!"

Set goals

You can achieve a lot as long as you are really determined. Set out goals, in writing if you can, and put dates by when you will achieve them. If you want to improve your running speed, set yourself a realistic target. Don't try for Olympic speeds straight away. Make it a gradual improvement, cutting a few seconds off your time every week. Be realistic about what you can achieve. Setting unrealistic goals leads to frustration no matter how single-minded you are.

Be yourself

If you have an argument with somebody at school, and you really feel that you are in the right, stick to your opinion. Make sure the other person knows you're arguing from commitment. You don't have to agree with everyone all the time to make sure that they like you. People respect others who stick to their own opinions. But don't lose your temper and shout. That's childish.

Try not to take life too seriously all the time. Relax and enjoy things as they happen. If you spend your time worrying about what might happen you won't have time to do anything.

HOW CONFIDENT ARE YOU?

1. You are invited to a party by somebody you don't know. Do you:

a) Feel delighted – you love meeting new people!
b) Say you'll go if you can bring a friend.

2. You win a prize, do you:

a) walk up and take it with a happy smile on your face?
b) blush, wriggle and act as if you're hating every moment.

3. You've bought something from the shops which breaks on the way home. Do you:

a) Turn round and take it straight back to the shop?
b) Go home and put the broken item away in a cupboard.

4. A teacher is organizing an outing and there is one place left. Do you:

a) Put up your hand straight away and ask if you can have the place?
b) Dither until the place is filled and then wish you'd put your hand up.

HOW DID YOU SCORE?

Mostly as
You are full of confidence! You are able to say what you want and go and get it!

Mostly bs
Have faith in yourself. Don't be afraid to do what you think is right. As long as you feel comfortable with yourself, you'll be fine.

You and the community

As you become more aware of the world around you, there are going to be things about it that you do and don't like. Many young people feel very passionate about moral issues and want to try and change things. They are concerned about poverty, sickness, wars and injustice generally and they want to do something meaningful.

You are probably especially concerned about the environment. The increasing destruction of our natural world, the burning of the rain forests and the growing hole in the planet's protective ozone layer, are environmental issues that you will already know about. Global organizations such as Greenpeace are challenging everyone to increase their awareness of environmental problems and their involvement in them.

*Stand up for a
cause you believe in.*

Local effort

When you look around your local community, you will see that there are things you can do to make life better for people who are less fortunate than yourself. For example, you could visit old or sick people or you could help look after the mentally or physically handicapped. Perhaps you like looking after children. If so, you could volunteer to help in a nursery or playgroup. You might organize a litter collection. You and your friends could make an open space or park a nicer place to walk or play in. You might learn first aid, which is always a useful skill. You never know when someone will need help which you know how to give. Every one of us can contribute something to make life a little more pleasant, however small the contribution might be. Any society is made up of the people who belong to it, so the more responsible, caring people there are, the more responsible and caring their society can be.

Find out about yourself

Work in the community also helps you to discover your own talents. Sometimes community work can lead to a full-time career when you leave school. For example, you may realize that you are good at raising money for organizations. This is a special talent. You need to be outgoing and very clear about what you say and think, to persuade people to give you money for any cause. You may discover that you are happiest working directly with disadvantaged people. You may be very good at looking after children. Whatever you find out about yourself will be positive. You will get a lot out of what you do and of course, the people you help will benefit enormously.

You can help make someone else's life easier and happier.

Recycling helps to preserve precious resources.

Global issues

Global issues concern events that are going on all over the world. Satellites beam powerful images of the world's calamities into our homes almost as they are happening. When you see pictures of war, sickness and famine on your television, you feel angry but also frustrated and powerless. What can you do about it?

Firstly you can speak out. You'll certainly not be on your own, and you'll swell the ranks of those who care enough to act. You can get involved with groups concerned about these issues, and go on organized, peaceful demonstrations. It's an active way of registering your protest. You'll undoubtedly feel better for that.

Large organizations like the International Red Cross, Oxfam and The Save the Children Fund will most likely have a group that you can join at local level. You can help by raising money or

by making things for the organization which will then be sold to raise funds.

If you want to help, get in touch with your local environmental group and volunteer to carry out some activity for them. You may find yourself working in the group's offices or distributing leaflets which present the latest information about environmental topics. Every little bit of help is important and will contribute to changing things.

When you join a group and start working for a cause that you believe in, you gain too. You will have the opportunity to meet people with the same views as yourself, as well as to learn more about the issue. The better informed you are, the more useful you'll be to your cause. You'll be able to explain its aims to other people and widen its impact on society.

Don't give up

Don't forget, water will wear away stone. Sometimes it may take a lifetime to see things change. When you're young, it's easy to feel frustrated with the delays and seemingly stupid hitches that take place. However, if you're aware of local and global issues when you're young, your commitment to making the world a better place for everyone will continue. And who knows what you might achieve.

NAMES AND ADDRESSES OF GLOBAL ORGANIZATIONS

Greenpeace
30-31 Islington Green
London N1 8XE
UK

International Committee of the Red Cross
19 Avenue de la Paix
CH-1202 Geneva
Switzerland

United Nations Children's Fund (UNICEF)
UNICEF House
3 UN Plaza
New York, NY 10017
USA

Worldwide Fund for Nature
Avenue du Mont-Blanc
1196 Gland
Switzerland

Your future

If you are taking exams at school, you will probably have begun to think already about what you want to do in the future. A choice of career is one of the most important decisions a young person has to make.

Don't be tempted to leave school too soon. A good education is the best qualification for life as well as for a career. An education teaches you how to make choices as well as how to pass exams. You need to be aware of the different options open to you and to know enough to be able to change your mind if you ever want to. The better educated you are, the easier it will be to do this.

Job influences

A few people make up their minds about their career very early on in their lives. They may be influenced by their parents' careers or by another adult whose job sounds interesting. They may be impressed by books, films or advertising, all of which create job images. It is a good idea to talk to adults who are actually doing the type of jobs you are interested in. Your school may well offer career guidance.

If you feel uncertain about your skills and talents, take time to decide what is best for you. Don't be pushed into something that you don't want to do. However, it's sensible to keep an open mind for as long as you can. You never know how things might change. And you may need to adapt and retrain for new technologies as they come along.

Changing course

It's an unfortunate fact that jobs are going to be harder and harder to find in the future. However desperate you are to do a particular job, you may sometimes have to change your mind. You may not find any jobs in your field, or you may be made redundant.

There may be periods in your life when you're out of a job altogether. If you are unemployed, try to keep busy, whatever happens. Even if there are no paid jobs around, you may find voluntary work to do. A future employer will appreciate that you've taken the initiative to do something. Sitting at home waiting for the phone to ring won't make you feel good. This is easier said than done, but it really is worth making the effort.

WHAT KIND OF A PERSON ARE YOU?

Different kinds of people are good at different kinds of job. It helps to think about yourself. What qualities do you have?

An ability to lead
Leadership qualities are useful in every career but in some jobs there is a need for one worker in a group to guide the others. Leaders must be mature and self confident.

An accurate and careful approach to detail
Some jobs depend upon a worker being very precise and careful in their work.

A sense of business
Businesses aren't set up to run at a loss. A business can only keep going if it makes a profit. This requires a good understanding of everything the business does – the goods it makes, the people and equipment who make them, the customers who buy and the price the goods are sold at. A lot depends on making the right decisions at the right time.

Eleven ways to make a good impression

When you go for your first interview – whether it is for a job or for a place in further education, there are things that can help you, quite apart from your qualifications.

1. Take advice from a teacher or parent on what to expect at an interview.

2. If you are nervous, try going through a practice interview with a parent or a friend the day before. You can make your mistakes at this interview and not at the real one.

3. Prepare your clothes for your interview the night before. Always wear something that you are comfortable in. Your clothes should be clean and tidy. Sew on any buttons that have come off.

4. Look at your hands. You are going to have to shake hands with your interviewers. Cut and clean your nails.

5. Make sure you have clean hair.

6. Arrive for your interview in good time. Five minutes early is ideal. Five minutes late will count against you – unless there's a spectacular reason for the delay.

7. When you greet your interviewer, use direct eye contact, and smile.

8. Don't chew gum or smoke at interviews.

9. As well as discussing your career, talk about what you like doing in your spare time.

10. Don't fidget, bite your nails or twist your hair. Try to look as relaxed as you can.

11. Towards the end of the interview, you will probably be asked if you have any questions arising from what you've been told about the job or the course. There may be something you do want to ask because it hasn't been explained. Be brave and come out with your question. If there's nothing you want to ask, say so.

A calm personality
People who work in difficult situations or for emergency services or under pressure, must be able to keep calm.

A wish to help people
There are many jobs which are mostly concerned with helping people in need. It is necessary to have strong qualities of tact and understanding and to be able to talk to people positively and constructively.

People who are sociable
In some careers, it is important to be able to mix with people, often strangers, and get on well with them.

People who can persuade others
A strong personality with strong opinions is an essential part of some jobs. You may need to persuade people to do something they don't particularly want to do for a good cause.

Willingness to work long hours
Some jobs involve working shifts, this may mean regularly working through the night or at weekends. Sometimes it is necessary to live on the job.

Creativity
Many people have a lively imagination and creative flair. But not so many manage to earn a living by their creativity.

Practicality
Being good with your hands is a great asset in many jobs.

Career choice

Not everyone can be a test pilot, a heart surgeon or a ballerina. And not everyone wants to be. We are all very different in our educational skills, our physical make-up and our personalities. An ideal career should combine your best points with your interests and qualifications. See if you can find something to suit you in this chart.

Career choice

Some of the subjects and skills you may find useful	Accountancy	Administration	Agriculture	Architecture	Armed services (army, navy, airforce)	Art	Astronomy	Banking	Building trade	Business management	Computers	Cook	Dance	Dentistry	Design	Drama	Economics	Engineering
Art				•		•							•		•	•		
Attention to detail	•	•	•	•	•	•	•	•	•	•	•	•	•	•	•	•	•	•
Biology			•											•				
Business sense	•	•	•	•				•	•	•							•	
Calmness	•	•			•			•			•	•		•				
Computer studies	•	•		•	•		•	•		•	•						•	•
Creativity				•		•						•	•		•	•		
Design technology				•		•			•						•			•
Economics	•	•						•		•	•						•	
Engineering				•	•				•									•
Hard work			•		•				•					•				
Helping people		•			•									•				
Home economics												•						
Languages		•						•		•								
Leadership		•		•	•					•								
Maths	•	•	•	•	•		•	•	•	•	•	•		•	•		•	•
Music													•			•		
Physical fitness			•	•					•				•			•		
Physics				•			•				•			•				•
Practicality			•		•	•			•			•		•				•
Sociability										•				•		•		
Social sciences		•															•	

	Farming	Film	Fire-fighting	Hotel	Journalism	Law	Librarianship	Management	Manufacturing	Medicine	Meteorology	Music	Nuclear power	Nursing	Oil industry	Pharmacy	Physical education	Police force	Secretarial	Shopkeeper	Social work	Teaching	Textiles	TV	Veterinary science
		●										●											●	●	
	●	●	●	●	●	●	●	●	●	●	●	●	●	●	●	●	●	●	●	●	●	●	●	●	●
	●									●					●	●									●
	●			●			●	●	●						●					●					
			●					●		●					●				●	●	●	●			●
								●	●		●			●			●	●							
		●											●										●	●	
								●															●		
				●				●	●																
													●		●										
	●	●								●				●				●				●			●
		●	●				●			●				●			●	●		●	●	●			●
				●																					
					●			●												●	●				
				●				●										●			●				
	●			●		●		●		●	●	●	●	●	●	●		●		●	●				●
													●								●			●	
	●																●	●			●				
								●			●		●		●										●
	●								●					●		●					●	●	●		●
			●		●					●				●				●		●	●	●		●	
			●		●	●								●				●			●	●			

243

HELPLINES

*Here's a list of organizations you could contact
in case you'd like to find out more about some of
the things discussed in this chapter. Whichever
part of the world you live in, there are
organizations that can answer your questions.
These organizations will be happy to give you
useful information and advice.*

Australia
AIDS Hotline

India
Asha Sadan, Umerkhadi
Children's Aid Society

Malaysia
AIDS, STDs, Unplanned
pregnancy

Philippines
Council for the Welfare of
Children

Singapore
AIDS Helpline
Association of Women for Action
and Research
Pregnancy Crisis Service
Singapore Planned Parenthood
Association

South Africa
Planned Parenthood
Association

UK
Brook Advisory Centre
(pregnancy)
National AIDS Helpline

*You should be able to find the telephone numbers
in your local telephone directory or by phoning
directory enquiries.*

5

CHANGING BODY

A young person's guide to puberty

You might think it would be useful if you could flick a switch and wake up tomorrow as an adult. But life isn't like that, of course. The changes that happen to your body happen over a number of years and you gradually develop into a physically mature person. Some of the changes are visible, but some happen inside your body. In this chapter you can find out all about the changes. If you know what to expect, you'll take everything in your stride!

Getting ready

This book deals with puberty — the physical development that happens to your body during your teenage years. Your body goes on changing all your life. Puberty is just part of this process of change. As you'll see from the photos on this page, a 12 year old can look very different from when they were younger. There are obvious differences such as size and strength. Then look at the way the shape of the face changes.

The physical development we call puberty is mostly to do with sex. Sex really just means whether you're male or female. We all belong to one or other sex, and part of growing up is becoming sexually mature and ready to make babies. As you notice your body gradually changing, you'll wonder why these changes have to happen. Are all your friends going through the same changes? Are you 'normal'? You probably want to ask a lot of questions about what's happening to you.

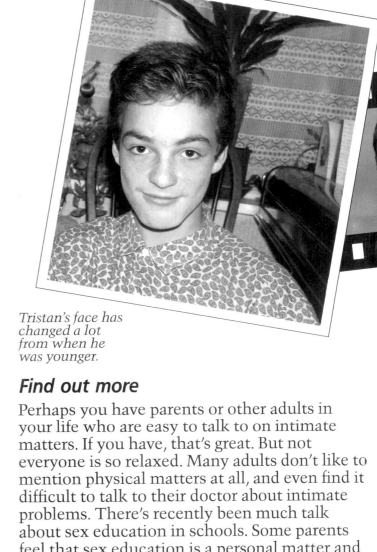

Tristan's face has changed a lot from when he was younger.

Find out more

Perhaps you have parents or other adults in your life who are easy to talk to on intimate matters. If you have, that's great. But not everyone is so relaxed. Many adults don't like to mention physical matters at all, and even find it difficult to talk to their doctor about intimate problems. There's recently been much talk about sex education in schools. Some parents feel that sex education is a personal matter and should be dealt with at home. They think that schools don't encourage high moral standards. Other people feel that sex education in school is a good thing. Whatever you think, it's good to know what will happen to your body, and why.

If your parents or your school have talked with you about sexual development, you may only have learned about what happens to people of your own sex. Girls often don't get to hear much about how the penis works, and boys aren't very clued up on menstruation. But it's extremely useful to know how someone of the other sex develops too. This will give you greater understanding of others, and will help you to appreciate their problems and the way they feel.

Here is Laura at 12 and Laura at 7.

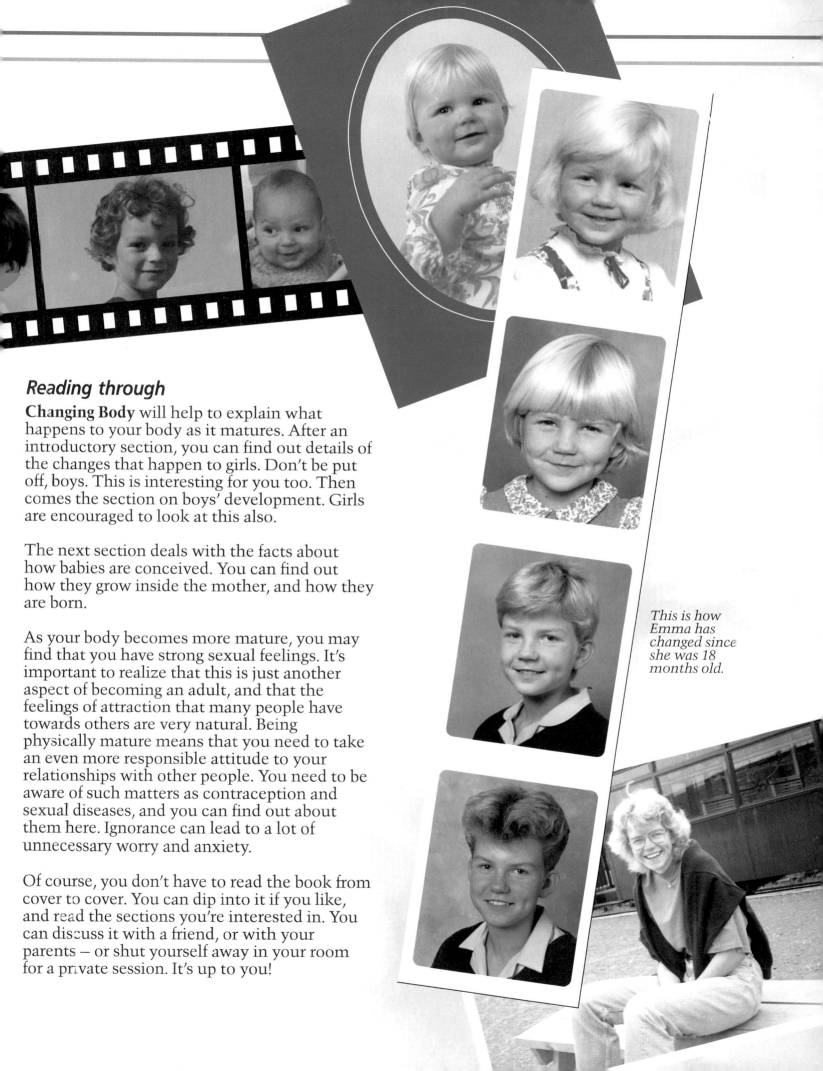

Reading through

Changing Body will help to explain what happens to your body as it matures. After an introductory section, you can find out details of the changes that happen to girls. Don't be put off, boys. This is interesting for you too. Then comes the section on boys' development. Girls are encouraged to look at this also.

The next section deals with the facts about how babies are conceived. You can find out how they grow inside the mother, and how they are born.

As your body becomes more mature, you may find that you have strong sexual feelings. It's important to realize that this is just another aspect of becoming an adult, and that the feelings of attraction that many people have towards others are very natural. Being physically mature means that you need to take an even more responsible attitude to your relationships with other people. You need to be aware of such matters as contraception and sexual diseases, and you can find out about them here. Ignorance can lead to a lot of unnecessary worry and anxiety.

Of course, you don't have to read the book from cover to cover. You can dip into it if you like, and read the sections you're interested in. You can discuss it with a friend, or with your parents — or shut yourself away in your room for a private session. It's up to you!

This is how Emma has changed since she was 18 months old.

You're all right!

The trouble with growing up is that for lots of people it doesn't happen quickly enough. You don't go to bed one day as a child and wake up the next as an adult.

In some cultures, events and ceremonies are staged to mark the moment of changing from a child to an adult. The Barasana tribe in the Amazon rain forest, for example, celebrate a girl's first period as the moment of entry into adult life. The girl is isolated in a screened-off section of her communal house. Her hair is cut and she will not be seen by men, women or children for around five days. During the five days the girl observes a strict diet. She is also expected to avoid certain 'luxury' objects such as her hammock or a mirror. At the end of the five days she undergoes a ritual bath and vomiting, which the Barasana tribe see as a very cleansing act. Now the girl is an adult.

In western countries, the usual definition of adulthood has nothing to do with our physical development. It's to do with the age at which the law allows you to do things like vote, drink or drive a car. The law is not interested in how much facial hair you have or how big your breasts are. In the west, people don't generally make a clear distinction between a physical child and a physical adult. The development from one to the other is accepted as a gradual process. People don't tend to celebrate a girl's first period with any great fun.

Media images

Whenever you watch TV or read magazines, you're constantly being presented with images of the ideal man or woman. Men are portrayed as hunky and athletic, and women as tall and slim. Throughout history, there have been different ideas of good looks. Two hundred years ago in Europe, boys might have tried for the thin and weedy look, while girls might have been padding themselves out to look more curvaceous. Different countries have their own ideas of beauty, too. Beauty really is in the eye of the beholder.

As you'll notice, not many real people match these ideals. Real people are short, tall, plump or skinny, hairy or smooth, bosomy or flat-chested. The way you look mostly depends on inherited characteristics, so you can't do a lot to change things, though you can alter your shape to some extent by dieting, exercising and generally looking after yourself. So learn to get used to your body. It's all yours. Nobody else looks quite like you!

Very few people look like the media version of the ideal man or woman.

We're all different

The way your body develops is individual, too. Think how different all your friends' faces are. You recognize them all as individuals, don't you? So you can see that their bodies are likely to be just as individual as their faces. We don't usually see each other's bodies much, but if we could, we'd see that everyone is different, from eyebrows to toenails! When you think of that, it becomes easier to accept that your body may not be changing in exactly the same way or at the same rate as your friends' bodies.

That's all very well, you may say. But my friend has perfect skin and I have two moles on my chin. My younger brother is really tall and broad-shouldered, and I look like a real weed when I stand next to him. Well, life isn't always fair. But the chances are that your friend and your brother may envy one or more of your features. Unfortunately, by comparing ourselves with others, we often end up being dissatisfied with our own bodies. Who says you have to be tall anyway, and if the moles on your chin really bother you, you may be able to have them removed by a doctor.

So try to accept what you are. You'll feel a whole lot happier if you're not endlessly wishing things were different. Anyway, think how uninteresting it would be if we all looked as if we'd walked off the same assembly line.

Introducing puberty

Once you reach your teens, it's not much fun being thought of as a kid any more. During this period of adolescence, your mind and your body are in the mood for change. You are in the throes of becoming an adult. This is an exciting period of life and most young people can't wait to get going.

You may feel that all your friends are growing up before you are. But no matter how hard you wish, your body has a mind of its own, and it will decide when it's ready to develop. The physical change from childhood to adulthood can start for girls as early as 8 years – or be delayed until 16 years of age.

Some girls have started their periods and are wearing bras by the age of 10. Others don't experience either until they are 14. Boys tend to start developing a little later than girls – around 10 years is probably the youngest, and at the latest, around 17 or 18.

Whatever age you notice that changes are starting to take place, you should at least understand why there are changes at all. Puberty is the process of physical change during which a child develops into an adult capable of making a baby. It would be helpful if your body adjusted at the same speed as your mind. But the necessary changes in your body may well start before you feel emotionally ready to cope with them.

THE CHANGEOVER
When puberty does start, it happens slowly. Some changes are obvious while others are going on discreetly inside you. You probably don't even realise they are happening. These changes are triggered off when a tiny part of your brain kicks from child into adult gear. From then on, chemical substances known as hormones start to become more active. During early childhood, all the parts of the body concerned with reproduction are relatively inactive. But as puberty starts, these areas are woken up and start to change the shape, size and function of certain organs in your body. And when the hormone levels are high enough, your body starts producing sex cells.

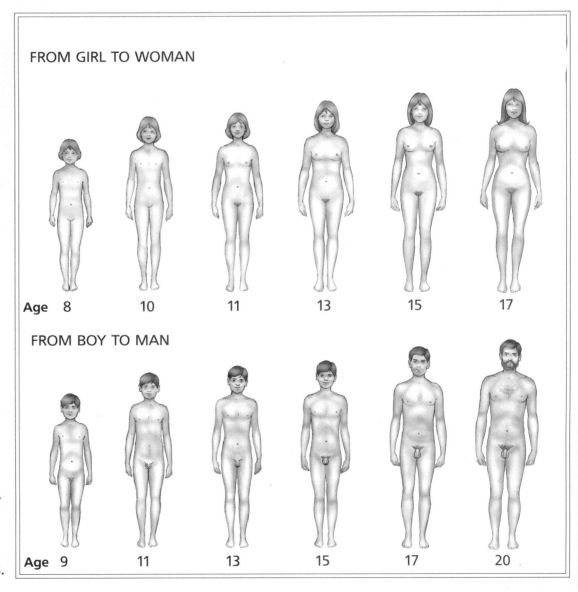

FROM GIRL TO WOMAN

Age 8   10   11   13   15   17

FROM BOY TO MAN

Age 9   11   13   15   17   20

GOING THROUGH PUBERTY

Puberty can be a great time in your life, once you understand what's happening. Changing schools or joining a new sports team can be worrying situations until you get used to them. Puberty is a bit like that. But if you know in advance what's about to happen, you'll cope better when it actually does. Whether you sail through your adolescent years or find them tough going, it will certainly help you to know as much as you can about the physical and emotional changes that will affect your body. This book aims to help you get through puberty by answering those questions which you find worrying or embarrassing.

Hormones

Puberty is the physical process whereby a child develops into an adult capable of reproduction. Puberty is controlled by hormones, which are special chemical messengers, that are released from endocrine glands, and travel around the body in the blood stream.

No one knows exactly what triggers the start of puberty. It starts in a part of the brain called the hypothalamus. This sends messages to the pituitary gland which is also in the brain. The pituitary makes a number of hormones involved in puberty. One is called the follicle-stimulating hormone or FSH, and another is the luteinizing hormone or LH. These act on the testes in the boy and the ovaries in the girl to produce the changes of puberty. In both sexes, the sex hormones work together with growth hormones, also produced by the pituitary, to cause a growth spurt in body height and weight. Later in this book you'll find out more about the parts of the body that are mentioned here.

In boys, LH acts on cells in the testes, called Leydig cells, causing them to secrete testosterone, the male sex hormone. Testosterone causes the growth of the penis and scrotum, the growth spurt and the growth of facial and body hair, a change in body odour, the deepening of the voice and the build-up of muscles. Testosterone is responsible for sexual feelings, erections and aggression. FSH stimulates the growth of the testicles.

In girls, the hormone known as FSH stimulates the growth of the follicles in the ovaries. These produce oestrogen, the female sex hormone. As the ovaries enlarge, more and more oestrogen is made. Oestrogen acts on the girl's body to produce the changes that we recognize as puberty. The breasts and nipples enlarge as the milk-producing glands are formed. Fat is laid down in the breasts and on the hips. The uterus, vagina and Fallopian tubes grow in size, the walls of the vagina thicken and become moist.

In girls small amounts of testosterone are made in the ovaries and other hormones are made in the adrenal glands. These are responsible for body hair, body odour, acne and sexual feelings.

The pituitary gland triggers production of hormones in the ovaries and testes. These hormones cause the changes of puberty.

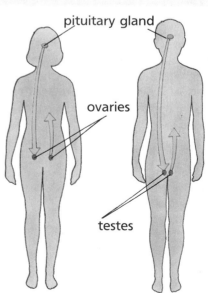

pituitary gland

ovaries

testes

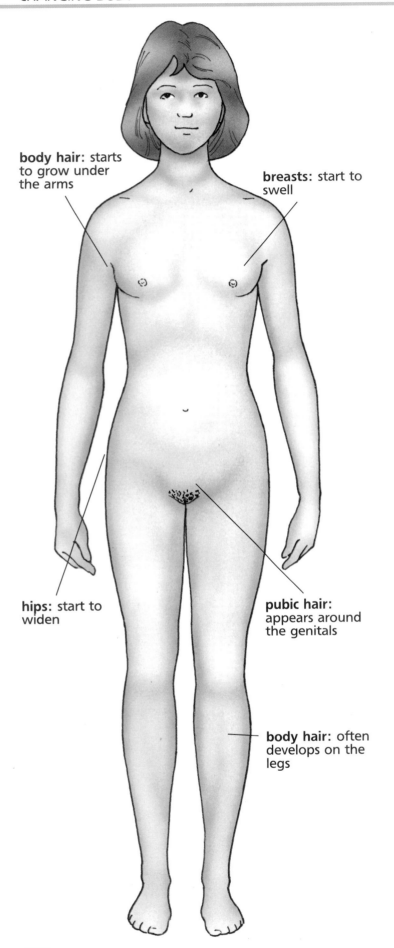

body hair: starts to grow under the arms

breasts: start to swell

hips: start to widen

pubic hair: appears around the genitals

body hair: often develops on the legs

A girl's new body map

You're probably discovering that puberty is made up of a whole series of changes. Your body, once a familiar place, is now becoming a bit like new, uncharted territory. If you know what is happening and why, you'll feel more at ease with yourself. It is important to remember that no matter in what order the changes come, they will all make sense in the end. Here are some signs of physical development you can watch out for.

Growth spurt

Around the beginning of puberty, you'll probably find you start to grow very fast – up to 100 millimetres in a year. The growth spurt lasts for a year or two, then it slows down to a more steady rate of about 25 to 50 millimetres a year. Girls usually reach their adult height within three years of having their first period. You can read about periods on pages 260 to 265.

You'll find that some parts of your body grow quicker than others. Your arms and legs usually grow faster than your body, and feet can reach their adult size long before the rest of you has caught up. You'll change shape, too. Your hips will get wider, and your face will alter.

Pubic hair

Probably the first place you'll notice bodily change is in the region of your sex organs or genitals. The hair which grows here as your body develops is called pubic hair. This normally starts off light coloured and fine, then gets darker over the years. To begin with you may only notice a few hairs on the fleshy mound on your lower pelvic region. This area is called the mons and it cushions and protects the bone underneath. If you look in a mirror you will see the outer lips or labia majora of your vagina. Pubic hair grows here, too. Hairs will gradually cover the mons and spread towards the thighs.

Just as eyelashes protect eyes from dirt, pubic hair protects the sensitive skin of the vagina. This is one reason why you should avoid plucking pubic hair. The other reason is that it's extremely painful!

Underarm hair

This usually starts to grow after pubic hair but it can appear before. Some women shave this hair off because they find it unattractive or for personal hygiene reasons. Many other women keep their underarm hair – the choice is yours.

Other body hair

As you get older your hair may turn darker and you will probably see more of it developing on your legs and arms. In some societies, girls choose to remove hair on their legs, but in other places, having leg hair is considered the usual thing. Again, it's up to you.

Breasts

As puberty develops, your breasts start to swell and become more noticeable. They won't reach their full size for quite a while yet. You can see how this happens on pages 254 and 255.

PERSPIRATION AND BODY ODOUR

During puberty you begin to sweat from many different areas – on your feet, the palms of the hands, underarms and around the genital areas between your legs. Everyone sweats, that's normal, but once air gets to the sweat and bacteria begin to breed, it starts to smell a bit unpleasant. However, you can stop odour becoming a problem by washing regularly with soap and sticking to a simple hygiene routine, such as using underarm antiperspirants or deodorants. Antiperspirants reduce the amount of sweat produced by your body. Deodorants destroy bacteria that cause body odour, and are sometimes perfumed.

Regular exercise is good for both your mind and body.

Your breasts

The swelling of your mammary glands, or breasts, is another early stage of puberty which you'll notice. Some girls are pleased when this happens. Others may prefer their old flat-chested look. You might feel slightly strange if you are the first girl in your class to need the support of a bra. At the same time, you will know that the development of breasts is one of the most obvious signs that you're becoming a woman.

Many people have breasts that are unequal in size. In fact, it's quite rare to find that both breasts are exactly the same. Normally the whole of your body is different one side from the other. The two sides of your face are different. One leg is often fatter or longer than the other and so on. So there's nothing wrong with you if one side of you and one breast is different from the other.

What are breasts for?

After childbirth, your breasts produce milk that your baby feeds on. The size of the breasts has nothing to do with how much milk they produce. Small breasts can produce just as much as large ones. The milk is made inside the lobes in the breast, and comes down the ducts or tubes to be sucked by the baby out of the little holes in the nipple. The milk comes out in a fine spray.

Breasts are for breast feeding.

PARTS OF THE BREASTS
All breasts work the same way, whatever their size.

The nipple
This is the most sensitive part. When it is cold or touched, tiny muscles pull together to make it hard, or erect. The shape of nipples varies a lot – some are large, others are small and some turn inwards instead of sticking out. Boys, of course, have nipples too, but theirs remain roughly the same size and shape throughout their lives.

The areola
This is the part that surrounds the nipple. Its colour can change as you grow up, from pale to dark brown. Sometimes, you'll see tiny lumps and bumps on this area especially if you're cold. You may see a few hairs growing here too.

The lobes
There are around 15 to 20 lobes inside each breast. As your breasts develop, the lobes in them get bigger. This is where the milk is made when you have a baby. In general, you shouldn't expect to see any fluid coming out of your nipples unless you're pregnant or have recently had a baby.

The fibres
The lobes are separated from each other by stretchy fibres. As they get older, some women breasts begin to droop because the fibres lose their elasticity. Wearing a properly fitting bra, specially during exercise, will help prevent this.

The rest of your breast
This is made up of fat which acts as protective padding and determines the size of the breast.

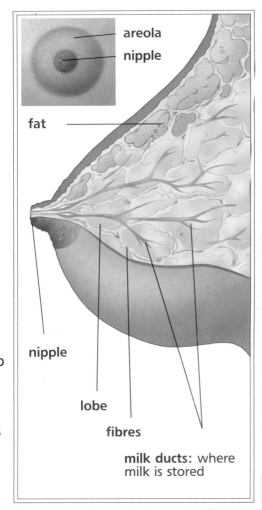

areola
nipple
fat
nipple
lobe
fibres
milk ducts: where milk is stored

The finishing tape

Nobody knows when your breasts will start to develop. It usually happpens between your ninth and fourteenth birthday, though you may be outside this span. You'll see that the eventual size of your breasts has nothing to do with when they start to grow. Just as some people have larger breasts than others, the different stages can last different lengths of time. Some girls go from stage one to stage four in six months. Others carry on growing for six years or more.

The size of your breasts does not have any affect on your ability to produce milk and breast feed your baby.

HOW THE BREASTS DEVELOP

It may take months, or even years for your breasts to develop fully.

Stage one
Before puberty your breasts are flat and the only part that sticks out is the nipple.

Stage two
This is sometimes called the breast bud stage. This is when the milk ducts or channels combine with fat tissue to form a small mound under each nipple and areola. The areola becomes wider and the area gets darker.

Stage three
Things have really started to happen now. The breast area becomes fuller and begins to be noticeable. Your breasts may now look like cones. This is perfectly normal.

Stage four
Nearly there! Some girls don't go through this stage, but others do. It occurs when your nipple and areola form a separate mound. They stand out just a little from the rest of the breast.

Stage five
You've made it! This is when your breasts take the shape and size that they'll be for the rest of your life, unless you put on or lose weight.

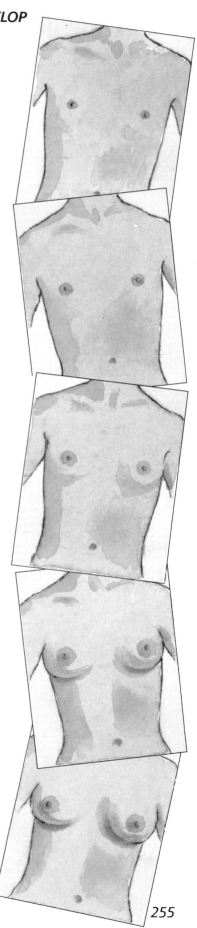

255

Breast care

The hormones in your body make your breasts react in certain ways. For instance, they often become fuller and a bit painful just before menstruation, when your hormones are at their most active. After a period they may feel softer and smaller.

Everyone's breasts feel different. Even the same breast can feel different as you get older as well as being influenced by the time of the month. Some breasts feel gritty or have lumpy areas in them, others feel like thick foam, smooth and even all over. Nipples vary too, in size, colour and shape. Some are turned inwards or flat, though they can usually be pulled out and massaged so that they stick out again. Consult your doctor if you are concerned about your nipples.

crop top

SUPPORT FOR YOUR BREASTS

Many girls like to wear a tight vest called a crop top which gives them some support before they get a bra for the first time. But when your breasts have reached stage 4, the cone-like stage, you'll probably start to think about wearing a bra.

If you are small-chested, there is no medical reason why you should wear a bra, though in many cultures and countries it's the accepted thing to do. If you are larger-breasted you will certainly feel more comfortable in a bra.

Although the breast has muscle underneath it, it is the ligaments which give it its shape. The ligaments do need support if you don't want your breasts to sag. Also, if you practise a lot of sport or exercise, you'll need the support of a bra, whatever your breast size.

Buying a bra

If people tell you that wearing a bra is uncomfortable, it's because they personally haven't got one that fits properly. If a bra fits well, you won't know you're wearing one.

Small breasts need no underwiring and are well suited to all-stretch cotton and Lycra with narrow back and shoulder straps.

Medium breasts choose a style with a deeper back, and preferably with light underwiring.

Large breasts choose a style with underwiring, preferably with support right around the ribcage beneath the breasts. Wide shoulder straps are most comfortable.

For sport look for support and plenty of flexibility to avoid any discomfort and strain that might damage ligaments.

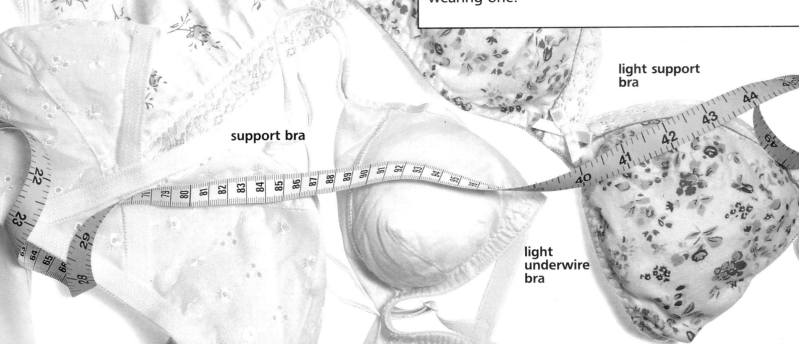

support bra

light support bra

light underwire bra

A bra is measured in centimetres and cup sizes. The centimetre measurement indicates the measurement round your chest underneath your breasts. The cup size is the measurement of the fullest part of your breast. To make sure you get one that's comfortable you need to measure both your chest and cup size.

1. Measure round your chest just under your breasts – where your rib cage is. Add 12 centimetres to that figure and write it down. This is your chest size.

2. Measure the fullest part of your breasts, which is usually round your chest and across the nipples. If this is the same measurement as your chest size you are an A cup.
If there is a 2.5 centimetre difference you are a B cup
If there is a 5 centimetre difference you are a C cup.

Bras come in many shapes, sizes and colours, just like breasts! There are plain bras and fancy bras, bras made from cotton, silk, satin, and polyester. Some are designed to do up in the front, some at the back, and some you pull on over your head. There are even strapless bras!

Examining your breasts

Breast examination is a good habit to get into. This doesn't mean you are likely to find anything wrong with your breasts. In fact, breast cancer is extremely rare among teenagers. But if you get to know what your breasts feel like, you'll know as soon as you find something out of the ordinary. Most of the lumps that women find in their breasts aren't cancer at all. They are usually pockets of fluid called cysts. A doctor can usually drain cysts quite easily by drawing off the liquid with a needle.

SELF EXAMINATION
The best time to examine your breasts is after your period has finished.

1. First stand in front of a mirror and look to see if there is any redness or swelling on the breasts. With your hands on your hips, press inwards and bend towards the mirror, tightening your muscles as you go. See if there are any changes in the shape of your breasts.

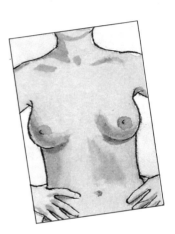

2. Lie down and put one hand behind your head. With three or four fingers of the other hand, press one breast in circular movements. Use the pads of your fingers, not the tips. Feel all the way round, right down to your chest and under your armpit, gradually working inwards towards the nipple.

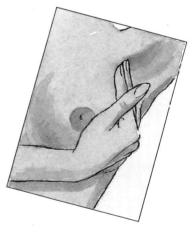

3. Repeat these steps for the other breast.

Your breasts are likely to feel quite bumpy, but if you've made a habit of examining yourself, you'll be able to notice any unusual lumps. If you do find any thickening or unusual spots, or unusual fluid coming from the nipples, get it checked out. Breast cancer in teenagers is very, very rare, but there are other breast disorders.

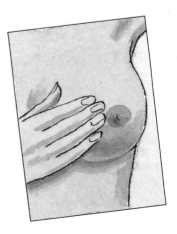

257

Female parts

Now you've seen how easy it is to examine your breasts you might like to explore the rest of your body too. In days gone by, women often had no idea of what their sex organs, or genitals, looked like. Perhaps this isn't surprising as unlike the penis, the vagina does not have to be handled every day and is not so much 'on show'.

Nowadays, knowing what your body looks like is far more accepted. If you feel comfortable, and have space and privacy, you might like to place a small mirror close to your genital area and have a look. Remember that the pictures in this book are diagrams, so your genitals won't look very much like them!

THE EXTERNAL ORGANS

This diagram shows where all the different parts are. The female genitals are known as the vulva. Don't be alarmed if your vulva looks different from pictures in this or other books. Genitals vary from person to person just like any other part of the body.

MONS

This is the mound of fat that cushions and protects the bone underneath. This will be covered in pubic hair when you are mature.

VAGINAL OPENING

The vaginal opening connects your internal and external sexual organs. This opening may be covered or partially covered by a small layer of skin called the hymen.

LABIA

The outer labia (labia majora) are two thick folds of skin. Labia is the latin word for lips, and majora means bigger. They have – or will have – pubic hair growing on them. Your labia almost certainly won't look neat and tidy like drawings in medical text books! When you're young, your labia are smooth, but will get more wrinkly during puberty. Underneath you may see some raised bumps. These are oil glands.

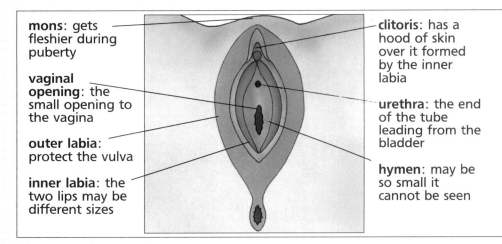

mons: gets fleshier during puberty

vaginal opening: the small opening to the vagina

outer labia: protect the vulva

inner labia: the two lips may be different sizes

clitoris: has a hood of skin over it formed by the inner labia

urethra: the end of the tube leading from the bladder

hymen: may be so small it cannot be seen

When you part the outer labia you will come to the inner labia, the labia minora, which is another set of lips. These are less thick and more sensitive. They usually stay inside the outer labia, but in some girls they do stick out a little. The inner labia don't have hair on them, and tend to be smoother than the labia majora.

CLITORIS

The clitoris is full of nerve endings. This small organ is the most sensitive part of the female body. The clitoris plays an important role in a woman's sexual excitement and pleasure.

URETHRA

Below the clitoris is the small hole called the urethra where urine is passed out of the body.

THE HYMEN

In some girls, but not all, you may see a thin piece of skin called the hymen stretched over the vaginal opening. Some girls find their hymen tears or stretches during exercise.

In some cultures the preservation of a hymen is considered to be very important, as it is supposed to show that a girl is a virgin. Technically, a virgin is someone who has not had sexual intercourse. In these cultures it is still thought to be shameful if a hymen is broken prior to marriage. But just because a girl doesn't have a noticeable hymen doesn't mean she's had sex. She may have broken it, or she may have a very small one that can't easily be seen.

INTERNAL SEX ORGANS

While all the changes that are happening to you on the outside can be seen – wonderful things are also happening inside that you can't see. You're born with all the equipment in place, and it's only during puberty that everything is activated and starts to function.

THE VAGINA

The vagina is a kind of tube inside your body. You can't actually see it. But you can see the vaginal opening, which is like a slit. The vagina itself isn't very big, but its elastic sides can expand a lot. It has to be able to expand enough to allow a baby through during childbirth.

THE UTERUS (WOMB)

This is roughly the same shape as an upside-down pear. It is where a fertilized egg or ovum implants itself and starts developing into a baby if it is fertilized by a sperm. Every month, the lining of your uterus will thicken to prepare itself for pregnancy. When you don't become pregnant, the egg disintegrates, the lining breaks down and passes out of your vagina together with the blood. This bleeding is called menstruation.

THE CERVIX

The cervix is a canal connecting the uterus with the vagina. As you can imagine, it is very stretchy during childbirth. It stretches from its normal width of one or two millimetres to allow the baby to pass through.

THE OVARIES

When you were born, you already had thousands of egg cells or ova in your ovaries. These ova are activated by the two hormones FSH and LH. These hormones cause the ova to mature and get ready to be released each month. One ovum is usually released from alternate ovaries each month.

FALLOPIAN TUBES

You have two thin Fallopian tubes not much wider than a strand of spaghetti, one each side of your uterus. They're also called uterine tubes, and they connect the ovaries to the uterus. Each has a fringe on the end called fimbria which almost cover – but don't touch – the ovary where eggs are released. Every month, the fringe reaches out in a wave type movement to catch the ovum and draw it into the tube. The ovum moves down the Fallopian tube.

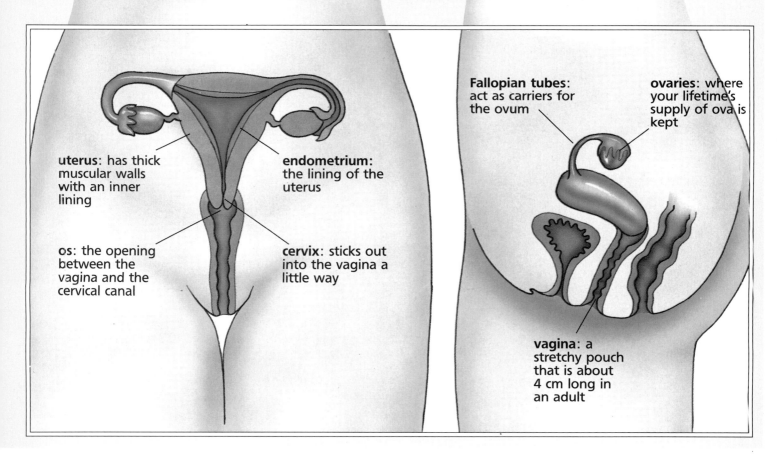

uterus: has thick muscular walls with an inner lining

os: the opening between the vagina and the cervical canal

endometrium: the lining of the uterus

cervix: sticks out into the vagina a little way

Fallopian tubes: act as carriers for the ovum

ovaries: where your lifetime's supply of ova is kept

vagina: a stretchy pouch that is about 4 cm long in an adult

Periods

Periods, or menstruating, are just part of growing up. It shows that your body is getting ready to have babies. You're becoming a woman. When you have a period, blood comes out of your vagina. Why? What is this blood, and where does it come from?

Why does menstruation happen?

Every month, an egg or ovum is released from one of the ovaries. You can see where these are on pages 258 and 259. You can't usually feel this happening, though some people do feel a slight twinge. The ovum makes its way down the Fallopian tube. If a sperm happens to find its way to the Fallopian tube at the same time, it may fertilize the ovum. If the ovum is not fertilized, it isn't needed any more, so it disintegrates in the uterus. The lining of the uterus breaks down, and comes out of your body as menstrual blood.

When do you start?

There's no fixed time when you'll start your periods. It may be any time between the ages of 10 and 16, though mostly it's between 11 and 14. You'll be able to get some clue when you'll start by asking your mother. Daughters very often have their first periods at around the same age as their mothers did.

The menstrual cycle

The menstrual cycle is controlled by your hormones which were explained earlier on page 251. You count your cycle from the first day of bleeding of one period to the first day of bleeding of the next. The average cycle is 28 days, although anything between 20 and 35 days is normal. The cycle may be irregular at first, but then usually follows a similar pattern every month.

Day 1 Your period starts. The bleeding is actually the lining of the uterus that sheds itself because no ovum has been fertilized and the lining is not needed. This bleeding usually lasts about five days. At the same time, a new ovum is maturing in one of your ovaries. Your pituitary gland has activated the hormone FSH to make this happen.

Day 5 The lining has now been shed and your bleeding stops. The new ovum carries on maturing and moves towards the surface of the ovary. At the same time the sac that contains the ovum, called a follicle, is producing another hormone called oestrogen. This makes the lining of the uterus thicken in case there is fertilization later in the cycle.

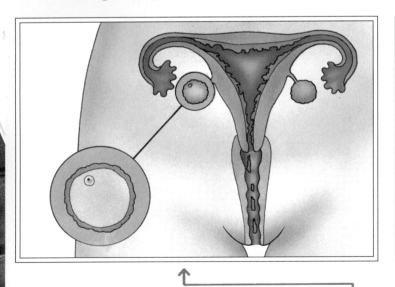

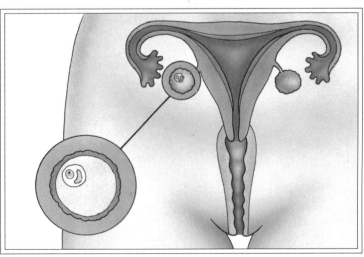

1

5

Reader's experience

"I had my first period six months ago, but I can never tell when the next one will be. Sometimes it happens every three weeks, others can be five to six weeks apart. It's really annoying".
Pauline

This is in fact quite common, especially for the first couple of years. It's because your hormones haven't had a chance to settle down into a regular rhythm yet. You might find that you don't have a period for several months, then have a couple only a few weeks apart. Give it time. Other factors that might make your periods irregular are worry, stress, being ill, or even going on holiday. People who lose a lot of weight quickly, or athletes who are doing too much serious training can also miss periods. With all the changes that are going on during puberty, it's not really surprising that things take a while to sort themselves out.

Day 14 Your body stops producing FSH and starts making a large amount of the hormone LH instead. LH helps the now mature ovum to burst through the surface of the ovary.

Another hormone called progesterone gets to work on the lining of the uterus making it soft and spongy. If an egg is now fertilized it will have something to embed itself on.

Day 21 The ovum travels along the Fallopian tubes to your uterus. The levels of oestrogen and progesterone fall. The ovum and lining of the uterus aren't needed so they

disintegrate, and start the slow journey down into your vagina. On day 27, your cycle is complete. Your next period will start tomorrow, Day 1 of your next menstrual cycle.

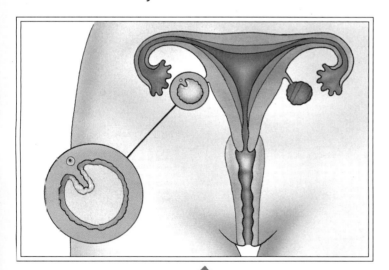

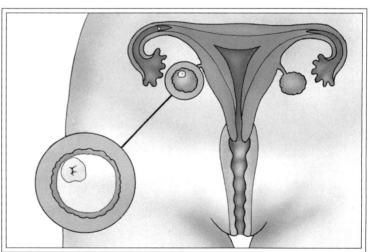

Be prepared!

Since you don't know when your periods will start, it's a good idea to be prepared. So you'll need to have something to soak up the blood. In some countries the old, tried and trusted methods that involve using natural materials like sponges, grasses, leaves and pieces of cloth are still used. But in most parts of the world, there's a range of sanitary products you can buy.

The product you choose will be up to you – you may have to try a few different ones before you find the one that suits you best. Ask someone you trust to help you choose. Some religions forbid the use of tampons, as they may break the hymen. However most young girls can safely and comfortably use a tampon even if they've never had sexual intercourse.

TAMPONS

A tampon is a smallish plug of densely packed cotton wool. You push it gently up into your vagina either with your finger or with an applicator. As the tampon absorbs the blood in your vagina, it expands. A string attached to the tampon makes it easy to pull the tampon out again. You can flush your used tampon down the toilet.

Many girls ask how they can tell if the opening in their hymen is large enough to use a tampon. In general, if a finger can be gently put in to the vagina, you can use a tampon. You may like to start with a junior size tampon when you first try. You can buy tampons in different sizes.

Fitting a tampon

Tampons can initially be quite hard to insert. Even the detailed instructions which come with every pack can make it look complicated. Push the tampon right up. If it's too low, it will feel uncomfortable. If you remember that your vagina slopes backwards a little, you should manage with a little practice!

Tampons are very comfortable to wear. When you've got one in, you won't notice it's there. But you must still remember to change it regularly – tampons can leak, just as sanitary towels can. Another possible problem is toxic shock syndrome. You can find out about this on the next page.

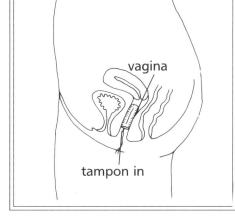

vagina

tampon in

Lost tampon?

A tampon can't get lost in your vagina. There's nowhere for it to go! Occasionally the string gets drawn up inside. If you reach your fingers gently inside the vagina (it helps to squat down) you'll soon find it.

tampon with and without applicator

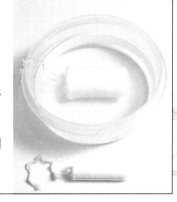

Absorbent tampons

When you look at a tampon, you wouldn't think it could absorb much liquid. But try this experiment. Put a tampon in a glass of water. You'll be amazed how much water it soaks up.

SANITARY TOWELS

These are rectangular pads of cotton wool encased in netting. They come in different sizes and thicknesses. They are easy to use and generally comfortable to wear. Some have sticky strips which you fix to your underwear, others have loops which are hooked onto a special sanitary belt. Many girls prefer to use them when they first start having their periods since using tampons takes a little practice.

As menstrual blood comes into contact with the air outside your body, it can develop a stale smell quite quickly. So you should change your sanitary towel every three or four hours to make sure there's no smell.

Don't flush used towels down the toilet – you could create a blockage. Wrap them in toilet paper and put them in a dustbin or disposal container.

Toxic shock syndrome

Toxic shock syndrome is a rare infection associated with the use of tampons.

The symptoms of toxic shock syndrome are fever, vomiting and diarrhoea, light-headedness or fainting, aching muscles and a sunburn-like rash. After 10 days the rash causes the skin to peel, especially on the palms and soles. In some people, the disease is severe enough to make them collapse and 10-15 percent of patients die. One third of patients who have one attack will have another.

Toxic shock syndrome is a rare but potentially lethal condition affecting about one in 20,000 menstruating women each year. Ninety five percent of cases are caused by a micro-organism called staphylococcus aureus. This lives in the vagina and releases a poison, or toxin, which causes the syndrome. Most cases, but not all, occur in adolescents and young women who are menstruating and using tampons. Men can get toxic shock syndrome too.

When you use tampons, it's important to take extra care over personal hygiene. Wash your hands before and after inserting them, and don't use tampons whose protective wrapper has come undone. Only use tampons during periods, and use the lowest absorbency that you need. Remember to change tampons every 4-6 hours. Never use a high absorbency tampon to make it last longer. Remove the old tampon before inserting a new one and remember to remove the last one at the end of a period.

If you are unwell during a period, and have symptoms of toxic shock syndrome, remove your tampon straight away. Consult your doctor and say that you have been using tampons. Toxic shock syndrome can usually be treated effectively with antibiotics provided you get medical help quickly.

Because tampons are so comfortable to wear, some people forget to take them out at the end of their period. Eventually this can cause a smell, and possibly a discharge, but both should disappear when you take out the tampon.

sticky-backed sanitary pads

More about periods

Normally, the menstrual cycle usually lasts about 28 days. But not everyone's periods work like clockwork. Your periods may not settle down into a routine until two or three years after you've started. And all through your life, there will be times when you're later than you expect, and times when you're earlier.

There can be lots of different reasons for irregular periods. You might have lost or gained a lot of weight, you may be worried, or ill. This is normal. But, if you're really worried or have bad pains or heavy bleeding for more than four or five days, you should go and see your doctor.

Period pains

Many people have no problems with periods. After you have become used to them, it's just another regular event. However there are women who become irritable, tired and generally feel unwell. Most women can tell when their period is coming from pain felt in their abdomen, the area below the stomach. In some it's a dull ache that comes in short spasms, for others it's a major cramping

sensation which lasts for a couple of days. It is thought that menstrual pain may be to do with the release of chemicals called prostaglandins. Severe menstrual cramping that persists for more than two or three days may be due to other medical conditions. See your doctor if this is the case.

PMT

You may have heard of PMT, or pre-menstrual tension, to give it its full name. It's caused by hormonal changes and may occur up to a week before the period starts. Symptoms include sore and swollen breasts, a bloated heavy feeling especially in the lower abdomen, headaches, spots and tiredness. PMT can also affect the way you are feeling about yourself. You may feel depressed, bad-tempered and unusually tense. PMT can really make your life a misery. There doesn't seem to be a proven medical remedy at the moment, but there are medications that can help with some of the symptoms. It's worth consulting your doctor if it's getting you down. Avoiding salty foods may help with the puffiness and bloating.

GENTLE EXERCISES

If you feel a bit uncomfortable when you have your period, you might like to try some of these exercises. They are not in any particular order, and you don't need to do them all. Try them out to see which ones suit you best. Any gentle exercise, such as walking around, might help to make you feel more comfortable.

2. Lie flat with your chin on the floor.

Lift your head and shoulder up for a count of three. Slowly relax, and then repeat the exercise several times.

1. Lie flat on the floor with your face to one side. Turn your head round to look in the other direction.

3. Push the upper part of your body up with your hands for a count of three.

Can I ...?

People often ask all sorts of questions about what they should and should not do during their period. Should they wash their hair? Should they swim? Should they go riding? Should they drink cold drinks?

The answer to all these questions is Yes. Questions like these arose at a time when people didn't know much about how the human body works. But we now know the truth – that menstruation is a completely natural part of all women's lives, and there's no reason at all why you shouldn't carry on with your life as normal.

What can you do?

Exercise like swimming, walking and dancing can help to relieve period pains. Or you could try one of the exercises on these pages. If you are really uncomfortable, you can take painkillers. You can buy painkillers that have been specially developed for dysmenorrhoea – the medical name for period pain. Lying down with a hot water bottle on your abdomen can help, too.

4. Lie on a low stool or table as shown. Put your hands on the ground in front of you.

5. Bend your knees and then push your legs out again as if you were swimming.

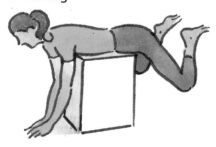

Your period doesn't have to stop you doing what you like.

Reader's experience

"When I have my period, I've noticed that I bleed very heavily on the first two days and then only have a brown trickle for the rest of the time. Is this normal?" **Mina**

Yes. Every woman has her own pattern of bleeding. Some people bleed for two or three days, some for seven. The bleeding may be heavier at the beginning or during the middle of the period. And the blood is only brown because it's taking a long time to trickle out of your vagina. You may think a lot of blood comes out of your body during your period, but it's actually only about two tablespoons.

265

Inner hygiene

It is entirely normal to have some wetness or discharge from your vagina. If it's clear and not smelly or itchy, you probably don't need to do anything about it. This discharge is the natural cleansing action of the vagina. But other discharges could indicate that something needs looking at. Some infections are caused by the fact that the vagina, the anus and the urethra are all very close together. Germs that live in one organ can be a problem if they get into another. After going to the lavatory you should always wipe yourself from front to back.

There are other reasons for infections. Taking antibiotics for a chest or other infection can kill the protective bacteria in your vagina, and allow harmful ones to grow. Other conditions that may result in problems are stress, the use of contraceptive pills, and certain medical conditions. Women who have had sexual intercourse may contract other infections.

Here are details of two of the most common infections that women get.

CYSTITIS
Fifty out of every hundred women get this and it can be extremely uncomfortable. It's basically an infection of the bladder and it can reoccur many times.

Symptoms
A burning sensation when you pass urine, and the need to go often and urgently. There may be a pain in your lower back or lower abdomen, and the urine may be dark, smelly or blood stained.

Solution
A single episode of mild burning on urination may be nothing serious. But if the symptoms persist, you should see your doctor. If a bladder infection is found, antibiotics will be prescribed and you may be encouraged to drink extra fluids to flush out the infection.

Prevention
As cystitis is often caused by the germs from the anus entering the bladder via your urethra, it's important to wipe yourself from front to back. Be sure to empty your bladder frequently, as overstretching it can make some women more susceptible to infection.

You should also avoid perfumed toiletries and talcum powder, and drink plenty of water. The acid contained in fruit drinks and the caffeine in tea, coffee and soft drinks can irritate the bladder, so water really is the best drink.

The cervix

"Why do I get vaginal discharge? Sometimes it feels sort of sticky. Is there anything wrong?"
Ruth

The vaginal discharge has two functions. The first is a way of cleaning out dead skin cells and excess fluid. The other is to help with the reproductive function of the vagina. It lubricates the vagina during sexual intercourse. When you reach puberty, you may notice an increase in the amount of secretions. This change in vaginal mucus is entirely normal in all women, whether they have had sex or not. The sticky fluid you mention usually occurs when you ovulate. If the mucus is clear and looks a bit like egg white, you have no need to worry. However if it is thick, yellowish and has a strong odour, it's wise to see a doctor.

The cervix has many jobs to do. It acts as a protective barrier to infections coming from the outside up the vagina and produces thick, sticky mucus which acts as a plug in the canal. The mucus is changed by hormones and becomes thin, clear and runny when the egg is produced (at ovulation). This change to thin mucus is so that the sperm can swim through the canal easily. The sperm has to swim up the canal through the uterus and along the tubes to reach the egg so that fertilization can occur. The cervix also holds the developing baby in the uterus and the tight ring of muscle at the os (the internal opening) is very important for this.

Cancer of the cervix is a common disease. It is happening more frequently and in younger and younger women. It is a preventable disease. Two main factors are known to increase the risk of cervical cancer. Girls who begin having sex in their early teens and those who have a lot of sexual partners are at higher risk. Cigarette smoking also increases the risk of cervical cancer.

If the cervix is examined and has a smear taken regularly, the earliest pre-cancer changes can be found and treated so that the cancer never develops. The pre-cancer changes that occur in the cervix are not visible to the naked eye and do not cause any symptoms. There is no pain, bleeding or discharge.

Every woman should have a smear taken within the first year of her first sexual intercourse. She should then have another smear a year later and then at least every three years for the rest of her life, or at least until the age of 70. All women are encouraged to be responsible for their own health and have regular smears.

A smear test is very simple to do. Having a smear taken is a bit uncomfortable but not painful. Very often the smear may be done by the nurse in the doctor's surgery or well-woman clinic. You lie on your back on a couch. A smooth metal or plastic instrument called a speculum is passed into the vagina and the cervix is looked at. A small brush or swab is inserted very gently. It scrapes the cervix to take off some of the cells. These are put on a slide and stained.

MONILIA (also called Thrush)
Ninety out of every hundred women will experience monilia at some time or another. It's caused by a fungus called Candida Albicans which lives naturally in your vagina. There's only a problem when there's an overgrowth of the fungus.

Symptoms
A change in your vaginal discharge – it may look white thick and lumpy, a bit like cottage cheese. The vaginal area may be red and sore or itchy. Urinating may be painful. Occasionally the infection spreads to the outer labia or thighs, causing a red rash.

Treatment
Visit your doctor who will take a sample of the discharge. This involves a gentle smear taken from your vaginal walls and does not hurt. This test will check the cause of the infection. If it is monilia, you'll be given medication to cure the infection and instructions on how to use it.

Prevention
Monilia does have a habit of coming back from time to time, so avoid tight, restricting clothes, wear cotton underwear if possible, avoid using tampons during your period if you have a thrush attack, avoid perfumed additives in your bath, and don't use vaginal sprays.

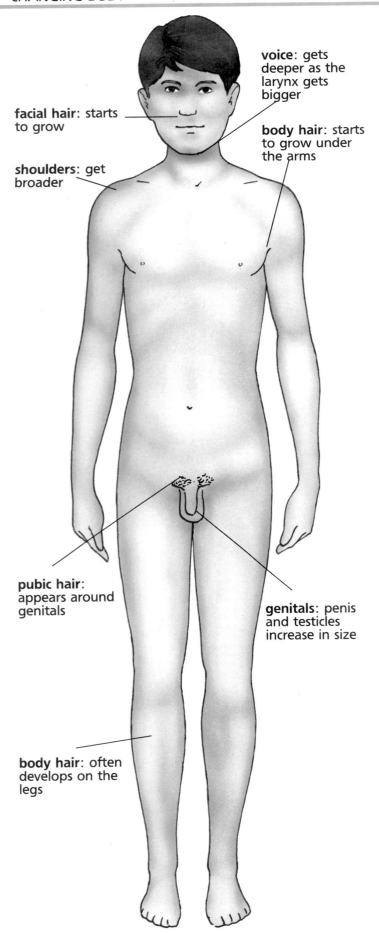

voice: gets deeper as the larynx gets bigger

facial hair: starts to grow

body hair: starts to grow under the arms

shoulders: get broader

pubic hair: appears around genitals

genitals: penis and testicles increase in size

body hair: often develops on the legs

A boy's new body map

When you think you've got used to your body, it starts to change! During puberty, even more perplexing things happen over which you have no control. It's a difficult time but one that's made a whole lot easier if you know what to expect. Here are the signs of physical development you'll see in your body.

Growth spurt

When you're 13 or 14, you'll probably notice that your jeans aren't long enough, and your shirtsleeves are too short! Many boys are older or younger than this when their growth spurt starts. Even when your rate of growth slows down after a couple of years, you'll probably go on growing till your late teens. Some boys grow as much as 120 millimetres in one year during this period.

Voice break

One of the most obvious changes that boys have to suffer is the difficult time when their voice 'breaks'. What this really means is that your voice loses its high pitched tone and deepens. This happens because the larynx in the throat gets bigger. It can take place between the ages of 11 to 16, but 13 to 14 is average.

You'll probably find that your voice won't break overnight. As the male hormone testosterone causes your vocal cords to get thicker and longer, you may well experience a little discomfort or frogginess of the throat as your voice deepens. You may also have embarrassing times when your voice sounds deep one minute, and high and squeaky the next. Whatever your experience, you can be sure that eventually your voice will settle down and you'll sound like a man.

Breast growth

Boys' breasts don't change as dramatically as girls', but the areola or ring of coloured flesh round the nipple will probably get wider and darker and your nipples may get larger with some bumps under the skin. The breasts may swell slightly too. If they do, the swelling will probably go down within 12 months.

Sport helps to strengthen growing muscles

Facial hair

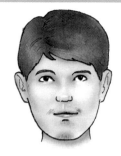

On average, boys start developing facial hair between the ages of 14 to 16. Many men don't develop full facial hair until they are in their 30s.

You will probably discover your first facial hairs appearing at the corners of your upper lip gradually filling inwards to form a thin moustache. Hair may also start to grow on upper parts of your cheeks, or below the centre of your lower lip. As you get older, your facial hair may become darker and thicker. It may well be darker than the hair on your head. Once you start growing facial hair you may want to shave it off. This is a matter of taste (unless your school or religion forbids it) but many boys look forward to shaving as a sign of growing up.

Body hair

Another sign of developing maturity is the appearance of body hair around your genitals, and on your underarms, face, chest, arms and legs. The development of all this body hair is triggered by the hormone testosterone which is made in the testicles. Testosterone doesn't influence how much hair will grow, as this is determined by what racial or ethnic group your family belongs to. White boys often grow more body hair than their black or oriental friends.

As well as the curly pubic hair that grows around the base of the penis, more hair might appear on your arms, the backs of hands, thighs and lower legs. It may grow on your chest and even your shoulders or back. There is no such thing as a normal amount of body hair — every man is different.

PERSPIRATION AND BODY ODOUR

It is normal for boys to perspire more at puberty and to develop a stronger, more musky body odour than when they were younger. Regular bathing or showering, plus the use of underarm anti-perspirant will keep you feeling — and smelling — fresh.

Male parts

No prizes for knowing where your penis is! But do you know what it really looks like, and how it and your other sex organs function? It's a good thing to understand all this, so that you can recognize any problems you might have, and won't be too embarrassed to ask a doctor if something is worrying you.

The names used in this book for the parts of the body are the medical ones but you probably have all sorts of other words for them.

The right temperature

Have you ever wondered why your testicles are outside your body and not inside where they'd be better protected? The reason is that the sperm that are made in the testicles need a cool temperature. It's too hot inside your body. Your penis is sensitive to temperature, too. At various times the penis may get temporarily smaller. Cold weather, feeling tired, tense or nervous may make your scrotal sac pull up closer to the body and your penis appear smaller for a while.

THE PENIS
The penis is the male sex organ on the outside of your body. It is made of spongy tissue and is covered with thin skin. When you're young, your penis is usually small and soft. Boys have penises of different size. Its length and width have nothing to do with how tall you are or how manly you are. As you get older, your penis gets longer and wider.

The penis itself has two parts, the shaft and the glans, which is the most sensitive area at the end of the penis. The glans has a small opening called the urethral opening, or meatus, through which both urine and semen leave the body.

THE SCROTUM
The scrotum or scrotal sac is the loose, wrinkly bag of skin beneath the penis. It contains two egg-shaped organs called the testes or testicles. The testicles are very sensitive. As puberty develops, the testicles get larger and the scrotal sac drops. One testicle normally hangs slightly lower than the other. This stops them from being squashed as you walk. The scrotum contains muscles that can pull the testicles up closer to the body.

As you get older, your testicles within the sac get larger and the scrotum becomes more wrinkly. The skin colour may also change, getting darker on dark-skinned boys or redder on fair ones.

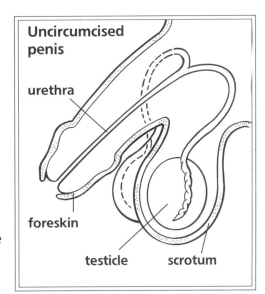

Uncircumcised penis

urethra

foreskin

testicle   scrotum

THE FORESKIN
Baby boys have a double fold of skin, called the foreskin, covering the glans of the penis. The foreskin can't be pulled back from the glans until a boy is about three years old.

270

Protection for sensitive parts

The penis and the testicles are extremely sensitive, as every boy knows. If you've accidentally been hit in the genital area, you'll know how painful that can be. For this reason, many boys and men wear protective supporters, specially when they're doing some kind of sporting activity. The footballers in the picture on the left seem to be very well protected all over their bodies!

Circumcision

Circumcision involves cutting off the double fold of the foreskin. If circumcision is done shortly after birth, it's a very simple procedure. In older boys and men, the cut edges need stitching together. The stitches dissolve by themselves over the next few days, and the patient can normally go home the same day. Like any cut, it is a little sore afterwards but, in young boys, paracetamol is usually a strong enough painkiller to control the discomfort.

Circumcision is a religious requirement of the Jewish faith and of Islam, and is a ritual act of many tribes throughout the world. There are a few medical reasons for performing circumcision. The commonest are:

1. Phimosis, when the foreskin is too tight and cannot be pulled back.

2. Paraphimosis, which occurs when a tight foreskin is pulled back over the glans and stays there. This causes swelling in the glans, which in turn stops the foreskin going back to its normal position.

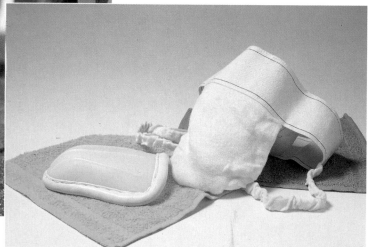

Many boys wear an athletic supporter or jockstrap.

PROBLEMS

A tight foreskin

A tight foreskin is one of the most common problems experienced by uncircumcised boys. Pulling the foreskin back over the glans is painful. You might discover this when masturbating – or even upon first intercourse when the act of penetration will probably hurt. A very tight foreskin can be put right by circumcision.

Spots or bumps on penis

Just like other parts of your body, your penis can get spots. White spots which are just blocked oil glands will eventually disappear. Warts on the penis can be spread by sexual activity and should be removed by a doctor – not as painful as it sounds.

Lumps in the genital area

These are normally caused by swollen lymph glands. This usually means your body is producing extra antibodies to fight an infection somewhere in your body. Even if you have never had sex it is possible to get infection in this area that causes pain and swelling. You should see a doctor.

Balanitis

Sometimes the end of the penis, the glans, becomes inflamed, itchy and sore. There may be a slight discharge. This is not usually serious, and mostly clears up with careful cleaning of the glans. See a doctor if the inflammation does not go away quickly.

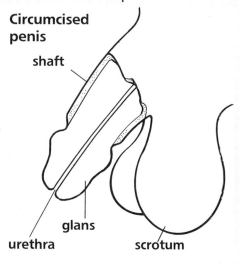

Circumcised penis

shaft

glans

urethra

scrotum

How the penis works

The penis has a dual function. It's used for urination and for ejaculation, or pumping out, of semen. The penis needs no 'warming up' in order to urinate, but for semen to come out, it needs to become stiff and erect.

How erections happen

Boys and men have erections throughout their lifetime – even small babies have them. During puberty, you'll find that you'll have erections more often, and they'll last longer. They may appear spontaneously, without warning, and disappear just as quickly. Or they may be long lasting, distracting and uncomfortable. When you have an erection, your penis becomes big and stiff, and sticks out from the body. During an erection, more blood than normal flows into the spongy tissue of the penis. The muscles at the base tighten, preventing the extra blood from flowing out. This means the penis gets wider and longer.

Why do erections happen?

Erections happen for all sorts of reasons. They happen when the penis is stroked or rubbed. You might have an erection when you're thinking sexual thoughts, or even when you're nervous or embarrassed. Sometimes erections happen for no apparent reason – these are called spontaneous erections.

Although having an erection is generally a nice feeling, there can be times when you just don't want it – especially if it happens in public. Spontaneous erections can happen any time. They often happen at night when you are asleep. But if this happens with other people around it can be an extremely embarrassing experience though your erection is probably much more noticeable to you than to other people. Most girls don't realize that boys worry about people seeing them have an erection, especially if they are wearing tight-fitting swimming trunks, or loose tracksuits on the sports field.

EJACULATION

This is the term used to describe the flow of fluid from a man's penis after the rhythmic contractions produced at the moment of orgasm, or sexual climax. At the moment of ejaculation, muscles in the genital area contract and seminal fluid is pumped out of the body, through the opening in the centre of the tip of the penis. This creamy white seminal fluid or semen contains fluids from the prostate, and sperm, which are made in the testicles. You can read about how sperm is made on pages 274 and 275.

The average man ejaculates less than a teaspoonful of semen, which carries around 400 million sperm. In sexual intercourse, sperm enter the woman's vagina and one of them may fertilize an ovum to make a baby.

You can read more about conception on pages 276 and 277.

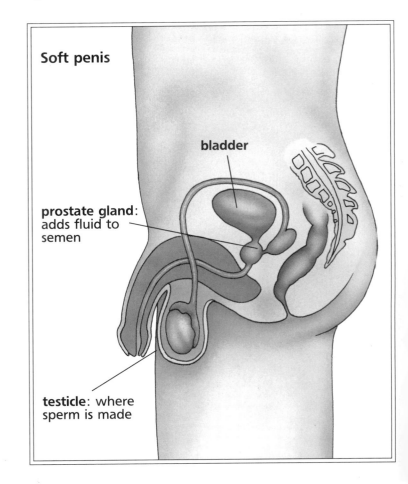

Soft penis

bladder

prostate gland: adds fluid to semen

testicle: where sperm is made

Retrograde ejaculation

Some people masturbate to orgasm but stop ejaculation by squeezing the penis. This may cause pain in the penis or testicles. The next time they urinate they may notice a clear or milky discharge before the urine comes out. This happens because the seminal fluid goes back down the penis and may be forced up into the bladder. This can lead to infection.

Masturbation

Lots of people masturbate, male and female. Masturbation means touching or rubbing the sexual organs. It does you no harm at all, but for some reason there's a myth about masturbation being harmful. You can find out more about masturbation on pages 288 and 289.

Wet dreams

A wet dream is the name given to spontaneous ejaculations which can occur while you're asleep. You'll begin to experience wet dreams from puberty onwards. In fact, a wet dream is frequently a boy's first experience of ejaculation. For many, the first wet dream comes as a bit of a shock. Fathers and mothers seldom prepare their sons for the time when they will start ejaculating. It is common for boys to wake up feeling wet, wondering whether they have cut themselves or wet the bed.

You can't control wet dreams, they just happen – but only when you are asleep. The biological reason for wet dreams is that they are the body's way of emptying testicles and making way for the production of new sperm.

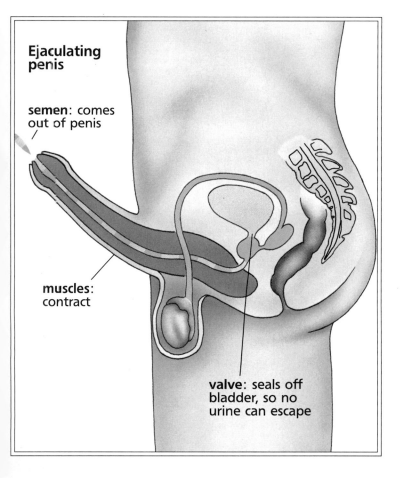

Ejaculating penis

semen: comes out of penis

muscles: contract

valve: seals off bladder, so no urine can escape

Reader's experience

"I knew all about wet dreams from reading a book my dad gave me about puberty. But it still came as quite a surprise when I got my first one. My best friend's experience was totally different. No-one in his family talks about sex. He told me how embarrassed he was, having to sneak down the stained sheets and throw them in the washing machine telling his mother he had spilled something on the bed."
Julian

The inside story

To understand exactly what happens when you ejaculate, it's helpful to know what goes on inside your body. We all know that sperm comes out of the penis at the moment of ejaculation. But before this, they have to be made and stored somewhere and this is what the testicles are for. Your testicles go on producing millions of sperm all your life, though production slows down in old age.

TESTICLES

Each of your two testicles, or testes, is made up of about 250 tiny separate compartments containing numerous tightly coiled thread-like tubes. From puberty onwards this is where sperm are made. Sperm are microscopic cells that look rather like long-tailed tadpoles. You produce millions of them in your testicles every day.

EPIDIDYMIS

After being made in the testicles, young sperm travel to the epididymis, a special compartment attached to the testicles, where they mature. This process takes between four and six weeks. Once they are fully mature, sperm are ready to travel up the scrotal sac to the ampulla where they are stored until you ejaculate.

AMPULLA

Near the bladder, the vas deferens widens out to form a sperm storage compartment called the ampulla. At the lower part of the ampulla little glands called seminal vesicles are connected to the vas. These glands make some of the white sticky fluid called semen which comes out of your penis when you ejaculate.

VAS DEFERENS

To get from your testicles to your urethra, the sperm travel along two tubes called the vas deferens, one in each testicle. Each tube is 355-455 millimetres long and winds up right over the bladder, where urine collects, and then down into the penis. When sperm leave the scrotal sac they are sluggish and slow-moving. But the vas deferens are lined with tiny hairs and have muscles which contract, sweeping the sperm along.

THE PROSTATE GLAND

This small, ring-shaped gland lies beneath the ampulla and the seminal vesicles and enlarges quite a lot during your teenage years. The vas deferens and other tubes run through the prostate. When a man ejaculates, the prostate contracts and squeezes the vas. This pushes sperm and semen into the urethra in the centre of the penis. The prostate gland also makes a fluid which combines with the semen.

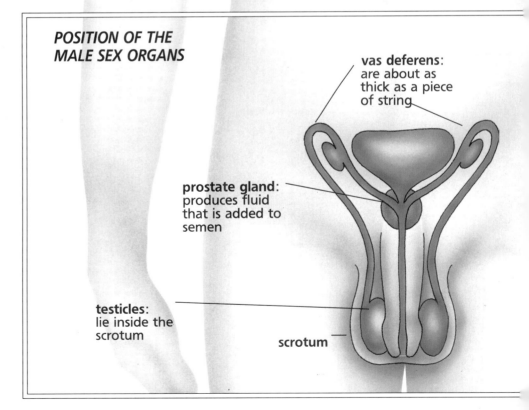

POSITION OF THE MALE SEX ORGANS

vas deferens: are about as thick as a piece of string

prostate gland: produces fluid that is added to semen

testicles: lie inside the scrotum

scrotum

SEMEN

Semen is rich in sugar and gives the sluggish sperm an energy boost sending them jumping around, whipping their tails in a frenzy. The sperm need this boost as once ejaculation has taken place they need to travel a long distance through the uterus to the Fallopian tube to fertilize a woman's ovum.

THE URETHRA

The urethra is a tube about 20 centimetres long on the inside of the penis. It is covered with soft, spongy tissue, and is connected to tubes from both the vas deferens and the bladder.

Sperm and seminal fluid travel through the urethra and spurt out through the opening in the centre of the glans during ejaculation.

The urethra is also the tube down which urine passes when you urinate. So how can you avoid urinating when you ejaculate? The answer is that just before ejaculation, a valve at the bottom of the bladder closes, preventing urine from getting into the urethra when sperm is about to pass through. So it's impossible to ejaculate and urinate at the same time.

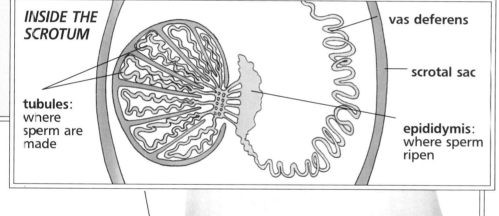

INSIDE THE SCROTUM

tubules: where sperm are made

vas deferens

scrotal sac

epididymis: where sperm ripen

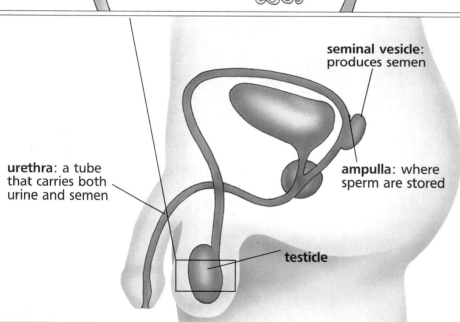

urethra: a tube that carries both urine and semen

seminal vesicle: produces semen

ampulla: where sperm are stored

testicle

Testicular cancer and other problems

Cancer of the testicles is very rare in adolescence but can occur in young men. In the early stages it can be cured, so it is important that it is identified early.

So just as girls are encouraged to examine their breasts for unusual lumps, boys in mid-adolescence should be taught how to examine their testicles. You only need to do it about once a month. During a warm shower or bath, when the testicles and scrotum are relaxed, is a good time.

A healthy testicle is smooth and soft, similar in size to a large grape, with a little ridge of tissue behind it. It is important to get to know what your own testicles are like. Hold your scrotum with both hands and gently roll each testicle between your fingers and thumbs for a few minutes.

If you notice a hard, pea-sized lump or one testicle larger than usual or a feeling of heaviness, consult your doctor. Testicular cancer is often painless until it is well advanced.

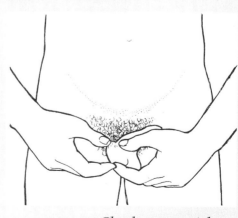

Check your testicles once a month.

Conception

The great mystery of life is how all of us came to be in the world. We know that somewhere along the line our parents met, they had sexual intercourse and we were conceived.

Conception, or the act of conceiving, is when a woman's egg, or ovum, is fertilized by a man's sperm. But it's amazing to think of the genetic miracle which makes sure that we are complete individuals. Each sperm and egg is unique so if another sperm from our father had fertilized our mother's ovum, each one of us would literally be somebody else!

Conceiving a baby

Two kinds of seed are needed to make a baby – an ovum from the woman's body, and a sperm from the man's body.

You saw on pages 260 and 261 how women make ova in their ovaries. Every month, an ovum ripens and bursts from one of the ovaries. The fringed ends of the Fallopian tube guide the ovum and gently push it down the tube towards the uterus. A man's sperm are made in his testes, and come out of his penis in the creamy fluid called semen. When a sperm and an ovum join together, the ovum is fertilized, and a baby is conceived.

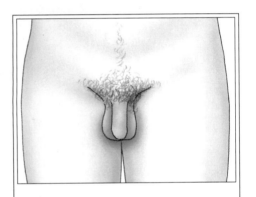

When a man and a woman have sexual intercourse, a baby may be conceived.

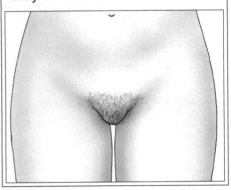

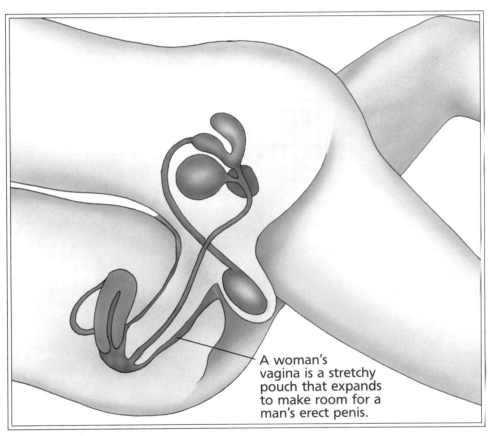

A woman's vagina is a stretchy pouch that expands to make room for a man's erect penis.

SEXUAL INTERCOURSE

The question is, how does the sperm reach the ovum? It usually gets there when a man and a woman have sexual intercourse. When a man is sexually aroused or excited, his penis usually becomes stiff and hard and stands out from his body. This is called having an erection. When a woman is aroused, the vagina releases fluid that lubricates the tissue. This makes it easy for the man's erect penis to enter the vagina during sexual intercourse.

During intercourse, movement of the penis in the vagina leads to ejaculation. When he ejaculates, the creamy fluid called semen gushes out of his penis into the woman's vagina. In the semen are millions of microscopic sperm.

A difficult journey

The sperm now take part in a sort of race. They all start swimming up through the cervix, the tiny opening at the top of the vagina, and on into the uterus. From there they continue their journey, wiggling up into the Fallopian tubes.

It's a long and difficult passage. Only about one hundred of the strongest sperm get this far. The rest fall away and die before dribbling back out of the woman's vagina or being absorbed. If the sperm meet an ovum, they cluster around it. One sperm may break through the ovum's outer barrier and fuse with it to form one new cell. Only one sperm can break into the ovum. This is the moment of fertilization. The fertilized ovum carries on down the Fallopian tube, and implants itself in the rich, nutritious and blood-enriched lining of the uterus. There it starts to grow into a baby.

Fertility

In general, an ovum can only be fertilized by a sperm during the 24 to 48 hours after the ovum comes out of the ovary, while it's on its way from the ovary to the uterus. This is the time when it is ripest. After this, the ovum cannot be fertilized.

Of course, people don't conceive every time they have sexual intercourse. Usually the ovum travels down the Fallopian tube without meeting a sperm. The ovum then disintegrates, and the spongy lining of the uterus breaks down and comes out of the woman's body through the vagina. You can read about this process on pages 260 and 261.

Being pregnant

It normally takes a few days for a fertilized egg to travel from the Fallopian tube into the uterus. There it attaches itself to the lining of the uterus, tapping into its mother's blood supply. After conception, the woman misses her period – that's when she discovers she's pregnant.

Hormones

Hormones in the woman's body prevent any more ova ripening during her pregnancy. So she doesn't have her normal periods while she is pregnant. The lining of the uterus is now needed by the fertilized ovum.

These sperm are travelling up the uterus.

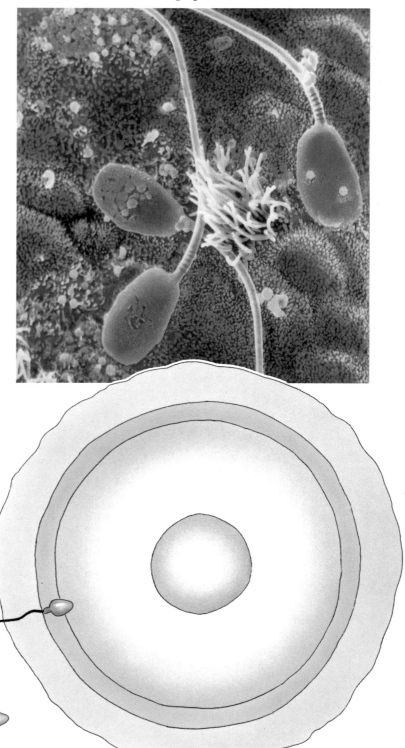

How a baby grows

When the sperm and ovum join together at the moment of conception, they form a single cell. The single cell divides many thousands of times to grow into a baby. A baby grows in the uterus at amazing speed. In fact, a baby is perfectly formed in miniature just three months after conception. When it is born, a baby will have developed from a single cell into an organism containing around 200 million cells.

8-9 weeks old

actual size

STAGES OF DEVELOPMENT

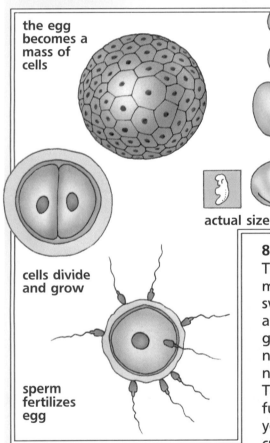

the egg becomes a mass of cells

cells divide and grow

sperm fertilizes egg

actual size

embryo at 4-5 weeks old

6-7 weeks old

actual size

6-7 weeks old
In the early stages of pregnancy, the developing baby is known as an embryo. The embryo floats in watery liquid in a transparent bag called the amniotic sac which protects it until birth. The heart starts to beat and the beginnings of a backbone, brain and nervous system form.

8-9 weeks old
The embryo is around 17 millimetres long. Four tiny swellings have developed – these are the arms and legs. The head grows rapidly, developing eyes, nostrils, ears and jaw. The baby now has a mouth and a tongue. The liver, kidney and lungs are fully developed but don't work yet. These early weeks are a crucial time for development. The limbs and organs are forming and can easily be damaged if the mother drinks, smokes cigarettes or takes certain drugs.

The baby is joined to its mother by a tube called the umbilical cord. This is the baby's lifeline. Oxygen and food pass along this cord from the mother to the baby.

The fleshy pad called the placenta rooted to the wall of the uterus separates the baby's circulation from the mother's.

10-14 weeks old
From this time on the baby is called a foetus. The foetus looks distinctly human. You can tell whether it's a girl or a boy. The foetus is now around 7.5 centimetres long. The uterus has enlarged and can be felt as a soft bulge above the pubic bone. The baby is moving around a lot, but the movements can't yet be felt by the mother.

15-22 weeks old
The baby is growing quickly, and the foetus, placenta and its waters now completely fill the uterus. The baby begins to grow downy hair called lanugo all over is body. It now has hair on its head, including eyebrows and eyelashes. Fingernails and toenails are growing, and the

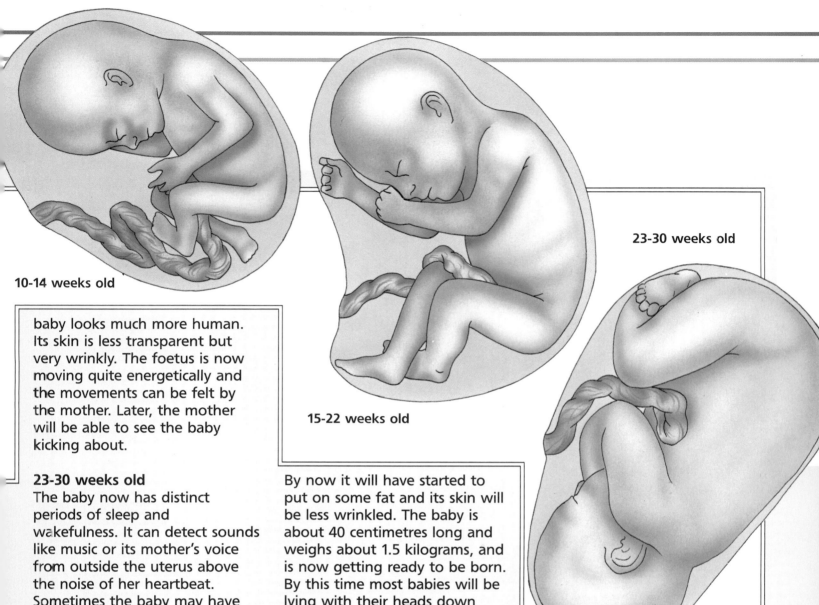

10-14 weeks old

15-22 weeks old

23-30 weeks old

baby looks much more human. Its skin is less transparent but very wrinkly. The foetus is now moving quite energetically and the movements can be felt by the mother. Later, the mother will be able to see the baby kicking about.

23-30 weeks old

The baby now has distinct periods of sleep and wakefulness. It can detect sounds like music or its mother's voice from outside the uterus above the noise of her heartbeat. Sometimes the baby may have hiccups. At this stage the baby is covered with a thick white grease called vernix which stops its skin becoming waterlogged.

At 28 weeks, the foetus is said to be viable – that means if the baby were born now it would have a good chance of survival. At this stage the lungs and other organs are still not very well developed, but if the baby is given specialist care in a Special Baby Care Unit, it may survive. Indeed, babies even younger than this often survive.

31-40 weeks old

The baby is perfectly formed and can open its eyes. It may even practise sucking its thumb!

By now it will have started to put on some fat and its skin will be less wrinkled. The baby is about 40 centimetres long and weighs about 1.5 kilograms, and is now getting ready to be born. By this time most babies will be lying with their heads down towards the cervix, having totally taken up all available space in the uterus.

At 36 weeks, the baby usually drops lower in the pelvis where its head is said to be engaged. This is normally a time of relief for its mother, whose internal organs have until now been getting increasingly squashed!

Around 40 weeks, the baby is now ready to be born. However, it is perfectly normal for a baby to be born at any time between the 38th and 42nd week. By this time, the lanugo or downy hair has usually disappeared though the baby's body may still be covered with vernix.

31-40 weeks old

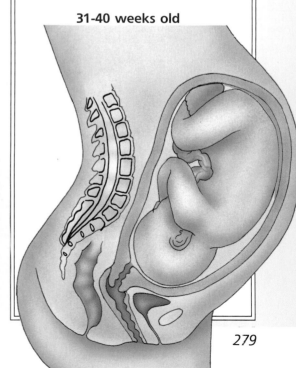

Childbirth

When a baby is ready to leave the uterus, its mother goes into a process called labour – perhaps because it's hard work! For most mothers-to-be, the first signs of labour are cramp-like pains coming at regular intervals perhaps 20 to 30 minutes apart. These spasms are usually felt low down in the uterus or near the bottom of the back. Although they are quite mild at first, these contractions become increasingly strong and more frequent. Sometimes the first sign of labour is when the amniotic sac breaks. This is the sac that holds the fluid in which the foetus lies. When it breaks, water gushes out through the vagina.

Going into labour

The length of time each stage lasts is different. On average, a woman can expect to go into labour for 12-15 hours for her first child. The more children a woman has, the more the process is speeded up.

Parents-to-be – both men and women – go to special classes before the birth to learn about ways of making the birth as easy as possible. Many mothers find that methods of breathing and relaxation can help a great deal. And the father can be very supportive, too.

Recovery

After giving birth, a woman's body usually takes some weeks to recover. Physical changes start the moment the placenta is expelled from the uterus. The uterus starts to shrink back to its original size. As it shrinks, it contracts and relaxes at irregular intervals. This feels a bit like

STAGES OF LABOUR

First stage
The cervix, the neck of the uterus, gradually opens to give the baby's head room to come through into the vagina. This passage from the uterus is normally only 1 or 2 millimetres wide. The cervix is opened by regular contraction and relaxation of powerful muscles at the top of the uterus.

With each contraction, the uterus pushes so that the baby's head presses against the cervix, gradually opening it until it is around 10 centimetres wide (an average baby's head measures 9.5 centimetres in diameter). The cervix is now said to be fully dilated. The doctor or midwife may now have to break the bag of water.

Second stage
The cervix is now fully open. The baby is pushed from the uterus through the cervix and down the woman's vagina or birth canal. This stretchy pouch expands to make room for the baby as it goes through.

All the time the uterus keeps contracting at regular intervals,

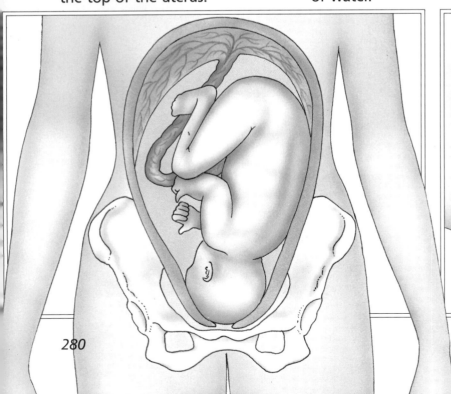

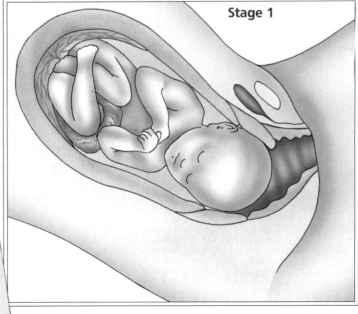

Stage 1

period pains. As the uterus shrinks, its thick lining disintegrates and passes out of the vagina rather like a period. This can last up to six weeks.

Feeding the baby

In the first few days after birth, the breasts produce a thick substance called colostrum. This is high in protein, and contains antibodies that protect the baby from infection. The breasts start producing milk about three days after birth. Breast milk contains all the nourishment the baby needs for the first few months of its life. Breast feeding also helps to make the uterus shrink more quickly. If a mother cannot breast feed her baby, she needn't feel guilty. There are plenty of healthy adults around today who were brought up on a bottle!

Caesarean section

A Caesarian section is a method of delivering a baby by cutting through the mother's abdomen and uterus and lifting the baby and placenta out. The complete operation takes about 40 minutes. While all this is going on the mother may have a general anaesthetic which makes her unconscious.

Alternatively she may have an epidural block, which is an injection at the base of the spine. The epidural takes away all feeling from the bottom half of the body. This means that the woman can stay awake and see her baby being born without feeling any pain.

There are several reasons why doctors might recommend a Caesarian section. The baby might be the wrong way up, with its feet facing the cervix. These so-called breech births can be difficult. Or maybe the mother's pelvis is too small or the placenta may be blocking the baby's path.

making the mother feel an urge to keep pushing the baby out. The baby's head moves down the vagina until it can be seen at the vaginal opening. Once the baby's head is out, the rest of its body normally slips out easily. The umbilical cord is cut, and the baby is born. Now, at last, the mother and father can hold their baby.

Third stage
Shortly after the baby is born, the placenta, with the umbilical cord still joined to it, detaches itself from the wall of the uterus. More contractions of the uterus push the placenta out through the vagina. The empty amniotic sac comes with it. The placenta, sac and cord are called the afterbirth.

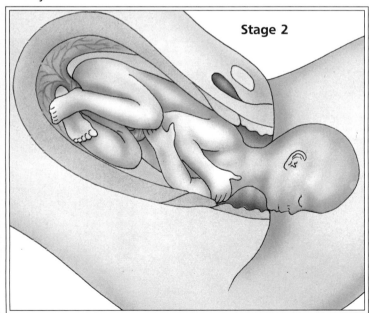
Stage 2

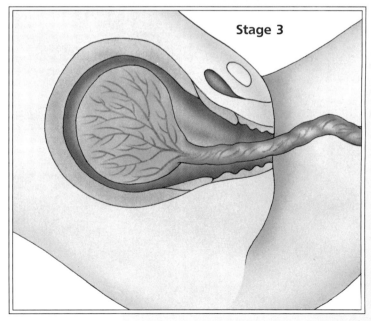
Stage 3

Attractions

Many teenagers are curious about the exciting romantic and sexual feelings they have. They become very aware of their own bodies, as well as of other people's sexuality. You may feel self-conscious when you are with someone of the opposite sex. Or you may find your eyes wandering over someone else's body when you think they are not looking.

Sometimes your romantic and sexual feelings seem to take over your life. It's hard to concentrate on school work when all you can think about is the first kiss with someone you really like. You may be worried that the girl next door doesn't fancy you. You may think that boy with the red jacket hasn't noticed you. You sometimes have to take your courage in both hands, and start up a conversation, or pick up the phone. You'll need to let the other person know how you feel.

Some people wonder why they don't have any particular feelings of physical attractions. They may be more interested in music, sport or school work. There's nothing wrong with that – it just means you're developing at your own rate, and these feelings haven't happened yet.

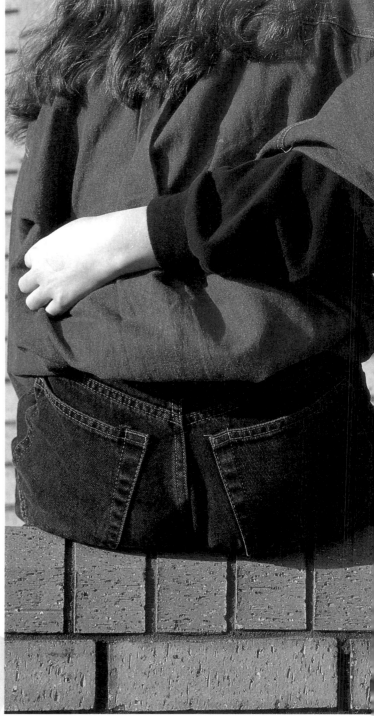

In love with love

Lots of teenagers have a crush on someone – a crush is an intense romantic longing for someone. It's a safe way of experimenting with your feelings, and usually remains a fantasy. The other person usually never guesses that they are an object of desire. If they do know, they may choose to ignore your feelings because they just don't think about you in the same way.

Same-sex friendships

Does it sometimes seem as if everyone expects you to have a girlfriend or boyfriend? Maybe you're somebody who doesn't feel attracted to people of the opposite sex. You may develop a very close friendship with someone of the same sex as yourself. This kind of friendship is very common among teenagers. It doesn't mean you're gay, in fact it's very normal.

Feeling different

Some people are only attracted to people who are the same sex as themselves. A person who is consistently physically attracted to someone of the same sex is called homosexual or gay. Female homosexuals are called lesbians.

Many young people have homosexual feelings or experiences as they grow up. This is perfectly normal and doesn't necessarily mean that they'll be homosexual all their lives. But other people continue to be physically and sexually attracted to people of their own sex. Adults are only considered homosexual if their strongest romantic and sexual feelings are towards people of the same sex as themselves.

Nobody really knows why some people are homosexual, but the fact is that there have been homosexuals since the beginning of time. Some people believe that homosexuality is wrong and unnatural. But nowadays most people accept that what people do with their own private lives is their own business, and if they are happy to be homosexual, then that's how they should be. It's much better to be a contented person than to be guilty and ashamed because you feel you're not the same as everyone else.

Crushes can be frustrating and painful, especially if strong feelings are not returned. Some people develop a crush on somebody who they're never likely to meet, such as a famous pop singer, actor or athlete. These kinds of crushes can be another good way of finding out how your feelings work, without you having to worry about whether the other person likes you or not.

283

Deciding about sex

Most young people feel confused about sex. This is not surprising! The information you get from television, magazines and films can be very different from the opinions expressed by your friends, your parents and teachers. One group appears to be saying that sex between teenagers is the norm. Then there is another clear message from the second group saying that teenage sex is wrong or immoral, and sex should only take place within a marriage. There is deep concern that young people are experimenting with sex too early – resulting in social problems like high levels of teenage pregnancy and infection.

Sex in society

Different countries and cultures have different ideas about when a young person is ready to have sex. In some countries it is illegal to have sex if you are under 16, in other countries girls are married by that age.

What is important is that you yourself take a carefully thought out approach to sex. The biological and therefore primary role of sex is to make sure that human beings continue to exist on our planet, although there's much more to it than that. However, if nobody had sex, populations would soon decline. Sex within a loving marriage or close, strong and lasting relationship should help to bond the relationship which in turn will provide a solid, loving environment in which to bring up children. When sex involves love and affection, it is a very powerful and exciting emotion. But sex without love or commitment can be an empty experience.

Tackle ignorance

As a teenager, you are going to be curious about sex and will want your questions answered. A lot of people find it hard to talk to their parents about sex. And indeed, research shows that many parents simply don't want to discuss the subject with their children. They feel it's up to the school. This is a great shame. Your parents were once young and inexperienced like you and may well be able to give you good advice. At the same time, many teenagers feel that the sex education they receive in school is not personal enough. Often young people learn about sex from each other. But sometimes the information shared around is not accurate and can be harmful. It's best to learn the facts.

First stirrings

Fancying someone, or feeling attracted to them is exciting. You may feel very nervous, too. Your hands may feel sweaty and shaky and your heart will pound away faster than usual. When you finally speak to the person in question you may find that the words come out all wrong. Although you usually chat away confidently to your friends and teachers, suddenly you may find yourself stuttering and stammering over a simple phrase.

If the object of your affections smiles at you it can make your day. If he or she ignores you, it can make you feel very depressed. You over-react emotionally. This means you are feeling things very strongly and even the smallest thing can worry or please you. These feelings are normal and natural. All young adults have to understand that.

Are you sure?

The decision to have a sexual relationship with somebody is an important one. The better informed you are about the sexual act itself, the consequences of making love, your own values and those of your girlfriend or boyfriend, the more you will realise how crucial it is to make the right decision. The difficulty is that sex is about people, and no two people approach it in the same way and for the same reason. Try to find out as much as you can through books and discussion. Establish your own ideas on teenage sex, on contraception, on abortion, on pregnancy, on unmarried mothers and on sexual diseases and HIV and AIDS. Read everything you can get your hands on. Don't be ignorant.

Being well-informed will help you reach decisions you are happy with.

Be safe

These days, the spread of AIDS and other sexually transmitted diseases means that everyone is gradually learning to be careful when they have sexual intercourse.

Somebody who has unprotected sex, that is when they take no precautions against pregnancy or sexual diseases, is taking great risks. Safe sex means being aware of important health issues and having a sense of responsibility, not only towards your partner but towards yourself as well – and then doing something about it! That means that males should always use a condom, with a spermicide containing nonoxynol-9. And females should insist that their partner wear a condom.

Young people who are becoming sexually aware have a lot to cope with. There are more problems to deal with now than when your parents were young. It's hard enough coping with physical changes and the first feelings of attractions towards other people. But when you actually start dating you need to consider a whole list of factors to make sure you stay healthy.

A sense of proportion

It's important to keep things in perspective. If you are sensible and educate yourself about the problems, you won't need to worry too much. Worrying takes a lot of the enjoyment out of life. However, you need to bear in mind that the more sexual partners you have the more you run the risk of catching a sexually transmitted disease – or of passing one on. The only really safe sex is between two people who have never had sex with anyone else and who use a reliable form of contraception.

SEX AND LOVE

Sex and love are not the same. This may sound surprising, but it's true. A sexual relationship without love doesn't usually work out. However there are varying degrees of love. You don't have to be passionately attached to someone to feel that you love them. Liking somebody, feeling warm and comfortable with them is a kind of love.

Sometimes, when a relationship isn't going well, people think that sex will improve things. But having sex doesn't necessarily mean you'll love each other any more. It's quite possible to have a loving relationship without becoming sexually involved. And the best relationships are those between friends.

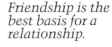

Friendship is the best basis for a relationship.

Saying yes, saying no

When people are strongly attracted to someone, they find themselves facing difficult questions. How should they deal with their feelings of attraction? How do they show their feelings towards the other person? When two people really like (or love!) each other, they naturally want to be physically close. But how close? Is it enough to hold hands? Should you kiss goodnight after your first date?

What girls need to know about boys

Most boys have stronger sexual urges than most girls. This is a generalization, of course, but you'll find that it's usually the boys who make the first move. What you need to know is that boys get sexually aroused very quickly. After one kiss, they could be ready for sexual intercourse. Girls don't usually get excited as quickly. So you need to be clear in your own mind that what you think is an innocent kiss may be taken by a boy for a green light! It may be easy for you to stop your sexual activity any time, but when a boy is sexually excited, the urge to have sexual intercourse may be hard for him to control. Girls should be sensitive to this.

Try to talk about how you feel about physical intimacy and having sex. If you feel strongly that you want to wait, say so. Likewise, if you want to have sex and your boyfriend doesn't, respect his feelings.

What boys need to know about girls

This is really the same as the previous paragraph only in reverse! Don't assume that just because a girl likes you, she is ready to have sex with you. The important thing is to talk about what you want to do and don't want to do. The time to have this conversation is when you can think straight, not when you are sexually excited and may lose control. Don't try to pressurize a girl into doing something she doesn't want to. It's not fair, and it's not right.

The first time

Many teenagers have mixed feelings about having sex for the first time, or losing their virginity – a virgin is someone who has never had sex. Some people are quite certain that they do not want to lose their virginity until they are married. Before someone decides they want to lose their virginity they need to ask themselves some searching questions. How does my partner feel about me and having sex with me? Will the relationship last? Will it lead to marriage? Will sex change the relationship we have at present, and how will our relationship change if there is no sex? Can I trust my partner in every sense? Which contraceptive method will we use? What is the danger of AIDS? What will happen if pregnancy occurs? Remember that drugs and alcohol can cloud your judgement. They could lead you to make decisions you'll regret.

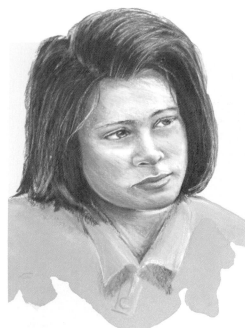

Readers' views

"My older sister told me that her boyfriend was trying to persuade her to have sex with him. He said 'If you love me, you'll have sex with me.' He put her under a lot of pressure, which I thought was really unfair. But she didn't give in, and now they've stopped seeing each other. He can't have loved her very much."
Tina

"I'm definitely going to wait until I get married before I have sex. My family is not especially religious, but I don't think it's right to have sex before marriage. I think by waiting I'll be showing that I really love my wife, and want to be with her always. I'll be able to show her that she's the most special person in my life, not just one in a line of girlfriends."
Mehmet

Holding hands is a good way of showing affection.

Say no

It's easy to give in to pressure when you're not certain one way or the other. Everyone gives you advice, everyone has an opinion. But the simple rule is, if you don't want to do something, or if you feel even vaguely scared or uncertain or under pressure, then say no. Be confident about your right to think things out for yourself in a grown-up way.

Neither girls nor boys should be afraid to say 'no' to sex. Sometimes people feel they should agree to have sex because their partner wants to, and they're afraid of losing the partner. Or it may be that all their friends seem to be sexually active, so they feel they should be the same. The most important thing is to do what you think is right. Anyone who really loves you will respect the way you feel. Saying no doesn't mean that you don't like the other person. In fact, it may mean you like them a lot!

Wait for it

Some people prefer to wait till they get married before they have sex. That way, sexual activity is special because both partners are learning together, and not comparing each other with previous partners. Other people think that when they are really in love, it's all right to have sex, because they feel confident that their relationship will last. Another thing to bear in mind is that in most countries there's a legal age of consent. This means that if anyone younger than the age of consent has sex, they are breaking the law.

There's no such thing as a 'correct' decision. Everyone is different, and everyone has different ideas of what's right and wrong. You have to take into account the religious and moral beliefs you've been brought up with. All religions have teachings, and all cultural groups have customs and morals. Do you think they are rules you can live by?

Whatever you decide, and whenever you start having sex, make sure you find out as much as you can about contraception, and about the risk of sexually transmitted diseases. You can start by reading pages 290-291 and 294-297 in this book!

Sexual feelings

Lots of people want to know what actually happens when people have sex. Of course, there's no right and wrong way to have sex. Certain parts of the body feel good when they are touched in certain ways, and when two people make love, they are making each other feel good and giving each other pleasure.

On this page, we're talking only about the physical side of sexual feelings. As you have read, this is only one element, since sex involves very strong emotions as well. Sex without emotional involvement isn't likely to be a very fulfilling experience.

"Do both boys and girls masturbate, and does it do you any harm?"
Ben

Because your hormones are racing about inside your body, sexual feelings are likely to be very strong. So many people – both girls and boys – find a release to these feelings in masturbation. Masturbation means stimulating or rubbing the clitoris or penis. When you reach the climax, or orgasm, you feel a sense of relaxation and relief from the sexual tensions that have been building up. Although some people have a religious or moral objection to self-stimulation, masturbation doesn't medically harm you at all.

You may think that once you're grown up and have had sex, you don't need to masturbate any more. This isn't so. Adults have strong sexual feelings too, and many people masturbate regardless of whether or not they are having sex regularly.

"What happens when people have oral sex?"
Ziggy

Oral sex describes when people stimulate each other's genital organs with their mouths and tongues. You might think this sounds unpleasant. In fact the genital organs carry no more germs than any other part of your body. But as with all sexual activity, nobody should feel they have to do anything they are not comfortable with.

"What is an orgasm, and what does it feel like?"
Jeanne

Orgasm is the feeling a man has when semen comes out of his penis. Women get an orgasm when their clitoris and/or vagina are rubbed.

As the orgasm begins, people's heartbeats get faster, and their skin may become flushed. They breathe heavily. An orgasm is a very private and individual experience. No two people will describe it in the same way. It's an intense wave of sensual feeling that people generally agree feels very good. After an orgasm, people often feel really relaxed and sleepy.

"I don't understand exactly how a man and a woman fit together when they have sexual intercourse."
Lori

When a man and woman have sexual intercourse, the man puts his erect penis inside his partner's vagina. This is called vaginal intercourse. Some young people think this may be painful. But when a woman is sexually excited, her vagina produces fluid. This makes it easy for the man's penis to slide in to the woman's vagina. As long as each partner is careful and considerate, they should both enjoy sexual intercourse.

The man moves his penis until he reaches sexual climax, or orgasm. Then the muscles in his penis and surrounding area contract, ejaculating semen into the woman's vagina in rhythmic bursts. The woman meanwhile may experience orgasm through intense contractions of the uterus and vagina. Not every woman has an orgasm each time she has sex. This doesn't mean there's anything wrong with her. It's a very individual thing.

"What's the first thing people do when they start to make love?"
Errol

Many people start their love-making by hugging, cuddling and kissing. Touching each other like this gives the two people warm, sensual feelings. Remember that making love like this doesn't have to lead to sexual intercourse. People can enjoy a kiss and an embrace and leave it at that.

"What are erogenous zones? Does everyone have them?"
Fatima

Certain parts of the body are very sensitive to touch, and are sexually exciting. These are called the erogenous zones. The most sexually stimulating are the sex organs themselves, but there are others. Exactly which others these are is different from person to person – somebody might be sexually excited, or turned on, by stroking the back of the neck, another by a foot-massage, and another by rubbing the nipples. You may well not know which your erogenous zones are until you discover them by discovering your own body, or when you're making love.

There are no rules!

Many young people are very unsure of how to act when they come to make love to another person. What should they do? What will the other person expect? But remember that there are no rules. If a person is sensitive to what their partner is feeling, they will soon find out what suits them best.

Contraception

Contraception is also called birth control or family planning. Contraception means preventing pregnancy and it works by stopping the man's sperm from meeting the woman's ovum or implanting in the uterus. A man and a woman who want to have sexual intercourse but don't want to have a baby need to use some kind of contraception. Although it's only the woman who gets pregnant, both partners have to be responsible for contraception. It takes two to make a baby, after all.

Even before you start having sex, it's a good idea to know what kinds of birth control are available when the time comes. And besides protecting against pregnancy, some contraceptives also give protection against sexually transmitted diseases.

What are contraceptives?

Contraceptives can be taken as pills or injections. There are sperm-killing foams and creams. There are barrier methods for the man and the woman that stops the sperm reaching the uterus, there is a sterilization operation, and several other choices. Different methods suit different people, and people often use several different methods during their lifetime, depending on what they feel comfortable with. Many young people start by using condoms as they're so convenient, inexpensive and easy to use.

As an alternative to the methods listed here, some people choose sterilization. This involves an operation to cut the man's vas deferens or the woman's Fallopian tubes. It is not reversible, and is only for people who are quite sure they won't want children in the future.

CONTRACEPTIVE METHODS
Contraceptives need to be used properly, otherwise they won't work.

CONDOM
The condom is made of very thin rubber. It is placed onto the man's erect penis. When the man ejaculates, the sperm is trapped inside the condom and can't get into the woman's vagina. But don't forget, it has to be thrown away after intercourse. The condom is easy to use and easy to buy. No prescription is needed. It protects both partners against sexually transmitted diseases (STDs) including AIDS.

FEMALE CONDOM
A female condom is a soft plastic bag that is placed inside the vagina. It is held in place by an inner ring with an outer ring that lies over the area outside the vagina. It is thrown away after use. Female condoms have only recently become available so it is not known exactly how reliable they are.

DIAPHRAGM
This is a soft rubber dome placed inside the vagina and over the cervix before intercourse. It is used with spermicidal gel or cream. Diaphragms come in different sizes, and need to be prescribed by a doctor.

CAP
The cap works in the same way as a diaphragm, but it's smaller. It fits snugly over the cervix, covering the os.

SPONGE

This is a soft, round sponge containing spermicide. The woman puts it into the vagina before intercourse, and it then works for 24 hours. It is relatively expensive and is not very reliable.

SPERMICIDES

These are sperm-killing chemicals put into the vagina before intercourse. They may be creams, jellies, pessaries (a kind of dissolving tablet) or foams. Spermicides are not a very effective contraceptive method on their own, but used with diaphragms, caps or condoms, they can work quite well.

COMBINED PILL

This is usually just known as the pill. The woman takes a series of pills every month. These pills contain hormones that prevent an ovum being released. The pill provides good protection against pregnancy, though the woman must be careful to take each pill on the right day. Even one day missed can result in pregnancy. The pill has to be prescribed by a doctor.

MINI PILL

This pill contains progesterone, which causes changes in the mucus around the cervix. This makes it difficult for the sperm to pass into the uterus.

CONTRACEPTIVE INJECTION

This is an injection of hormones that works by preventing ovulation. Each injection stays effective for two or three months.

In some countries it is possible to get contraceptive implants which are similar to the injections but last for five years.

VAGINA RING

This is a soft rubber ring which is placed high in the vagina and left there. Each ring lasts for three months. It releases hormones that change the mucus around the cervix and in some women it prevents ovulation.

INTRA UTERINE DEVICE (IUD)

This is a small copper and plastic device that is placed inside the woman's uterus by a doctor. It needs to be changed about every five years. It is reliable, but is not a good choice for women who have never been pregnant.

NATURAL METHODS

These rely on knowing when the woman is most likely to get pregnant and avoiding intercourse at those times. The woman has to check what her cervical mucus is like, and monitor her body temperature every morning – a change in her temperature shows when she has ovulated. She can then predict when she will no longer be fertile. She must also keep track of the days of her menstrual cycle. This method is only effective if the woman's menstrual cycle is very regular, and if the couple are extremely careful. For this reason it's not a good choice for most young couples. It is the only method currently allowed by the Roman Catholic church.

Unplanned pregnancy

There's a good chance that a woman will become pregnant if she and her partner don't use contraceptives. Even if a couple has been using contraceptives, a woman can still get pregnant because no method is one hundred percent effective.

Signs of pregnancy

The first sign that a woman might be pregnant is usually a missed period. People sometimes also have nausea or have sore breasts. But there are other reasons for these things, so it's not the only way to tell. Anyone who thinks they might be pregnant should have a pregnancy test. The best place to go for a test is to a doctor or family planning clinic. But some people like to find out the truth in private first, by buying a pregnancy test kit at a chemist's. These kits are easy to use – they just involve testing the woman's urine.

Who can she tell?

If the pregnancy test proves positive, how will the woman feel about it? Will she be pleased or will she be upset? She'll have to decide what to do. First, she'll need to talk to someone. There's probably nobody better to talk to than her mother, but if that's not possible, then she could try to tell an adult she trusts. It may not always be easy to tell her partner – she won't know how he'll react. Will he be shocked, will he be scared or angry, or will he be pleased, and able to give her the support she needs? In the end, he'll have to know. After all, he is the potential father.

A pregnancy test kit.

What should she do?

There are three choices in the case of an unplanned pregnancy – having the baby and keeping it, having the baby and giving it up for adoption, or having an abortion. This may be an extremely difficult decision to make, and there's no easy option. It's really the woman's choice. But there are people who can give sympathetic advice, and help the woman to reach her decision. Even if she knows what she wants to do, it's helpful to discuss things with a counsellor.

Having the baby

Not all teenagers with an unplanned pregnancy are unhappy about it. In some situations, the couple may have been planning to get married anyway, and the baby's coming just moves up the plans. The couple should feel they are ready for marriage, and ready for the demanding commitment of raising a child. It is helpful if they have finished school, and also if the couple's parents and other family members are supportive of the situation. The couple should also consider where they will live and whether they will have jobs that allow them to support themselves financially.

COUNSELLING
When a teenager is faced with an unplanned pregnancy, she needs to seek advice. First, she'll probably turn to her family. But then she may find it helpful to seek advice from a trained counsellor.

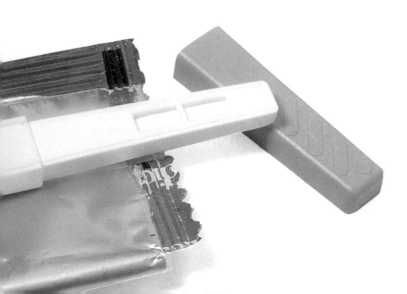

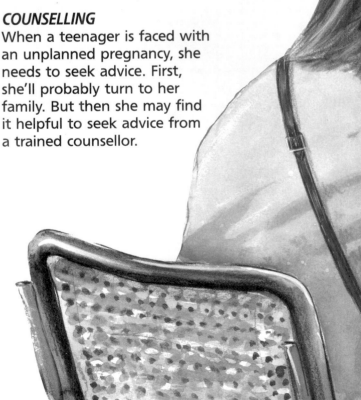

If marriage or a supportive long-term relationship with her partner are not likely, the woman will need to consider many important issues. Will her family be supportive and help her raise the child? Can she cope with the constant demands of the baby? Will having the child interfere with plans for a future career? Can she afford all the expenses? Is she emotionally mature enough to be a parent? These questions are important for a couple to consider, too. Nobody should decide to have a baby just to have someone to love or to bring them closer to their partner. Neither of these works out very well!

When the mother is a young teenager, there are other problems as well. Pregnancy puts great strain on a body – any body – but if the body is not fully grown, it can create problems with the teenager's own development. For instance, the growing foetus has to use calcium that should be used for the teenager's bones.

COUNSELLORS

Counsellors are trained to give sensible advice on problems of all kinds. A counsellor on matters of pregnancy can be a very useful person to talk to. They will have come across a wide range of difficulties, and will be able to suggest ways of dealing with them. Many people find it easy to talk to someone who is not personally involved with their problem. Counsellors don't usually make judgements that could embarrass their clients.

Having carefully considered all these matters, many girls choose to keep their babies. Again, the most important thing is to think through the matter carefully, and be sure this option is the right one.

Adoption

Some people feel they would like to have their baby, rather than have an abortion, and then to give it up for adoption afterwards. This may seem like a good idea during pregnancy, but many women have second thoughts once they have actually seen the baby they've been carrying for nine months. Mothers can still change their mind at that stage.

Some teenagers give their baby up because they feel it will have a better chance of a happy life with adoptive parents who are ready and able to provide love, care and support. Even so, the mother may feel just as sad as a woman who's had an abortion. It is a difficult and painful decision to take, and it should be made only after careful counselling.

Abortion

Abortion is a way of ending a pregnancy. But it's not always easy to get an abortion – some countries have strict anti-abortion laws, and don't allow abortion at all. People have very strong feelings about abortion. Some think that abortion is the same as murder – that by removing the embryo from the mother's body, a human being is being killed. Others think that the woman should be able to decide what happens to her own body, and that she should have the right to choose whether or not to have an abortion. Very often, a woman must be able to give very good reasons why she should have an abortion.

Abortions are carried out at a hospital or clinic. A doctor passes a tube through the cervix into the uterus, and the embryo and the lining of the uterus are sucked out. If it's properly done, the operation is very safe. Some women feel rather sad afterwards, while at the same time being relieved that their pregnancy is over.

Sexually transmitted diseases

Herpes virus.

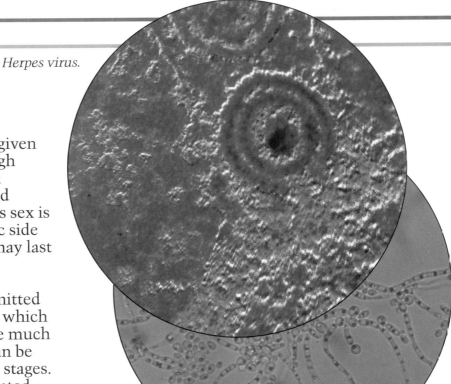

Sexually transmitted diseases (STDs) are given this name because they are caught through sexual contact. They are easily passed on between partners and affect both men and women. This means that anyone who has sex is potentially at risk. This is the unromantic side of sex! The long-term effects of an STD may last throughout a person's life.

There are various sorts of sexually transmitted diseases. Some are only minor infections which can be easily treated. Other infections are much more dangerous, and can kill, but they can be treated successfully if caught in the early stages. Others, such as genital herpes, can be treated and the symptoms relieved but not cured. Most importantly, the Human Immunodeficiency Virus (HIV) which may lead to AIDS (Acquired Immune Deficiency Syndrome) has no permanent cure.

(above) Candida albicans causes candidiasis.

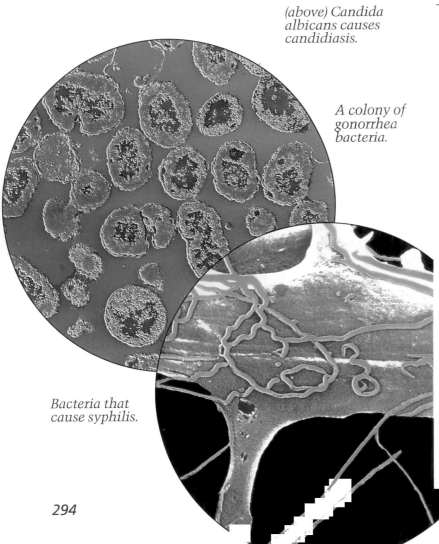

A colony of gonorrhea bacteria.

Bacteria that cause syphilis.

SOME STDs

Disease	Symptoms
pubic lice	lice that live in pubic hair and cause itching
non-specific urethritis (NSU)	painful urination and discharge from penis or urinary opening
trichomonas	watery, foul-smelling discharge, painful irritation
genital warts	start as pinhead-sized swellings
genital herpes	painful blisters on the penis or labia
gonorrhea	painful urination and thick yellow discharge
syphilis	first, a painless sore appears on the mouth, anus, vagina or penis. Then a rash and flu-like symptoms develop.
AIDS	many different symptoms
candidiasis	inflammation in the vagina or penis

(you can read more about AIDS on pages 296 and 297)

How can you catch STDs?

STDs are nearly always passed on through sexual contact but you can, rarely, catch them from certain objects. In theory, if you use a towel or share bathing trunks with someone with an STD discharge from their penis or vagina, it is just possible that you may contract the same disease. Similarly, if someone with a herpes simplex sore on their mouth gave you a friendly kiss on the lips you could catch the virus too.

Many people are worried about catching something from toilet seats. This is not very likely. Someone who has been sexually active should be aware of any of the following signs and symptoms – genitals itching, soreness, blisters, pain when passing urine, genital warts. Any of these symptoms may be accompanied by general feelings of tiredness and lethargy. Anyone who thinks they may have caught a sexually transmitted disease should go to see a doctor. Doctors are used to treating problems like this. Most sexually transmitted diseases are easily treated, and they clear up quickly if they are caught at an early stage.

How to avoid catching STDs

There are a number of ways to avoid getting a sexually transmitted disease. The safest is not to have sex until marriage to a partner who has not had sex, and remains faithful to you.

If you have never had sexual contact with anyone, you are very unlikely to catch a sexually transmitted disease. You will not catch STDs from masturbating, from holding someone's hand or sitting on someone's lap.

Choose carefully

When you're going to have a sexual relationship, be selective about your partner. Doctors have classified a number of groups that they call high risk in passing on STDs. These include people who are promiscuous, that is they sleep with many partners; homosexual men, bi-sexual men (those who have sex with men and women) and intravenous drug users, who inject drugs direct into their veins. Anyone who has had sex with a member of the high risk groups is also high risk.

In other words, never have any form of sexual contact with someone you don't really know. If a potential partner is a friend, you can find out a lot about their sexual history before you get involved. As you get older and meet more and more potential partners this precaution could save your life. Every time you have sex with someone, you are potentially exposing yourself to the diseases of every single person your partner slept with before you.

Safe sex

People who do have sex should always use a condom. When a condom is used with spermicides containing nonoxynol 9, it is very successful in preventing the transmission of some STDs.

In terms of catching diseases from other people's belongings, the best precaution is to use your own. Don't share flannels, toothbrushes, bathing suits or underpants.

Personal hygiene is very important.

Sexually active people should always use a condom.

HIV and AIDS

Many people think that HIV is the same as AIDS. It's not. HIV is the name given to the virus that causes the illness (or collection of illnesses) called AIDS. Someone who is infected with HIV may go on to develop AIDS, though some HIV infected people show no symptoms for many years. During this time, the infected person can pass the infection on to other people.

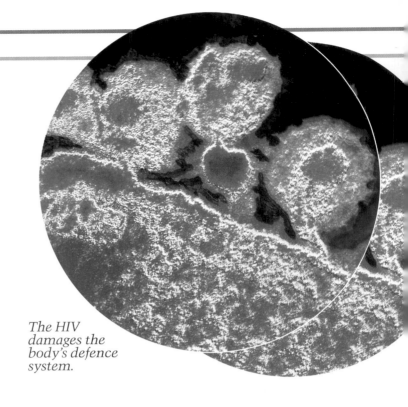

The HIV damages the body's defence system.

What is HIV?

HIV stands for Human Immunodeficiency Virus. This virus lives mainly in the defence or immune system of the body, and in particular in one sort of the white blood cell called the T lymphocyte or 'helper cell'. These cells are important for fighting the bacteria and viruses which cause infection. The HIV can remain hidden in the T cells for a long time, and during this time a person can remain quite healthy and well. However, with time, the HIV gradually destroys the T cells and can also spread to other cells. The immune system is now damaged. If someone has been exposed to the HIV virus, their body produces antibodies to fight the virus. So if a blood test shows that these antibodies are present, it proves that the person has been exposed to the HIV virus. This is referred to as being HIV positive.

Once somebody knows they have an HIV infection, it is important to have regular physical check ups and blood tests. Among the blood tests is a test for immunity which shows how many T cells there are in the blood.

Using condoms helps to make sex safer.

Treating HIV infection

There are medicines available which help to prevent the HIV from spreading throughout the body. Although they do not cure the disease they may keep the person well for longer. There are also other medicines which can be taken when the immunity is poor, and can prevent other infections from occurring.

What is AIDS?

AIDS stands for Acquired Immune Deficiency Syndrome. AIDS isn't an illness in itself. It's any one of a number of illnesses which can occur in a person with HIV infection who has very poor immunity. The major illnesses are due to other infections, but other problems can include loss of weight, lung problems and difficulties with concentration, balance and walking if the HIV affects the brain. Even when AIDS has developed, both adults and children may be relatively well in between periods of illness. In adults with HIV infection, it takes an average of 10-12 years for AIDS to develop from the time of getting HIV. Some children get HIV from their mothers during pregnancy (15-20 out of every hundred babies born to HIV positive mothers will get HIV infection) and for them, AIDS can sometimes develop more quickly.

All over the world, education programmes teach people about HIV and AIDS.

Living with AIDS

So a person with AIDS may have to take medicines every day to prevent illnesses from occurring and to treat infections if they do get them. If they get sick and if the illness is severe, they may have to go into hospital for treatment. This may be just for a few days or sometimes for longer. Some hospitals have school teachers or a school so young patients don't have to miss lessons! Having HIV or even AIDS does not mean that someone has to make drastic changes in their life – they can carry on doing many of the things that they have been doing or would like to do.

Prevent the spread of AIDS

There is no known cure for AIDS. The only answer is to avoid it. So how can you do this?

HIV is passed from person to person through the body fluids of an infected person – that is blood, semen or secretions from the vagina. Remember that an HIV infected person is not necessarily sick – in fact they may be completely well. An infected person can pass on the virus by having sex with someone without using a condom, or by letting their blood come in contact with someone else's blood, for example through sharing needles and razors. Someone won't be infected by touching or kissing unless one person has HIV and both have mouth ulcers. You can avoid the risk of infection by always using a condom when you have sex.

The future

Every year, there are more and more cases of AIDS throughout the world. The World Health Organization now estimates that there are one and a half million cases of AIDS, with a further eleven to thirteen million people who are HIV positive. One million of those who are HIV positive are children.

Research is being undertaken into a vaccine to prevent AIDS, but the virus so far has proved to be very complicated. Education programmes all over the world are helping to make people aware of how to avoid AIDS.

Dispelling the myths

All over the world some people have strange ideas about sexuality and sexual behaviour. Many of these strange ideas arose because people didn't understand what was happening. But myths and old wives' tales continue to frighten and mislead people. Here are some myths that you may have heard and the truth that lies behind them.

"My sister says you can't get pregnant if you have a bath straight after having sex. Is this true?"
Clio

No, it isn't. You can get pregnant however well you wash. Sperm are not going to be washed away by you having a bath, and they won't fall out of your body until they discover there's no ovum to fertilize. You won't avoid pregnancy by having sexual intercourse standing up, either. The only way to be sure is to use a reliable method of contraception.

"My penis is rather small. I'm quite tall and athletic, and I get teased a lot about the size of my penis. Is it true that it won't be able to fit into a woman's vagina when I have sexual intercourse?"
Adri

No. A penis is almost never too small to have intercourse. In any case, when you have an erection, you'll find your penis gets much bigger. Adult penises vary a lot in size when they are soft, from about 83 to 108 millimetres long. When they are erect, the penises grow to around 160 millimetres long, regardless of how long
they were when soft. A short penis grows during an erection more than a long one, that's all. A small penis is just as efficient in every way as a large one. Just because your penis is short, it doesn't mean that you're any less manly than anyone else. And those myths about men with big feet or big thumbs having a big penis? Nonsense!

"I've been told all sorts of things about what I should and shouldn't do when I have my period. I'm really confused. Someone said I shouldn't eat ice-cream. Is this really right?"
Rita

No. You can do anything during your period that you normally do. There are hundreds of myths about menstruation. People used to believe that menstruating women were ill. Men were meant to have no contact with them because they were unclean. They were said to have all sorts of effects on things – make mayonnaise curdle, or milk go sour, and prevent cakes from rising. People built up stories around the menstrual bleeding because they didn't understand it. We are now better informed. Menstruation is not an illness. Your period is proof of your womanhood, and you can be proud of it!

"I've noticed a creamy white discharge behind my foreskin. What is it, and should I do anything about it? Have I caught some kind of sexual disease?"
Lee

No. This discharge is called smegma. Its appearance generally means that you are not washing the head of your penis as thoroughly as you should. If you are not circumcised, you should gently pull back your foreskin every day to remove any smegma which may have accumulated. Leaving it can cause an unpleasant odour or irritation to occur.

"My grandfather really scared me the other day when he said that if I masturbated too much, it would affect my brain and I'd go crazy. Is this true?"
Julian

No. Masturbation does your body no harm at all. People used to think that all sorts of things would happen to you if you masturbated. They said you'd grow hairs on the palms of your hands, you'd go blind, you'd go mad, or you'd use up your supply of sperm. None of this is true. As you've read in this book, masturbation is just a natural way of releasing tension.

"I've heard that gays are really people who want to change sex – that gay men really want to be female, and gay women want to be men. Is this so?"
Josie

No. Gays feel attracted to people of the same sex as themselves, and want to be loved by them. Some gay men appear effeminate, and seem to prefer things that women are traditionally expected to like, and some lesbians seem to be butch and wear masculine type clothes. But this doesn't mean they want to change sex. There are some people who feel they've been born in a body of the wrong sex. These people are called trans-sexuals, but that is completely different from homosexuality.

"When I went to public toilets when I was young, my mother made me cover the toilet seat with paper before I sat on it. She said it was to protect me against catching a disease. Could I really catch a disease from a toilet seat?"
Nadine

You could contract a skin infection such as impetigo from toilet seats. However it's not very likely that you'd catch a sexually transmitted disease that way. That's because STDs just don't survive that long outside the human body.

Healthy relationships

Nobody ever said puberty was easy. At times, you may be uncertain, anxious, confused or down in the dumps. There are good things and bad. You are excited at the thought of being more independent, but maybe you're not so keen on the additional responsibilities this independence demands. You may not always welcome the changes that are happening to your body. But you can't tell your body to stop developing. Neither can you tell it to hurry up and develop more quickly. So accept what's happening. Your body will mature gradually in its own good time. As your body develops, you become aware that your feelings are developing too. You feel excited about becoming grown up, but may not be sure about how to deal with the sexual feelings you're experiencing.

Changing attitudes

You may find your attitude to other people alters. The boys or girls you got on with fine at school become people for whom you find you have sexual feelings. Once you've recognized this, you may find you're a bit in awe of them. Being with someone of the other sex suddenly becomes awkward. The most comfortable way of dealing with this awkwardness is often to go around in a group. That way you can be with a mixed group without having to be on a single date.

One to one

When you've gained a bit of confidence, you may start going out with someone. Going out on a date is fun – you go out to enjoy yourselves. There's another aspect to the enjoyment. You get an added kick because

you like each other — you like being together, and doing things together. You realize that you are physically attracted to each other. The first physical contact is really exciting — just brushing your friend's arm, holding hands, or putting an arm round their waist can send a thrill up your spine and make your heart beat faster.

A natural urge

The sexual feelings that people have are as natural an impulse as feeling thirsty. Humans, like all other animals, have a powerful sex drive. But as human beings we keep this sex drive in check, and keep it as a private and intimate matter between two people.

Enjoy your feelings

If you're prepared for what your sexual feelings might be like, you'll feel happier about dealing with them. By reading this book, you'll have found out lots about the changes that take place in your body, as well as your changing attitudes to other people. Don't be afraid that knowing in advance what might happen will take the excitement out of your sexual encounters. It won't! Your feelings are yours, and yours alone. No two people have exactly the same experiences. By being well-informed about sexuality, you'll feel confident and relaxed in your relationships with others. And you'll be able to enjoy a happy and loving sex life when you're ready for it.

The friendships you make when you are young can be very important.

Making sense of puberty

Your body will never again undergo such radical changes as during puberty. Do you know what will happen? Can you disentangle fact from fiction? Do you feel confident about dealing with the changes? Try this quiz and find out!

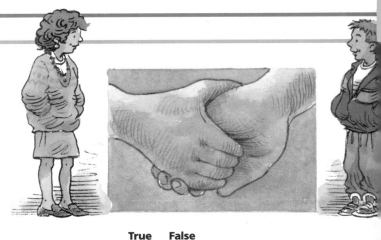

True **False**

☐ ☐ **1.** A man with big feet has a big penis.

☐ ☐ **2.** HIV is the same as AIDS.

☐ ☐ **3.** Girls don't have any of the male hormone testosterone.

☐ ☐ **4.** A man can't pass urine and semen at the same time.

☐ ☐ **5.** A man with a hairy chest is more masculine than a man with smooth skin.

☐ ☐ **6.** A girl should not swim when she has her period.

☐ ☐ **7.** A baby inside its mother gets its nourishment from the amniotic fluid.

☐ ☐ **8.** When they are born, baby girls already have thousands of ova in their ovaries.

True **False**

☐ ☐ **9.** A boy should never touch his testicles.

☐ ☐ **10.** An embryo is what a baby is called until it is about 10 weeks old.

☐ ☐ **11.** A woman doesn't need to use contraceptives when she has her period.

PICK YOUR ANSWER

1. The male hormone is called:

☐ **a.** testosterone
☐ **b.** testimony
☐ **c.** oestrogen

2. The dark area surrounding the nipple is the:

☐ **a.** areola
☐ **b.** aroma
☐ **c.** aurora

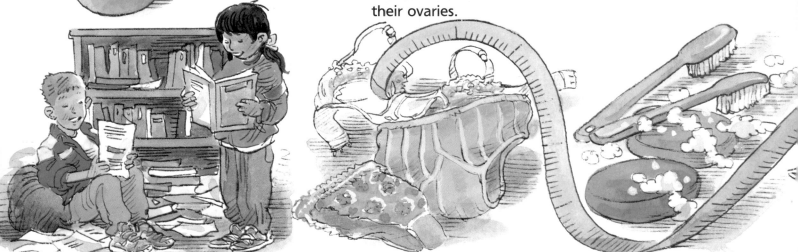

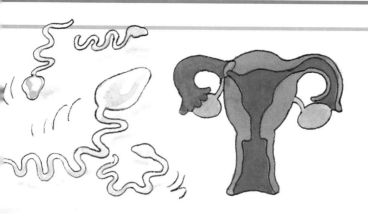

3. The thin piece of skin over the vaginal opening is the:

☐ **a.** hilum
☐ **b.** hymen
☐ **c.** lumen

4. What fruit does the shape of a uterus make you think of?

☐ **a.** melon
☐ **b.** pear
☐ **c.** mango

5. Dysmenorrhoea is the medical name for:

☐ **a.** vomiting
☐ **b.** hair growth
☐ **c.** period pains

6. Sperm ripen in the:

☐ **a.** epidermis
☐ **b.** epididymis
☐ **c.** epidural

7. The chemicals that cause puberty to take place are called:

☐ **a.** hummus
☐ **b.** ferromones
☐ **c.** hormones

8. How long does a baby stay inside its mother's body?

☐ **a.** 30 weeks
☐ **b.** 40 weeks
☐ **c.** 50 weeks

9. Where does pubic hair grow?

☐ **a.** around your genitals
☐ **b.** on your legs
☐ **c.** on your chest

10. How much blood does a woman usually lose during her period?

☐ **a.** 2 tablespoons
☐ **b.** 2 cups
☐ **c.** 2 teaspoons

Answers:

1. False. The size of a penis has nothing whatever to do with the size of a man's body.
2. False. HIV is the virus that causes AIDS.
3. False. They produce a little.
4. True. A valve ensures this.
5. False. The amount of body hair a man has doesn't have any bearing on his manliness.
6. False.
7. False. The baby is fed through the umbilical cord by the placenta.
8. True. Their lifetime's supply is already in place.
9. False. Every boy should get used to examining his testicles.
10. True. After 10 weeks, the baby is known as a foetus.
11. False. She can never be sure she will be safe.

Pick your answer:

1. **a** Testosterone
2. **a** Areola
3. **b** Hymen
4. **b** Pear
5. **c** Period pains
6. **b** Epididymis
7. **c** Hormones
8. **b** 40 weeks
9. **a** Around your genitals
10. **a** 2 tablespoons

HOW DID YOU SCORE?
Give yourself a point for each correct answer.

16-21 points: Cool! It sounds as if you know a lot about the changes that happen during puberty, both to you and to friends of the other sex.

9-15 points: Don't get put off by the long words. As long as you know why things happen, you'll be on the right track.

under 8 points: Maybe you need to read this book again. The more you know, the better prepared you'll feel.

Index

oxygen 11, 32, 37
    breathing 30, 31, 34-35

packaging (food) 129, 176
Pakistan 60, 172-173
pancreas 150
pantothenic acid 145
papilla 80
paraphimosis 271
parasite 181
parents 188, 192, 194-195, 210
    feelings about 198
    problems with 220
    separation/divorce 196-197
    talking to 220
passive smoking 214
pasta 128, 130-131
pasteurisation 175
peanut 132, 141
peanut butter 164
peas 132, 134, 138
pectin 139
peer group 187
peer pressure 204
Pelé 57
pelota 61
penis 270, 271, 272-273, 277
    discharge 271, 294, 299
    size 298
pepsin 150
peptic ulcer 215
period 250, 259, 260-265, 298
    breasts and 256
    first 248, 261
    irregular 261, 264
    pains 264, 265
permed hair 85
personal appearance 66-67, 68-69,
    248-249
    confidence and 211
    for job interview 241
personality 240-241, 242
perspiration 253, 269
phagocyte 114
phalange 39
phimosis 271
phosphorus 145, 146, 147
physical development 246-247
    boys 250-251, 268-269, 270
    girls 250-251, 252-255
physical disability 58-59
pierced ears 97
pill (contraceptive) 291, 266
pimples 74-75
ping pong see table tennis
pituitary gland 251, 260
pivot joint 44

pizza 154
placenta 278, 281
plantar wart 101
plaque 102, 103, 104, 137
pleurisy 35
pneumonia 35
pores (skin) 70, 72, 74-75, 79
port-wine stain 71
positive thinking 5, 224, 229, 236
    moods and 227
posture 9, 18, 42, 47
    exercises for 108-109
potassium (dietary) 147, 149, 178
potato 143, 178-179, 139
    starch 128, 134
    storage 176, 177
    vitamins 145, 178
pre-menstrual tension 264
pregnancy 133, 277, 278-279, 293,
    298
    HIV and 296
    smoking and 215
    unplanned 292-293
pregnancy test 292
preserving food 170-171, 174-175
press-ups 37, 40
processed food 164, 170, 171,
    172-173
progesterone 74, 261, 291
prostrate gland 272, 274
protein (dietary) 128, 132-133, 152,
    154, 158
    agricultural supply 166-167
    requirement 26, 129, 167
    sources 128, 130, 135, 165,
        178-179
protein (keratin) 70, 80, 85, 99
Prozumenshchikova, Galina 57
puberty 88, 159, 246, 250-251
    boys 268-269, 270, 272, 273
    girls 252-253, 254-255, 261
    muscular changes 41
pubic hair 294
    female 252, 253
    male 268, 269
puffy eyes 95
pull-ups 37, 40
pulmonary artery 32
pulmonary vein 32
pulse rate 33, 215
pulses 132, 138
pupil (eye) 90, 91
pyridoxine 145
pyroligneous acid 174

qualifications 230
quarrelling 196

rabies 119
radiology 117
rape 213
rapid eye movement 111
rash 168
razor 86, 87
rebelling 192-193
red blood cell 145
Red Cross 239
reflexes 49
relationships 300-301
    family 194-195
    opposite sex 206, 207, 208
    sex and 284, 285, 295
relaxation 10, 29, 36, 110-111
    and breathing 11, 34
relaxing hair 85
resentment 196
resistance training 37
resorcinol 72
rest 110-111
retina 90, 91
riboflavin 145
rice 135, 138, 172-173
    protein 128, 132
    starch 128, 134
rickets 144
road bowling 56
road safety 25
rod cell 91
roller skating 23, 31, 60
    balance 7, 50
rotation ball 15
roughage 134, 150
rowing 23, 27, 30, 40
rugby 23, 27, 45, 61
rules 192, 193, 195
runner's high 11
running 11, 23, 27, 28-29
    marathon 28-29, 59, 60
running away 199
Russia 127, 172-173
rye 172-173

saccharin 171
saddle joint 44
sadness 200, 226
safe sex 285, 295, 297
sailing 23, 25, 27
saliva 150, 151
salmonella 113, 180
salt 55, 146, 147, 170
    fast food 164
    preserving food 174
saltpetre 171
Salute to the Sun 10-11
sanitary towel 263

Acknowledgements

The publishers would like to thank the following for permission to use photographs in this book: Adams Picture Library 28/29, 97, 112–113, 202; Allsport 16, 20/21, 54/55, 58/59, 156/157, 252/253, 270/271; Art Directors 180, 181, 294; Barnaby's Picture Library 20, 24, 50; Collections 202, 204, 206, 214, 231, 300, 301; David Hoffman Photolibrary 192/193, 216; Dr D Roberts-Harry, University of Bristol Dental Hospital 105; Format 238; Martin Potter 44; National Medical Slidebank 168, 217; Network Photographers 216; Pictorial Parade 37; Picturepoint Ltd 106, 137, 172, 174, 175, 200/201, 239; Rex Features 162, 163, 199, 202/203; Robert Harding Picture Library 44, 58; Sally and Richard Greenhill 127, 137, 139, 192, 198, 202, 203, 224, 228, 231, 236; Science Photo Library 71, 75, 81, 92, 101, 104, 112, 113, 115, 121, 137, 146, 166, 175, 181, 215, 277, 294, 296; Still Pictures 297; The Hutchison Library 166; The Image Bank 13, 14/15, 42, 50, 176, 300, 301; The Metropolitan Police Service, New Scotland Yard 218/219; Tony Stone Worldwide 9, 16, 24, 68/69, 80/81, 210, 216, 282, 300/301; Tropix 85; Vandystadt 50; Zefa Picture Library 265, 269.

The extract from an article that appeared in the Amateur Swimming Association bulletin is reprinted by permission of Adrian Moorhouse.

The extract from *Workout* by Jane Fonda, © 1981 by The Workout Inc., is reprinted by permission of Simon & Schuster Inc. and Penguin Books Ltd.

The publishers would also like to give special thanks to Aurora Scientific, Corston, Bath, UK for the loan of scientific equipment; Cole and Son Ltd, Chippenham, UK for the loan of sports equipment; Haine and Smith, Chippenham, UK for the loan of optical equipment; to everyone who acted as photographic models; and to Jannean Donson and Tisha for assistance with make-up.